FARM JOURNAL'S COMPLETE
PIE cookbook

700 BEST DESSERT AND MAIN-DISH PIES
IN THE COUNTRY

Other cookbooks by *Farm Journal*

FARM JOURNAL'S COUNTRY COOKBOOK
FARM JOURNAL'S TIMESAVING COUNTRY COOKBOOK
FREEZING AND CANNING COOKBOOK

FARM JOURNAL'S COMPLETE
PIE cookbook

700 BEST DESSERT AND MAIN-DISH PIES

IN THE COUNTRY · · · · EDITED BY

Nell B. Nichols FIELD FOOD EDITOR

WITH THE ASSISTANCE OF THE FOOD STAFF
OF *FARM JOURNAL* · PHOTOGRAPHY SUPER-
VISED BY AL J. REAGAN, ART DIRECTOR
OF *THE FARMER'S WIFE*

DOUBLEDAY & COMPANY, INC.

GARDEN CITY, NEW YORK

Library of Congress Catalog Card Number 65-16174

CONTENTS

MAIN-DISH PIES

COLOR ILLUSTRATIONS

FARM JOURNAL'S COMPLETE
PIE cookbook

700 BEST DESSERT AND MAIN-DISH PIES
IN THE COUNTRY

CHAPTER 1

ALL ABOUT PIES

We invite you to the largest showing of American pies ever presented between the covers of one book. You'll find tested recipes for almost every pie you ever heard of, and for others so new they've never been made outside our Test Kitchens. We've also included pies so old-fashioned you've probably never seen written-down recipes for them—treasures of your heritage.

Pie is America's top dessert. It appeared on New World tables almost from the start—long before the Stars and Stripes flew from a flagpole or the Fourth of July was an extraordinary day. The early pies had more crust than filling—thrifty ingenious pioneer wives stretched scarce ingredients in this way. But pies caught on at once, and each generation of women has widened the variety, improved quality and invented new recipes. Pie has kept in step with the times and new ingredients.

Fruit pies lead the array in our biggest chapter. Recipes using 28 different kinds of fruits and berries—those that grow wild along roadside fence rows or in the woods, those scientifically cultivated, as well as some fruits imported from other countries, all in Chapter 3.

Delicate, velvety custard and cream pies, rich with fresh country eggs, milk and cream, follow. Then the beauty queens—a whole chapter of those refrigerator and ice cream specials (Chapter 5). They are desserts made ahead and held in the controlled, low temperatures of up-to-date refrigerators and freezers until serving time. You'll find some spectacular ones that will bring praise from your guests.

Homey deep-dish pies, the serve-in-bowl desserts practical for every day, are long on fruit and short on pastry. They've always been the farm woman's favorite way to salvage fruit that might otherwise be wasted when the orchard yields a bumper crop. Today, they're good calorie savers, too. You ladle their colorful juices over the servings and set a pitcher of "pour cream" on the table (each individual can be guided by his calorie conscience). Country cobblers—maybe you call them family pies—are a variation of the deep-dish pies. They're so easy to make and ideal for serving a hungry family, especially with unexpected drop-in guests.

You'll find samples of the old-time cake pies (cake baked in pie shells) in our Cookbook. Not merely in memory of Grandfather who ate them with such enthusiasm, but also for the hostess who wants something unusual and good for her coffee party.

New fast-fix pies, modern as space travel, make a bow in this book. The cream pies which use modern packaged ingredients in a new way will delight you on busy days. Our Frozen Strawberry Pie is another example. You whip it up with the electric mixer, put it in the freezer and forget about it until you need a luscious dessert in a hurry. Then all you have to do is bring it out, cut the pieces and take it to the table. Like many country specials, the recipe makes two pies.

Tarts and turnovers, the dainty pastries for receptions, teas and parties, are attractive and appetizing served from a tray (Chapter 7). Also among the hostess specials in this book are the toppings (Chapter 9) that touch pies with glamour and make them excitingly different.

No section of our Cookbook holds more surprises than the two chapters (Chapters 10 and 11) of hearty, main-dish pies. Their great variety is impressive, their taste rewarding. Grandmother's Sunday-best and church-supper chicken pies and such new inventions as meaty chicken pieces topped with crunchy, brown popover crust get equal billing.

Many kinds of crusts—rice, potato, biscuit, pastry and corn pone—contribute to the wonderful flavors and texture contrasts of these main dishes. Frozen mashed-potato pie shells and toppings, developed in FARM JOURNAL'S Test Kitchens, will help you bake compliment-winning main dishes on short notice and with small effort. And the vegetable pies in this book are a mother's answer on how to get the children to eat most everything that grows in the garden.

You may wonder why so many apple, cherry and pumpkin pies are featured in our showing. Our reason is simple: They are the pies most often named as favorites. We asked members of our Family Test Group, farm women in all states, to name their families' favorite pies. They listed them in this order: apple, cherry, pumpkin, lemon, chocolate, pecan and coconut —a vote that tallies with other surveys. We felt duty bound to offer you both the traditional versions and creative new ways with these seven wonders of our pie world!

Pioneer Pies—Why Were They Round?

The history of pies fascinates most women. So find an easy chair or prop yourself up in bed—you'll enjoy the next few pages particularly. The creativity of pioneer homemakers, who were as eager as you are to prepare food to please family and friends, will inspire you.

Why were the first pies round instead of square or oblong, for instance? What happened in the New World that shaped pies for centuries to come? Sparse food supplies had much to do with it. Colonial women used round pans literally to cut corners and stretch the ingredients. For the same reason they baked shallow pies. When the orchards and berry patches they planted on cleared, fertile land started to supplement the fruits of the wilderness and "garden sass" became plentiful, truly American pies, plump and juicy, came from ovens. Rhubarb, a New World garden plant, was called pieplant to designate its major use. Increasingly generous amounts of filling were held or wrapped in crisp, golden pastry made with three available staples: flour, lard and water.

Pastry itself was originated on the other side of the Atlantic by the Greeks during their Golden Age. The Romans, sampling the delicacy, carried home recipes for making it—a prize of victory when they conquered Greece. It spread throughout Europe, via the Roman roads, where every country adapted the recipes to their customs and foods. American women followed suit. When they experimented in their colonial kitchens, they came up with different pastries than they had made in their former homes.

Gradually regional pies developed—pumpkin (a native vegetable) in New England, chess and pecan in the South and "nervous pies," or quivering custards teamed with fruits, in Pennsylvania Dutch kitchens. For pies were important taste pleasures in pioneer life. Once, when a sailing ship bringing molasses to Connecticut colony was delayed on the high seas, the Thanksgiving celebration was postponed until the homemakers could have molasses to make pumpkin pies. So it's not surprising that Thanksgiving dinner isn't complete in New England today without pumpkin pie.

Early homemakers were limited by the foods grown on their farms. They of course had to "make do" as much as possible with what they could produce. In contrast, we now draw on the wide world for pie ingredients—chocolate, vanilla, bananas, pineapple and coconut, for example. In our devotion to creamy chocolate pies we sometimes think we are the great chocolate fans of all time. Far from it! The ancient Aztec Indians in Mexico loved the chocolate taste. They prized the native evergreen trees with their clusters of pale pink blossoms that produced the football-shaped pods from which chocolate is made. They even paid their taxes with chocolate —the same as money to them. These ancient Mexicans also revered their "climbing orchid" with its green-yellow flowers—one flower in about a thousand produces a vanilla bean from which the fragrant flavoring is extracted to this very day.

When pioneers traveled inland by waterway and in covered wagons, cherished pie recipes went along. But soon new pies also were created in log cabins and frontier homes—Hoosier Cream Pie, for one (Chapter 4). This is the pie in which the ingredients for the filling were mixed right in pastry-lined pans by fingers so deft that they did not tear the tender pastry.

So from pioneer beginnings to this very day pie recipes have multiplied, and keep multiplying. There is nothing static about pie recipes. Women continually adapt them to changing conditions and ingredients. Trained home economists in test kitchens of research and business perfect techniques and ingredients, too.

Chiffon pies, served originally in a restaurant located by the railroad tracks in Marshalltown, Iowa, are typical of the evolution that takes place. Chiffon pies retain many of the characteristics of their forerunners, the fluff pies, which are still enjoyed (see recipes for Lemon Fluff and Fluffy Pineapple Pies in Chapter 4). Their fluffiness derives from beaten egg whites folded into the filling, as does that of chiffon pies. But it's the addition of gelatin that transformed the old fluff pies into the gorgeous chiffons, and the refrigerator makes them practical.

Pies Are Party Fare

Because pies were enjoyed so much, they became a part of neighborhood festivities from the start. Pie-eating contests were highlights at gatherings like county fairs. The champion—the man who could eat the most pie—was the envy of his neighbors, many of whom secretly wished for a greater capacity for their pie favorites.

Young women, as recently as a generation ago, practiced to bake pretty pies of exceptional quality for pie-supper auctions in one-room country schoolhouses. They toted these pies in boxes they had covered with pastel colored tissue or crepe paper or wallpaper scraps and decorated with paper flowers made by their nimble and artistic fingers. The auctioneer was a clever fellow who used all the showman's tricks. He hinted who baked the pie he held, removing the lid of the box just enough to give the tantalized young beaux a glimpse of the treat within.

Pies went along in carriages and spring wagons to all-day picnics in the grove and showed up at family reunions in quantity and variety. They pleased and satisfied the hungry threshing crews in the steam engine era. The men always had a choice: "Raisin? Apple? Do try this berry!"

No wonder pie baking stimulated a friendly, competitive spirit in country kitchens. Women vied with one another, as they do today, to see who could bake the best to take to church suppers, bake sales and other social gatherings. We guarantee that the tested, unusual recipes in this Cookbook will win prizes and praises.

Pies Stimulate Baking Contests

Today baking contests, sponsored by food manufacturers, thrive on a national scale, enlisting the interest, efforts and imagination of thousands of homemakers. The 4-H Club baking demonstrations, judged by home economics experts coast-to-coast, who hand out the blue, red and white ribbons, promote good baking among future homemakers. The Cherry Pie Baking Contest for girls, formerly national, still is held in some regions. And home-baked pies are entered year after year in state and county fairs to win coveted prizes and recognition for the women who make them.

Pies Capture Hearts

Pies have won their way into our culture—and our sentiments. You've heard a doting grandmother call a grandchild, "Sweetie Pie," an expression of endearment. Husbands and wives use the same affectionate term. The lonely cowboy, returning from a long day in the saddle to the brightest spot on the cattle spread, the chuck wagon, called it the pie box.

Now, the chuck wagon is likely to be a pickup truck, complete with a bottled-gas stove, refrigerator and running water. The dishpan still is the "wreck pan" in which the workers at roundups stack their dishes after a meal. Canned goods are "airtights," sweet syrups are "lick," knives and forks are "artillery." But the bread is usually the commercial loaf. Not the pies, though! They are baked on the spot. A New Mexico roundup helper puts it this way: "Freshly baked pies are the men's favorite dessert. We demand them. And we hope for luck—occasional servings of fresh peach and berry pies."

Some young men still refer to their homes as "the pie house"—a tribute to their mothers' baking skills. One homemaker says: "I've wiped away more than one tear over a letter from my son, far away in military service, when he writes, 'What wouldn't I give for a piece of your chocolate pie!' To cheer myself up, I start planning all the pies I'm going to bake when my boy comes home." And some FARM JOURNAL readers tell us they bake birthday pies for their husbands by request. These men prefer to have lighted candles on pies rather than cakes.

Pies Like Mother Used to Make

It's one of our national traits to hold on to the best of the old that's practical under present conditions and to accept the best of the new with enthusiasm, like chiffon and ice cream pies. Almost all women at one time feel the urge to bake an old-fashioned pie whose appeal has been proved through the generations. Frequently the spur is the husband with a yen for a wonderful pie his mother used to make. Some old baking techniques worth holding on to (although more work than most women would put into everyday pie) are the maneuvers with crust.

New England, most food historians agree, was the cradle of American pies. The tricks with crust which women there used were not glamorous; they created good eating, not beauty. Indeed they were as free of adornment as a Puritan hat. Take-off crusts, for example. Some homemakers still make apple pies (and peach) this way. They place the apples in the pastry-lined pan and gently lay the crust on top, but do not seal it to the undercrust. After baking the pie, they carefully lift off the top crust, add the sugar and spices and return the pastry lid to the pie. Champions of this old-fashioned pie insist that the fruit sweetened after baking has an unusually fresh-from-the-orchard taste. (For peaches, they usually combine

½ cup sugar with the fruit before baking and pour a cool, delicate custard instead of sugar and spices, into the finished pie.)

Old-time pour-through crusts have a somewhat larger band of loyal supporters (see Dutch-Style Apple Pie, Chapter 3). The apple pie, for instance, is made in the standard way, except that the steam vents in the top crust are cut larger. About 5 minutes before the pie is done, early-day homemakers would take it from the oven and pour ½ cup heavy cream (for a nine-inch pie) through the vents, then finish the baking. A similar custom, with some ardent admirers, is performed with baked apple pie. Just before serving, the cook cuts around the pie with a small sharp knife, through the crust, near the fluted edge. She lifts the cut-out circle and pours the cream into the pie, places the crust back on the pie, cuts and serves it.

Bake an Old-Fashioned Pie

There are times when a truly old-fashioned pie becomes a great conversation piece. You'll find some in this Cookbook—2-Crust Lemon, Shoofly, Lemon Whey, Brown-Butter Butterscotch and Marlborough, to name a few. For the butterscotch pie (Chapter 4), you brown the butter and then add dark brown sugar. Requires close skillet watching to avoid scorching the butter, but it has its own taste that some people rave over. Certainly it's not as foolproof as the recipe for Butterscotch Cream Pie in the same chapter, one of our own Test Kitchen specials.

Try the historic Marlborough Pie (Chapter 3), a glorification of everyday apple pie, that is thickened with eggs; lemon juice and grated peel point up the flavors. This pie is still served in New England, and during the Thursday-through-Sunday Thanksgiving holiday it shares honors with pumpkin, mince and cranberry pies. Sometimes slivers (small triangles) of the four pies are served together to make the proper traditional meal ending at this season.

Pies for Calorie Counters

Perhaps the greatest compliment to pies is the way the dessert holds its own in a weight-conscious age—proof that they're too good to give up. True, some of the exceptionally rich treats have been abandoned. Hoosier

Cream Pie, for instance, the old-fashioned pie previously mentioned. Its filling contained only pure cream, sugar, flavoring and a little flour for thickening. Apple-Pork Pie (Chapter 6) is disappearing even from farm tables. Part of its decline can be attributed to the changing farm scene. Now that farm animals usually are slaughtered, processed and the meat frozen in locker plants, there's rarely the former excess of salt pork that must be used. So naturally, apple pie with salt pork, cut in pieces the size of small peas, combined with the fruit and baked in pastry, would be baked less frequently, regardless of its calorie content. (Good, though!)

The excellent cooks of this country have, however, found ways to reduce calories, either in a meal they'll end with pie, or in the pie itself. You'll find lower-calorie pies scattered throughout this Cookbook. And in Chapter 2 there are special recipes for crusts that contain minimum amounts of fat.

We serve more single-crust pies today—one gesture to weight control. We often substitute whipped dry milk and packaged whip mix for whipped cream. Frequently we cut pies in smaller pieces—especially the rich ones. You'll notice that the recipes in this Cookbook give pan sizes, but rarely suggest the number of servings. How a woman divides a pie is an individual matter controlled by the rest of the meal, the family's appetite and degree of weight consciousness.

No Matter How You Cut It

All country homemakers know that, traditionally, an eight-inch pie cuts 4 to 6 wedges, a nine-inch, 6 and a ten-inch, 8. Frequently, if the pie is not being served to men who do hard physical labor, women cut more wedges. Or they cut the pieces of uneven size, the larger ones for grownups, the smaller for the children. And for preschool youngsters, often only the filling, baked in custard cups instead of in pastry, is served.

You can easily cut a pie in 5 pieces of equal size if that arrangement fits your family. Here's the way to do it. Start at the center of the pie and cut a straight line to the edge of the pie. From the center above the line, cut a V. You then will have a capital Y, the upper part making a wedge. Divide the 2 remaining large pieces in half. You will have pieces the same size. Practice with pencil and paper before you use a knife on a pie, to make certain the V is the right width. Of course, you can cut a narrower V if you wish to cut 1 wedge smaller than the other 4.

When our recipe indicates that an eight- or nine-inch pie makes more than 6 servings, that's our way of saying the pie is extremely rich.

Freezers Revolutionize Pie Storage

Home food freezers have practically banished seasons for pies—like pumpkin in autumn, cherry at cherry-picking time and dewberry and boysenberry when the berries are ripe in the patch. Even the wild fruits—blueberries, blackberries, huckleberries, raspberries, elderberries, mulberries and the West's service berries (pronounced sarvis)—are frozen when ripe for year-round pie baking. Colorado mountain ranchwomen often complain that bears get more than their share of the raspberry crop, Minnesota women that bears are too fond of blueberries. So we still have our frontiers where wild animals interfere with pie baking!

Freezers also have changed the pattern of storing pies. Less than a century ago, pie safes with pierced tin panels were standard equipment in Pennsylvania Dutch and other farm kitchens. The perforations in the tin formed decorative designs, which partly explains why these safes today are antique-fanciers' prizes. The tiny openings provided ventilation for the rows of pies on the shelves waiting for hungry people, and also gave protection from flies in an age when windows were unscreened and fly sprays were unknown.

New England homemakers often baked from 50 to 100 mince pies in November, stacked them in covered stone crocks and stored them in the woodshed or some other service room attached to the rear of the house. The pies were protected by a roof. And so was the homemaker; she did not have to step out in the snow and cold to bring them, when needed, to the kitchen to thaw and warm on the shelves of the pie cupboard in the fireplace chimney. (In Boston, this was after mince pies "came back." Originally they were baked in manger-shaped pans at Christmastime, with the shape of the pies symbolic of the Christ child's manger and the spices of the gifts of the Three Wise Men. The Puritans considered these pies idolatrous and abolished not only the pies by law, but also the outward celebration aspects of Christmas.)

Today's farm homemakers usually bake at least a couple of extra pies while they have the rolling pin out and the ingredients handy. A member of FARM JOURNAL's Family Test Group says: "I seldom bake one pie at a time. Ordinarily, I make 4 to 6 and the same number of crusts and put them in the freezer. I make these pies in assorted sizes so that I can select the one that best fits the number of people to be served."

Modern Pie-making Bees

It's not too unusual for two or more farm women to spend a day together in one of their kitchens making pies to freeze when a fruit is plentiful. They socialize while they work—a new kind of get-together, replacing the quilting bee. (Some homemakers prefer to fix and freeze pie fillings instead of the finished pie. This Cookbook gives the directions.)

Cars become pie wagons as visiting neighbors take their share of the pies home to their freezers. Convenient pie carriers, plastic and metal, simplify toting one or two pies to community suppers, bake sales and other places. Compare the ease of this system with the Southern custom of horse-and-buggy days, when women stacked transparent pies (a form of chess pie) and fastened them together by spreading on a cooked frosting so they could be carried safely in a basket to all-day picnics once so popular.

What's Your Pie Appeal?

How attractive are your shut, open and bar pies, as Grandmother classified the pies she baked? (We refer to them as 2-crust, 1-crust and open-face pies.) Many of today's cooks are not the top-crust artists their mothers and grandmothers were. If you want to fix pies with fancy tops and pretty edges, read the suggestions in Chapter 2. Perhaps we also can take a few lessons from old-time Dutch or German women in Pennsylvania, Virginia, Connecticut and North Carolina, who excelled in creating beautiful pies (extra good) with tools commonplace in their kitchens—the 4-tined fork, for instance.

One of their homespun tricks was to run a fork in one direction over the top of an unbaked 2-crust pie, then the other direction. The lines formed a plaid. In baking, the surface at different levels took on variegated shades of brown—most attractive and it cost no more. Or they would cut a design (steam vents) in the top crust with a sharp knife—through the pastry in some places, not quite through in others. With a thin knife blade, they carefully lifted the cut edges (in places where the cut was not through the crust) to ruffle during the baking. Again uneven browning made the pie top intriguing.

Take a thimble from your sewing basket. Wash and use it for a pattern, as your grandmothers did, to cut steam vents and a Coin Edge (Chapter 2). Today there are tiny cookie and canapé cutters of many shapes that make interesting steam vents and trims for pie edges. And some homemakers paint pastry cutouts with egg-yolk paint—a few drops of food color added to egg yolk—and bake them separately from the 1-crust pie. They arrange them over the baked pie.

Hearty Main-Dish Pies

While the major part of this book features dessert pies, the last two chapters are filled with tempting meat, chicken, fish, sea food, cheese and vegetable pies. Many of these main-dish pies are outstanding enough to serve on special occasions. All of them are simply delicious. Explore these pages and use the recipes to give your meals a pleasing change, your meat platters a rest. Interestingly enough, main-course pies have not caught on in America the way dessert pies have. But in Europe they are great favorites. We think our recipes will make fans out of you and your family.

Try a cheese pie some evening. Or shrimp pie. Treat your family to Brunswick Chicken Pie. Or make the crusty chicken pie with the light meat on one side, the dark on the other. Notice the tantalizing effect the fragrance has on everyone around the table when the serving spoon cuts through the flaky crust into the steaming gravy and chicken. Guaranteed to fascinate guests! Serve updated Shepherd's Pie with pride—there are farmers who say no better way of serving leftover roast beef or lamb, mashed potatoes and brown gravy has ever been invented. You'll wonder why main-dish pies could be neglected.

Perfect Pies Every Time

Never were pies so good as they are today. Research has improved and standardized ingredients and techniques. For instance, you'll observe that many of the pies in this Cookbook are baked at a constant temperature—

no adjusting of the oven regulator during baking is necessary. And top-notch ingredients are universally available. (Especially has rancid fat become rare in home kitchens!)

But the best part of all is that any woman who wants to bake perfect pies can realize her ambition—quickly. All she need do is follow the recipes and directions in this Cookbook. If she does this, the old expression "easy as pie" will come true for her.

Every neighborhood has a few women experienced in cooking who are locally famous for their crusts and pies. Some beginners (often brides) believe these homemakers are born with special talents in baking. They don't realize how many of them learned by the discouraging "trial and error" method no longer necessary with up-to-date recipes and directions. What suggestions do these wonderful home bakers have for new cooks?

Universally, their first tip is: Use a light hand with pastry. The next one: roll the dough lightly from the center in all directions to make a circle, lifting the rolling pin near the edges to avoid splitting the pastry or getting it too thin. Lift the pastry to the pie pan gently—as carefully as you'd handle a full-blown rose—and avoid stretching it. Bend your right index finger (if you're right-handed) and fit the pastry into the pan. One expert pie maker, remembering her first pies, sympathetically adds: "Don't despair if you tear the pastry. Pinch the edges together or put on a pastry patch so the juices can't run away. But do avoid a repeat of the mishap when you bake the next pie."

First Things First—Pastry

Turn the pages of this Cookbook—cooking adventure and success are that near. For with pie, it's pastry first, and the next chapter is all about pastry. Master the making of pie crusts and you've won more than half of the victory in achieving perfect pies. When you're proud of the traditional and oil pastry you make, branch out and try some of the marvelous specialties in this chapter—like cheese, orange, egg, cornmeal and peanut pastry. And when you're making a lemon pie, do use the pastry designed especially for pies made with sunny, citrus fruit. Make many kinds of crusts, not only those with graham cracker crumbs. Use those made with coconut, cereals, nuts, cookie dough and pretzels, for instance, and the light, crunchy-crisp meringues.

From the chapter on pie crusts turn the pages of this book to plump and juicy fruit pies; delicate, browned-topped custards; flavorful cream pies and the make-ahead beauties; refrigerator and ice cream pies. Continue your recipe tour to deep-dish fruit and cake pies, homey cobblers, apples and peaches baked in flaky dumpling jackets, party-pretty tarts and dainty turnovers. You'll want to stop long enough to get acquainted with the appealing fast-fix pies if ever you're short on time for cooking. Your dessert journey ends with glamorous, sweet pie toppings that offer new flavor blends and a new look. By this time, we believe you'll have a long list of pies you'll want to bake soon.

But keep reading and get acquainted with the main-dish pies. You'll find their succulent tastes a big help in putting new zip and surprise in your meals.

Round Out a Square Meal

"Cutting the pie" has come to mean dividing something good. And that's exactly what we are doing with this Cookbook—sharing with you favorite pie recipes from farm women in all parts of the country and from our own Test Kitchens. We hope you will enjoy making and serving many of these luscious pies. You can do so with complete confidence that your family will compliment you on your baking skill and guests will beg for your recipes.

Remember that pies please men. Since men are the great pie eaters and promoters, let's give a rancher friend the last word—his definition of his favorite dessert: "A triangle of pie is the best way ever discovered to round out a square meal."

CHAPTER 2

PIE CRUSTS OF ALL KINDS

Pie crust is one of the great kitchen discoveries of all time. Women who transform flour, salt, fat and water into flaky, fork-tender, golden pastry are magicians in their way. They pull gorgeous pies from ovens rather than colored-silk handkerchiefs from hats. Think of the pleasure they bring— velvet-smooth pumpkin pies for Thanksgiving reunions, juicy cherry pies for February parties and plump apple pies for friendly Sunday dinners.

Country women know you can't have a good pie without a good crust. What some homemakers don't appreciate is the way you can introduce tasty variety in pies by using different crusts. This chapter has two impor- tant purposes—to help you make perfect pies every time and to encourage you to experiment with the many kinds of pie crusts we give you.

You'll first find basic pastry, both that made with solid vegetable short- ening or lard, and with salad oil. Perfecting these basics is the initial step in successful pie making. There also are recipes for Electric-Mixer Pastry, Homemade Pie Crust Mixes, special crusts for tarts and turnovers, one particularly luscious with butter, Beginner's Pastry (the paste method) and a short-cut version that you mix in the pie pan.

Then we have the specialty crusts, mentioned in Chapter 1—everything from fancy pastry to crumb, cereal, coconut and crispy-firm meringue pie shells, large and individual sizes, for angel pies. Biscuit Toppers for Main- Dish Pies (the recipe also makes wonderful hot biscuits) with nine varia- tions are included. At the chapter end you'll find our Pie Clinic, which gives you the reasons your pies may fall short of perfection and answers your pastry questions.

Many suggestions for making pretty pies and fancy edges are described. You'll enjoy using these dress-up ideas for pies to tote to church and com- munity suppers and bake sales.

Perfect Pastry for Country Pies

Country cooks need no introduction to perfect pastry; they know a good pie crust when they see, cut and taste it. The top of the pie is light-golden to golden in the center, the brown deepening slightly toward the edges. It has what our grandmothers called "bloom," a soft luster rather than a dull look.

The surface of the baked crust is a little blistery or irregular, although pastry made with hot water or oil usually is smoother (it also is more mealy than pastry made with lard or other shortening). The crust is thin. It's delicately crisp and flaky, easy to cut, fork-tender and not crumbly; it holds its shape when cut.

Blandness in taste is characteristic and desirable—the filling provides heightened flavors. The taste depends primarily on just the right amount of salt and on the kind of fat used. It's important, of course, to use high-quality fat, free of rancidity.

In this chapter's recipes, use all-purpose flour unless another kind is listed. If you use flour that does not require sifting, follow package directions. Or use the special pastry recipe we give for instant-type flour.

There's no mystery about pastry making. All you need do to achieve success is to be loyal to the recipe you are following in this chapter.

Do not improvise. Heed the technique suggested and *do not change the ingredients*—their proportions are balanced. Just one warning—be careful when adding water. If you add too much, you'll have to increase the flour to take care of it and the ratio of fat to flour is upset. This is one of the common causes of inferior pie crusts.

When it comes to making *attractive* pies, every woman is largely on her own. We do give you tips for pretty pie tops and fancy edges, which may help. Be an observing pie scout—look at the pies you see at parties, church suppers, bake sales and other places. Notice why some of them are especially attractive. Don't be afraid to copy some of the ideas you see.

Do serve your pies the day you bake them unless you are freezing them or making one by a recipe that specifies otherwise. It's the fresh-baked quality that won first place among desserts for pies on the farms and eventually in the entire United States. Their supremacy constantly is challenged by other desserts, but never successfully. Country cooks have had much to do with keeping pie the top-ranking American dessert—a tribute to the women on farms and ranches.

Basic Pastry-making Tools

Standard measuring spoons and cup

Mixing bowl (large enough to hold all ingredients with ample room for measuring)

Pastry blender, 2 table knives or an electric mixer at low speed (to cut shortening or lard into flour)

Fork (to combine water with flour-shortening mixture)

Evenly floured pastry cloth or board or waxed paper (for rolling pastry)

Rolling pin that rolls easily (floured stockinette cover helps prevent sticking when pastry is not rolled between sheets of waxed paper)

Pie pans of size (check by measuring top inside diameter) recommended in recipe (members of FARM JOURNAL's Family Test Group have more 9″ pans, but many kitchens have 8″ and 10″ pans)

Pie pans that absorb and distribute heat evenly, such as glass or dull aluminum (shiny pans reflect heat and interfere with browning)

Pie server (wedge-shaped spatula)

Flaky Pastry

This is the traditional or standard pie crust. Make it with solid fats, except butter and margarine. Measure shortening or lard in nested measuring cups. Press it into the cup to avoid air pockets and level it off with a knife or spatula.

FLAKY PASTRY FOR 2-CRUST PIE

(*Traditional Method*)

2 c. sifted flour
1 tsp. salt
¾ c. vegetable shortening or ⅔ c. lard
4 to 5 tblsp. cold water

• Combine flour and salt in mixing bowl. Cut in shortening with pastry blender or with two knives until mixture is the consistency of coarse cornmeal or tiny peas.

• Sprinkle on cold water, 1 tblsp. at a time, tossing mixture lightly and stirring with fork. Add water each time to the driest part of mixture. The dough should be just moist enough to hold together when pressed gently with a fork. It should not be sticky.

• Shape dough in smooth ball with hands, and roll. Or if you are not ready to make the pie, wrap it in waxed paper and refrigerate 30 minutes or until ready to fill and bake pie.

• Makes crust for 1 (8″ or 9″) 2-crust pie, 2 (8″ or 9″) pie shells, 8 or 9 (4″) tart shells, 1 (9″ or 10″) pie with latticed top or topping for 2 (8″ or 9″) deep-dish pies.

To Make 2-Crust Pie

• Divide dough in half and shape in 2 flat balls, smoothing edges so there are no breaks.

Bottom Crust: Press 1 dough ball in flat circle with hands on lightly floured surface. Roll it lightly with short strokes from center in all directions to ⅛" thickness, making a 10" to 11" circle. Fold rolled dough in half and ease it loosely into pie pan with fold in center. Unfold and fit into pan, using care not to stretch dough. Gently press out air pockets with finger tips. Make certain there are no openings for juices to escape.

• Trim edge even with pie pan. Then roll top crust.

Top Crust: Roll second ball of dough like the first one (for bottom crust). Put filling in pastry-lined pan. Fold pastry circle in half; lift it to the top of the pie with fold in center. Gently unfold over top of pie. Trim with scissors to ½" beyond edge of pie. Fold top edge under bottom crust and press gently with fingers to seal and to make an upright edge. Crimp edge as desired.

• Cut vents in top crust or prick with fork to allow steam to escape. (Or cut vents before placing pastry on top of pie.) Bake as pie recipe directs.

Lattice Pie Tops Display Filling

Country women especially like to top their pies with a pastry lattice when the filling is colorful—cherries, for instance. For the same reason, this peek-a-boo topping is traditional for cranberry pies in Cape Cod communities.

Many farm women roll pastry slightly thicker than usual for a lattice top. That's because the strips are easier to handle.

There are several ways to make the lattice. Here are a few of the favorites, including the new Wedge Lattice, developed in our Test Kitchens.

LATTICE PIE TOP: Line pie pan with pastry as described, leaving 1" overhang. Cut rolled pastry for top crust in strips ½" wide. Add filling to pastry-lined pan. Moisten rim of pie with water and lay half of the strips over

the pie about 1" apart. Repeat with remaining strips, placing them in opposite direction in diamond or square pattern. Trim strips even with pie edge. Turn bottom crust's overhang up over rim and ends of strips. Press firmly all around to seal strips to rim. Flute edge as desired.

FANCY LATTICE TOP: Twist strips of pastry placed over pie to make the lattice; cut strips with rippled pastry wheel to give a pretty edge.

WOVEN LATTICE TOP: Lay half the pastry strips 1" apart over the filled pie. Weave the first cross strip through the center. Add another cross strip, first folding back every other strip to help in weaving crosswise strips over and under. Continue weaving until lattice is complete. Fold lower crust over pastry strips, press firmly around the edge to seal strips to the rim. Flute edge as desired. You may find it easier to weave lattice on waxed paper, lifting it on to pie.

SPIRAL TOPPING: Cut pastry strips ¾" wide and fasten them together by moistening ends with water and pressing with fingers. Twist strip and swirl in spiral from pie's center, covering pie's filling.

WEDGE LATTICE: Cut long strips of pastry ½" wide. Place on top of pie in the same number of wedge shapes as you plan to cut pieces of pie (see color photo elsewhere in book), keep sides of wedges inside lines where you will cut serving pieces. Use more pastry strips to make smaller V shapes inside the larger wedges, trimming off excess pastry. Press ends to moistened pastry on pan edge. Fold pastry overhang to cover ends of pastry strips and seal. Finish with decorative edge.

FLAKY PASTRY FOR 1-CRUST PIE

(*Traditional Method*)

1   c. sifted flour
½   tsp. salt
⅓   c. plus 1 tblsp. vegetable short-
      ening or ⅓ c. lard
2   to 2½ tblsp. cold water

· Combine ingredients as directed for Pastry for 2-Crust Pie, traditional method. Shape 1 smooth ball of dough. Makes enough for 1 (8" or 9") pie shell or top crust for 1½ qt. casserole.

TO MAKE PIE SHELL

Unbaked: On lightly floured surface roll Pastry for 1-Crust Pie. Roll it lightly from the center out in all directions to ⅛" thickness, making a 10" to 11" circle. Fold rolled dough in half and ease it loosely into pie pan, with fold in center. Gently press out air pockets with finger tips and make certain there are no openings for juices to escape.

· Fold under edge of crust and press into an upright rim. Crimp edge as desired. Refrigerate until ready to fill.

Baked: Make pie shell as directed for Unbaked Pie Shell, pricking entire surface evenly and closely (¼" to ½" apart) with a 4-tined fork. Refrigerate ½ hour. Meanwhile, preheat oven. Bake pie shell in very hot oven (450° F.) from 10 to 15 minutes, or until browned the way you like it. Cool before filling.

PASTRY FOR (10") 2-CRUST PIE

(*Traditional Method*)

3   c. sifted flour
1½   tsp. salt
1   c. plus 2 tblsp. vegetable short-
        ening or 1 c. lard
6   tblsp. water

· Combine as directed in recipe for Flaky Pastry for 2-Crust Pie.

GOOD IDEA: Draw a circle on waxed paper to use for a guide in rolling pastry. Make the circle about 1½" to 2" larger than your pie-pan diameter.

HOMEMADE PASTRY MIX

With Lard:

7   c. sifted flour
4   tsp. salt
2   c. lard

With Vegetable Shortening:

6   c. sifted flour
1   tblsp. salt
1   (1 lb.) can vegetable shortening (about 2 ⅓ c.)

• Mix flour and salt in large bowl. Cut in lard or shortening until mixture resembles coarse meal. Cover and store mix made with lard in refrigerator. It will keep about a month. Store mix made with vegetable shortening in a cool place. It does not require refrigeration. Makes from 8 to 9 cups.

How to Use Pastry Mix

To Make a 1-Crust Pie: Use 2 to 4 tblsp. cold water and:

1 ¼   c. mix for 8″ pie
1 ½   c. mix for 9″ pie
1 ¾   c. mix for 10″ pie

To Make a 2-Crust Pie: Use 4 to 6 tblsp. cold water and:

2   to 2 ¼ c. mix for 8″ pie
2 ¼   to 2 ½ c. mix for 9″ pie
2 ½   to 2 ¾ c. mix for 10″ pie

• Measure mix into bowl. Sprinkle on water, a small amount at a time, mixing quickly and evenly with fork until dough just holds together in a ball. Use no more water than necessary.
• Proceed as with traditional pastry.

GOOD IDEA: Spread a sheet of aluminum foil directly on bottom of oven under a 2-Crust fruit pie to catch runaway juices. When so placed, it will not deflect the heat from the pie.

GOOD IDEAS FROM OUR TEST KITCHENS

Home economists in FARM JOURNAL's Test Kitchens prefer to use ice water instead of cold water in pastry making. They recommend that beginners put the water in a salt shaker to sprinkle over the flour-shortening mixture. This helps to add the water evenly.

They like to cut two thirds of the shortening or lard into the flour until it resembles cornmeal, then to cut in the remaining third until the particles are the size of small peas.

Pastry with Instant-Type Flour

There are two methods of making pastry with instant-type flour. The ingredients for both are combined with the electric mixer. Follow directions carefully and accurately.

METHOD NUMBER ONE

PASTRY FOR 2-CRUST PIE

1 ¾   c. instant-type flour
1   tsp. salt
¾   c. vegetable shortening
¼   c. cold water

Glamorize your favorite pie filling *by serving it in an unusual Walnut-Cereal Crust or Cheese Pastry shell (recipes, pages 37, 33). Our colorful berry pie features a new simple wedge lattice and fancy edge (see pages 21 and 27).*

• Measure flour and salt into electric mixer's small bowl. Stir to mix. Add shortening and mix at low speed about 1 minute, scraping bowl constantly. Add water and continue mixing until all flour is moistened, about 1 minute. Scrape bowl constantly. (You may need to add 1 to 2 tsp. more water, but be careful not to add too much.) Shape in smooth ball with hands.

• Follow directions for making 2-Crust Pie from Flaky Pastry.

• Makes 1 (8″ or 9″) 2-crust pie.

Note: You can use ½ c. plus 2 tblsp. lard instead of vegetable shortening.

PASTRY FOR 1-CRUST PIE

1   c. instant-type flour
½   tsp. salt
⅓   c. plus 1 tblsp. vegetable short-
       ening
2   tblsp. cold water

• Combine as for Pastry for 2-Crust Pie. Shape in smooth ball of dough. Makes 1 (8″ or 9″) pie shell.

Note: You can use ⅓ c. lard instead of the vegetable shortening.

METHOD NUMBER TWO

PASTRY FOR 2-CRUST PIE

⅓   c. plus 1 tblsp. cold water
¾   c. shortening
2   c. instant-type flour
1   tsp. salt

• Measure all ingredients into electric mixer's bowl. Mix on lowest speed until dough begins to form, 15 to 30 seconds. Shape in firm, smooth ball with hands. Follow directions for 2-Crust Pie from Flaky Pastry.

• Makes 1 (8″ or 9″) 2-crust pie.

PASTRY FOR 1-CRUST PIE

¼   c. water
½   c. shortening
1 ¼ c. instant-type flour
½   tsp. salt

• Combine as for pastry for 2-Crust Pie. Shape in firm, smooth ball.

• Makes 1 (8″ or 9″) pie shell.

ELECTRIC-MIXER PASTRY

Blending is done with mixer—no cutting of shortening into flour and salt

2-Crust 8″ or 9″ Pie
⅔   c. vegetable shortening
1 ¾ c. flour
1   tsp. salt
¼   c. cold water

1-Crust 8″ or 9″ Pie
¼   c. vegetable shortening
¾   c. flour
½   tsp. salt
2   tblsp. cold water

• Place shortening, flour and salt in mixer bowl. Blend at low speed about ½ minute or until mixture is consistency of coarse cornmeal.   *more*

Sing a song of spring *by baking our Fresh Rhubarb Pie shown in photo at left. In this garden-fresh, country favorite, the pink, juicy sweet-tart filling has a delicate orange taste. You'll find this wonderful recipe on page 96.*

· Add all water at one time and mix on low speed about 15 seconds, or until dough clings together. Shape dough in ball. It should feel moist. Follow directions for crusts mixed by traditional method.

Freezing Pastry

Busy farm women sometimes find it easier to make pies and tarts if they have the frozen pastry shells on hand. Other homemakers prefer to freeze pastry dough to thaw and shape when they're ready to use it. Here are directions to follow:

BAKED PIE AND TART SHELLS: Freeze without wrapping. When frozen, wrap with sheet freezer material and seal or place in freezer bags.

To use, unwrap and heat in moderate oven (375°F.) about 10 minutes. If more convenient, let thaw, unwrapped, at room temperature.

UNBAKED PIE AND TART SHELLS: Freeze without wrapping. Stack when frozen, placing crumpled waxed paper between them for easier separation. Package or place in freezer bags, and return to freezer.

To use, unwrap and bake in very hot oven (450°F.) 5 minutes. Then prick with 4-tined fork and continue baking until browned, about 15 minutes.

UNBAKED PASTRY: Roll it before or after freezing. If rolled, stack the circles with 2 or 3 sheets of waxed paper between them. Freeze and then package or place in freezer bags. Wrap unrolled pastry dough in freezer paper or plastic wrapping and place in freezer.

To use frozen pastry, unwrap and let it thaw at room temperature; then proceed as if it had just been made.

Note: The recommended storage time for unbaked pie and tart shells and pastry is 2 months; for baked pie and tart shells and pastry, 4 to 6 months.

Pie Crusts Made with Oil

The pastry dough is tender. Be sure to roll it between sheets of waxed paper. One advantage of using oil is that it's easy to measure.

PASTRY FOR 2-CRUST PIE

(*With Oil*)

2   c. sifted flour
1   tsp. salt
½   c. cooking or salad oil
3   tblsp. cold water

· Sift flour and salt into mixing bowl. Add oil, mix well with fork. Sprinkle cold water over mixture and mix well.

· With hands press mixture into a smooth ball. (If mix is too dry, add 1 to 2 tblsp. more oil, a little at a time and then shape ball.) Divide ball in half and flatten both parts slightly. Makes 1 (8″ or 9″) 2-crust pie or 2 (8″ or 9″) pie shells.

PASTRY FOR 1-CRUST PIE

(*With Oil*)

1⅓   c. sifted flour
½   tsp. salt
⅓   c. cooking or salad oil
2   tblsp. cold water

• Combine ingredients as directed for Pastry for 2-Crust Pie with cooking oil. Make 1 smooth ball of dough. (If mixture is too dry, add 1 to 2 tblsp. more oil, a little at a time.) Makes 1 (8″ or 9″) pie shell.

To Make 2-Crust Pie
(With Oil)

Bottom Crust: Wipe countertop or board with a damp cloth so waxed paper will not slip. Roll out 1 dough ball to circle between 2 (12″) square sheets waxed paper to edge of paper. Peel off top sheet of paper and gently invert pastry over pie plate; peel off paper. (The pastry is tender. If it tears, press edges together or lightly press a patch over it.)
• Fit pastry carefully into pie pan, using care not to stretch. Trim evenly with edge of pan.

Top Crust: Roll out remaining dough ball between two sheets of waxed paper as directed for Bottom Crust. Peel off top paper. Add filling to pastry-lined pan. Arrange rolled pastry over filled pie and peel off paper. Cut vents for steam to escape. Trim crust ½″ beyond edge of pie pan; fold top crust under bottom crust. Flute edge. Bake as pie recipe directs.

To Make Pie Shell
(Oil Pastry)

Unbaked Pie Shell: Wipe countertop or board with a damp cloth so paper will not slip. Roll out pastry between 2 (12″) sheets waxed paper to edge of paper. Peel off top sheet of paper and gently invert pastry over pie pan; peel off paper. Fit pastry into pie pan, pressing gently with finger tips toward center of pan.
• Trim crust ½″ beyond edge of pie pan, fold under edge of crust and crimp to make upright rim. Refrigerate until ready to fill and bake.

Baked Pie Shell: Make pie shell as directed for Unbaked Pie Shell, only prick entire surface evenly with 4-tined fork. Refrigerate ½ hour. Meanwhile, preheat oven. Bake pie shell in very hot oven (450°F.), 10 to 15 minutes, until browned. Cool before filling.

GOOD IDEA: Roll pastry between waxed paper to the desired size. Chill in waxed paper while you fix the pie filling. You'll find the paper will peel off easily from the pastry. This is one way to avoid rolling too much flour into the dough.

Pastry with Less Fat

If someone in the family is counting calories, or if you're cutting down on fat in your diet, we have two recipes for satisfactory pastry with less than the usual amount of fat. Follow mixing directions closely—they were worked out by U. S. Department of Agriculture scientists. Do not try to freeze either of the recipes. The low-oil pastry and pastry made with less than ⅓ c. shortening to 1 c. flour do not freeze satisfactorily.

SOLID-FAT PASTRY

Breaking the solid fat into fine particles and sprinkling in water distributes them evenly—makes for flakiness

- 2 c. sifted flour
- ¾ tsp. salt
- ½ c. lard or vegetable shortening (room temperature)
- 3 tblsp. water

· Sift flour and salt together into mixing bowl. Using an electric mixer on lowest speed, blend lard into dry ingredients for 2 minutes, then sprinkle in the water gradually while blending 1 minute. Or, cut in fat with pastry blender or two knives until finely distributed. The dough will look dry and crumbly, but will shape into a ball. Roll out between sheets of waxed paper. Makes 1 (8″ or 9″) 2-crust pie.

OIL PASTRY

Even distribution of oil and water makes melt-in-the-mouth pastry

- ½ c. minus 1 tblsp. cooking or salad oil
- ¼ c. water
- 2 c. sifted flour
- ¾ tsp. salt

· Shake together oil and water (both at room temperature).
· Sift dry ingredients together into mixing bowl; sprinkle with water-oil mixture while blending with electric mixer at lowest speed for 3 minutes. Or, stir it in with a fork. Dough will seem dry but it can be molded easily by hand. Shape it into ball, flatten slightly, roll out between sheets of waxed paper. Makes 1 (8″ or 9″) 2-crust pie.

Pretty Tops for Country Pies

Country cooks have many last-minute, quick, glamorous touches for 2-crust pies. They use the ingredients in their kitchens and obtain attractive results. Here are the favorites of FARM JOURNAL readers and of our food staff.

SPARKLE TOPS: With fingers, moisten top crust with cold water and sprinkle evenly with a little sugar.

SHINY TOPS: Brush top pastry crust lightly with beaten egg or egg yolk, cream, milk, undiluted evaporated milk or melted butter, margarine, shortening or salad oil. Sprinkle with sugar, if desired.

DECORATIVE VENTS: Use tiny cookie cutters or cut around homemade patterns with sharp knife to make steam vents in the shape of the fruit in the pie—cherries, apples or a cluster of grapes, for instance.

INITIAL TOPS: Farm women frequently cut initials with a knife or prick them with a fork for steam vents —A for apple, B for blueberry or C for cherry. These steam vents are especially helpful at bake sales because they indicate the kind of pie at a glance.

Fancy Pie Edges

FLUTES: Trim pastry ½″ beyond rim and fold under to make double rim. Make a stand-up rim. Place left index finger inside pastry rim. With right thumb and index finger on outside of rim, press pastry into V shapes ½″ apart. Pinch flutes to make points, if desired. For 1- or 2-crust pies.

SCALLOPS: Form like flutes but do not make points. Flatten each flute with a 4-tined fork. For 2-crust pies.

FORK TRIM: Make a high-standing rim. With 4-tined fork, press pastry to rim at ½″ intervals. For 1- or 2-crust pies.

ROPE: Turn overhang under and make a stand-up rim. Press right thumb into pastry at an angle. Press pastry between right thumb and knuckle of index finger. Repeat around the pie. For 1- or 2-crust pies.

COIN: Trim overhang even with pie pan. Cut circles the size of pennies from pastry scraps with toy cookie cutter, thimble or bottle cap. Moisten rim with cold water and place circles on rim, overlapping them slightly. Press lightly to rim. For 1-crust pies.

FLUTED COIN: Fold under overhang; make stand-up rim; flute pastry. From extra pastry, cut rounds of dough to size that will fit the indentations of fluting; moisten outside edges of fluting and press into each flute a round of dough standing on edge. (See Cream Pies photo.)

CORNUCOPIA: Leave ¾″ overhang, cut with scissors in sawtooth design, making "teeth" that are 1″ wide at pan edge; roll from one angled side of each to make cornucopia that rests on pan edge.

BEAN CUTTER: Fold under overhang; use cutter for French-style green beans to press design all around edge. (See photo of unusual pie shells.)

WREATH: Fold under overhang; make stand-up rim. Snip pastry with scissors at ¼″ intervals. Lay cut pieces alternately toward pie and away from pie.

SAWTOOTH: Cut pastry overhang with scissors in sawtooth design; moisten rim and fold the triangles of pastry up on rim, pointing to center of pie; press down. (See Lemon Pies photo.)

LOOPED: Trim pastry even with pan edge; cut extra strip of pastry same width as pan edge; mold pastry strip over pencil held at right angles to pan edge to make loop; press bottom of loop to seal; keep pastry moistened to seal strip to edge. (See Lemon Pie photo.)

RUFFLE: Fold overhang over pastry on pan edge loosely; press left index finger under fold of pastry, press right index finger firmly next to lifted portion.

BUTTON: Fold under overhang; use handle end of measuring spoon to press design into edge (hole in end of handle makes button design).

FLUTED FORK: Fold under overhang; make 1″ wide flutes that rest on pan edge, with ¼″ flute between them that stands up and points to pan center. Press floured 4-tined fork into each wide flute. (See Rhubarb Pie photo.)

QUARTER-MOON: Trim pastry even with pan edge; cut long strip of pastry same width as pan edge and press down onto moistened pastry on pan edge; with inverted ½-teaspoon measuring spoon, press design of two semi-circles (one inside the other) around edge. (See photo of unusual pie shells.)

Pastry Shells for Miniature Pies

Take your pick of the following methods we suggest for shaping tart shells—the plain and the fancy. Then turn to the tart and turnover recipes in Chapter 7. Once you've read them, you'll start planning an excuse to bake the tiny pies and show them off!

TART SHELLS FROM BASIC PASTRY (FROM 2-CRUST PIE RECIPE)

· Divide pastry into 5 parts. Roll out each part to make 4½″ to 5″ circles.

In Tart Pans: Fit pastry circles into 3½″ tart pans, pressing them evenly over bottoms and sides of pans, removing air bubbles. Let them extend about ½″ beyond pans' edges, turn under and flute. Prick well on bottoms and sides with 4-tined fork. Refrigerate 30 minutes.

On Muffin-Cup Pans or Custard Cups: Fit pastry circles over backs of inverted 3½″ muffin-cup pans. Make pleats so pastry will fit snugly. Prick entire surface with 4-tined fork. Or fit pastry over inverted custard cups, prick well and set on baking sheet. Refrigerate 30 minutes before baking.

Muffin-Cup-Pan Measurements: Regardless of the size of your muffin-cup pans, you can bake tart shells on them. With a string, measure one of the inverted cups down one side, across the bottom and up on the other side. Cut the string this length. Find a bowl, saucer or small plate in the kitchen that has the same diameter as the string. Or cut a cardboard this size. Use for a pattern to cut the rolled pastry in circles. Fit pastry rounds on alternate muffin cups—6 on a pan with 12 cups. Pleat pastry to fit snugly.

With Aluminum Foil: Cut circles of heavy-duty aluminum foil same size as pastry circles (use small saucer as pattern, trimming around it with knife). Lay pastry on them. Shape tart shells by bringing the foil and pastry up and pinching to make flutes or scallops. Or shape as desired. Set shaped tarts on baking sheet and chill 30 minutes.

· *To Bake Tart Shells:* Meanwhile preheat oven to 450°F. Bake tart shells 10 to 12 minutes or until golden. Cool on wire racks. Then carefully remove from pans, custard cups or foil. Fill as desired. Makes 10 tarts. (By rolling pastry thinner, 12 tarts; thicker, 8 tarts.)

VARIATIONS

BUTTER-RICH TART SHELLS: Divide pastry for 2-crust pie in half. Roll first half ⅛" thick and dot with 3 tblsp. firm butter (if too hard or soft, butter breaks through). Fold pastry from two sides to meet in center. Press with fingers to seal. Fold other two ends to center and seal. Wrap in waxed paper and chill. Repeat with other half of pastry. When ready to use, roll out, cut in circles and bake like Tart Shells from Basic Pastry for 2-Crust Pie.

PETAL TART SHELLS: You will need 6 (2¼") circles of pastry for each tart shell. (Cut circles with cookie cutter if you have the right size.) Place 1 circle in bottom of each 2¾" muffin-cup pan or 6 oz. custard cup. Moisten edge of circle with cold water. Press remaining 5 pastry circles to sides and bottom of the cup, overlapping them slightly and pressing firmly to sides and bottom. Prick entire surface with 4-tined fork and bake like Tart Shells.

FLOWER TART SHELLS: Cut pastry in 4" or 5" squares instead of circles. Fit a square in each 3" muffin-cup pans, letting corners stand up. Prick entire surface with 4-tined fork and press pastry firmly to sides and bottoms of pans. Bake like Tart Shells.

TINY TART SHELLS: Use 1¼" muffin-cup pans. Cut rolled pastry with 1¾" cookie cutter or use cardboard circle as pattern and cut around it with knife. Prick, chill and bake like Tart Shells

from Basic Pastry for 2-Crust Pies. Use Cheese Pastry for variety. Makes about 60 tart shells, 1- or 2-bite or canapé size.

READY-TO-GO PASTRY: Prick entire surface of the pastry circles with 4-tined fork. Stack them with waxed paper between. Wrap in aluminum foil or freezer wrap and freeze. To use, preheat oven to 450°F. Remove pastry from freezer and lay rounds over inverted muffin-cup pans or custard cups set on baking sheet. Let thaw just enough so you can pleat it. Bake 10 to 12 minutes or until tart shells are golden. Cool, remove from pans or cups and fill as desired.

Note: Packaged pie-crust mix may be used to make tart shells.

TART SHELLS MADE WITH BUTTER

½   c. soft butter or margarine
¼   c. sugar
¼   tsp. salt
1   egg yolk
1 ½ c. sifted flour
2   tblsp. milk

• Combine butter, sugar and salt in medium bowl and beat until light. Beat in egg yolk.
• Beat in flour and then milk (on low speed if using electric mixer).
• Shape into ball, wrap in waxed paper and refrigerate at least 1 hour.
• Divide chilled dough in 8 equal parts and pat each part into 3¾" tart pans or muffin-cup pans. Set tart pans on large baking sheet. Refrigerate 30 minutes.
• Prick over entire surface of tart shells with 4-tined fork. Bake in mod-

erate oven (375°F.) about 20 minutes, or until golden.
· Partially cool in pans (about 10 minutes); remove from pans and complete cooling. Fill as desired. Makes 8.

VARIATIONS

LEMON TART SHELLS: Substitute 2 tblsp. lemon juice for milk and add 1 tsp. grated lemon peel.

ORANGE TART SHELLS: Substitute 2 tblsp. orange juice for milk and add 2 tsp. grated orange peel.

NUT TART SHELLS: Add ½ c. finely chopped walnuts with the flour.

COCONUT TART SHELLS: Add ½ c. flaked coconut with the flour.

GOOD IDEAS FROM OUR TEST KITCHENS

Home economists in FARM JOURNAL's Test Kitchens, who bake many tarts, find it is easier to prick the pastry after rolling than after it is fitted in or on inverted muffin-cup pans or shaped in foil. They prick it either before or after cutting.

They also roll out pastry scraps, trimmed from 8″ and 9″ pies, cut them in circles for tarts and freeze for later use. It's a thrifty trick. And you'll be surprised how soon you have enough circles to make all the tart shells you need for a party or a meal.

BASIC PUFF PASTRY

The most elegant pastry of all—extra-rich and extra-flaky

1 lb. butter, chilled thoroughly
4¼ c. sifted flour

1 c. ice water
2 tblsp. lemon juice

· Cut ½ lb. butter into flour in large mixing bowl, using pastry blender or two knives, until mixture is crumbly and pale yellow. Add ice water and lemon juice all at once; stir with fork until mixture is moistened completely and pastry is stiff. Shape in a ball, wrap in waxed paper, foil or plastic wrap. Chill at least 30 minutes.
· Roll out on a well-floured pastry cloth into an 18″ × 12″ rectangle, ¼″ thick. Roll pastry straight, lifting rolling pin at edge of pastry so pastry will be of even thickness.
· Slice remaining ½ lb. chilled butter into thin, even pats. Arrange pats over two thirds of pastry, making a 12″ × 12″ square.
· Fold uncovered third of pastry over the middle third. Then fold butter-covered pastry end over the top. Now fold pastry in thirds, crosswise, to make a block. There are 9 layers of pastry with butter between each.
· Roll out again to an 18″ × 12″ rectangle. Fold again as above. Chill 30 minutes.
· Continue rolling, folding and chilling 3 more times. Before each rolling, pastry will be stiff. First pound with rolling pin to flatten, using care to keep thickness uniform.
· After last folding, chill pastry 30 minutes before using. You can wrap in waxed paper and refrigerate or freezer-wrap and store in freezer for use within a month.
· Use to make: Elegant French Pastries (Chapter 7).

PATTY SHELLS

Professional-looking, crisp, golden main-dish or dessert pastry holders

½   recipe Basic Puff Pastry

· Chill 2 baking sheets.
· Roll pastry on lightly floured surface to make a rectangle ¼″ thick. Cut 10 rounds with 3″ plain or fluted cookie cutter.
· Rinse chilled baking sheets with cold water. Place rounds 3″ apart on baking sheets. You can reroll trimmings of pastry to make two more rounds.
· Press 2″ cookie cutter into each pastry round, cutting only halfway through. Refrigerate 30 minutes.
· Bake, one sheet at a time, in very hot oven (450°F.) 15 minutes. Reduce temperature to 350° and bake until lightly browned, about 15 minutes.
· With sharp knife, cut around center circles and carefully remove tops; place tops on baking sheet. Scoop out any uncooked pastry in centers and discard. Return shells and tops to oven and continue baking 5 minutes.
· Repeat with remaining pastry circles on second baking sheet. Use at once, or freeze.
· Serve filled with creamed chicken or shellfish; replace pastry tops. Or use the tops as the base for canapés. Makes 12 patty shells.

Note: Shells also may be used for desserts. Fill with Pastry Cream (recipe in Chapter 7) and garnish with berries or fruit.

Specialty Pie Crusts

Several recipes from farm women are featured in this section. Try them to find out why they are such favorites —and to treat your family and friends to something different. Many good country cooks like to include egg, vinegar and lemon juice and other special ingredients in their pastry. It's wise to use recipes designed especially for such additions.

SHORT-CUT PASTRY FOR FRUIT PIES

You skip the rolling pin—mix pastry in pie pan. Use this for fruit pies

2   c. sifted flour
2   tsp. sugar
1 ¼   tsp. salt
⅔   c. cooking or salad oil
3   tblsp. milk

· Combine flour, sugar and salt; sift into an 8″ or 9″ pie pan.
· Whip oil and milk together with a fork and pour over flour mixture.
· Mix with fork until all flour is moistened. Save out about one third of dough to top pie.
· Press remaining dough evenly in pie pan, covering bottom and sides. Crimp the edges. Add the fruit filling. Crumble reserved dough over filling to make top crust. Bake as fruit-pie recipe directs.

BEGINNER'S PASTRY

(*Paste Method*)

2   c. sifted flour
1   tsp. salt
⅔   c. vegetable shortening
4   tblsp. cold water

• Mix flour and salt in a bowl. Cut in shortening with pastry blender until mixture is like coarse meal. Combine ⅓ c. of this mixture with the water; add to the remaining flour-shortening mixture. Mix with fork and then with fingers just until dough holds together and will shape into a ball. Divide dough in two parts. Follow directions for rolling, etc., given with Flaky Pastry for 2-Crust Pie. Makes 1 (8″ or 9″) 2-crust pie.

HOT-WATER PASTRY

¾   c. vegetable shortening
¼   c. boiling water
1   tblsp. milk
2   c. sifted flour
1   tsp. salt

• Put shortening in medium bowl. Add water and milk; break up shortening with a 4-tined fork. Tilt bowl and beat with fork in quick, cross-the-bowl strokes until mixture is smooth and thick like whipped cream and holds soft peaks when fork is lifted.
• Sift flour and salt onto shortening. With vigorous, round-the-bowl strokes, stir quickly, forming dough that clings together and cleans bowl. Pick up dough and work into a smooth, flat round. Then divide in half and form in two balls. Roll out, following directions given in Flaky Pastry for 2-Crust Pie. Makes enough for 1 (8″ or 9″) 2-crust pie.

EGG PASTRY

2   c. sifted flour
1   tsp. salt
⅔   c. vegetable shortening
1   egg, slightly beaten
2   tblsp. cold water
2   tsp. lemon juice

• Sift flour with salt into mixing bowl. Cut in shortening until particles are the size of small peas.
• Combine egg, water and lemon juice. Sprinkle over dry ingredients, tossing and stirring with fork until mixture is moist enough to hold together. (You may need to add a few more drops of water.)
• Divide in half; shape in two flat balls. Roll. Makes 1 (8″ or 9″) 2-crust pie.

COUNTRY TEAROOM PASTRY

4   c. sifted flour
1   tblsp. sugar
1½   tsp. salt
1½   c. lard
1   egg
1   tblsp. vinegar
½   c. cold water

• Blend flour, sugar and salt. Cut in lard until particles are the size of peas.
• Beat egg, blend in vinegar and water. Sprinkle over flour mixture, a tablespoonful at a time, tossing with fork to mix. Gather dough together with fingers so it cleans the bowl. Chill before rolling. Makes 2 (9″) 2-crust pies and 1 (9″) pie shell.

Note: This is the pastry used by a Wisconsin woman in the tearoom she operates in her home. (Also see Egg Yolk Pastry, Chapter 3.)

CREAM CHEESE PASTRY

½ c. butter
1 (3 oz.) pkg. cream cheese
1 c. sifted flour
⅛ tsp. salt

· Cream butter and cheese, beating until smooth. Combine flour and salt and add half at a time to cheese mixture. Mix thoroughly.
· Shape in ball, wrap in waxed paper and chill until pastry will roll and handle easily. (Or shape in 2" rolls, wrap, refrigerate overnight and slice in about 18 circles.) Roll, cut in 2" circles and bake in (2") muffin-cup pans in very hot oven (450°F.) about 12 minutes, or until lightly browned. Cool before filling. Makes 18 (2") tart shells.

CHEESE PASTRY

Marvelous for apple and many kinds of pies—see recipes in this Cookbook

1⅔ c. sifted flour
½ tsp. salt
1 c. grated sharp natural Cheddar cheese
½ c. vegetable shortening
4 to 6 tblsp. cold water

· Sift flour with salt into medium bowl. Add cheese and toss with a fork to mix thoroughly with flour. Cut in shortening until mixture resembles small peas.
· Sprinkle water over pastry mixture, 1 tblsp. at a time, until dough will hold together. Shape into a ball with hands, wrap in waxed paper and refrigerate until ready to use. Divide in halves, flatten each half with hand. Make bottom and top crusts as directed in Flaky Pastry for 2-Crust Pie. Makes pastry for 1 (8" or 9") 2-crust pie.

CHEESE PIE SHELL: Follow recipe for Cheese Pastry but reduce flour to 1 c. and use ¼ tsp. salt, ½ c. grated Cheddar cheese, ¼ c. shortening and 2 to 3 tblsp. water. Proceed as with Baked Pie Shell made with Flaky Pastry. Makes 1 (8" or 9") pie shell or top crust for 1½ qt. casserole.

VARIATION

· Use grated process Cheddar or American cheese instead of sharp Cheddar cheese.

CALIFORNIA ORANGE PASTRY

3 c. sifted flour
1 tsp. salt
1 c. vegetable shortening
6 to 8 tblsp. orange juice

· Sift together flour and salt. Cut in shortening until mixture resembles cornmeal.
· Add orange juice, a small amount at a time, tossing lightly with fork until dough is moist enough to hold together. Shape into ball and roll or refrigerate. Pastry, wrapped in waxed paper, may be kept in refrigerator several days. Makes 1 (8" or 9") 2-crust pie and 2 (8" or 9") pie shells.

Note: Another way to introduce orange flavor to pastry is to add 1 tblsp. grated orange peel and 1 tsp. sugar to the flour for a 1-crust pie before cutting in shortening.

PEANUT PIE SHELL

Fascinating flavor blend with cream, chocolate and butterscotch pies

1   c. sifted flour
½   tsp. baking powder
½   tsp. salt
⅓   c. vegetable shortening
¼   c. crushed salted peanuts
3   to 4 tblsp. cold water

• Sift flour, baking powder and salt into mixing bowl. Cut in shortening with knives, or blend with pastry blender until mixture resembles coarse cornmeal. Add peanuts.
• Sprinkle cold water over mixture, a little at a time, stirring with fork until dough is just moist enough to hold together and form a ball.
• Roll out on lightly floured surface to a circle 1½" larger than an 8" or 9" pie pan inverted over it. Fit loosely into pan and flute edges. Prick over entire surface with a 4-tined fork.
• Bake in hot oven (425°F.) 12 to 15 minutes. Cool.

CHOCOLATE CANDY PIE SHELL

Try this for chiffon-pie fillings

1   (12 oz.) pkg. semisweet chocolate pieces
2   tblsp. vegetable shortening
2   tblsp. sifted confectioners sugar

• Form pie shell by pressing 12"-square heavy-duty aluminum foil in 9" pie pan. Cut off excess at rim. Carefully remove foil pie shell. Sprinkle in chocolate pieces and place on baking sheet in very slow oven (250°F.) for 5 minutes. Remove and set aluminum shell in pie pan. Add shortening and blend with back of spoon. Add confectioners sugar; blend. Spread mixture evenly on bottom and sides of foil shell. Chill until well set.
• Carefully remove foil and return chocolate liner to pie pan. Fill with chiffon-pie filling.

Note: Pie shell is crispy hard like coating on chocolate bonbons. It will soften some for easier cutting if allowed to stand at room temperature 20 minutes.

CHOCOLATE PIE SHELL

1   c. sifted flour
½   tsp. salt
3   tblsp. sugar
3   tblsp. cocoa
⅓   c. vegetable shortening
¼   tsp. vanilla
3   to 4 tblsp. cold water

• Sift flour with salt, sugar and cocoa into bowl. Cut in shortening until particles of mixture resemble small peas in size. Blend in vanilla.
• Sprinkle water over cocoa mixture, stirring lightly with fork, until dough is moist enough to hold together. Shape into ball.
• Roll between two sheets of waxed paper to ⅛" thickness. Gently peel off top paper. Cut dough in circle 1½" to 2" larger than an 8" or 9" pie pan inverted over it. Fit dough loosely into pan, remove paper and pat out all air pockets. Fold edge to make a standing rim and flute as desired. Prick generously with a 4-tined fork.
• Bake in hot oven (400°F.) 8 to 10

minutes. Cool and fill as desired. Makes 8″ or 9″ pie shell.

Note: Cut scraps of leftover rolled dough with fancy cookie cutters, place on baking sheet and bake in hot oven (400°F.). Use to garnish top of pie.

PASTRY FOR LEMON PIES

It accents that wonderful lemon taste

1 ½   c. sifted flour
1 ½   tsp. sugar
½   tsp. salt
½   c. vegetable shortening
1   tblsp. lemon juice
2   tblsp. cold water

· Sift together flour, sugar and salt. Take out 2 tblsp. of shortening. Cut remaining shortening with two knives or blend with pastry blender into flour mixture until mixture resembles coarse meal. Cut in the 2 tblsp. shortening in pieces the size of large peas. Add lemon juice and cold water gradually, mixing lightly with fork. Form into ball.

· Roll out on lightly floured pastry cloth to ⅛″ thickness. Cut in circle 1½″ larger than inverted 9″ pie pan. Fit loosely in pan; pat out air bubbles; turn edge under and flute. Prick sides and bottom with fork.

· Bake in very hot oven (450°F.) 10 to 12 minutes. Cool. Makes 1 (9″) pie shell.

SESAME SEED CRUST: Toast ⅓ c. sesame seeds in moderate oven (375°F.) 12 to 15 minutes, or until light golden brown. Add to pastry for a 1-crust pie after cutting in shortening.

Graham Cracker Crusts

Graham cracker crumbs, finely rolled, are available in packages. Each (13¾ oz.) package will make 3 (9″) pies. Or you can make the crumbs in a jiffy by blending the crackers in an electric blender. If you crush and roll the crackers, place them in a plastic bag or between sheets of waxed paper before using the rolling pin.

Baking gives a firmer and more crunchy crust, but the unbaked type is satisfactory for chiffon and other light and fluffy pie fillings.

BAKED GRAHAM CRACKER CRUST

1 ⅓   c. graham cracker crumbs (16 to 18)

¼   c. sugar
¼   c. soft butter or margarine
¼   tsp. nutmeg or cinnamon (optional)

· In medium mixing bowl combine graham cracker crumbs, sugar, butter and nutmeg; blend until crumbly. Save out ⅓ c. crumbs to sprinkle on top of pie, if desired. Press remaining crumbs evenly on bottom and sides of 9″ pie pan, making a small rim.

· Bake in moderate oven (375°F.) 8 minutes, or until edges are lightly browned. Cool on wire rack and fill as pie recipe directs.

UNBAKED GRAHAM CRACKER CRUMB CRUST: Use the same ingredients as for the baked crust; do not make rim on pie shell. Chill about 1 hour, or until set before filling.

VARIATIONS

WALNUT GRAHAM CRACKER CRUST: Reduce crumbs to 1 c. and add ½ c. finely chopped walnuts. Follow directions for Baked Graham Cracker Crumb Crust. (You can use finely chopped pecans, almonds or Brazil nuts instead of walnuts.)

CHOCOLATE GRAHAM CRACKER CRUST: Reduce crumbs to 1 c. and add 2 squares unsweetened chocolate, grated. Follow recipe for Baked Graham Cracker Crumb Crust.

Wafer and Cereal Crusts

An excellent way to introduce change in crumb crusts is to use wafers or cereals instead of graham cracker crumbs. Here are a few good examples.

CHOCOLATE WAFER CRUMB CRUST: Mix 1⅓ c. fine chocolate wafer crumbs, about 18 (2¾″) wafers, with 3 tblsp. soft butter or margarine until crumbly. Press on bottom and sides of 8″ or 9″ pie pan, saving out 3 tblsp. crumbs to sprinkle on top of pie, if desired. Bake in moderate oven (375°F.) 8 minutes.

VANILLA WAFER CRUMB CRUST: Mix 1⅓ c. fine vanilla wafer crumbs, about 24 (2″) wafers, with ¼ c. soft butter or margarine until crumbly. Press on bottom and sides of 8″ or 9″ pie pan, reserving 3 tblsp. mixture to sprinkle on top of pie, if desired. Bake in moderate oven (375°F.) 8 minutes, or until edge is lightly browned.

GINGERSNAP CRUMB CRUST: Mix 1⅓ c. fine gingersnap crumbs, about 20 (2″) gingersnaps, with 6 tblsp. soft butter or margarine until crumbly. Press mixture on bottom and sides of 8″ or 9″ pie pan, reserving 3 tblsp. crumbs to sprinkle on top of pie, if desired. Bake in moderate oven (375°F.) 8 minutes.

PRETZEL CRUMB CRUST

¾ c. coarsely crushed pretzel sticks
¼ c. soft butter or margarine
3 tblsp. sugar

• Combine ingredients in medium mixing bowl. Press into bottom and on sides of 9″ pie pan. Refrigerate until ready to fill as pie recipe directs.

CORN FLAKE CRUMB CRUST: Mix 1⅓ c. corn flake crumbs (3 c. corn flakes) with 2 tblsp. sugar and ¼ c. soft butter until mixture is crumbly. Press on bottom and sides of 8″ or 9″ pie pan, saving out 3 tblsp. crumbs to sprinkle on top of pie, if desired. Bake in moderate oven (375°F.) 8 minutes. (Packaged corn flake crumbs are available.)

VARIATION

RICE CEREAL CRUMB CRUST: Follow directions for Corn Flake Crumb

Crust, substituting rice cereal flakes for corn flakes.

WALNUT-CEREAL CRUST

1 c. uncooked rolled oats (quick cooking)
3 tblsp. brown sugar
⅛ tsp. salt

⅔ c. chopped walnuts
⅓ c. melted butter or margarine

• Spread rolled oats in large, shallow pan. Toast in moderate oven (350°F.) 10 minutes.
• Combine with sugar, salt, nuts and melted butter. Press on bottom and sides of 9″ pie pan. Chill while you prepare filling.

Nut and Coconut Crusts

Nuts, finely ground, are delicious substitutes for graham cracker crumbs in pie crusts. If you add the finely ground nuts to a beaten egg white and line the pie pan with the mixture, you get a "chewy" crust that's a favorite of many people. Here are recipes for these crusts, along with several for coconut pie shells. Crunchy coconut crusts are wonderful for chiffon-pie fillings and for holding balls or scoops of ice cream. Add the ice cream just before serving and cut at the table. And do vary the coconut crusts using some of the recipes that follow.

NUT BROWN PASTRY

1 c. finely ground blanched almonds, filberts, Brazil nuts, pecans, peanuts or walnuts
2½ tblsp. sugar

• Blend nuts and sugar, mixing well. Press firmly with spoon on bottom and sides of 8″ or 9″ pie pan. Do not make rim. Bake in hot oven (400°F.) 6 to 8 minutes. Cool.

NUT MERINGUE CRUST: To 1½ c. finely ground Brazil nuts, pecans or walnuts (put through food chopper using medium blade), add ¼ c. sugar and ⅛ tsp. salt. Beat 1 egg white until soft peaks form; add nut mixture. Line bottom of greased 9″ pie pan with circle of waxed paper, cut to fit. Press nut mixture over bottom and sides of pan, not on rim. Bake in moderate oven (375°F.) until lightly browned, about 12 to 15 minutes. Remove from oven and loosen crust around edges with spatula; let cool on rack in pan about 10 minutes. Lift out crust with care, removing waxed paper. Cool thoroughly, then return to pan, before filling.

UNBAKED COCONUT CRUST

1½ c. packaged grated coconut
½ c. confectioners sugar
3 tblsp. melted butter

• Combine fine grated coconut with confectioners sugar. Gradually stir in butter. Press evenly over bottom and sides of an oiled 8″ or 9″ pie pan. Refrigerate until firm, about 1 hour.

TOASTED COCONUT CRUST

2 c. flaked coconut
¼ c. butter or margarine   *more*

• Place coconut and butter, mixed together, in 9″ pie pan. Toast in moderate oven (300°F.) 15 to 20 minutes, stirring occasionally, until golden brown. Press over bottom and sides of pie pan. Cool before filling.

SHORT-CUT TOASTED COCONUT CRUST

2 c. moist toasted coconut (1 7 oz. pkg.)
¼ c. melted butter or margarine

• Combine coconut and butter. Press evenly over sides and bottom of an oiled 8″ or 9″ pie pan. Chill until firm, about 1 hour. Crust may be frozen.

CHOCONUT PIE SHELL

A chocolate-flavored nut crust

1 c. sifted flour
2 oz. sweet cooking chocolate, grated or ground
¼ tsp. salt
¼ c. vegetable shortening
3 tblsp. milk
½ tsp. vanilla
¼ c. finely chopped pecans

• Stir together flour, grated chocolate and salt. Cut in shortening with two knives or blend with pastry blender until mixture resembles coarse meal. Combine milk and vanilla; add gradually to dry mixture, tossing lightly with a fork. Form into ball.
• Roll out on lightly floured pastry cloth to ⅛″ thickness. Cut in circle 1½″ larger than inverted 9″ pie pan. Fit loosely in pan; pat out air bubbles; turn edge under and flute.
• Sprinkle with chopped pecans and press gently into pastry. Prick sides and bottom with a fork.
• Bake in hot oven (400°F.) 10 to 12 minutes. Makes 1 (9″) pie shell.

MARSHMALLOW-COCONUT CRUST

¼ c. butter or margarine
1 c. marshmallow creme
½ c. flaked coconut
¼ tsp. vanilla
1½ c. crushed bite-size rice cereal

• Butter a 9″ pie pan. Heat and stir marshmallow creme and butter over hot water. Add coconut, vanilla and rice cereal crumbs. Press on bottom and sides of pie pan. Chill.

Cookie-Type Pie Shells

When a recipe calls for a baked pie shell, a sweet, rich crust may be made with cookie dough. Many superior farm cooks have favorite refrigerator cookie recipes they enjoy using to make pie shells for chiffon and other fluffy, light pie fillings. You can roll the thoroughly chilled dough and fit it, like pastry, into the pie pan. Or you can shape the dough in the traditional roll, chill and then slice it ⅛″ thick.

Cover the bottom and sides of the lightly greased pie pan with overlapping slices. It takes about 30 to 33 slices for an 8″ pie pan. The overlapping cookies on the sides of the pie pan will make an attractive scalloped edge. Chill for at least 15 minutes, prick the entire surface with a 4-tined fork and bake in a moderate oven (375°F.) until lightly browned, about 10 minutes.

We give you two recipes for these crusts, one you pat into the pie pan and one that you roll and fit into the pan. Packaged refrigerator cookies, available in supermarkets, also may be used (Hawaiian Pineapple Pie, Chapter 8).

COOKIE PIE SHELL

1   c. sifted flour
½   c. butter (room temperature)
Grated peel of ½ lemon
⅛   tsp. salt
2   tblsp. sugar
1   egg yolk, slightly beaten
Ice water

• Combine flour, butter, lemon peel and salt in medium bowl. Blend in sugar.
• Add egg yolk and just enough water to make particles adhere. Shape into ball, wrap in waxed paper and refrigerate 1 hour or longer.
• Roll out dough on a lightly floured surface and fit into a 9″ pie pan, making pie shell. Chill at least 15 minutes.
• Prick entire surface of pie shell and bake in hot oven (400°F.) until light-golden, 15 to 20 minutes. Cool thoroughly on wire rack.

VARIATION

ORANGE COOKIE PIE SHELL: Substitute grated peel of ½ orange for lemon peel.

RICH COOKIE CRUST

1   c. sifted flour
¼   c. sugar
1   tsp. grated orange or lemon peel
½   c. butter
1   egg yolk, slightly beaten
¼   tsp. vanilla

• Combine flour, sugar and lemon peel in bowl. Cut in butter until mixture resembles coarse meal. Stir in egg yolk and vanilla and mix with hands until blended.
• Pat evenly into a 9″ pie pan. Make a small edge on pie shell. Prick with fork.
• Bake in hot oven (400°F.) until a light brown, about 10 minutes. Cool on rack before filling.

Glamorous Meringue Crusts

Meringues make dramatic crusts for special-occasion pies and tarts. Rarely are variations made in the basic recipe, which follows, but good country cooks, especially in the South, frequently add pecans. They fold ½ c. finely ground nuts into the meringue just before spreading it into the pie pan.

Meringue pie shells are perfect for holding fresh strawberries, raspberries or sliced peaches, lightly sweetened, and whipped cream or ice cream. During the seasons when fresh fruits are unavailable, custard-type fillings are favorites. Not for flavor alone, although it's important, but also because custard-filled meringues are make-ahead desserts. Most homemakers prefer to chill them overnight, adding the whipped-cream topping shortly before serving time.

PERFECT PUFFY MERINGUE FOR PIE AND TART SHELLS

Here are the rules to follow for success every time.

· Choose a cool, dry day to make meringue shells, if possible. Humidity often softens meringues.
· Be sure your tools are dry and clean. It takes only a tiny speck of fat to ruin meringues.
· Use egg whites at room temperature. Take eggs from the refrigerator, separate and let whites stand at least 1 hour before beating.
· Let your electric mixer do the work —save your arm. The beating takes from 25 to 30 minutes. The sugar must be completely dissolved or the meringue will weep. To test, rub a little of the meringue between the fingers. It should feel smooth. If grainy, continue beating until it feels smooth.
· Cool before filling.

BASIC MERINGUE PIE SHELL

3   egg whites (room temperature)
¼   tsp. cream of tartar
⅛   tsp. salt
¾   c. sugar

· Combine egg whites, cream of tartar and salt. Beat until frothy. Gradually add sugar and beat until stiff glossy peaks form. Meringue should be shiny and moist and all sugar dissolved.
· Spread over bottom and sides of a well-greased 9″ pie pan. Build up sides. (You can make fancy edge with cake decorator, if desired.)
· Bake in very slow oven (275°F.) 1 hour, or until light brown and crisp

to touch. Let cool in pan away from drafts. Spoon in filling and chill.

Note: Don't be disturbed if the meringue pie shell falls and cracks in the center—it usually does.

MERINGUE TART SHELLS

3   egg whites (room temperature)
¼   tsp. cream of tartar
¼   tsp. salt
½   tsp. vanilla
¾   c. sugar

· Combine egg whites, cream of tartar, salt and vanilla in large mixer bowl. Beat until very soft peaks form when beater is lifted slowly. Beat in sugar, 2 tblsp. at a time, beating after each addition. Continue beating until stiff peaks form. The meringue should be glossy and moist.
· Line baking sheets with heavy brown paper. Drop spoonfuls of meringue on paper to make 8 mounds of even size, 3″ apart. With back of spoon hollow out each mound to make tart shell.
· Bake in very slow oven (275°F.) 1 hour. Turn off oven heat and let shells remain in oven, with door closed, until cold.
· At serving time, fill with ice cream and top with berries, cut-up fruit or butterscotch, chocolate or other sauce. Or fill with berries or fresh fruit and top with whipped cream.
· To store Meringue Tart Shells for a few days, loosely wrap them, when cool, in waxed paper. Keep in a cool, dry place, such as a cupboard. Do not put in airtight containers or meringues will soften.

DO'S FOR BAKING PIES

· Follow package directions when using commercial pie crust mixes.
· Use the ingredients specified in all pastry recipes—don't substitute or change.
· Use cold water unless otherwise specified. It helps make flaky pastry.
· Measure accurately—it's important.
· Use pan size recommended by recipe so your filling will fit.
· Check pie-pan size by measuring top inside diameter.
· Use pans that are not shiny, such as glass or dull aluminum that do not reflect heat away from pie during baking.
· Use pie tape or a narrow strip of foil to cover pie edge if it gets too brown when baking.
· Cool baked pies on a wire cooling rack to let air circulate under and prevent sogginess.

PIE CRUST CLINIC

If you're troubled with pie crust problems, all you need to do is follow the recipes in this chapter. But if you wonder why your crust sometimes goes wrong, here are some answers. They show how important it is to follow recipe directions carefully.

WHAT MAKES PIE CRUST . . .

Tough?
1. Use of too little fat or too much flour
2. Failure to blend flour, fat and water enough

3. Handling or rerolling dough too much
4. Incorrect proportion of ingredients —too much flour and too little fat
5. Too much water

Crumbly?
1. Too much fat or too little water
2. Insufficient blending of flour, fat and water
3. Use of self-rising flour without special recipe

Shrink and lose its shape?
1. Stretching of dough when fitting it into pie pan or when fluting edge
2. Rolling dough to uneven thickness, too much rerolling or patching
3. Not pricking dough enough when baking pie shell

Soggy?
1. Underbaking—too short baking time or too low oven temperature
2. Using shiny pie pans that reflect heat so crust does not bake thoroughly
3. Placing pie pan on aluminum foil or baking sheet, deflecting oven heat from pie
4. Pricking, a break or tear in bottom crust of 2-crust pie or filled 1-crust pie
5. Allowing filled 2-crust pie to stand too long before baking

Fail to brown?
1. Same reasons as for soggy crusts
2. Too little fat or oil
3. Too much liquid
4. Overmixing or overhandling of dough
5. Too much flour used when rolling dough
6. Rolling crust too thin

Brown unevenly?
1. Rolling dough to uneven thickness or shaping it unevenly
2. Edge too high
3. Not enough filling for 2-crust pie
4. Pie baked too high or too low in oven
5. Pie placed too close to oven wall or pies baked too close together
6. Oven shelf that is not level

Stick to bottom of pan?
1. Filling boils over
2. Break in crust allowing juice from filling to leak

Have an unpleasant flavor?
1. Raw taste from underbaking
2. Scorched taste from overbaking
3. Bitter or rancid fat or oil
4. Too much or too little salt

COMMON PASTRY QUESTIONS

Q. Why does my pie dough handle differently at times?
A. Temperature, humidity and atmospheric conditions affect it. In hot, humid weather the dough often is soft; when the humidity is low, it may be dry. Chill soft dough. Add a few drops of cold water to dry doughs (use caution—it's easy to add too much).

Q. When do you put the filling in the crust for best results?
A. Follow the pie recipe when adding filling to a baked pie shell. Fill 1-crust pie just before baking; a 2-crust pie after the top crust is rolled and ready to be transferred to top of pie.

Q. Why does my pie dough sometimes crack around the edges when rolled?
A. Either the dough is too dry or it was not mixed sufficiently after water was added. The edges also may not have been smoothed after ball of dough was flattened before rolling.

Q. Why does my 2-crust fruit pie sometimes boil over?
A. Too much filling or insufficient thickening of filling, top and bottom crust edges not sealed completely or inadequate vents cut in top of crust for escape of steam or vents cut too near edge of pie, overbaking, oven shelf not level or uneven thickness of top crust.

Q. What makes my pie shells shrink?
A. Stretching pastry, when putting it in the pan, is one cause. (Unfold pastry in pan and ease it gently and loosely into pan. Press out air bubbles lightly with finger tips and then fit pastry into pan with bent index finger.)

Use of too much shortening or lard in proportion to flour encourages shrinkage.

Baking pie shells in an oven at too low temperature results in shrinkage. The oven temperature generally recommended is 450°F., but some home economists prefer to use a higher one, 475°F.

GOOD IDEA: To prevent a pastry shell from shrinking during baking, a farm woman says she places a foil pan of the same size in the pie pan containing the pastry. She bakes the pie shell in a very hot oven (450°F.) 8 minutes, then removes foil pan and continues the baking until pastry is browned, about 7 minutes.

pastry, others with biscuit dough. Here are examples of recipes you'll find:

COBBLER CRUSTS

Look in Chapter 6 for cobbler toppings. You'll see several made with

Cobbler Topping
Orange Biscuit Topping
Batter Topping
Biscuit Lattice

Biscuit Toppers for Main-Dish Pies

BAKING POWDER BISCUITS

(*Basic Recipe*)

2   c. sifted flour
3   tsp. baking powder
1   tsp. salt
6   tblsp. shortening
⅔ to ¾ c. milk

· Sift flour, baking powder and salt into bowl. Cut in shortening with pastry blender or two knives until mixture resembles cornmeal.

· Make a well in center of flour mixture and pour in ½ c. milk. Mix lightly and quickly with fork. Add more milk, just enough to make dough moist enough to leave the sides of the bowl and to cling to the fork in a ball. Turn on a lightly floured surface.

· Knead dough gently 6 or 8 times. Lightly roll from center in all directions, lifting rolling pin at edges. Roll ⅛" to ¼" thick. Cut as desired for topping main-dish pies. Place on hot pie filling and bake as directed in pie recipe.

VARIATIONS

DROP BISCUITS: Increase milk to 1 c. and drop from spoon on hot pie filling and bake as in basic recipe.

EXTRA-RICH BISCUITS: Increase shortening to ½ c.

CHEESE: Add ½ c. grated sharp Cheddar cheese to sifted dry ingredients.

BUTTERMILK: Reduce baking powder to 2 tsp. and add ¼ tsp. baking soda. Substitute buttermilk for sweet milk.

ONION: Sauté ¼ c. finely chopped onions in 2 tblsp. butter or margarine until light golden brown. Add to sifted dry ingredients with milk.

CURRY: Add ¼ to ½ tsp. curry powder to sifted dry ingredients (for chicken pies).

CARAWAY: Add 1 to 2 tsp. caraway seeds to sifted dry ingredients (for pork pies).

HERB: Add ¼ c. chopped fresh parsley or chives to sifted dry ingredients.

SAGE: Add ¼ tsp. dry mustard and ½ tsp. crumbled dried sage to sifted dry ingredients (for chicken and pork).

CHEESE-HERB: Add ½ c. grated sharp Cheddar cheese and 1 tsp. caraway or celery seeds to dry ingredients (for beef, pork and chicken pies).

Note: To make hot biscuits to serve as bread, roll dough ½″ to ¾″ thick for fluffy biscuits, ⅛″ for crusty, thin biscuits. Makes about 18 (2″) biscuits.

Frozen Mashed Potatoes to Hold Pie Fillings and to Top Pies

If the men who eat at your table are meat-and-potato fans, you'll welcome the new method of successfully freezing mashed potatoes developed in FARM JOURNAL's Test Kitchens. You can use them to top main-dish pies or to make nestlike shells to hold chicken, meat, vegetable, fish and other hearty fillings.

There's one important precaution to heed: Shape the potatoes ready for use before freezing. Thawing softens potatoes and makes them mushy.

A convenient way to stock your freezer is to cook and mash double the amount of potatoes when you are getting a meal. Use one half, freeze the other. You can store frozen mashed potatoes up to 2 months. Here is the basic recipe with some suggestions of what to do with it. You'll find many more ways to make pies with frozen potatoes once you start keeping the shells or nests and the topping in your freezer.

BASIC MASHED POTATOES

Play it smart and keep a supply in your freezer to use at busy seasons

4   lbs. boiling potatoes
1   c. milk (amount varies with moisture in potatoes)
¼   c. butter or margarine
1 ½ tsp. salt

· Peel potatoes. Boil until soft; drain. Press potatoes through ricer, or mash.
· Heat milk, butter and salt together. Gradually whip into potatoes; whip until smooth and fluffy. Makes 2 pie shells for 1½ qt. casserole.

POTATO PIE SHELLS

· Line 1½ qt. casserole with aluminum foil. Spoon half of hot Basic Mashed Potatoes into casserole. Shape into nestlike pie shell, building up sides to top of casserole. Remove from casserole with foil to hold shape of potato mixture. Repeat with remaining half of potatoes. Cool; freeze until firm. Remove from freezer; package, seal and label. Return to freezer.

To Use: Remove wrap from frozen Potato Pie Shell. Place in casserole in which it originally was shaped. Drizzle with 2 tblsp. melted butter or margarine. Cover and bake in hot oven (400°F.) 30 minutes. Uncover and bake 30 minutes. Fill with hot filling for chicken or meat pie and serve.

PIMIENTO-POTATO PIE SHELLS: Add ½ c. chopped pimiento to hot Basic Mashed Potatoes. Shape, freeze, bake and fill like Potato Pie Shells.

CHEESE-POTATO PIE SHELLS: Add ½ c. grated Cheddar cheese to hot Basic Mashed Potatoes. Shape, freeze and bake like Potato Pie Shells.

POTATO PIE TOPPING

SNOWCAPS: Add 2 egg yolks to Basic Mashed Potatoes; whip until blended. Spoon hot potatoes in mounds on baking sheet. Cool; freeze until firm. Remove from baking sheet; place in plastic bags. Seal, label and return to freezer.

To Use: Place frozen Snowcaps on top of hot meat-pie mixture. Bake in moderate oven (375°F.) 30 minutes, or until potatoes brown lightly. Use them to convert the thickened beef-vegetable stew into a main-dish pie. (See Hamburger-Potato Pie, Chapter 10.) Makes 24 Snowcaps.

Dessert Pies

Dessert Pies

CHAPTER 3

FRUIT PIES

You don't need a calendar to tell you when a new pie season is about to start. When the wiry willows brighten to yellow-green and the light lingers in the evening sky, country cooks know that before too long there will be fresh fruit in their yards and gardens. Already they can visualize the plump strawberries glistening under shiny glazes in flaky pastry or teamed up with pink rhubarb in a luscious beauty, colorful Latticed Strawberry-Rhubarb Pie, pictured on this Cookbook's jacket. Other berries, cherries, currants, peaches, pears, plums and grapes follow, to the joy of pie bakers—and pie eaters.

Later in the year when, with little warning, sugar maples turn flame-colored and orchards glow with the deep red and blush-gold of apples, farm women concentrate their talents on the greatest of all American pies . . . apple. Often the season's nuts and fresh cider add their flavors to apple pie (for tasty examples, see Apple-Pecan and Apple Strip Pies).

Children used to keep track of the seasons by visiting Grandmother's kitchen to see, smell and taste the pies she was baking. The old rhythm is less obvious today. With improved canned, frozen and dried fruits widely available and transportation and storage methods greatly improved, fresh-tasting fruit pies come from home ovens the year around. And country women capture the elusive flavors of ripe fruit when it is plentiful by making pies and fillings and freezing them.

On the farm, the bounty of fresh fruits encourages their lavish use in summer. Twenty-six different kinds show up in our recipes. Fruit pies are a logical answer to the busy woman's eternal question: What can I fix for dessert that will glorify my otherwise ordinary meal?

Not to be overlooked is the fact that most men will vote a fruit pie their favorite dessert! We predict that after reading through the pages of this chapter you will get out your rolling pin and go on a pie-baking spree. Good luck and good pies!

Perfect Pies Have Flaky Crusts

Even if your family and neighbors consider you the best pie baker in the country, do read the preceding chapter, Pie Crusts of All Kinds, before you make any of the fruit pie recipes in this chapter. Remember that no pie is better than its pastry. And much of the success with pie crusts depends on you—because the ingredients are really quite simple. It's how you handle them that counts.

You will find a wide variety of pastry recipes. Some of them are new; you'll want to give them a try. (And when you don't have time to make pie crust, don't forget you can buy the mix in packages or frozen rolled pastry.)

You will notice that many of our pies are baked at one temperature, so you won't have to change the regulator setting once the pie is in the oven. Do look at your pie occasionally, though, especially the first time you use a recipe, to make certain that it doesn't brown too much. Remember that the higher the crimped edges of the rim are, the more quickly they brown. Here are suggestions for baking pies with tops browned just the way you like them.

Top-Crust Pointers

Some good pastry makers fold the rolled pastry for the top crust in quarters, cut vents near the center and lift it to the top of the pie. Other pie bakers prefer to cut their own designs (vents) in the pastry and then roll the pastry around the rolling pin and unroll it over the pie. Another school of farm cooks find it easier to avoid stretching the pastry when they cut the vents or prick the top crust after it is adjusted on the pie. Take your choice of methods, but REMEMBER TO CUT VENTS, plain or decorative, or to prick the top crust to allow steam to escape.

To keep pie edges from getting too brown while baking, cover them with 1½" strips of aluminum foil. Remove the foil about 15 minutes before end of baking time so edge will brown lightly. Another good way to protect the pie edges is to cut a circle of aluminum foil 1½" larger than the pie pan. Then cut out center of foil circle so only pie edges will be covered by the ring. Keep a few of these foil rings ready for quick and easy use.

Thickening Fruit Pies

The juiciness of fruit varies from one variety and from one season to another—and from different areas in the same season. Our measurement is for average juiciness. You may want to add a little more or less thickening (flour, cornstarch, quick-cooking tapioca) than the amount specified in the filling recipes. Then, too, you may like your pie fillings a little thicker or thinner than some other cooks. The accepted rule for a fruit filling is that it should be juicy, but not "runny."

Apple Pie—the Top Farm Favorite

To a farmer, an apple tree covered with blossoms is a lovely sight. He may watch the birds shake a shower of the petals to the earth and rejoice in trees glistening after an early morning rain. But you can bet he also has thoughts of a juicy wedge of apple pie. We predict that any of the apple pie recipes in this Cookbook will bring you his compliments. Try them all to find his very favorite!

For who can decide which apple pie is best? Members of FARM JOURNAL's Family Test Group voted the traditional Old-Fashioned Apple Pie their families' first love, but there were bountiful praises of others. Open-Face Apple Pie won the second most votes, and nutmeg fans were excited and enthusiastic about Country Apple Pie. Then there's Apple-Pecan Pie . . . but why attempt to select the champions from the many pies we share with you? They all deserve blue ribbons!

Try the different recipes and find out for yourself which pies are best liked at your house. Maybe your final decision will be like that of one farmer who says: "Makes little difference what dessert my wife fixes—so long as it's apple pie."

OLD-FASHIONED APPLE PIE

First choice of all farm pies, it's juicy, plump and luscious

Pastry for 2-crust pie
¾   to 1 c. sugar
2   tblsp. flour
½   to 1 tsp. cinnamon
⅛   tsp. nutmeg
¼   tsp. salt
6   to 7 c. sliced peeled apples (2
    to 2½ lbs.)
2   tblsp. butter or margarine

· Combine sugar, flour, cinnamon, nutmeg and salt. Mix lightly through apples (sliced ¼" thick). Heap in pastry-lined 9" pie pan. Dot with butter. Adjust top crust and flute edges; cut vents.
· Bake in hot oven (425°F.) 50 to 60 minutes, or until crust is browned and apples are tender.

Note: Amount of sugar you will need varies with tartness of apples.

VARIATIONS

DUTCH-STYLE APPLE PIE: Cut large vents in top crust and omit butter. Five minutes before baking time is up, remove pie from oven and pour ½ c.

heavy cream into pie through vents. Return to oven and complete baking.

CINNAMON APPLE PIE: Omit cinnamon and nutmeg and add 3 tblsp. red cinnamon candies (red hots) to sugar. Use a lattice pastry top if desired.

CRUMB APPLE PIE: Use ¾ c. sugar. Omit pastry top crust; instead, sprinkle filling with crumbs made by mixing ½ c. butter, ½ c. light brown sugar, firmly packed, and 1 c. flour. Bake in hot oven (400°F.) 45 to 55 minutes. Serve warm with ice cream or pass a pitcher of cream for pouring over pie.

SPEEDY APPLE PIE: Substitute 2 (1 lb. 4 oz.) cans sliced apples for the fresh apples.

GREEN APPLE PIE: Add ½ c. more sugar. Omit spices completely, or reduce amounts. If apples are very juicy, add 2 tblsp. more flour.

APPLE-PECAN PIE

You'll like what the nuts do to apple pie—both in flavor and texture

Unbaked 9″ pie shell
¼ c. chopped pecans
6   c. sliced peeled apples
1   c. sugar
2   tsp. flour
½   tsp. cinnamon
¼   tsp. nutmeg
Spicy Pecan Topping

• Sprinkle chopped pecans in bottom of pie shell. Combine apples, sugar, flour, cinnamon and nutmeg. Turn into pie shell and spread topping (see recipe) over apple mixture.
• Bake in hot oven (425°F.) 40 to 45 minutes, or until apples are tender and pie top is a rich brown.

SPICY PECAN TOPPING: Mix ¼ c. butter or margarine, ½ c. brown sugar, ⅓ c. flour and ½ tsp. cinnamon until completely blended. Stir in ¼ c. chopped pecans.

OPEN-FACE APPLE PIE

Farmers voted this the best 1-crust apple pie—with ice cream on top!

Unbaked 9″ pie shell
1   c. sliced peeled apples
5   c. quartered peeled apples
1 ⅓ c. sugar
3   tblsp. flour
¾   tsp. salt
⅓   c. light cream
¼   tsp. cinnamon

• Thinly slice 1 apple and lay across bottom of pie shell. Arrange quartered apples to fill the shell, overlapping pieces, rounded side up. (Cut apples in eighths if they are not quick-cooking.)
• Combine sugar, flour and salt; add cream, mixing well. Sprinkle top with cinnamon.
• Bake in moderate oven (375°F.) 1½ to 2 hours, or until apples are tender. Cover top with aluminum foil (tucking corners under edge of pie pan) during first hour of baking to prevent overbrowning of crust.

COUNTRY APPLE PIE

Nutmeg and lemon flavors blend in this pie that tastes wonderful

Pastry for 2-crust pie
½ c. heavy cream
2 tblsp. quick-cooking tapioca
1 c. sugar
¼ tsp. salt
½ tsp. nutmeg
¼ tsp. cinnamon
2 tsp. lemon juice
5 c. sliced peeled apples
2 tblsp. butter or margarine

• Combine cream, tapioca, sugar, salt, spices and lemon juice in bowl.
• Add thinly sliced apples and toss to mix. Spoon half of mixture into pastry-lined 9″ pie pan. Fill around edges and pack well. Dot with butter. Add remaining apples. Adjust top crust and flute edges; cut vents. Brush top lightly with milk.
• Bake in hot oven (400°F.) 50 to 60 minutes, or until apples are tender and crust is golden brown.

APPLE STRIP PIE

When cider presses are busy, make this unforgettable autumn pie

Pastry for 2-crust pie
3 c. grated peeled apples
½ c. sugar
½ tsp. cinnamon
¼ tsp. nutmeg
⅛ tsp. salt
2 tsp. grated lemon peel
1 tblsp. lemon juice
3 tblsp. butter or margarine

3 tblsp. flour
1 c. apple cider
½ c. raisins
1 egg white
1 tsp. water
Cinnamon Nut Topping

• Combine apples, sugar, cinnamon, nutmeg, salt, lemon peel and juice.
• Melt butter in saucepan; add flour and blend. Add cider and cook over medium heat, stirring constantly, until mixture comes to a boil. Add apple mixture and raisins. Bring to a boil and cool.
• Line a 9″ pie pan with pastry. Beat together egg white and water. Brush part of mixture over pie shell. Turn apple mixture into pie shell. Roll out remaining pastry and cut in three (1½″) strips. Lay across top of pie, leaving space between; brush strips with remaining egg white.
• Sprinkle topping between strips.
• Bake in moderate oven (350°F.) until crust is brown and filling is bubbly, 40 to 50 minutes.

CINNAMON NUT TOPPING: Combine ¼ c. chopped pecans with 1 tblsp. sugar and ¼ tsp. cinnamon.

APPLE-CHEESE PIE

Cheese bakes in pie and unites with apples in this tasty dessert

Pastry for 2-crust pie
5 c. sliced peeled tart apples (about 2 lbs.)
½ tsp. grated lemon peel
2 tsp. lemon juice
¾ c. sugar
2 tblsp. flour *more*

⅛   tsp. salt
½   tsp. cinnamon
¼   tsp. nutmeg
1   tblsp. butter or margarine
4   thin slices sharp process cheese
    (¼ lb.)
Cream to brush top

• Combine apples, sliced ¼″ thick,
with lemon peel and juice.
• Combine sugar, flour, salt, cinnamon and nutmeg. Sprinkle 2 tblsp.
mixture over bottom of pastry-lined 8″
pie pan.
• Toss apples in remainder of sugar
mixture. Turn into pie shell. Dot with
butter. Lay slices of cheese over
apples, leaving space for steam to escape. Adjust top crust; flute edges, cut
vents and brush on cream.
• Bake in hot oven (400°F.) about
40 minutes, or until apples are tender
and crust is golden.

APPLE PIE GLACÉ

*Spiral of apple slices under apricot
glaze makes this a festive pie*

Unbaked 9″ pie shell
7   large apples
½   c. water
½   c. plus 1 tblsp. sugar
5   tblsp. butter or margarine
1   tblsp. lemon juice
½   tsp. cinnamon
¼   tsp. nutmeg
⅛   tsp. salt
2   small apples
¼   c. apricot jam
1   tblsp. hot water

• Peel and quarter large apples; cook
with water and ½ c. sugar until soft

(about 35 minutes). Put through
sieve; add butter, lemon juice, spices
and salt. Pour into pie shell.
• Peel small apples; slice thinly
lengthwise. Arrange in spiral starting
at center of pie; sprinkle with 1 tblsp.
sugar.
• Bake in hot oven (400°F.) 35 minutes, until apples on top are tender
and the pastry is golden. Melt jam in
hot water; pour over top.

FROSTED BIG APPLE PIE

*Jumbo apple pie for treating a crowd
—have a pot of coffee ready to pour*

Egg Yolk Pastry
4   tsp. lemon juice
5   lbs. peeled, thinly sliced, tart
    apples (about 12 to 15 c.)
¾   c. granulated sugar
¾   c. brown sugar, firmly packed
1   tsp. cinnamon
¼   tsp. salt
½   tsp. nutmeg
Confectioners sugar frosting

• Roll out half the pastry into rectangle and use to line 15½″ × 10½″
jelly-roll pan. Sprinkle lemon juice on
apples. Place half the apples in bottom
of pastry-lined sheet.
• Combine remaining ingredients, except apples and frosting. Sprinkle half
the mixture over apples in pan. Spread
remaining apple slices on top and
sprinkle with remaining sugar-spice
mixture.
• Top with remaining pastry, rolled
out; seal and crimp edges. Brush with
milk and sprinkle with a little sugar.
(Cut vents or prick with fork as for
all 2-crust fruit pies.)

A fresh-flavor miracle—Concord Grape Cobbler (recipe, page 188)—you can bake and take to the table during the snowy season. The trick—you freeze the filling, add crust at baking time. We show it with Lattice Biscuit Topping.

NORTH POLE CHERRY PIE

GOLDEN PEACH PIE

• Bake in hot oven (400°F.) 50 minutes. When cool, drizzle with confectioners sugar mixed with milk to make a thin icing. Cut in squares to serve. Makes 24 servings.

EGG YOLK PASTRY

5	c. sifted flour
4	tsp. sugar
½	tsp. salt
½	tsp. baking powder
1 ½	c. lard
2	egg yolks
Cold water	

• Combine dry ingredients; cut in lard. Beat egg yolks slightly in measuring cup with fork and blend in enough cold water to make a scant cupful.
• Roll out like any pastry. Makes pastry for 1 Frosted Big Apple Pie or 3 (2-crust) 9″ pies.

APPLE MOLASSES PIE

Good way to salvage windfall apples —pie has that brown-sugar butter taste

Pastry for 2-crust pie
¾	c. light molasses
¼	c. water
1	tblsp. lemon juice
½	tsp. salt
6	c. sliced peeled apples
¼	c. melted butter or margarine
¼	c. flour

• Combine molasses, water, lemon juice and salt and bring to a boil.
• Add apples, cook until tender and remove from syrup.
• Blend butter and flour and add to hot syrup gradually, stirring constantly. Cook until thick and smooth. Fold apples lightly into syrup. Cool slightly. Turn into pastry-lined 9″ pie pan, top with pastry lattice.
• Bake in hot oven (425°F.) 30 minutes.

Men Praise This Two-Fruit Pie

The Massachusetts homemaker who shares the recipe for Apple-Cranberry Pie which follows, likes to bake it in autumn when harvesting is in full swing in the local cranberry bogs and juicy apples are fresh from orchards. She prefers Baldwin and McIntosh apples if they're available. Jonathans are a splendid choice, but any good cooking apple will fill the bill.

This New England pie baker brushes the tops of the unbaked pies with milk and sprinkles on a little sugar. "One time I made 25 of these pies for a men's dinner," she says. "I served them with cheese slices and the pies really made a hit."

Try this recipe yourself any day during Indian summer when you want to end a meal with something special.

Feast your winter guests on Golden Peach Pie, *photo at left, made with frozen peaches (recipe, page 106), or quick North Pole Cherry Pie (recipe, page 228) made with vanilla ice cream topped with color-bright canned cherry pie filling.*

HARVEST APPLE-CRANBERRY PIE

It's a bit tart—to sweeten, top with scoops of vanilla ice cream

Pastry for 2-crust pie
¾ c. sugar
3 tblsp. cornstarch
¼ tsp. salt
¾ c. light corn syrup
¼ c. water
1 ½ c. raw cranberries
2 tsp. grated orange peel
1 ½ c. chopped peeled apples
2 tblsp. butter or margarine

· Mix sugar, cornstarch and salt in saucepan; gradually add corn syrup and water. Cook, stirring constantly, until mixture thickens slightly.
· Add cranberries and continue cooking until skins break. Add orange peel; cool.
· Add apples to cranberry mixture and turn into pastry-lined 9″ pie pan. Dot with butter. Adjust top crust and flute edges; cut vents.
· Bake in hot oven (425°F.) 40 to 50 minutes.

APPLE-APRICOT PIE

Apricots provide the tart flavor that makes this apple pie unusual

Pastry for 2-crust pie
½ c. sugar
1 tblsp. flour
½ tsp. cinnamon
¼ tsp. salt
4 c. sliced peeled apples (about 5 medium)
1 c. coarsely chopped, drained, canned apricots

· Combine sugar, flour, cinnamon and salt. Toss apples and apricots with sugar mixture.
· Turn into pastry-lined 9″ pie pan; adjust top crust and flute edges; cut vents.
· Bake in hot oven (400°F.) until apples are tender and pie is golden, about 40 minutes.

FROSTED APPLE-RAISIN PIE

A FARM JOURNAL *5-star recipe—from our* COUNTRY COOKBOOK

Pastry for 2-crust pie
¾ c. sugar
2 tblsp. flour
⅛ tsp. salt
½ tsp. cinnamon
6 c. sliced peeled tart apples
½ c. seedless raisins
2 tblsp. orange juice
3 tblsp. butter or margarine
Orange Frosting

· Combine sugar, flour, salt and cinnamon; mix with apples and raisins; place in pastry-lined 9″ pie pan. Sprinkle with orange juice; dot with butter. Adjust top crust and flute edges; cut vents.
· Bake in hot oven (400°F.) about 40 minutes, or until crust is browned and apples are tender.
· Spread Orange Frosting over hot pie.

ORANGE FROSTING: Mix 1 c. confectioners sugar, 3 tblsp. strained orange juice and 1 tsp. grated orange peel.

Apples, Blackberries Join Flavors

About the time yellow-green, summer apples are coming into their own, lustrous, black-purple blackberries ripen. The wild berries, available in many parts of the country, have superb flavor and relatively small seeds. Gather them; put up with stained fingers and thorn pricks—it's worth it. Combine them with early apples for a pie that can't be surpassed.

Summer apples are juicy, tart and fast-cooking—ideal for pies. They make superior applesauce, too, but brown too quickly when cut for salads and they're too tart to eat out of hand. But don't weep over these shortcomings . . . they make superior pies.

BLACKBERRY-APPLE PIE

Use either wild or cultivated berries

Pastry for 2-crust pie
3   c. fresh blackberries
1   c. thin, peeled green apple slices
2½ to 3 tblsp. quick-cooking tapioca
1   c. sugar
½   tsp. cinnamon
2   tblsp. butter or margarine

• Pick over and wash berries in cold water. Lift out and drain. In large bowl, combine berries, apples, tapioca, sugar and cinnamon, mixing well.
• Turn into pastry-lined 9" pie pan. Dot with butter and adjust top crust and flute edges; cut vents.

• Bake in hot oven (425°F.) until crust is golden brown and juices start to bubble up in vents, 40 to 50 minutes.

Note: For a change use Cheese Pastry (see Chapter 2).

SWISS APPLE-CHERRY PIE

This pie's double popularity is no mystery—it combines two tasty fruits

Pastry for 2-crust pie
1¼ c. sugar
¼   c. flour
1   tsp. cinnamon
¼   tsp. nutmeg
5   medium apples, thinly sliced and peeled (3½ c.)
1   (1 lb. 4 oz.) can tart cherries, drained
2   tblsp. butter

• Combine sugar, flour, cinnamon and nutmeg. Divide mixture in four parts.
• Arrange one third of apple slices over bottom of pastry-lined 9" pie pan. Sprinkle with one fourth of sugar-spice mixture. Cover with half of the cherries; sprinkle on second fourth of sugar-spice mixture. Repeat, using all of sugar-spice mixture, apples and cherries. Dot with butter. Adjust top crust; flute edges and cut vents.
• Bake in hot oven (400°F.) 50 minutes, or until pastry is browned and filling is bubbly in vents.

Note: For an interesting pie top, sprinkle with 1 tsp. sugar and ⅛ tsp. cinnamon before baking pie.

Try Hawaiian Apple Pie

Hawaiian cooks are famed for dishes made with coconut, which grows in the Islands. So you'd expect them to add coconut to apple pie, but you'll be surprised how wonderful the combination of the two tastes when baked in pastry. Here's a recipe from the palm-fringed shores of our fiftieth state worthy of adoption across country.

COCONUT-CRUNCH APPLE PIE

A 2-layer, 1-crust pie—crisp coconut tops the juicy, spiced apples

Pastry for 1-crust pie
1	c. granulated sugar
¼	c. brown sugar, firmly packed
2	tblsp. flour
½	tsp. cinnamon
5	c. sliced peeled apples
2	tblsp. butter or margarine
2	c. shredded coconut
1	egg, beaten
¼	c. milk
½	tsp. salt

• Combine ½ c. white sugar, the brown sugar, flour and cinnamon. Place half the apples in pastry-lined 9" pie pan; sprinkle with half the sugar-spice mixture. Repeat. Dot with butter.

• Cut two layers of aluminum foil in a circle to cover filling only. Bake, foil-covered, in moderate oven (375°F.) 30 minutes.

• Combine coconut, egg, the remaining ½ c. sugar, milk and salt.

• Remove pie from oven and lift off foil. Spread coconut mixture on top. Return to oven and bake 30 minutes longer.

BUTTERSCOTCH APPLE PIE

Introduce this new apple pie to your family—they'll ask for a repeat

Unbaked 9" pie shell
5	c. sliced peeled apples
1	(6 oz.) pkg. butterscotch morsels
	Cinnamon
¼	c. sugar
¼	c. flour
1	tsp. salt
½	c. light cream

• Combine apples and butterscotch morsels; put into pastry shell. Sprinkle generously with cinnamon.

• Combine sugar, flour and salt; then add cream. Drizzle over apples so that slices are coated.

• Place pie in large paper bag; fasten bag securely. Bake in moderate oven (375°F.) about 70 minutes.

• Remove from bag at once. Cool.

APPLE-DATE PIE

Cherries are scattered like garnets in filling to show through lattice

Pastry for 2-crust pie
4	c. peeled and diced tart apples
½	c. dates, cut into pieces

½ c. maraschino cherries, cut into quarters
½ c. coarsely chopped walnuts
¾ c. sugar
¼ c. flour
¼ tsp. salt
¼ c. light cream
¼ c. lemon juice

• Combine apples, dates, cherries and nuts; put into pastry-lined 9" pie pan.
• Combine sugar, flour and salt. Add cream, mix well. Add lemon juice. Pour cream mixture over fruit. Top with lattice design of strips made from remaining pastry.
• Place pie in large paper bag. Close and fasten bag. Bake in hot oven (400°F.) 60 minutes (pie will brown, bag keeps steam around pie). Remove from oven; remove pie from bag at once.

APPLE-GRAPEFRUIT PIE

Grapefruit fans like the tart taste

Baked 9" pie shell
5 apples peeled (3 c. thin slices)
2½ c. sweetened grapefruit juice (canned)
3½ tblsp. cornstarch
⅔ c. sugar
¼ tsp. salt
Sweetened whipped cream

• Cook apple slices in grapefruit juice until tender. Remove apples from juice.
• Mix cornstarch, sugar and salt; add to juice and cook about 10 minutes, or until thickened and clear. Cool.
• Place apples in pie shell. Pour thickened juice over them.
• Serve with sweetened whipped cream.

STREUSEL APPLE-MINCE PIE

Version of mince pie men brag about

Unbaked 9" pie shell
2 c. prepared mincemeat
3 c. sliced peeled apples
½ c. sugar
1 tblsp. lemon juice
Brown Sugar Streusel

• Spoon mincemeat into pie shell. Combine apples, sugar and lemon juice. Spread over mincemeat.
• Sprinkle Brown Sugar Streusel over apples.
• Bake in hot oven (425°F.) until apples are tender and pie browned the way you like it, about 45 minutes.

BROWN SUGAR STREUSEL: Blend ½ c. flour and ½ c. brown sugar. Cut in ¼ c. butter or margarine until well mixed.

MARLBOROUGH PIE

Rich yellow pie has sharp lemon taste but texture of apples—cuts like jelly

Unbaked 9" pie shell
1 c. unsweetened applesauce
3 tblsp. lemon juice
½ tsp. lemon peel
1 c. sugar
4 eggs, slightly beaten
2 tblsp. butter, melted
½ tsp. salt

• Chill pie shell while preparing filling.
• Combine applesauce, lemon juice and peel, sugar, eggs, butter and salt. Blend thoroughly and pour into pastry-lined pie pan.   *more*

· Bake in very hot oven (450°F.) 15 minutes; reduce heat to 350°F. and bake 10 to 15 minutes longer, or until silver knife inserted halfway between center and edge of pie comes out clean. Cool on rack.

Note: New England homemakers steam peeled and cored apples and put them through food mill or sieve to make sauce.

ROSY CRAB APPLE PIE

A FARM JOURNAL *5-star recipe—from our* FREEZING & CANNING COOKBOOK

Pastry for 2-crust pie
1   c. sugar
1   tblsp. flour
¼   tsp. salt
6   c. finely chopped unpeeled crab apples
1   tsp. vanilla
1 ½   tblsp. lemon juice
⅓   c. water
1 ½   tblsp. butter

· Combine sugar, flour and salt; toss together with apples.
· Pour apple mixture into pastry-lined 9″ pie pan. Sprinkle with mixture of vanilla, lemon juice and water. Dot with butter. Adjust top crust and flute edges; cut vents.
· Bake in hot oven (400°F.) 50 minutes, or until filling is tender and crust is browned.

Note: If you wish to freeze pie, steam apple bits in colander over boiling water 1 to 2 minutes before mixing filling and cool quickly. This will preserve color.

APRICOT-STRAWBERRY PIE

Wonderful served slightly warm with a topknot of vanilla ice cream

Pastry for 2-crust pie
4   c. pitted quartered fresh apricots
1   c. crushed fresh strawberries
1   c. sugar
1   tblsp. lemon juice
2   tblsp. quick-cooking tapioca
⅛   tsp. salt
2   tblsp. butter or margarine

· Combine apricots, strawberries, sugar, lemon juice, tapioca and salt in mixing bowl. Pour into pastry-lined 9″ pie pan. Dot with butter. Adjust top crust, cut steam vents and flute edges.
· Bake in hot oven (425°F.) about 35 to 45 minutes, or until crust is browned and juices start to bubble in vents. Cool on rack.

Note: The natural sweetness of apricots dictates the amount of sugar to use. Fully ripe fruit requires less than the firm apricots usually available in markets in areas where the fruit is not grown, the kind used in testing this recipe.

Summer's Best—Berry Pies

Early summer mornings, when the air's still dewy, farm children gather ripe, juicy berries for Mother's superb pies. Step into the farm kitchen mid-morning and a taunting fragrance greets you. Visit and sip coffee for a half hour and you'll see sugar-sprinkled pies with color-bright juice bubbling in the vents being carried from oven to cooling racks on the counter. You'll want to accept that invitation to linger longer for dinner—fresh berry pie for dessert!

We'll give you several berry pie recipes, but we'll start with a plus: basic directions that will insure your success with fresh berry pies.

Tips for Success with 2-Crust Fresh Berry Pies

BERRIES: You can use blueberries, blackberries, boysenberries, gooseberries, loganberries, raspberries, strawberries, etc. If the strawberries are large, cut them in half.

Pick over and wash berries, removing stems and hulls. Combine 1⅓ c. sugar and ⅓ c. flour. Add 4 c. ripe berries and toss gently to mix. Pour mixture into pastry-lined 9″ pie pan. Dot with 2 tblsp. butter or margarine. Adjust top crust, cut vents or prick with 4-tined fork, seal and flute edges to make a high-standing rim.

Bake in hot oven (425°F.) until crust is golden, about 35 to 45 minutes. Serve faintly warm.

SUGAR: The amount of sugar you need depends on the ripeness and tartness of the berries—also on how sweet you like your pies. Sometimes 1 c. is adequate, but if berries are very tart or not fully ripe, you may need as much as 2 c. but 1⅓ c. is the average amount.

SPICE: A few country cooks like to add a touch of spice to berry pies, usually ½ tsp. cinnamon or ¼ tsp. cloves or nutmeg.

LEMON JUICE: Most pie bakers add from 1 to 2 tblsp. lemon juice to berry pie fillings. They find it brings out the best flavors. Its addition is optional, of course.

SUGAR-SPARKLE TOPS: It's standard procedure in country kitchens to brush the top crust of berry pie with milk or cream and sprinkle on 1 tsp. sugar before baking.

FAVORITE TOPPING: Vanilla ice cream on faintly warm pie can't be beat.

Note: Some cooks prefer a thinner pie with runaway juices under firm control. They use 3 c. berries, ⅔ to 1 c. sugar, 2 tblsp. cornstarch or 4 tblsp. flour and 1½ tblsp. butter.

FARM KITCHEN IDEA: A Kansas homemaker's first choice is pie made with half blackberries and half red raspberries. Do try the combination—serve the pie faintly warm with scoops of ice cream on top.

COUNTRY KITCHEN IDEA: Make larger than usual vents in top crust of blueberry pie. Omit butter. Five minutes before pie is baked, remove from oven and pour ½ c. heavy cream into pie through vents. Return to oven to complete baking.

Country Blueberry Pies

Many farm women prefer wild blueberries to the prettier, larger cultivated fruit with softer seeds. They hold that domesticating the berry tamed its flavor, too! Both have their champions—both make excellent pies.

If you live where you can pick your own, use the berries soon after taking them from the bush. We especially recommend our 1-Crust Double-Good Blueberry and Lemon-Blueberry Pies. The first, a New England special, is a half-and-half pie—contains both raw and cooked berries. In the second, grated lemon peel enhances the berry taste. The recipe comes from a Wisconsin farm kitchen in which the pie shows up on the dinner table the year around. Frozen berries do the honors when fresh ones are unseasonal.

Blueberries freeze successfully. It's easy to fix them. Just wash the stemmed fruit in cold water, the colder the better. Lift out and drain. Package and freeze without sweetening and use like fresh berries.

DOUBLE-GOOD BLUEBERRY PIE

Secret of the pie's popularity is its remarkably fresh berry taste

Baked 9" pie shell
¾ c. sugar
3 tblsp. cornstarch
⅛ tsp. salt
¼ c. water
4 c. blueberries
1 tblsp. butter
1 tblsp. lemon juice
Whipped cream (optional)

· Combine sugar, cornstarch and salt in saucepan. Add water and 2 c. blueberries; cook over medium heat, stirring constantly, until mixture comes to a boil and is thickened and clear. (Mixture will be quite thick.)
· Remove from heat and stir in butter and lemon juice. Cool.
· Place remaining 2 c. raw blueberries in pie shell. Top with cooked berry mixture. Chill. Serve garnished with whipped cream.

LEMON-BLUEBERRY PIE

Money-making pie—a favorite in a successful farm-home tearoom

Pastry for 2-crust pie
4 c. frozen blueberries or 2
   (10 oz.) pkgs.
1 c. sugar
⅓ c. flour

1   tsp. grated lemon peel
⅛   tsp. salt
2   tblsp. butter

• Combine berries, sugar, flour, lemon peel and salt. Place in pastry-lined 9" pie pan. Dot with butter. Adjust top crust and flute edges; cut vents.

• Bake in hot oven (425°F.) 40 to 50 minutes, or until crust is lightly browned and juice bubbles through steam vents.

BLUEBERRY-LEMON SPONGE PIE

Blueberries combine with lemon sponge in a delectable 2-layer pie

Baked 9" pie shell

Blueberry Layer:
2   c. fresh blueberries
¾   c. sugar
2   tblsp. flour
⅛   tsp. salt
2   egg yolks, well beaten
¼   c. orange juice

Sponge Layer:
½   c. sugar
2   tblsp. flour
⅛   tsp. salt
½   c. cold water
1   egg yolk, slightly beaten
1   tblsp. lemon juice
1   tsp. grated lemon peel
3   egg whites

Blueberry Layer: Heat berries in heavy saucepan over low heat. Blend dry ingredients and add to egg yolks. Add orange juice and beat until smooth. Pour over berries and cook over low heat until thick, stirring constantly. Pour into pie shell.

Sponge Layer: Add blended ¼ c. sugar, flour, salt and cold water to egg yolk; blend and cook over low heat until thick, stirring constantly. Remove from heat; add lemon juice and peel.

• Beat egg whites until soft peaks form; add remaining ¼ c. sugar gradually, beating until mixture is stiff and glossy. Fold cooked lemon mixture into meringue. Pile onto blueberry layer, making sure it touches crust all around.

• Bake in slow oven (325°F.) 35 minutes, or until lightly browned.

Elderberry Pie

Creamy, white blossoms on elderberry bushes start daydreams of summer pies. Elderberry is a pioneer pie that never has gone out of style. The edible blue or black berries have a tart flavor of their own, which country cooks frequently point up with a touch of vinegar or lemon juice. Some pie bakers prefer to combine elderberries with other fruits—apples, gooseberries, cherries, for instance.

Elderberries, like blueberries, freeze successfully without sweetening. During seasons when bucketfuls of berries may be picked free as all outdoors, some cooks put packages of elderberries in their freezers for around-the-year pie baking. They use the frozen berries like fresh ones.

One rule of country cooking is to serve elderberry pie hot from the oven. Frequently a pitcher of sweetened pour cream is passed—a traditional custom. Today, with vanilla ice cream kept on hand in many farm freezers, it also often tops elderberry pie at serving time.

Whenever you talk elderberry pies with farm women, you discover that almost every good cook has tricks of her own. An Iowa homemaker likes to combine 1 part elderberries with 3 parts gooseberries or tart cherries in pies. Then she omits the vinegar or lemon juice and adds a trifle less sugar than when she bakes either a plain gooseberry or cherry pie.

A Kentucky homemaker says: "When I bake apple pies, I often scatter from ½ to 1 cup stemmed elderberries among the apples, sprinkle on a little lemon juice and add a lattice top to show off the beautiful color of the filling. One taste brings compliments—the second bite, requests for my recipe! I always suggest that everyone make her favorite apple pie, adding the ½ or 1 cup of elderberries for a special touch."

The amount of thickening—tapioca, cornstarch or flour—required varies somewhat with the season—depending on the juiciness of the berries. Our recipe suggests the amount usually needed, but you may have to make some adjustment from one year to another.

PIONEER ELDERBERRY PIE

A dessert that makes the search for elderberries along fence rows pay off

Pastry for 2-crust pie
3 ½ c. washed, stemmed elderberries
1 tblsp. vinegar or lemon juice
1 c. sugar
¼ tsp. salt
⅓ c. flour
1 tblsp. butter or margarine

• Spread elderberries in pastry-lined 9″ pie pan. Sprinkle with vinegar.
• Combine sugar, salt and flour; sprinkle over berries. Dot with butter.
• Adjust top crust and flute edges; cut vents. Bake in hot oven (400°F.) 35 to 45 minutes, or until juices show in vents and crust is golden brown.

Note: A farm kitchen trick—use a wide-tooth comb to strip elderberries from their stems.

ELDERBERRY-APPLE PIE

An old-time FARM JOURNAL *favorite*

Unbaked 9″ pie shell
2 c. elderberries
1 ½ c. chopped peeled tart apples
1 c. sugar
⅛ tsp. salt
3 tblsp. quick-cooking tapioca
2 tblsp. butter

• Wash and stem elderberries. (Hold berries in palm of hand and pull stems off with wire egg beater, the kind shaped like tennis racquet.)

• Combine elderberries, apples, sugar, salt and tapioca, crushing berries with spoon.
• Spoon mixture into pie shell; dot with butter; top with pastry lattice.
• Bake in hot oven (400°F.) 35 to 40 minutes, or until apples are tender and crust is golden.

Gather Mulberries for Pies

The recipe for mulberry pie properly starts: "Select a sunny summer day when the breezes are light. Stand on the shady side of the mulberry tree and fill your pail with the knobby, long, glistening berries. Do a little bird watching while you work." Or if you are of a different berry-picking school: "Spread a worn sheet on the emerald grass beneath the tree, shake the branches lightly and run from the shower of juicy, warm, sweet berries that plop down. Get your exercise bending over to pick up berries."

Certainly mulberries are one of the easiest berries to transfer directly from tree to pail. There's no stooping, kneeling or squatting the way there is when you are picking strawberries, raspberries and blackberries, for instance.

Bake a wonderful country pie that day—a pie most city people never are fortunate enough to see or taste. Combine the sweet mulberries with a tart fruit, like gooseberries, or rhubarb. The sweet-tart blend is extra-delicious. We give you a recipe for the berry-rhubarb team that makes one of the most economical farm fruit pies—and one of the best.

MULBERRY PIE

Enjoy this summer pie every month—freeze berries and rhubarb to make it

Pastry for 2-crust pie
2 c. mulberries
1 c. finely sliced rhubarb
1 c. sugar
4 tblsp. flour
2 tblsp. butter or margarine

• Combine mulberries and rhubarb in medium bowl.
• Combine sugar and flour. Sprinkle about ⅓ of mixture in bottom of pastry-lined 9″ pie pan. Turn mulberries and rhubarb into pie pan and add remaining sugar-flour mixture. Dot with butter. Adjust top crust, cut steam vents and flute edges.
• Bake in hot oven (425°F.) 40 to 50 minutes, or until crust is browned and juices bubble in vents.

Two-Berry Pie—Popular with Men

Among popular fruit pies in the Pacific Northwest are the luscious cranberry-blueberry specials. A Washington farm homemaker says: "We have a cranberry bog and my favorite Cranberry-Blueberry Pie recipe comes in handy during the harvest season when I cook for a crew of men. They all seem to enjoy this dessert best. For company, I often put a lattice top on this pie—sometimes spoon vanilla ice cream on top.

"We have enough blueberry bushes to yield fruit for fresh berry pies, and to freeze to combine with fresh cranberries and pastry."

If you want to bake a pie with both blueberries (frozen) and cranberries, follow our famous recipe for Burgundy Berry Pie, which also originated in a Washington country kitchen.

CRANBERRY-BLUEBERRY PIE

Latticed pastry top will display rich color of luscious fruit filling

Pastry for 2-crust pie
 2 c. fresh cranberries
 2 c. frozen, unsweetened blueberries
1 ½ c. sugar
 ⅓ c. flour
 ⅛ tsp. salt
 2 tblsp. butter or margarine

• Put cranberries through food chopper. Combine with frozen blueberries, sugar, flour and salt. Place in pastry-lined 9″ pie pan. Dot with butter. Adjust top crust and flute edges; cut vents.
• Bake in hot oven (425°F.) 45 to 50 minutes or until crust is golden.

CRANBERRY-RAISIN PIE

Colorful Cape Cod pie that's perfect with turkey, chicken and pork

Pastry for 2-crust pie
 3 c. fresh cranberries

 2 tblsp. flour
 2 c. sugar
 ¼ tsp. salt
 ⅔ c. boiling water
 1 c. seedless raisins
 2 tsp. grated lemon peel
 2 tblsp. butter or margarine

• Remove stems from cranberries.
• Combine flour, sugar and salt in saucepan. Stir in cranberries, water, raisins and lemon peel. Cover and cook until cranberries start to pop. Remove from heat and add butter. Cool until lukewarm.
• Pour filling into pastry-lined 9″ pie pan. Arrange lattice of pastry strips on top (see Chapter 2).
• Bake in hot oven (425°F.) 40 to 50 minutes, or until juices bubble in lattice openings and crust is browned.

BURGUNDY BERRY PIE

A Farm Journal *5-star recipe—from our* Freezing & Canning Cookbook

Baked 9″ pie shell and cutouts
1 ¼ c. sugar
 5 tblsp. cornstarch
 ⅛ tsp. salt
 2 tblsp. water
1 ½ c. frozen whole cranberries, unsweetened
 2 c. frozen blueberries, unsweetened

• Combine sugar, cornstarch and salt in heavy saucepan; stir in water and cook over very low heat until mixture melts and comes to a full boil. Add cranberries; cook gently until soft. Remove from heat, and add frozen blueberries. Cool.

• Pour into cooled pastry shell and top with pastry cutouts.

Note: To make pastry cutouts, cut rolled pastry for top crust in fancy shapes with cookie cutter. Brush with water and sprinkle with sugar. Bake on baking sheet in very hot oven (450°F.) a few minutes, or until lightly browned. Cool. Place on pie, one cutout per wedge.

CRANBERRY RELISH PIE

Fine with chicken dinners—make it with frozen cranberries in summer

Pastry for 2-crust pie
2 ½ c. ground fresh cranberries
1 c. ground unpeeled apple (about 2 medium)
½ c. ground orange pulp and peel (1 small)
½ c. chopped nuts
1 ½ c. sugar
2 tblsp. flour
½ tsp. cinnamon
¼ tsp. nutmeg
2 tblsp. butter

• Combine cranberries, apple, orange, nuts, sugar, flour, cinnamon and nutmeg. Place in pastry-lined 9″ pie pan. Dot with butter.
• Adjust latticed top crust; flute edges. Bake in hot oven (425°F.) until pastry is browned and juice begins to bubble through openings in lattice, 40 to 50 minutes.

FRESH GOOSEBERRY PIE

Old-time favorite with as big-time popularity as in pioneer days

Almond Pastry for 2-crust pie
3 c. fresh gooseberries

1 ½ c. sugar
3 tblsp. quick-cooking tapioca
⅛ tsp. salt
2 tblsp. butter or margarine

• Crush ¾ c. gooseberries and add to sugar, tapioca and salt. Stir in remainder of berries. Cook and stir until mixture thickens.
• Turn into pastry-lined 9″ pie pan. Dot with butter. Adjust top crust and flute edges; cut vents. Brush with milk.
• Bake in hot oven (425°F.) 35 to 45 minutes, or until crust is golden. Serve slightly warm.

ALMOND PASTRY: Before adding water to blended flour and shortening in making pastry for a 2-crust pie, add 1 tsp. almond extract. Also good for peach and cherry pies.

RASPBERRY GLACÉ PIE

"My company special," says the Minnesota woman who shares her recipe

Baked 9″ pie shell
1 qt. red raspberries
1 c. water
1 c. sugar
3 tblsp. cornstarch
Few drops red food color
2 tsp. lemon juice
1 (3 oz.) pkg. cream cheese (room temperature)
1 tblsp. milk
Whipped cream (optional)

• Wash berries gently in cold water, lift out and spread on paper toweling to drain thoroughly.   *more*

• Place 1 c. berries and ⅔ c. water in saucepan; simmer 3 minutes. Run through strainer to remove seeds.

• Blend sugar, cornstarch and remaining ⅓ c. water. Add to cooked raspberries and cook until mixture is thick and translucent, stirring constantly. Remove from heat, add food color and lemon juice. Cool.

• Combine cream cheese with milk and spread evenly over bottom of pie shell. Pour remaining berries into pie shell, reserving a few of the prettiest ones for garnishing. Spread cooled, cooked berry mixture over berries. Chill until firm, at least 2 hours. Serve garnished with whipped cream and whole berries.

STRAWBERRY GLACÉ PIE

Hostess idea—substitute individual tart shells for the big pie shell

Baked 9″ pie shell
1 ½ qts. strawberries
1   c. sugar
3   tblsp. cornstarch
½   c. water
1   tblsp. butter or margarine
1   c. heavy cream, whipped
2   tblsp. sifted confectioners sugar

• Hull, wash in cold water and thoroughly drain berries. Crush enough (with potato masher) to make 1 c.

• Combine sugar and cornstarch. Add crushed berries and water. Cook over medium heat, stirring constantly, until mixture comes to a boil. Continue cooking and stirring over low heat 2 minutes. The mixture will be thickened and translucent. Remove from heat and stir in butter. Cool.

• Place whole berries in pie shell, reserving a few choice ones for garnishing. Pour cooked mixture over berries and chill at least 2 hours.

• Serve topped with whipped cream, confectioners sugar added. Garnish with remaining strawberries.

VARIATION

STRAWBERRY CHEESE GLACÉ PIE: Combine 1 (3 oz.) pkg. cream cheese (room temperature) with 1 tblsp. milk and spread over bottom of pie shell before adding berries.

STRAWBERRY FESTIVAL PIE

Crunchy topped, red-bright filling—a beauty that tastes as good as it looks

Baked 9″ pie shell
3   tblsp. cornstarch
¾   c. sugar
¼   c. water
4   c. strawberries
Few drops red food color
Toasted Oat Topping
Whipped cream (optional)

• Combine cornstarch and ½ c. sugar in saucepan; blend in water. Add 2 c. berries and cook, stirring constantly, until thickened and translucent (mixture will be very thick).

• Remove from heat, add food color, remaining ¼ c. sugar and 2 c. berries. Chill.

• Turn strawberry mixture into pie shell and scatter Toasted Oat Topping over pie. Serve with whipped cream if you like.

TOASTED OAT TOPPING: Combine 1 c. quick-cooking rolled oats, ¼ c. brown sugar and ¼ c. melted butter or margarine. Spread in shallow pan. Toast in moderate oven (350°F.) 10 minutes. Toss lightly with a fork.

STRAWBERRY-APRICOT PIE

These fruits ripen at the same time in California's Santa Clara Valley where this pie is a favorite

Baked 9″ pie shell
12 fresh unpeeled apricots, pitted and halved
¾ c. water
½ c. sugar
2 tblsp. cornstarch
½ tsp. salt
2 tblsp. lemon juice
1 qt. ripe strawberries, sliced
1 c. heavy cream, whipped

· Combine apricots and ¾ c. water in saucepan. Bring to a boil and remove from heat at once. Drain, saving liquid. Measure liquid into cup and add water to make ¾ c.
· Purée apricots in blender with a little of the measured liquid, or by putting through sieve or food mill. Return puréed apricots and cooking liquid to saucepan; bring to a boil.
· Combine sugar, cornstarch and salt, mixing thoroughly. Stir into apricot purée. Continue cooking and stirring until mixture thickens and becomes clear. Stir in lemon juice. Cool.
· Fill pie shell with berries; cover with apricot glaze. Top with whipped cream.

STRAWBERRY CREAM PIE

Pie filling contains both cooked and uncooked berries—extra-good flavor

Baked 9″ pie shell
1 qt. hulled strawberries
3 tblsp. cornstarch
1 c. sugar
2 tblsp. lemon juice
⅛ tsp. salt
Whipped cream

· Crush half of berries with potato masher or fork; stir in cornstarch, sugar, lemon juice and salt. Cook over medium heat until mixture is thickened and clear. Cool.
· Cut remaining 2 c. berries in halves, saving out 6 whole berries; fold into the cooked mixture. Pour into pie shell and chill.
· To serve, garnish with puffs of whipped cream and a few choice berries.

STRAWBERRY-CANTALOUPE PIE

Cool-looking, colorful, tempting and refreshing with luscious flavor blend

Baked 9″ pie shell
1 (3 oz.) pkg. cream cheese
1 tblsp. milk
1 c. ripe strawberries
½ c. water
½ c. sugar
2 tblsp. cornstarch
⅛ tsp. salt
1 tblsp. butter
1 tsp. finely grated lemon peel

more

Red food color
3 c. fresh cantaloupe balls, drained

• Spread cream cheese, softened with milk, over bottom of cool pie shell.
• Crush strawberries slightly and combine with water; simmer 5 minutes and press through sieve. Discard seeds.
• Blend sugar, cornstarch and salt; stir into strawberry mixture. Cook over medium heat, stirring constantly until mixture comes to a boil. Continue cooking and stirring over low heat 2 minutes. The mixture will be thickened and translucent. Remove from heat and stir in butter and lemon peel. Add a few drops of red color. Cool until lukewarm.
• Place cantaloupe balls in pie shell on top of cheese; spoon strawberry glaze over them. Let glaze set before serving.

STRAWBERRY-PINEAPPLE PIE

Competes with strawberry shortcake for blue ribbons—try it for a change

Pastry for 2-crust pie
1 c. sugar
4 tblsp. cornstarch
½ tsp. salt
4 c. fresh strawberries, sliced
½ c. drained crushed pineapple (canned)
2 tblsp. butter
Whipped cream (optional)

• Combine sugar, cornstarch and salt. Stir in strawberries and pineapple. Turn into pastry-lined 9″ pie pan. Dot with butter. Adjust top crust (use latticed top for greatest appeal); flute edges. Brush top of pie with milk.
• Bake in hot oven (400°F.) 40 to 50 minutes. Cool on rack before serving. Garnish with fluffs of whipped cream and choice, ripe berries.

Red Cherry Orchard Pie

If you have a cherry tree, the chances are you race with the birds to see who will get the juicy, red fruit. Country homemakers refuse to let their feathered friends win—a determination that has their families' approval. Cherry pie is one of the royal American desserts—it competes with apple pie for top honors. Here's our best recipe for the classic, a simple, unadorned one. For who always wants to try to improve on the bright cherry flavor and color?

FRESH CHERRY PIE

Every forkful of our best cherry pie brings delight—an easy one to make

Pastry for 2-crust pie
1 ⅓ c. sugar
⅓ c. flour
⅛ tsp. salt
3 drops almond extract (optional)
4 c. pitted tart cherries
2 tblsp. butter or margarine

• Combine sugar, flour and salt. Add almond extract to cherries and toss with sugar-flour mixture to mix thoroughly. Turn into pastry-lined 9″ pie pan. Adjust lattice top; flute edges.

• Bake in hot oven (425°F.) about 40 minutes. If edges brown too much, cover loosely with strip of aluminum foil.

Note: Use 1½ c. sugar if you do not like a cherry pie on the tart side.

CRISSCROSS CHERRY PIE

A FARM JOURNAL *5-star recipe—from our* COUNTRY COOKBOOK

Rich Pastry
2   (1 lb.) cans pitted tart cherries
      (water pack)
2½ tblsp. quick-cooking tapioca
¼   tsp. salt
¼   tsp. almond extract
1   tsp. lemon juice
4   drops red food color
1¼ c. sugar
1   tblsp. butter or margarine

• Drain cherries. Measure ⅓ c. liquid into mixing bowl. Add tapioca, salt, almond extract, lemon juice and food color, then cherries and 1 c. sugar. Mix and let stand while making pastry.

• Fit pastry into bottom of 9″ pie pan. Trim ½″ beyond outer rim of pan. Fill with cherry mixture. Dot with butter. Sprinkle with remaining sugar. Moisten rim with water. Adjust latticed top; flute edges. (To keep high rim from browning faster than crisscross strips, circle pie with a stand-up foil collar. Fold foil over rim and leave on during entire baking.)

• Bake in hot oven (425°F.) 40 to 45 minutes. Serve warm.

RICH PASTRY

2¼ c. sifted flour
1   tsp. salt
1   tblsp. sugar
¾   c. vegetable shortening
1   egg yolk
1   tblsp. lemon juice
¼   c. milk

• Sift flour with salt and sugar. Cut in shortening until mixture resembles coarse cornmeal.

• Beat egg yolk and lemon juice. Blend in milk. Add to dry ingredients, tossing with fork into a soft dough.

• Divide dough in half. Form each into ball. Flatten each on lightly floured surface. Roll to about ⅛″ thickness. Use half for bottom crust. Cut second half into 18 strips with sharp knife or pastry wheel. Interlace 14 strips, pressing ends against moistened rim and folding lower crust up over them. Moisten rim again and circle it with remaining 4 strips. Press down firmly.

CHERRY PIE GLACÉ

Dessert they'll praise—open-face pie filled with shiny, red cherries

Unbaked 9″ pie shell
4   c. pitted fresh tart cherries
1   c. sugar
⅛   tsp. salt
¼   c. flour
1   tblsp. lemon juice
2   tblsp. butter or margarine
Cinnamon Jelly Glaze
Whipped cream (optional)   *more*

• Combine cherries, sugar, salt, flour and lemon juice. Pour into pie shell. Dot with butter.
• Bake in moderate oven (375°F.) 40 minutes. Cool on rack.
• Spoon Cinnamon Jelly Glaze over cherries. To serve, garnish with spoonfuls of whipped cream.

CINNAMON JELLY GLAZE: Melt ¾ c. red currant or other tart jelly over hot water. Add ¼ tsp. cinnamon.

VARIATIONS

CHERRY PIE GLACÉ WITH CANNED FRUIT: Substitute 2 (1 lb. 4 oz.) cans tart cherries, well drained, for fresh pitted cherries.

CHERRY PIE GLACÉ WITH FROZEN FRUIT: Substitute 2 (1 lb.) cans frozen tart cherries (packed in syrup), thawed and well drained, for fresh pitted cherries. Reduce sugar from 1 c. to ½ c.

Filling:
2 (1 lb. 4 oz.) cans tart cherries, drained
1 c. sugar
¼ c. cornstarch
½ c. cherry juice
1 tsp. almond extract
Few drops red food color
Meringue (3 egg whites)

Crust: Sift together flour, salt, baking powder and sugar. Cut in butter. Add egg yolks mixed with water. Stir until dough clings together.
• Press mixture into a 10″ pie pan, lining bottom and sides evenly. Bake in moderate oven (375°F.) 15 minutes.
Filling: Combine cherries, sugar, cornstarch and cherry juice. Cook until thickened. Stir in almond extract and food color. Cool; turn into cool baked pie shell.
• Spoon meringue over pie (see Perfect Meringue for Topping Pies, Chapter 9).
• Bake in moderate oven (350°F.) 12 to 15 minutes, or until meringue is browned. Cool. Makes 8 servings.

REGAL CHERRY PIE

Crust and filling bake separately—good way to curb runaway juices

Crust:
1 ¾ c. sifted flour
¼ tsp. salt
1 tsp. baking powder
1 tblsp. sugar
¾ c. butter or shortening
3 egg yolks, slightly beaten
1 tblsp. water

CHERRY-MINCEMEAT PIE

No need to get in a pie rut—bake a double-good cherry-mincemeat treat

Pastry for 2-crust pie
1 (1 lb. 4 oz.) can pitted tart cherries
½ c. sugar
Few drops red food color
2 c. prepared mincemeat
3 tblsp. flour
⅛ tsp. salt
1 egg, beaten

• Drain cherries (you should have 2 c.).
• Combine cherries and the sugar. Let stand while you make pastry.
• Combine cherry mixture, food color, mincemeat, flour, salt and egg. Pour into a pastry-lined 9″ pie pan. Top with a lattice crust.
• Bake in hot oven (425°F.) 35 to 40 minutes.

CHERRY-WALNUT PIE

No wonder it's a holiday favorite—so festive, colorful, delicious

Crust:
    1   c. flour
    2   tblsp. confectioners sugar
    ½   c. butter or margarine

Filling:
    2   eggs, slightly beaten
    1   c. sugar
    ¼   c. flour
    ½   tsp. baking powder
    1   c. chopped walnuts
    ¾   c. flaked coconut
    1   (5 oz.) jar maraschino cherries
Whipped cream

Crust: Combine flour, sugar and butter in small bowl. Use mixer at low speed and mix only until dough forms. Press dough, with fingers, in bottom and sides of 9″ pie pan. Bake 10 minutes in moderate oven (350°F.). Cool.
Filling: Beat eggs and add sugar gradually. Stir in flour and baking powder, sifted together. Stir in walnuts, coconut, cherries and cherry juice, saving out some nuts, cherries and coconut for garnishing. Spread in cooled pie shell, mounding slightly in center.
• Bake in moderate oven (350°F.) 30 to 35 minutes. Spread with whipped cream and top with reserved nuts, cherries and coconut. Makes 8 servings.

Change-of-Pace Cherry Pie

Cherry pies take the spotlight in February—thanks to George Washington and the month's many parties. Why not surprise your family and friends by baking a pie with canned *sweet* cherries? They have a distinctive flavor and an appealing deep-red color. And you can buy them pitted if you don't have your own canned fruit. Here's a country-style pie to make ahead and refrigerate a few hours—one bound to be praised.

SWEET CHERRY PIE

Bake this pie once and you'll make it again and again—ever so good

Baked 9″ pie shell
    2   (1 lb.) cans pitted dark sweet cherries
    ⅔   c. sugar
    3   tblsp. cornstarch
    ⅛   tsp. salt
    1   tblsp. butter   *more*

2   tblsp. lemon juice
1   (3 oz.) pkg. cream cheese
Whipped cream (optional)

• Drain cherries, reserving juice. Combine sugar, cornstarch and salt in saucepan. Add 1 c. cherry juice. Cook, stirring constantly, over medium heat until mixture comes to a boil. Continue cooking and stirring 2 minutes. Add cherries and cook 2 minutes.

• Remove from heat; add butter and lemon juice, stirring until butter melts. Cool.

• Let cream cheese stand at room temperature to soften. Spread over bottom of pie shell. Pour cooled cherry mixture into pie shell. Chill several hours. Serve garnished with whipped cream.

CHERRY MACAROON PIE

An exquisite party pie worth its cost in ingredients and in time

Macaroon Crust:

1   c. sifted flour
½   tsp. salt
1   tsp. granulated sugar
⅓   c. shortening
½   c. crushed macaroon cookie crumbs (8 two-inch cookies)
1   egg yolk, slightly beaten
4   tblsp. cold water

Filling:

1   (8 oz.) pkg. cream cheese (room temperature)
½   c. dairy sour cream
⅓   c. brown sugar, firmly packed
1   tsp. cinnamon
1   (1 lb. 4 oz.) can pitted tart cherries

½   c. sugar
⅛   tsp. salt
2½   tblsp. cornstarch
⅛   tsp. almond extract
Few drops red food color
1   (3½ oz.) can flaked coconut
Meringue (3 egg whites)

Crust: Sift together flour, salt and sugar. Cut in shortening until mixture resembles small peas. Blend in macaroon crumbs. Combine egg yolk and water; gradually sprinkle over crumbs, tossing with fork. (You may need a few more drops of water to make dough workable.)

• Form dough into ball, flatten and roll on a lightly floured surface to make a 10½″ circle. Fit dough into 9″ pie pan. Flute edge and prick well with 4-tined fork.

• Bake in hot oven (400°F.) 15 minutes. Cool.

Filling: Combine cream cheese, sour cream, brown sugar and cinnamon. Spread on bottom of cool pie shell.

• Drain cherries, saving juice. Add enough water to juice to make 1 c.

• Combine sugar, salt and cornstarch. Slowly stir in cherry juice. Cook, stirring constantly, until thick and clear. Remove from heat, add almond extract and a few drops of food color; add cherries and coconut, mixing well. Spoon mixture into pie shell. Top with meringue (see Perfect Meringue for Topping Pies, Chapter 9) and bake in moderate oven (350°F.) until tipped with gold, 12 to 15 minutes. Cool away from drafts.

Note: For an especially pretty pie, sprinkle meringue with ¼ c. flaked coconut before baking.

Red and Green Currant Pie

Country cooks are skillful in using the fruits of the woods and field—currants, for instance. Some pie bakers choose red-ripe fruit, but most of them prefer currants that are either half ripe or mostly green with a few berries starting to blush or turn color.

You may be able to buy or grow red currants if you live where the wild fruit is not available. (Most of the commercial production goes to the producers of that marvelous spread, currant jelly.) In the majority of neighborhoods fresh currants are becoming a rare treat. Their season is short, so farm homemakers lose no time in making pies when currants are ripe.

Our grandmothers' recipes for currant pie always started: "Take a scant quart of currants." If you use 4 cups of berries in a 9" pie pan, you may end up with part of the juice in the oven instead of in the pie. Modern recipes almost always call for 3 cups of fruit.

The unwritten farm-kitchen rule is to bake green currants between two pie crusts, the ripe with a latticed top to display the attractive color. If you haven't baked a currant pie and decide to make the adventure, you'll wonder why you never baked this dessert before. Almost incomparable!

FRESH CURRANT PIE

Just tart enough, very juicy; the filling has gorgeous color

Pastry for 2-crust pie
3 c. washed, stemmed currants
1½ c. sugar
3 tblsp. quick-cooking tapioca
½ tsp. salt
1 tblsp. butter or margarine

· Drain currants. Place in a bowl and crush lightly with spoon.
· Combine sugar, tapioca and salt. Add to currants and stir gently to mix.
· Turn into pastry-lined 9" pie pan; dot with butter. Adjust top crust; flute edges and cut vents.
· Bake in hot oven (425°F.) until crust is golden and the juices are bubbly, 35 to 45 minutes.

Concord Grape Pie—Extra-Delicious

It's a fragrant, tantalizing moment in the farm kitchen when grape pie comes from the oven bubbling with sweet-tart juices. Everybody wants to have dinner at once!

Today's homemakers extend the short Concord grape pie season by fixing, packaging and freezing a few pie fillings ready to add to pastry. They bake a pie or two during the holiday season or between Thanksgiving and Christmas to bring a welcome remembrance of summer to meals. The frozen filling holds its flavor three to four months.

Many women feel that the superlative taste of this old-fashioned dessert pleases their families and friends enough to justify labor and time costs. It does take a little time to slip the skins from the blue-black grapes, to heat the pulp, strain out the seeds and reunite pulp and skins before you can fix the filling.

Unfortunately, these juicy, winy native American grapes aren't grown across the nation. They are available in largest amounts in the Northeast, upper Midwest and the Middle Atlantic States.

But pie bakers on Western ranches and other places where fresh Concords are not available do not deprive their tables entirely of the rich, fruity flavor combined with tender, flaky pastry. They use frozen grape juice concentrate or bottled juice to make their pies (see Chapter 5).

Concord grape cobblers are another wonderful farm dessert. See our recipe in Chapter 6.

STREUSEL CONCORD GRAPE PIE

You can bake this filling in 2 crusts if you prefer pastry to streusel

Unbaked 9″ pie shell
4 ½ c. Concord grapes
1   c. sugar
¼ c. flour
2 tsp. lemon juice
⅛ tsp. salt
Oat Streusel

· Wash grapes and remove skins by pinching at end opposite stem. Reserve skins.
· Place pulp in saucepan and bring to a boil; cook a few minutes until pulp is soft. Put through strainer or food mill, while pulp is hot, to remove seeds.
· Mix strained pulp with skins. Stir in sugar, flour, lemon juice and salt.
· Place grape mixture in pastry-lined pie pan. Sprinkle on Oat Streusel.
· Bake in hot oven (425°F.) 35 to 40 minutes.

OAT STREUSEL: Combine ½ c. quick-cooking rolled oats, ½ c. brown sugar and ¼ c. flour. Cut in ¼ c. butter or margarine to distribute evenly.

Seedless Grapes—Pie-Fancier's Joy

Here's a pie that captures the honeylike sweetness of the yellow-green grapes—and the enthusiasm of all tasters. Thompson seedless grapes, developed less than a century ago in California by William Thompson, are still grown most extensively in the Golden State's vineyards. More than half the world's seedless raisins are made from them. Although the grapes have been developed to a larger size in recent years, they have retained their pleasing flavor.

If you live where you can get the immature Thompson seedless grapes, you can fashion a pie with them using your recipe for gooseberry pie. Just substitute the unripe grapes for the berries, suggests an Arizona ranch cook.

The ripe grapes are greenish-white to pale-gold color; they are sweet and have tender skins. That's the kind we used in the recipe that follows. There's no worry about stray seeds in this grape pie!

GREEN GRAPE-APPLE PIE

Grapes blend their honey sweetness with tart, juicy summer apples

Pastry for 2-crust pie
2 c. seedless green grapes

3 c. sliced peeled apples
1 c. sugar
3 tblsp. quick-cooking tapioca
¼ tsp. ground cardamon
¼ tsp. cinnamon
¼ tsp. salt
2 tblsp. butter

• Combine grapes, apples, sugar, tapioca, spices and salt. Turn into pastry-lined 9″ pie pan. Dot with butter.
• Adjust top crust; flute edges and cut vents. Bake in hot oven (425°F.) 50 to 60 minutes.

Big Red Grapes—the Tokays

Never had Tokay pie? You've missed something! When the firm, compact clusters of brilliant-red Tokay or Flame Tokay grapes are ripe, surprise your family and company by making a pie with them. It's a fine way to introduce a change of pace in your autumn meals.

RED GRAPE PIE

They'll ask what it's made of and beg for your recipe

Pastry for 2-crust pie
5 c. seeded, cut-up Tokay grapes
⅔ c. sugar

1 tsp. grated lemon peel
1 tsp. lemon juice
2½ to 3 tblsp. quick-cooking tapioca
2 tblsp. butter or margarine
2 tsp. sugar
⅛ tsp. cinnamon

• Combine grapes, ⅔ c. sugar, lemon peel and juice and tapioca. Place in pastry-lined 9″ pie pan. Dot with butter.
• Adjust top crust, flute edges and cut vents; sprinkle with mixture of 2 tsp. sugar and cinnamon. Bake in hot oven (425°F.) 45 to 50 minutes.

Peach Pies for Summer Suppers

"Peach pie is a reward tired and hungry men who have worked late in the field trying to finish a job really appreciate," one farm woman says. "A cool evening and a peach pie are country joys to sample together."

Here are some of the best peach pies that farm women across the country bake. Take your pick and give your family a taste treat.

OLD-FASHIONED PEACH PIE

*One of summer's best treats. For a
pretty pie, use a latticed pastry top*

Pastry for 2-crust pie
¾	c. sugar
3	tblsp. flour
¼	tsp. cinnamon or nutmeg
⅛	tsp. salt
5	c. sliced fresh peaches
1	tsp. lemon juice
⅛	tsp. almond extract (optional)
2	tblsp. butter or margarine

· Combine sugar, flour, cinnamon and
salt. Add to peaches; sprinkle on
lemon juice and almond extract.
· Pour into a pastry-lined 9″ pie pan.
Dot with butter.
· Adjust top crust, flute edges and cut
steam vents.
· Bake in hot oven (425°F.) 40 to
45 minutes, or until peaches are
tender and crust is browned.

BROWN SUGAR PIE

*Give this old-time pie a new twist—
top servings with lemon sherbet*

Pastry for 2-crust pie
½	c. granulated sugar
¼	c. brown sugar, firmly packed
3	tblsp. flour
¼ to ½	tsp. cinnamon
⅛	tsp. salt
5	c. sliced peeled fresh peaches
1	tblsp. lemon juice (optional)
¼	tsp. almond extract (optional)
2	tblsp. butter or margarine

· Combine sugars, flour, cinnamon
and salt.

· Sprinkle peaches with lemon juice
and almond extract.
· Add sugar-flour mixture to peaches
and mix gently. Turn into pastry-lined
9″ pie pan. Dot with butter. Adjust
top crust and flute edges; cut vents.
(Use lattice top, if desired.)
· Bake in hot oven (425°F.) about
35 to 45 minutes, or until juices start
to bubble in vents and crust is golden.
Serve slightly warm with ice cream, if
desired.

VARIATION

PEACH-BLUEBERRY PIE: Spread 2 c.
blueberries in pastry-lined pan. Sprinkle with half the sugar-flour mixture
and half the lemon juice. Top with
2½ c. sliced fresh peaches. Sprinkle
with remaining sugar-flour mixture
and lemon juice. Omit almond extract.
Dot with butter. Add top crust and
bake like Brown Sugar Pie.

PEACH CREAM PIE

A new version of peaches and cream

Unbaked 9″ pie shell
1	qt. sliced peeled peaches
½	c. sugar
½	tsp. cinnamon
1	egg
2	tblsp. cream

Lemon Crumb Topping

· Arrange peaches in pastry-lined pie
pan; sprinkle with sugar and cinnamon. Beat together egg and cream;
pour over peaches. Sprinkle Lemon
Crumb Topping over peaches.
· Bake in hot oven (425°F.) until
lightly browned, 35 to 40 minutes.

LEMON CRUMB TOPPING: Combine ¼ c. brown sugar, ½ c. flour and 1 tsp. grated lemon peel. Cut in ¼ c. butter or margarine until mixture is crumbly.

CHEESE-TOP PEACH PIE

Sour cream and cheese enhance flavor

Unbaked 9″ pie shell
- 1   c. sugar
- 3   tblsp. flour
- ⅛   tsp. salt
- ½   tsp. cinnamon
- 5   c. sliced fresh peaches
- ½   c. dairy sour cream
- ½   c. grated Cheddar cheese

· Chill pie shell 30 minutes.
· Meanwhile, combine sugar, flour, salt and cinnamon. Sprinkle about 2 tblsp. of this mixture over bottom of chilled pie shell.
· In large mixing bowl, lightly toss together sliced peaches and remainder of sugar mixture.
· Pour peach mixture into pie shell. Dot with sour cream and sprinkle with grated cheese.
· Bake in hot oven (425°F.) 35 to 40 minutes.

SOUR CREAM PEACH PIE

Summer's treat—peaches and cream under spicy, sparkly pastry cover

Pastry for 2-crust pie
- 4   c. sliced peeled peaches (7 to 8 medium)
- 1   c. sugar
- 5   tblsp. flour
- ⅛   tsp. salt
- ½   c. dairy sour cream
- ¼   tsp. cinnamon
- ¼   tsp. nutmeg

· Spread peaches in pastry-lined 9″ pie pan. Combine sugar (reserving 2 tblsp.), flour, salt and sour cream. Spread over peaches. Adjust top crust and flute edges; cut vents.
· Mix remaining 2 tblsp. sugar, cinnamon and nutmeg. Sprinkle over top.
· Bake in hot oven (400°F.) about 40 minutes or until peaches are tender and crust is browned.

VARIATION

SOUR CREAM PEACH PIE WITH CANNED FRUIT: Substitute 2 (1 lb.) cans sliced peaches for fresh peaches. Drain canned peaches; you should have 3 c. after draining.

OPEN-FACE PEACH PIE

Rich, shortbreadlike crust holds ripe peaches in spicy custard

Crust:
- 2   c. flour
- ¼   tsp. baking powder
- ½   tsp. salt
- 2   tblsp. sugar
- ½   c. butter or margarine
- 1   egg white, beaten

Filling:
- 5   medium-size freestone peaches
- ¾   c. sugar
- ½   tsp. cinnamon
- ¼   tsp. nutmeg
- 3   egg yolks, beaten
- ⅔   c. heavy cream   *more*

Crust: Combine flour, baking powder, salt and 2 tblsp. sugar in a bowl. Cut in butter until mixture resembles coarse crumbs. Pat evenly on sides and bottom of a 10″ pie pan. Brush bottom of crust with beaten egg white and chill while you fix the filling.

Filling: Peel, halve and pit peaches. Arrange cut side up in crust.

• Combine ¾ c. sugar and spices and sprinkle evenly over fruit.

• Bake in hot oven (400°F.) 15 minutes.

• Blend egg yolks with cream; pour over fruit, letting some of mixture run into center of peaches. Continue baking until filling is set, about 30 minutes. Cool at least 1 hour before serving. Makes 8 servings.

Note: If you do not have a 10″ pie pan, bake this pie in an 8″ square pan. And if you're not calorie conscious, top servings with vanilla ice cream.

PEACHY PRALINE PIE

Pecans and brown sugar give this summer Dixie pie superb flavor

Unbaked 9″ pie shell
  ¾   c. granulated sugar
  3   tblsp. flour
  4   c. sliced peeled peaches
  1 ½ tsp. lemon juice
  ⅓   c. brown sugar, firmly packed
  ¼   c. flour
  ½   c. chopped pecans
  3   tblsp. butter or margarine

• Combine granulated sugar and 3 tblsp. flour in large bowl. Add peaches and the lemon juice.

• Combine brown sugar, ¼ c. flour and pecans in small bowl. Mix in butter until mixture is crumbly. Sprinkle one third of pecan mixture over bottom of pie shell; cover with the peach mixture and sprinkle remaining pecan mixture over peaches.

• Bake in hot oven (400°F.) until peaches are tender, about 40 minutes.

ALL-SEASON PEACH PIE

A FARM JOURNAL *5-star recipe—great favorite at Maine church suppers*

Unbaked 9″ pie shell
  2   (1 lb.) cans peach halves, well drained
  ⅓   c. sugar
  3   tblsp. cornstarch
  ¾   tsp. nutmeg
  ¼   tsp. salt
  ¾   c. heavy cream
  ¾   tsp. vanilla
Whipped cream

• Arrange peach halves, cut side up, in pie shell.

• Combine sugar, cornstarch, ½ tsp. nutmeg, salt, cream and vanilla. Pour over peaches in shell; sprinkle with remaining nutmeg.

• Bake in hot oven (400°F.) 40 minutes, or until peaches are tender. Serve with whipped cream.

Note: Extra-good made with fresh peaches. Use ½ c. instead of ⅓ c. sugar.

Peaches off the Cupboard Shelf

Home-canned peaches on the shelf and your own pie-crust mix nearby in the kitchen! No wonder country cooks are famed for their baking talents. They keep the ingredients handy for turning out golden-topped pies in a hurry. They appreciate that a marvelous dessert, like Butterscotch Peach Pie, is the best answer to the menu maker's age-old question: What dessert can I fix that will make an otherwise commonplace meal something special? This old-fashioned, sugar-sprinkled pie is a farm favorite. Do try it.

BUTTERSCOTCH PEACH PIE

Butter, brown sugar and peaches make this homey pie a praiseworthy treat

Pastry for 2-crust pie
3 ½ c. home-canned peaches, drained
½   c. brown sugar, firmly packed
2   tblsp. flour
⅛   tsp. salt
½   c. syrup from canned peaches
¼   c. butter or margarine
2   tsp. lemon juice
¼   to ½ tsp. almond extract
1   tsp. granulated sugar

• Place peaches in pastry-lined 9" pie pan.
• Combine sugar, flour, salt and peach syrup; add butter. Cook until thick, stirring. Remove from heat; add lemon juice and almond extract. Pour over peaches. Adjust top crust; flute edges and cut vents. Sprinkle with granulated sugar.
• Bake in hot oven (425°F.) 30 minutes. Cool on rack.

Note: You can use 1 (1 lb. 13 oz.) can peaches if you do not have a supply of home-canned fruit.

PEACH MARSHMALLOW PIE

Sweet sauce brings out fruit flavor in this country kitchen pie

Pastry for 2-crust pie
¼   c. sugar
1 ½ tblsp. quick-cooking tapioca
¼   tsp. salt
1   tblsp. lemon juice
¼   tsp. almond extract
1   (1 lb. 13 oz.) can sliced peaches, drained
⅓   c. peach juice
2   tblsp. butter or margarine
Marshmallow Sauce

• Mix sugar, tapioca and salt. Add lemon juice, almond extract, peach juice and drained peaches (2 c.). Let stand 15 minutes.
• Pour into pastry-lined 8" pie pan. Dot with butter. Adjust top crust; flute edges and cut vents.
• Bake in hot oven (425°F.) about 45 minutes, or until crust is browned and juices start to bubble in vents.
• Serve with Marshmallow Sauce.

MARSHMALLOW SAUCE: Measure ½ c. marshmallow creme into small bowl. Beat in 1 tblsp. milk with fork until smooth. Serve to pour over pie.

CHAMPION PEACH PIE

Top winner in a national bake-off

Crust:
1   (1 lb. 13 oz.) can peach slices
2   c. sifted flour
1   tsp. salt
⅔   c. vegetable shortening

Filling:
½   c. sugar
2   tblsp. cornstarch
2   tblsp. corn syrup
2   tsp. pumpkin pie spice
2   tsp. vanilla
2   tblsp. butter

Topping:
2   eggs, slightly beaten
⅓   c. sugar
1   (3 oz.) pkg. cream cheese
½   c. dairy sour cream
1   tblsp. lemon juice

Crust: Drain peaches; reserve juice. Combine flour with salt in mixing bowl and cut in shortening until mixture is the size of small peas. Sprinkle 6 to 7 tblsp. peach juice, a little at a time, over mixture, tossing and stirring lightly with fork. Add juice to driest particles, pushing lumps to side, until dough is just moist enough to hold together. Roll out half of dough on floured surface to a circle 1½" larger than inverted 9" pie pan. Fit loosely into pan.

Filling: Combine reserved peach slices, sugar, cornstarch, corn syrup, pumpkin pie spice and vanilla. Place in pastry-lined pie pan. Dot with butter.

Topping: Combine eggs, sugar and 2 tblsp. reserved peach juice in small saucepan. Cook over low heat, stirring constantly, until mixture thickens. Soften cream cheese in small mixing bowl.

· Blend in sour cream and lemon juice. Gradually add hot mixture, beating constantly until smooth. Spread on peach filling.

· Adjust top crust, flute edges and cut vents. Brush with peach juice.

· Bake in hot oven (425°F.) for 10 minutes; reduce heat to 350°F. and continue baking 30 to 35 minutes until golden brown. (Cover edge with foil the last 20 minutes.)

Sample This Nectarine Pie

If you grow or can get nectarines, they make elegant summer pies. There are many kinds of nectarines, as there are peaches, but most of them produce extra-special pies with a peachy flavor. Some California cooks, including the one who sent us the recipe, believe nectarines have more flavor and aroma than peaches. Our recipe testers agreed the fruit makes really good "peach" pies!

NECTARINE PIE

Nectarines retain good color and texture when baked in pies

Pastry for 2-crust pie
5   c. sliced peeled and pitted nectarines
1   tsp. lemon juice
1   c. sugar
⅓   c. flour
¼   tsp. mace
⅛   tsp. salt
¼   tsp. grated lemon peel
1 ½   tblsp. butter or margarine

· Combine nectarines, lemon juice, sugar, flour, mace, salt and lemon peel. Place in pastry-lined 9″ pie pan. Dot with butter.
· Adjust top crust and flute edges; cut steam vents. Bake in hot oven (425°F.) about 45 minutes or until crust is browned and juice begins to bubble through the slits.

Plum-Delicious Pie

By the time school bells ring in September, silver-dusted purple Italian plums, grown extensively in Idaho, appear on fruit counters. Pies made with "blue plums," as farm women commonly call them, end many autumn meals in fine fashion.

A spicy, buttery crumb topping complements the tart-sweet fruit flavor of this juicy Purple Plum Pie, the favorite recipe of an Iowa homemaker, who bakes it in a heavy paper bag from her grocery store. The bag catches any runaway juices that bubble over and prevents the edges and top of the pie from browning too much. Also, she doesn't have to watch the pie as it bakes.

PURPLE PLUM PIE

Best faintly warm with nippy cheese slices or scoops of ice cream

Unbaked 9″ pie shell
4   c. sliced, pitted purple plums
½   c. sugar
¼   c. flour
¼   tsp. salt
¼   tsp. cinnamon
1   tblsp. lemon juice
Spicy Topping

· Remove pits and cut plums in quarters. Combine with sugar, flour, salt and cinnamon. Turn into pie shell and sprinkle with lemon juice. Add Spicy Topping.
· Place pie in heavy brown paper bag from supermarket. Be sure bag is large enough to cover pie loosely. Fold over open end twice to close, and fasten with paper clips. Set on baking sheet in hot oven (425°F.); bake 1 hour. Remove from oven, let rest a few minutes before removing pie from paper bag. Partially cool on rack.

SPICY TOPPING: Combine ½ c. flour, ½ c. sugar, ¼ tsp. cinnamon and ¼ tsp. nutmeg. Cut in ¼ c. butter or margarine until mixture resembles coarse crumbs. Sprinkle over plums, mounding crumbs up in center of pie.

FRESH PLUM PIE

Use sweet, blue-to-purple prune plums to make this open-face pie

Press-in-Pan Pastry:
1 ½ c. sifted flour
¼ tsp. baking powder
½ c. soft butter
1 egg
⅓ c. sugar
⅛ tsp. salt

Filling:
1 ½ lbs. fresh prune plums, quartered and pitted
2 tblsp. granulated sugar
1 tsp. grated orange peel
½ tsp. cinnamon
1 tblsp. butter
3 tblsp. confectioners sugar

Pastry: Sift flour and baking powder into bowl; blend in butter until mixture is smooth.

• Beat egg until frothy; gradually add sugar and salt, beating until egg thickens. Add to flour mixture, stirring until smooth.

• Turn dough into greased 9″ pie pan and press evenly over sides and bottom of pan, but do not make rim. Refrigerate.

Filling: Circle plums in pastry-lined pie pan to make rows. Sprinkle with granulated sugar, orange peel, cinnamon and dots of butter.

• Bake in hot oven (400°F.) 15 minutes; reduce heat to 350°F. and bake about 45 minutes longer, or until plums are tender. Remove from oven and sift confectioners sugar over pie. Cool on rack. Serve slightly warm with a scoop of vanilla ice cream, if desired, or garnish with whipped cream.

FRESH PINEAPPLE PIE

Excellent way to point up the fruit's natural tart-sweet, fresh flavor

Pastry for 2-crust pie
1 medium pineapple
2 eggs, slightly beaten
1 ½ c. sugar
2 tblsp. flour
1 tblsp. grated lemon peel
1 tblsp. lemon juice
⅛ tsp. salt

• Cut peeled and cored pineapple in bite-size chunks. You should have about 3 c. fruit.

• Place eggs in bowl and beat in sugar, flour, lemon peel and juice and salt. Turn into pastry-lined 9″ pie pan. Adjust top crust (or use lattice top); flute edges and cut vents.

• Bake in hot oven (425°F.) 45 minutes, or until crust is lightly browned.

PINEAPPLE-APRICOT PIE

Combination of fruits that complement each other, with ginger top

Crumb Pie Shell:
1 ½ c. sifted flour
3 tblsp. confectioners sugar
¾ c. butter or margarine
½ c. granulated sugar
½ tsp. ginger

Filling:
1 (11 oz.) pkg. dried apricots (about 2 c.)
2 c. water
½ c. sugar
2 tblsp. flour
1 (1 lb. 4 oz.) can crushed pineapple
⅛ tsp. salt

Shell: Sift flour and confectioners sugar into mixing bowl. Cut in butter until mixture resembles coarse crumbs. Remove 1 c. crumbs; mix with ½ c. granulated sugar and ginger; set aside. Pat remaining crumbs in bottom and on sides of 9″ pie pan. Bake in hot oven (425°F.) about 8 minutes, or until lightly browned. Cool.

Filling: Cook apricots, cut in pieces, in 2 c. water over low heat until very tender, stirring occasionally. Add a little more water during cooking, if necessary. Apricot mixture should be thick when cooked. Remove from heat; add sugar, flour, pineapple and salt.

• Spoon pineapple-apricot mixture in pie shell; sprinkle rest of ginger crumbs on top. Broil at least 5″ to 9″ from heat until crumbs are browned, watching carefully (crumbs brown very fast). Partially cool before cutting.

• Combine cornstarch and ¼ c. brown sugar in saucepan. Add lemon juice and pineapple syrup mixture; cook, stirring constantly, until mixture is thick and clear. Remove from heat and add 2 tblsp. butter, stirring until it melts. Add pineapple.

• While preheating oven to 425°F., place remaining 4 tblsp. butter in bottom of 9″ pie pan; place in oven until butter is melted. Sprinkle with remaining ½ c. brown sugar and 1 tblsp. water. Arrange pecan halves, rounded side down, around bottom and sides of pie pan. Carefully line pan with pastry. Spoon in pineapple mixture.

• Adjust top crust, flute edges; cut vents. Place pie on square of foil in oven to catch drippings.

• Bake in hot oven (425°F.) 25 minutes. Turn out, upside down, on serving plate immediately. Cool on rack before cutting. Serve with ice cream or whipped cream, if desired.

PINEAPPLE UPSIDE-DOWN PIE

New, nut-topped pie makes its own luscious caramel sauce while it bakes

Pastry for 2-crust pie
1   (1 lb. 4½ oz.) can pineapple tidbits
Water
3   tblsp. cornstarch
¾   c. brown sugar, firmly packed
2   tblsp. lemon juice
6   tblsp. butter
½   c. pecan halves

• Drain pineapple. Add water to pineapple syrup to make 1¼ c.

SPRINGTIME "PINE-APPLE" PIE

Candy spices the filling and gives color —a becoming blush of spring

Pastry for 2-crust pie
1   (8¾ oz.) can crushed pineapple (1 c.)
¼   c. red cinnamon candies (red hots)
¼   c. brown sugar, firmly packed
⅔   c. granulated sugar
½   tsp. salt
2   tblsp. quick-cooking tapioca
3   c. thinly sliced peeled apples
2   tblsp. butter   *more*

· Combine pineapple and red hots, cook over low heat until candies melt.
· Combine sugars, salt, tapioca and apples. Let stand 15 minutes.
· Combine pineapple and apple mixtures, turn into pastry-lined 9″ pie pan.

· Adjust top crust and flute edges; cut vents. Bake in hot oven (425°F.) 40 to 50 minutes, or until filling is tender and crust golden. Partially cool on rack.

Winter-Pear Pies

Now that juicy, meaty fresh pears are available the winter through, you can bake pear pies from late summer, when the Bartletts are ripe in many places, until May. Try using Bosc pears, the fruit with a rich russet exterior and tender, buttery, sugar-sweet flesh, or the Anjou variety, the pear shaped like a huge teardrop. The Anjou is green, but turns a creamy-yellow when ripe, is fine-grained and has a delicate spicy flavor. It is available from October through April, the Bosc from September through January. Either kind will make a perfect Ginger Pear Pie.

GINGER PEAR PIE

Elegant!   Lemon-and-ginger-flavored fresh pear slices enveloped in pastry

Unbaked 9″ pie shell
¾ c. sugar
2 tblsp. flour
¾ tsp. ginger
¼ tsp. salt
3 ripe winter pears
2 tblsp. soft butter
2 eggs, separated

1 tsp. grated lemon peel
3 tblsp. lemon juice
¾ c. milk

· Combine ¼ c. sugar, 1 tblsp. flour, ginger and salt. Sprinkle in pie shell.
· Peel and core pears, slice thinly and lay slices over sugar-flour mixture.
· Cream butter; add remaining ½ c. sugar and 1 tblsp. flour. Add egg yolks, lemon peel and juice. Beat thoroughly.
· Add milk and mix.
· Beat egg whites until stiff. Fold into lemon mixture. Pour over pears.
· Bake in hot oven (425°F.) 10 minutes; reduce heat to 350°F. and bake 30 minutes.

PEAR-APPLE PIE

A pie you'll bake again and again— unusual but makes new friends quickly

Unbaked 9″ pie shell
3 c. thinly sliced peeled Anjou pears
3 c. thinly sliced peeled apples
¾ c. sugar
3 tblsp. flour

Best cherry pie you've ever tasted! *You can stake your baking reputation on FARM JOURNAL'S famous Crisscross Cherry pie shown at right (recipe, page 71). Almond flavor in the fruit filling and the unusual rich pastry make it superior.*

Chocolate and cream cheese blend superbly in this velvet-smooth Chocolate Cheese Pie, a specialty on the menu of a famous old inn in New Mexico. This is one of those conversation-piece desserts. You can make it ahead and keep it in your refrigerator ready to serve. It's rich—you'll want to cut it into small wedges. However, we also give you Short-cut Chocolate Cheese Pie, lower in calories (see page 175).

½ tsp. cinnamon
¼ tsp. salt

Topping:
½ c. brown sugar, firmly packed
¼ c. flour
½ c. finely chopped pecans
¼ c. butter

· Combine pears, apples, sugar, flour, cinnamon and salt. Place in pie shell. *Topping:* Combine brown sugar, flour, pecans and butter. Sprinkle over top of pie.
· Fold a 14″ circle of foil loosely over top and around sides of pie. Bake in hot oven (425°F.) 40 minutes. Remove foil and continue baking 20 minutes.

FRENCH PEAR PIE

Spices, orange and lemon flavors and ripe, juicy pears blend deliciously

Unbaked 9″ pie shell
5 large Bartlett pears
3 tblsp. frozen orange juice concentrate
½ tsp. grated lemon peel
¾ c. flour
½ c. sugar
⅛ tsp. salt
1 tsp. cinnamon
½ tsp. ginger
⅓ c. butter or margarine

· Peel, core and slice pears thinly. Toss lightly with undiluted orange juice concentrate and lemon peel. Arrange in pie shell.
· Mix together remaining ingredients until crumbly. Sprinkle evenly over pears, being careful to cover all.
· Bake in hot oven (400°F.) 40 minutes, or until fruit is tender.

OPEN-FACE PEAR PIE

Use fully ripened Bartlett pears to make this unusual, interesting pie

Unbaked 9″ pastry shell
4 medium-size pears
Juice of ½ lemon
¼ c. butter or margarine
1 c. sugar
¼ c. flour
3 eggs
1 tsp. vanilla
⅛ tsp. salt
⅛ tsp. mace
Whipped cream (optional)

· Peel, halve and core pears. Brush with lemon juice. Place pears cut side down in pie shell with narrow ends toward center.
· Cream together butter and sugar. Beat in flour, eggs, vanilla and salt. Pour over pears. Sprinkle lightly with mace.
· Bake in moderate oven (350°F.) 45 minutes or until filling is set and lightly browned. Cool on cakerack 1 hour or longer before cutting. Top with whipped cream. Serve the same day you bake the pie—pear filling may darken if you keep pie overnight.

PEAR ANISE PIE

Serve thin slices of Parmesan cheese with this gourmet pie

Pastry for 2-crust pie
5 c. sliced peeled Anjou pears (6 medium)
⅔ c. granulated sugar
4 tblsp. cornstarch
1 ½ tsp. whole anise seed   *more*

2   tsp. grated lemon peel
Lemon juice
2   tblsp. butter or margarine
½   c. confectioners sugar

• Combine pears, sugar, cornstarch, anise seed and lemon peel. Mix gently. Place in pastry-lined 9″ pie pan.
• Sprinkle pie filling with 1½ tsp. lemon juice. Dot with butter. Adjust top crust and flute edges; cut vents.
• Bake in hot oven (400°F.) until pears are tender and crust is lightly browned, about 40 minutes.
• While pie is hot, brush with glaze made by mixing confectioners sugar with enough lemon juice for spreading consistency (about 2½ tsp.). Cool.

CRUNCH TOP PEAR PIE

Luscious flavor—oranges and pears, deftly spiced, sweetened crunchy top

Unbaked 9″ pie shell
6   sliced peeled and cored large
       winter pears
½   c. granulated sugar
1   orange
½   c. brown sugar, firmly packed
½   c. flour
½   tsp. cinnamon
¼   tsp. ginger
¼   tsp. mace
⅓   c. butter
1   c. heavy cream, whipped

• Gently mix pears with sugar, 2 tsp. grated orange peel and 3 tblsp. orange juice. Arrange in pie shell.
• Combine brown sugar, flour and spices. Cut in butter until mixture is crumbly. Sprinkle over pears.

• Bake in hot oven (400°F.) until pears are tender, about 45 minutes. Partially cool. Serve warm with whipped cream.

Note: For a tasty topping, sweeten whipped cream lightly and flavor it with 1 tsp. vanilla. When it is on the pie, scatter on a little grated orange peel.

SUMMER PEAR PIE

Cheese pastry and faintly spiced pears —an unsurpassable flavor team

Cheese Pastry for 2-crust pie (Chapter 2)
2   tblsp. lemon juice
4   c. sliced peeled Bartlett pears
⅓   c. granulated sugar
⅓   c. brown sugar, firmly packed
2   tblsp. cornstarch
¼   tsp. salt
¼   tsp. mace
2   tblsp. butter or margarine

• Sprinkle lemon juice over pears.
• Combine sugars, cornstarch, salt and mace.
• Place half of pears in pastry-lined 9″ pie pan.
• Sprinkle with half the sugar mixture. Add remaining pears; sprinkle with remaining sugar mixture. Dot with butter. Adjust top crust; flute edges and cut vents.
• Bake in hot oven (425°F.) 35 to 40 minutes, or until pears are tender, crust is browned and juices bubble in vents.

Pies from Country-Cupboard Fruits

Grandmother had her snow cupboard—a well-chosen cache of foods to meet emergencies. Like awakening on a winter morning to find the roads had vanished in the night's blizzard!

Among the choice contents of her kitchen warehouse were dried fruits—raisins, prunes and apricots, to name a few. With sugar and flour in bins and plenty of home-rendered lard on hand, she had the makings for unforgettable winter pies. Her family rejoiced at her cleverness in outwitting the swirling snow.

Farm life changes and, nowadays, with highways and country roads cleared of snow promptly and freezers filled with many good things to eat, even severe storms rarely are much of a problem. But the habit of keeping generous supplies of dried (as well as canned) fruits hasn't changed. There's a good reason why—farm people like the wonderful pies made with dried fruit. They're really tasty!

Raisin pies, according to the number of recipes shared by FARM JOURNAL readers, are a prime favorite. We give you samples of the different kinds—those made with seedless, seeded, and golden or light raisins, along with one in which the raisins are put through a food chopper. Don't miss the 5-star recipe offered in this chapter to meet repeated requests for it—Frosted Apple-Raisin Pie.

Look at all the raisin pie recipes in this chapter. You'll find the traditional one in which vinegar supplies the classic tart taste. And you'll notice new touches for old-time pies, like walnuts and citrus fruits. And recipes for new unusual ones. There are also many pies in this book in which raisins team with other fruits—cranberries and apples, for instance.

You'll also find our famous recipes for homemade mincemeats, rich with raisins, and for pies made with commercially prepared mincemeat to save the cook's time.

Don't overlook the elegant prune and dried apricot pies. We'll be surprised if you don't agree that Prune Crumble Pie is a gourmet dessert to serve on special occasions. You will notice that a Montana ranchwoman combines dried fruits for a wonderful pie filling.

We hope you will agree with our taste testers when you eat our dried fruit pies. They repeatedly gave these desserts a score of "Excellent" or "Outstanding."

VIENNESE APRICOT PIE

A gourmet pie to serve to fastidious guests who are expert cooks

Unbaked 10" pie shell
2   eggs, slightly beaten
2   c. dairy sour cream
1 ½   c. sugar
¼   c. flour
½   tsp. salt
4   drops almond extract
1 ½   c. dried apricots
Crumbly Topping   *more*

• Combine eggs, sour cream, sugar, flour, salt and almond extract; beat with rotary beater until blended. Stir in apricots, cooked, drained and cut in small pieces.

• Pour mixture into pie shell. Bake in hot oven (400°F.) 25 minutes. Remove from oven and sprinkle with Crumbly Topping. Return to oven and continue baking 20 to 25 minutes, or until filling is set. Cool to room temperature or chill before serving. Makes 8 servings.

CRUMBLY TOPPING: Combine ½ c. light brown sugar and ⅓ c. flour, mixing well. Cut in ¼ c. butter or margarine until mixture resembles coarse crumbs.

FRESNO RAISIN-NUT PIE

Spices accent raisin flavor, fluffy meringue topping provides eye appeal

Baked 8″ pie shell
 ¾ c. sugar
 2 tblsp. cornstarch
 ¼ tsp. salt
 ½ tsp. cinnamon
 ½ tsp. cloves
 2 eggs, separated
 1 c. dairy sour cream
 1 c. seedless raisins
1 ½ tsp. lemon juice
 ½ c. chopped walnuts
Meringue (2 egg whites)

• Combine sugar, cornstarch, salt and spices. Blend in egg yolks. Add sour cream, raisins and lemon juice. Cook over moderate heat, stirring constantly, until mixture thickens. Cool. Stir in walnuts. Pour into pie shell. Top with meringue (see Perfect Meringue for Topping Pies, Chapter 9).

• Bake in moderate oven (350°F.) about 15 minutes, or until meringue is browned.

RAISIN CREAM PIE

Country cook's trick—put raisins through food chopper for rich flavor

Pastry for 2-crust pie
 3 c. seedless raisins
 ½ c. sugar
1 ½ c. light cream
 ¼ tsp. salt
 2 tblsp. lemon juice

• Rinse raisins in warm water; drain thoroughly. Put through food chopper, using medium blade.

• Add sugar, cream and salt. Heat, stirring constantly, until sugar is dissolved and mixture thickens. Remove from heat and stir in lemon juice.

• Pour into pastry-lined 9″ pie pan. Adjust top crust; flute edges, cut vents.

• Bake in hot oven (425°F.) until lightly browned, 30 to 35 minutes.

HOMESTEAD RAISIN PIE

Like Grandmother used to make— GOOD! Be sure to try this

Baked 9″ pie shell
1 ⅓ c. seeded raisins (muscat)
 2 c. water
 3 eggs, separated
 1 c. sugar
 2 tblsp. vinegar
 2 tblsp. flour
 2 tblsp. butter
Meringue (3 egg whites)

• Add raisins to water in saucepan and simmer 5 minutes. Beat egg yolks,

sugar, vinegar and flour until light and creamy. Slowly add to raisins. Cook, stirring constantly, until filling is thick, 4 to 5 minutes. Remove from heat, stir in butter and cool until lukewarm.
· Pour raisin mixture into pie shell

and top with meringue (see Perfect Meringue for Topping Pies, Chapter 9).
· Bake in moderate oven (350°F.) until meringue browns, 12 to 15 minutes. Cool away from drafts.

Vineyard-Country Favorite

Here's a pie that cuts like a charm, suggestive of a rich chess pie, but accented with raisins. It's one of the many unusual raisin pie recipes in the much-thumbed collections of farm women.

HARVEST FESTIVAL RAISIN PIE

Pie full of suntanned raisins made a hit at a California harvest festival

Unbaked 9" pie shell
2 c. seedless raisins
1 c. water
½ c. butter or margarine
¾ c. sugar
1 tblsp. flour
2 eggs, separated
¾ c. broken walnuts

· Simmer raisins in water 10 minutes. Remove from heat and stir in butter, sugar, flour and beaten egg yolks. Return to heat; cook, stirring constantly, until mixture is slightly thickened. Cool briefly and stir in nuts. Fold in stiffly beaten egg whites.
· Spoon into pie shell, mounding slightly in center.
· Bake in slow oven (325°F.) 55 minutes.

GOLDEN RAISIN PIE

Sour cream raisin meringue pie with medley of spices and orange undertone

Baked 8" pie shell
¼ c. sugar
1 ½ tblsp. cornstarch
½ tsp. salt
½ tsp. ginger
½ tsp. cinnamon
⅛ tsp. cloves
⅛ tsp. nutmeg
½ c. light corn syrup
3 egg yolks, beaten
1 c. dairy sour cream
1 c. light raisins
1 tblsp. grated orange peel
Meringue (3 egg whites)

· Mix sugar, cornstarch, salt and spices in top of double boiler. Stir in corn syrup, egg yolks, sour cream, raisins and orange peel.
· Cook over hot water, stirring, until smooth and thick, about 15 to 18 minutes. Pour into cool pie shell.
· Top with meringue (see Perfect Meringue for Topping Pies, Chapter 9) while filling is hot.
· Bake in moderate oven (350°F.) until brown, 12 to 15 minutes.

GOOD COUNTRY IDEA: When the California ranch cook bakes raisin pies containing either orange juice or grated peel, she often adds a little red and yellow food color to the filling for deepening the tawniness.

MINCEMEAT PIE

Top warm pie with vanilla ice cream

Pastry for 2-crust pie
1 (1 lb. 12 oz.) jar prepared mincemeat (2½ c.)
1 c. diced apples
½ c. raisins
⅓ c. grape or orange juice
¼ tsp. grated lemon peel

• Combine mincemeat, apples, raisins, grape juice and lemon peel in bowl. Pour into 9″ pie pan lined with pastry. Adjust top crust, cut steam vents and flute edges.
• Bake in hot oven (425°F.) 40 to 45 minutes or until pastry is golden.

VARIATION

CHRISTMAS MINCEMEAT PIE: Add 2 tblsp. thinly sliced candied cherries and 2 tblsp. chopped walnuts to mincemeat pie filling.

FRUIT AND NUT MINCE PIE

Wintertime ranch favorite in Montana —recipe makes two marvelous pies

Pastry for 2 (2-crust) pies
1 c. dried apricots
1 c. dried prunes
1 c. raisins

Juice of 1 medium orange
½ tsp. cinnamon
¼ tsp. nutmeg
¼ tsp. cloves
1 c. sugar
¼ c. chopped walnuts
¼ c. shredded almonds

• Pour boiling water over apricots and prunes. Drain; cover with cold water and let stand 3 hours. Drain, reserving water, and cut fruits in small pieces. Cook in water in which fruits soaked until ¾ c. liquid remains. Remove from heat.
• Add other ingredients to apricot-prune mixture. Divide in half. Pour each half into pastry-lined 8″ pie pan. Adjust top crusts; flute edges and cut vents.
• Bake in hot oven (400°F.) until crust is browned, about 30 minutes.

Note: For a sparkly top crust, brush pie tops with milk and sprinkle lightly with sugar before baking.

MINCEFRUIT PIE FILLING

Here's a filling for pies to keep on your cupboard shelf ready-to-go

4 lbs. pears
3 lbs. apples
4 medium oranges
2 (15 oz.) pkgs. seedless raisins
5 c. sugar
1 tblsp. salt
4 tsp. cinnamon
1 tsp. cloves

• Cut unpeeled pears, apples and oranges in quarters. Remove cores and seeds. Run through food chopper, using medium blade.

• Add remaining ingredients; stir to combine. Bring to a boil over medium heat. Simmer until thick, about 1 hour. Stir frequently.

• Pack at once in hot pint jars. Adjust lids. Process in boiling-water bath (212°F.) 25 minutes.

• Remove jars from canner and complete seals unless closures are self-sealing type. Makes 8 pints, or about enough for 4 (9″) pies.

MINCEFRUIT PASTRY SQUARES

Just the pie to serve a crowd; pieces also carry successfully in lunches

2 ½ c. sifted flour
1 tblsp. sugar
1 tsp. salt
1 c. lard
1 egg, separated
Milk
3 c. Mincefruit Pie Filling
1 c. confectioners sugar
2 tblsp. lemon juice

• Sift together flour, sugar and salt; cut in lard with pastry blender or two knives, until like coarse meal.

• Put egg yolk into measuring cup and add milk to make ½ c. Add to lard mixture; mix just enough so dough shapes into a ball. Roll out half to 15″ × 11″ rectangle; transfer to baking sheet. Spread Mincefruit Pie Filling evenly over dough to within ¾″ of edges.

• Roll out other half of dough for top crust; place over filling; pinch edges together, cut vents.

• Beat egg white until stiff; spread on top crust. Bake in hot oven (400°F.) 25 to 30 minutes.

• Mix confectioners sugar and lemon juice. Drizzle over top of crust while hot. Makes 16 servings.

CHEESE CRUMBLE PRUNE PIE

Prunes have exciting fresh plumlike taste in this cheese-crumb pie shell

1 ½ c. flour
¾ c. brown sugar, firmly packed
½ tsp. salt
¾ c. butter
1 ½ c. (6 oz.) shredded mild Cheddar cheese
2 c. coarsely cut cooked prunes

• Combine flour, sugar and salt in a mixing bowl. With pastry blender or two knives, cut in butter and cheese until particles are fine. Press two thirds of the crumb mixture over bottom and sides of 8″ pie pan to form a shell. Fill with prunes. Spread remaining crumbs over prunes.

• Bake in moderate oven (350°F.) 25 minutes, or until crumbs are golden brown. Place on rack and cool slightly. Cut into slender wedges and serve warm. Makes 10 servings.

CALIFORNIA PRUNE PIE

Four-seasons pie—as tempting and rewarding in June as in January

Baked 9″ pie shell
2 c. cooked prunes
1 orange, peeled and diced (⅓ c.)
½ c. brown sugar, firmly packed
¼ tsp. salt
2 tblsp. cornstarch   *more*

1 c. liquid from prunes
1 tblsp. grated orange peel
2 tblsp. butter
2 tblsp. granulated sugar
1 c. heavy cream, whipped
Orange sections
Walnut halves

· Drain cooked prunes, reserving 1 c. liquid, pit and measure. Remove all white inner peel when peeling orange.
· Combine sugar, salt and cornstarch. Add prune liquid and bring to a boil, stirring constantly. Cook until thick. Add prunes, orange, orange peel and butter; cook 10 minutes, stirring occasionally. Cool.
· Pour into pie shell. Refrigerate until mealtime. To serve, add 2 tblsp. sugar to whipped cream and spread on pie. To dress up pie, garnish with orange sections and a few walnut halves.

PRUNE MERINGUE PIE

One look, one delicious taste—this old-fashioned pie is a great success

Baked 8" pie shell
1 c. sugar

¼ c. cornstarch
¼ tsp. salt
1 c. boiling water
2 eggs, separated
3 tblsp. lemon juice
2 tsp. grated lemon peel
2 tblsp. butter or margarine
1 c. cooked pitted prunes, drained
Meringue (2 egg whites)

· Combine sugar, cornstarch and salt. Stir in boiling water. Cook over direct heat until mixture thickens and boils, stirring constantly.
· Place in double boiler and cook 10 minutes. Beat egg yolks slightly; gradually beat in hot mixture until half of it has been added. Pour quickly into mixture in double boiler; cook 5 minutes, stirring constantly.
· Remove from hot water and blend in lemon juice and peel and butter. Cool.
· Arrange prunes in cool pie shell.
· Pour lemon mixture over prunes. Top with meringue (see Perfect Meringue for Topping Pies, Chapter 9).
· Bake in moderate oven (350°F.) 12 to 15 minutes, or until browned. Cool.

Dates Are Grand in Pies

Fresh dates are widely available today. Women who are expert pie bakers make excellent use of them. They keep the fruit in their freezers for around-the-year use. The dates you use should be soft if pies are to be at their best. If the fruit has become dry or hard, steam it for a few minutes. The moisture has a marvelous softening effect.

CHEESE-DATE PIE

Cottage cheese imparts its flavor to this tasty country-kitchen pie

Baked 9" Graham Cracker Crumb Crust (Chapter 2)
2 c. creamed cottage cheese
2 eggs
⅓ c. sugar

¼ c. dairy sour or sweet cream
2 tblsp. flour
1 tsp. grated lemon peel
1 tblsp. lemon juice
1 c. chopped dates
4 tblsp. chopped walnuts

• Beat cottage cheese in electric mixer until smooth. Add eggs, one at a time, beating until well blended. Add sugar, cream, flour, lemon peel and juice and blend thoroughly. Mix in dates.
• Pour into cool crust and sprinkle with nuts. Bake in slow oven (300°F.) until set, about 1 hour.

FRESH DATE-NUT PIE

Rich, but not so sweet as some date pies—lemon peel adds subtle touch

Unbaked 9" pie shell
3 eggs
½ c. sugar
1 c. dark corn syrup
¼ c. melted butter
1 ½ tsp. vanilla
¼ tsp. salt
1 c. finely cut fresh dates
¾ c. chopped walnuts
1 ½ tsp. grated lemon peel
1 c. heavy cream, whipped

• Beat eggs until thick and light; gradually beat in sugar. Beat in corn syrup, butter, vanilla and salt. Fold in dates, walnuts and lemon peel. Turn into pie shell.
• Bake in moderate oven (375°F.) 30 minutes, or until filling is set and browned. Cool. Top each serving with whipped cream. Makes 8 servings.

BUTTERMILK DATE PIE

Buttermilk adds just the right touch of tartness to the sweet fruit filling

Baked 9" pie shell
1 c. sugar
¼ c. cornstarch
½ tsp. nutmeg
½ tsp. cinnamon
¼ tsp. salt
2 ½ c. buttermilk
2 egg yolks, beaten
1 c. chopped dates
Meringue (2 egg whites)

• Combine sugar, cornstarch, spices and salt in saucepan; blend thoroughly. Gradually stir in buttermilk and egg yolks. Add dates. Cook over medium heat, stirring constantly until mixture boils and thickens. Cool slightly. Pour into pie shell. Top with meringue and brown (see Perfect Meringue for Topping Pies, Chapter 9). Or chill pie thoroughly and serve topped with whipped cream.

CALIFORNIA DATE PIE

For a really rich version, omit the meringue and spoon on whipped cream with a little Date Butter added

Unbaked 9" pie shell
3 eggs, separated
1 ½ c. Date Butter
1 tsp. grated lemon peel
2 c. milk
Meringue (3 egg whites)

• Beat egg yolks, add Date Butter, beating until well blended.
• Stir in lemon peel and milk.   *more*

• Pour into pie shell. Bake in hot oven (400°F.) 15 minutes; reduce temperature to 350°F. and bake 25 minutes, or until set.
• Spoon meringue over pie (see Perfect Meringue for Topping Pies, Chapter 9).
• Bake in moderate oven (350°F.) 12 to 15 minutes.

DATE BUTTER

2   (7 oz.) pkgs. pitted dates
¾   c. water

• Chop or cut up dates. Add water.
• Cover; cook over medium heat until mixture boils; reduce heat, cook about 10 minutes, or until dates are mushy. Stir occasionally. Makes about 1¾ cups.

ORANGE-DATE PIE

This rich, delicious pie serves 8

Unbaked 9″ pie shell
½   c. butter or margarine
1¼   c. sugar
4   eggs, separated
1   c. chopped dates
1   c. flaked coconut (or chopped nuts)
1   tblsp. grated orange peel
2   tblsp. frozen orange juice concentrate, undiluted

• Cream butter and sugar; add egg yolks, one at a time, beating well after each. Add dates, coconut, orange peel and juice.
• Beat egg whites until stiff but not dry. Fold into filling. Turn into pie shell. Bake in slow oven (300°F.) 1 hour. Cool before serving.

Garden Is Pie Baker's Friend

Many farm women eagerly watch their gardens in spring for the first tender, strawberry-pink rhubarb stalks. And in autumn, when trees are tinted red by summer's afterglow and the pleasing warmth of country kitchens invites baking, they pick tomatoes green to cheat Jack Frost. And to make pies! Both of these tart vegetables make excellent pie fillings. Surrounded by flaky pastry, they behave like fruits and actually rival them in flavor. For this reason they're at home in the company of pies made with the gifts of orchards and berry patches.

We include some of our best rhubarb and green tomato pie recipes in this collection of dessert fruit pies. You will find several other vegetable pies in this Cookbook; pumpkin, for instance. Also in main-dish pies, Chapter 11.

FRESH RHUBARB PIE

This rosy rhubarb pie has a fascinating, though subtle, orange taste

Pastry for 2-crust pie
1⅓   c. sugar
⅓   c. flour
½   tsp. grated orange peel
⅛   tsp. salt
4   c. (½″ pieces) rhubarb
2   tblsp. butter

• Combine sugar, flour, orange peel and salt. Add to pink rhubarb.
• Place in pastry-lined 9″ pie pan and dot with butter.
• Adjust top crust (lattice top is attractive) and flute edges to make high-standing rim, cut vents.
• Bake in hot oven (425°F.) 40 to 50 minutes, or until juice begins to bubble through vents and crust is golden brown. Partially cool.

Note: If your rhubarb is not the pink variety, add a few drops of red food color to filling. To eliminate peeling rhubarb, use tender, young stalks. The amount of sugar varies with the tartness of the rhubarb—from 1⅓ c. to 2 c. Usually rhubarb is less tart early in the season.

VARIATIONS

SPICED RHUBARB PIE: Omit the grated orange peel and add ¼ tsp. nutmeg.

PINEAPPLE-RHUBARB PIE: Substitute 1 c. drained crushed pineapple (canned) for 1 c. rhubarb.

GLAZED STRAWBERRY-RHUBARB PIE

Luscious spring dessert: Serve pie warm with sour cream spread on top

Pastry for 2-crust pie
1 ¼ c. sugar
⅛ tsp. salt
⅓ c. flour
2   c. fresh strawberries

2   c. (1″ pieces) fresh rhubarb
2   tblsp. butter or margarine
1   tblsp. sugar

• Combine 1¼ c. sugar, salt and flour.
• Arrange half of strawberries and rhubarb in pastry-lined 9″ pie pan. Sprinkle with half of sugar mixture. Repeat with remaining fruit and sugar mixture; dot with butter.
• Adjust top crust and flute edges. Brush top of pie with cold water and sprinkle on 1 tblsp. sugar. Cut steam vents.
• Bake in hot oven (425°F.) 40 to 50 minutes or until rhubarb is tender and crust is browned.

VARIATION

LATTICED STRAWBERRY-RHUBARB PIE: Use a lattice top to show off the beauty of this spring pie. See its picture on the jacket of this Cookbook.

Quick Oven-to-Table Pie

You'll never find a more tasty and satisfying jonquil-time dessert than this homey, last-minute pie. It will make practically any meal a success. Good idea to finish baking the pie while everyone is enjoying the main course (put it in the oven about 10 minutes before you sit down to eat). Just before serving, make the sweet, caramel-tasting syrup that contrasts so delightfully with the crisp, hot crust and cold ice cream.

RHUBARB POPOVER PIE

Spring comes to the table in this superb flavor-texture combination

2   eggs
¾   c. milk
¾   c. flour
½   tsp. salt
¼   c. butter
1 ½ c. (¾" slices) fresh cut-up rhubarb
½   c. drained pineapple chunks (canned)
Brown Sugar Syrup
1   pt. vanilla ice cream

· Beat eggs and milk; add flour and salt and beat until smooth.
· Put butter in a 9" pie pan and heat in oven until it bubbles. Immediately pour in batter. Combine and drop rhubarb and pineapple in center of batter, within about 2" of pan edges.
· Bake in hot oven (425°F.) 25 minutes, or until batter is puffed and brown. Immediately cut in 6 wedges for serving, topping each with a big spoonful of warm Brown Sugar Syrup and a small scoop of ice cream. Serve at once.

BROWN SUGAR SYRUP: Melt ⅓ c. butter. Stir in 1 c. brown sugar, firmly packed, making a thick syrup. Serve at once.

VARIATION

RHUBARB POPOVER PIE: Omit pineapple in Rhubarb Popover Pie.

HONEYED RHUBARB PIE

A FARM JOURNAL 5-star recipe

Pastry for 2-crust pie
4   c. (½" pieces) rhubarb
1 ¼ c. sugar
6   tblsp. flour
¼   tsp. salt
2   tsp. grated lemon peel
⅓   c. strained honey
4   to 5 drops red food color
2   tblsp. butter or margarine

· Combine rhubarb, sugar, flour, salt and lemon peel; mix well. Blend in honey and food color. Let stand several minutes.
· Spoon rhubarb mixture into pastry-lined 9" pie pan; dot with butter. Adjust top crust and flute edges; cut vents. (For sparkling top, brush with milk and sprinkle with sugar.)
· Bake in hot oven (400°F.) 50 to 60 minutes.

RHUBARB-APPLE PIE

Rhubarb adds refreshing flavor to canned apples in this homey pie

Pastry for 2-crust pie
1   (1 lb. 4 oz.) can sliced apples
2   c. (½" pieces) rhubarb
1   c. sugar
¼   tsp. salt
½   tsp. cinnamon
3   tblsp. quick-cooking tapioca
2   tblsp. butter or margarine

· Combine apples and their syrup, with rhubarb, sugar, salt, cinnamon and tapioca; mix well. Turn into pastry-lined 9" pie pan. Dot with butter. Cover with lattice pastry top.

• Bake in hot oven (425°F.) about 50 minutes, or until filling starts to bubble and crust is golden.

SPICED RHUBARB-STRAWBERRY PIE

Pink of perfection in springtime pies —pastry lattice shows bright filling

Pastry for 2-crust pie
3 c. cut-up rhubarb (1 lb.)
1 pt. strawberries, cut in halves
¾ c. sugar
4 tblsp. flour
⅛ tsp. salt
¼ tsp. pumpkin pie spice or mace
2 tblsp. butter or margarine

• Combine rhubarb, cut in ¾" pieces, and strawberries in bowl. Sprinkle on sugar, flour, salt and pumpkin pie spice; mix gently. Turn into pastry-lined 9" pie pan; dot with butter. Adjust lattice pastry top, flute edges.
• Bake in hot oven (400°F.) 40 minutes, or until crust is browned and juices bubble. Cool on rack.

RHUBARB-ORANGE PIE

Orange and rhubarb flavors taste as good together as peaches and cream

Pastry for 2-crust pie
2 eggs
1 ¾ c. sugar
¼ c. flour
⅛ tsp. nutmeg or mace
¼ c. orange juice
4 c. cut-up rhubarb (1 ½ lbs.)

• Beat eggs in large bowl; add sugar, flour, nutmeg and orange juice; stir in rhubarb. Turn into pastry-lined 9" pie

pan. Adjust top crust; flute edges and cut vents.
• Bake in hot oven (425°F.) 50 minutes, or until crust is browned and juices bubble in vents. Cool.

Note: Recipe was tested with early hothouse rhubarb, which sometimes is less juicy than stalks grown in outdoor gardens.

PARTY RHUBARB PIE

Definitely a special-occasion pie—it suggests spring even if it is snowing

Unbaked 9" pie shell
2 (1 lb.) pkgs. frozen rhubarb in syrup
3 tblsp. flour
1 c. sugar
4 (3 oz.) pkgs. cream cheese
2 eggs
1 c. dairy sour cream

• Thaw and drain rhubarb. You should have 1 qt. fruit. Blend with flour and ½ c. sugar. Turn into pie shell; bake in hot oven (425°F.) 15 minutes.
• Meanwhile, blend together cream cheese, eggs and remaining ½ c. sugar. Remove pie from oven and spread cheese mixture over top of rhubarb filling. Return to oven and bake in moderate oven (350°F.) 30 minutes. Cool. Spread sour cream over top. Refrigerate until ready to serve.

Note: You will have about 1 c. pretty, pink rhubarb juice which you won't use in this recipe. But do use it for part of the liquid in making gelatin salads or desserts. Or combine with orange juice and chill for a refreshing breakfast starter.

Green Tomato Pies

One of the joys of having a garden is that you can gather green tomatoes for cooking. Spicy pies made with them have a distinctive flavor of their own. No wonder they're farm favorites! Many country women bake them with immature tomatoes on the vines at frost time. But some gourmet cooks like to pick a few of the mature full-size green tomatoes earlier in the season for a couple of special pies.

Mature tomatoes turn color quickly, however. Once they are in the kitchen, use them promptly—or at least refrigerate them. Also use immature green tomatoes soon after you bring them to the house. They rarely ripen, but often rot, especially if left standing at room temperature.

Many FARM JOURNAL readers have told us they like to use our recipe for Green Tomato Mincemeat in autumn when they have lots of tomatoes. We'll give you this famous recipe, too.

Green tomatoes combined with peeled apple slices make one of the tastiest of all country pies. (And you can substitute apples for the green tomatoes in the following recipe for a *good* apple pie!) Try our recipes and see if you don't agree.

GREEN TOMATO-APPLE PIE

Once you try it, we predict you'll have it several times every year

Pastry for 2-crust pie
2 c. skinned, quartered and thinly sliced green tomatoes

3 c. thin, peeled apple slices
⅔ c. brown sugar, firmly packed
⅓ c. granulated sugar
2 to 3 tblsp. flour
½ tsp. cinnamon
⅛ tsp. salt
2 tblsp. butter

• To peel green tomatoes easily, place in boiling water. Let stand 2 to 3 minutes, or until skins can be slipped off.
• Combine tomatoes, apples, sugars, flour, cinnamon and salt. Place in a pastry-lined 9″ pie pan. Dot with butter.
• Adjust top crust and flute edges; cut steam vents. Bake in hot oven (425°F.) 50 to 60 minutes.

SLICED GREEN TOMATO PIE

A gardener's dessert-time special

Pastry for 2-crust pie
4 c. peeled, thinly sliced green tomatoes
1¼ c. sugar
½ tsp. cinnamon
½ tsp. nutmeg
¼ tsp. salt
4 to 5 tblsp. flour
2 tblsp. lemon juice

• To peel tomatoes easily, immerse in boiling water until skins will slip off (about 3 minutes).
• Blend together sugar, cinnamon, nutmeg, salt, flour and lemon juice in bowl. Toss with green tomatoes.

· Place in pastry-lined 9″ pie pan. Adjust top crust and flute edges; cut vents.

· Bake in hot oven (425°F.) until tomatoes are soft and crust is lightly browned, about 50 to 60 minutes.

Country-Good Homemade Mincemeat

When a big kettle of simmering mincemeat fills the kitchen with its tantalizing aroma, everyone in the house starts looking forward to plump winter pies. One of our readers says: "Almost always someone in our family, sniffing the spicy fragrance of cooking mincemeat, asks if we have to wait until Thanksgiving and Christmas to have pie made with it. My answer comes a few days later when I carry the season's first mincemeat pie to the table. It's one of the best ways to please my family and to round out an otherwise light meal."

We are reprinting in this chapter a popular and balanced collection of mincemeat recipes from our FREEZING & CANNING COOKBOOK. All five of them have their ardent champions. Pear-growers' wives perfected the pear version, ranchwomen in the Mountain West laud the venison special and Midwestern gardeners vote for the Green Tomato Mincemeat, for instance.

Canning directions accompany each recipe, but you can freeze mincemeat if you prefer and have freezer space. Don't forget the commercial mincemeats available in food markets—they are such a help for busy cooks. (You'll also find recipes using them in this book.) Regardless of what kind of mincemeat pie you bake, do serve it slightly warm, with a topping of soft vanilla ice cream for special.

GREEN TOMATO MINCEMEAT

Decidedly different—on the tart side

6	lbs. green tomatoes
2	lbs. tart apples
2	c. raisins
4	c. brown sugar, firmly packed
2	c. strong coffee
1	lemon (grated peel and juice)
2	tsp. grated orange peel
½	c. vinegar
1	tsp. salt
1	tsp. nutmeg
1	tsp. allspice

· Core and quarter tomatoes and apples; put through food chopper with raisins.

· Combine all ingredients in large saucepan. Simmer 2 hours, stirring frequently.

· Pack at once in hot pint jars. Adjust lids. Process in boiling-water bath (212°F.) 25 minutes.

· Remove jars from canner and complete seals unless closures are self-sealing type. Makes about 10 pints.

BLUE RIBBON MINCEMEAT

Cider gives this fascinating flavor

6	c. ground beef
12	c. chopped apples
6	c. seedless raisins

more

1   c. cider
1   tblsp. cinnamon
1   tblsp. allspice
1   tblsp. nutmeg
3½   c. sugar

• Cook beef thoroughly, but do not brown.
• Put meat and apples through food chopper, using medium blade.
• Combine all ingredients in large kettle. Simmer 30 minutes.
• Pack at once in hot pint jars. Adjust lids. Process in pressure canner 60 minutes at 10 pounds pressure (240°F.).
• Remove jars from canner and complete seals unless closures are self-sealing type. Makes 8 pints.

STATE-OF-THE-UNION MINCEMEAT

California-style, fruited mincemeat

3   lbs. lean beef
1   qt. water
1   c. chopped dates
1   c. washed suet, finely chopped
3½   lbs. apples
1   lb. seedless raisins
1   lb. white raisins
4   c. orange marmalade
2   qts. cider
2   tblsp. cinnamon
1   tsp. cloves
1   tsp. nutmeg
3   tblsp. salt

• Simmer beef in water until tender (add more water if needed). Drain. Trim away bone and gristle. Put meat through food chopper, using medium blade.

• Combine all ingredients in large kettle. Mix well. Bring to a boil; reduce heat and simmer 1½ hours, stirring often.
• Pour at once into hot pint jars. Adjust lids. Process in pressure canner 60 minutes at 10 pounds pressure (240°F.).
• Remove jars from canner and complete seals unless closures are self-sealing type. Makes about 10 pints. Store in cool, dark place.

Note: Takes time to make, but this recipe, adapted by a California homemaker from the Alaska favorite, is rich in blended fruit flavors.

VENISON MINCEMEAT

Hunters vote for that venison taste

4   lbs. venison "trim" meat with bones
Water
¾   lb. beef suet
3   lbs. apples, peeled and quartered
2   lbs. seedless raisins
1   (15 oz.) pkg. seeded raisins
1   (12 oz.) pkg. currants
1   tblsp. salt
1   tblsp. cinnamon
1   tblsp. ginger
1   tblsp. cloves
1   tblsp. nutmeg
1   tsp. allspice
1   tsp. mace (optional)
2   qts. cider, grape or other fruit juice
1   lb. brown sugar

• Trim fat from venison. Cover with water; simmer until meat is tender.

Refrigerate venison in cooking liquid overnight. Remove all fat from top of liquid. Separate meat from bones and put meat through food chopper—using coarse blade. (There should be enough ground venison to make at least 2 qts.)

• Put suet and apples through food chopper.

• Combine all ingredients in large kettle. Simmer 2 hours to plump fruit and blend flavors. Stir often to prevent sticking.

• Pack at once in hot pint jars. Adjust lids. Process in pressure canner at 10 pounds pressure (240°F.) 60 minutes.

• Remove jars from canner and complete seals unless closures are self-sealing type. Makes about 11 pints.

Note: You can freeze mincemeat. Recommended storage time: 3 months.

OLD-TIME PEAR MINCEMEAT

Good way to salvage pear-crop windfalls or the less choice fruit

7	lbs. ripe Bartlett pears
1	lemon
2	(1 lb.) pkgs. seedless raisins
6¾	c. sugar
1	c. vinegar
1	tblsp. cloves
1	tblsp. cinnamon

1	tblsp. nutmeg
1	tblsp. allspice
1	tsp. ginger

• Core and quarter pears.

• Cut lemon into quarters, removing seeds.

• Put pears, lemon and raisins through food chopper.

• Combine remaining ingredients in large kettle. Add chopped-fruit mixture. Bring to a boil over medium heat; simmer 40 minutes.

• Pack at once in hot pint jars. Adjust lids. Process in boiling water bath (212°F.) 25 minutes.

• Remove jars from canner and complete seals unless closures are self-sealing type. Makes 9 pints.

BASIC HOMEMADE MINCEMEAT PIE

• You will need 4 c. homemade mincemeat for a 9″ pie. Dot the filling with 1 tblsp. butter, adjust top crust, cut vents and flute edges. Brush top with light cream, if desired. (It's a good idea to cover pie edges with 1½″ strip of aluminum foil the first half hour of baking to prevent excessive browning.)

• Bake in hot oven (425°F.) 40 to 45 minutes, or until pastry is golden. Partially cool on rack before serving.

Freezing Fruit Pies

You can freeze baked or unbaked 2-crust fruit pies successfully. Many people believe frozen unbaked pies have a fresher fruit taste and a crisper crust than pies baked before freezing.

But busy farm homemakers sometimes find it more convenient and time saving to bake and then freeze their pies. Follow the system that works best for you.

If you freeze apple or peach pies, pretreat the fruit to prevent darkening. Add 1 tblsp. lemon juice (or ¼ tsp. ascorbic acid, mixed with 1 tblsp. water) to peaches for a pie. Steam apple slices 3 to 5 minutes. Or use a commercial color protector, following label directions. Good pie bakers like to coat sweet cherries and berries with the sugar-flour mixture before adding them to a pie for freezing.

UNBAKED PIE: Freeze pie and then wrap. You can place pie in tin, aluminum or special paper pie pan designed for the freezer. Cover with a second pan to protect pie top. Tape top pan in place and insert pie in plastic bag or wrap in freezer wrapping; seal, label, date and return to freezer.

To serve pie, unwrap, cut vents if not cut before freezing and bake on lower shelf of hot oven (425°F.) 10 to 20 minutes longer than regular time for unfrozen pie. If rims of pie brown too quickly, cover with 1½" strips of aluminum foil.

BAKED PIE: Remove pie from oven when only lightly browned. It will finish browning when reheated for serving. Cool, then freeze without wrapping. Package frozen pie like frozen unbaked pie.

To serve, partially thaw in original wrap at room temperature, about 30 minutes. Unwrap and place on lower shelf of moderate oven (375°F.) 30 minutes, or until warm, and the juices in center are bubbling.

To Freeze Fruit-Pie Fillings

Many farm women find it more convenient to freeze pie fillings, when fresh fruit is plentiful, than finished pies. The fillings take less time and are economical of freezer space.

Here are the basic directions:
• Combine 1 qt. of any of the following ripe fruits—blueberries, pitted cherries, sliced strawberries, peaches, apples or pears—with ¾ to 1 c. sugar, depending on tartness, 3 tblsp. quick-cooking tapioca, ¼ tsp. salt and 1 to 2 tblsp. lemon juice. Before adding sugar, stir ¼ to ½ tsp. ascorbic acid into fruit that darkens. (Or use commercial color protector as directed on label.)
• Line 8" pie pan with heavy-duty aluminum foil, several layers of saran or freezer wrap. Let lining extend 6" beyond rim of pie pan. Add pie filling

and cover loosely with lining. Freeze. When frozen firm, wrap with lining to cover completely and seal with freezer tape. Label, date and return to freezer.
• To make pie with frozen filling, unwrap, but do not thaw. Place in pastry-lined 9" pie pan. Dot with 1½ tblsp. butter or margarine. Adjust top crust, cut vents and flute edges. Bake in hot oven (425°F.) about 1 hour, or until juices in vents boil with thick bubbles that do not burst.

Here are two FARM JOURNAL filling recipes that have many boosters among farm women who freeze them. The combination of cornstarch and tapioca thickens the fruit mixture just right. The recipes were first printed in our FREEZING & CANNING COOK-BOOK.

APPLE-CRANBERRY PIE FILLING

Almost magic—making pie with au-
tumn fruit favorites when lilacs bloom

- 3   c. sliced peeled apples
- 2   c. fresh cranberries
- 1 ¾ c. sugar
- ¼   c. flour
- 1   tsp. cinnamon
- 1 ½ tsp. melted butter

• Combine all ingredients. Arrange in
a foil-lined 8″ pie pan. Cover loosely
with aluminum foil and freeze. Remove frozen filling from pan, wrap,
seal, label, date and return to freezer.
Recommended storage time: up to 3
months.

• To make pie, place unwrapped, unthawed filling in pastry-lined 9″ pie
pan. Top with pastry strip lattice.

• Bake in hot oven (425°F.) 1 hour
and 10 minutes.

PEACH PIE FILLING

Let it snow! You can treat your guests
with fresh-tasting peach pie

- 4   qts. sliced peeled peaches (9
      lbs.)
- 1   tsp. ascorbic acid
- 1   gal. water
- 3 ½ c. sugar
- ½   c. plus 2 tblsp. quick-cooking
      tapioca
- ¼   c. lemon juice
- 1   tsp. salt

• Place peaches in large container.
Dissolve ascorbic acid in water and
pour over peaches. Drain.

• Combine peaches, sugar, tapioca,
lemon juice and salt.

• Line 4 (8″) pie pans with heavy-
duty aluminum foil, letting it extend
5″ beyond rim. Divide filling evenly
between pans. Makes fillings for 4
(9″) pies.

To Freeze: Fold foil loosely over fillings; freeze. Remove from freezer,
turn filling from pans and wrap snugly
with foil. Return to freezer. Recommended storage time: 6 months.

To Bake: Remove foil from frozen pie
filling and place it, unthawed, in a pastry-lined 9″ pie pan. Dot with butter
and, if you like, sprinkle on ¼ tsp. nutmeg or cinnamon. Add top crust; seal
and flute edges. Cut slits in top crust
with kitchen scissors or knife.

• Bake in hot oven (425°F.) 1 hour
and 10 minutes, or until syrup boils
with heavy bubbles that do not burst.

COUNTRY BLUEBERRY PIE

Brings summer flavor to winter meals

- Pastry for 2-crust pie
- 3   c. frozen blueberries (unsweet-
      ened)
- Blueberry juice
- Water
- ¾   c. sugar
- 2   tblsp. quick-cooking tapioca
- 1 ½ tblsp. cornstarch
- 1   tsp. lemon juice

• Thaw berries until most of free ice
has disappeared. Drain off juice, measure and add water to make ½ c. liquid;
stir into mixture of sugar, tapioca and
cornstarch in saucepan. Heat rapidly
until thickening is complete. Boiling is
not necessary. Set aside to cool.

• Add berries and lemon juice to
cooled, thickened juice. Pour filling

into pastry-lined 9″ pie pan. Cut steam vents and adjust top crust; flute edges.
• Bake in hot oven (425°F.) 30 minutes, or until nicely browned. For a brown undercrust, bake on lowest oven shelf.

PERFECT CHERRY PIE

It deserves its name—try it and see

Pastry for 2-crust pie
- 3 c. pitted tart frozen cherries
- 1 c. tart cherry juice
- 3 tblsp. sugar
- 2 tblsp. quick-cooking tapioca
- 1 ⅔ tblsp. cornstarch (5 tsp.)
- ⅛ tsp. almond extract

• Thaw cherries until most of the free ice has disappeared. Drain off the juice; measure and stir it into mixture of sugar, tapioca and cornstarch in saucepan. Heat rapidly until thickening is complete. Boiling is not necessary. Set aside to cool.
• Add cherries and extract to cooled, thickened juice. Pour filling into pastry-lined 9″ pie pan. Cut vents and adjust top crust; flute edges.
• Bake in hot oven (425°F.) 30 to 35 minutes, or until nicely browned. For a brown undercrust, bake on lowest oven shelf.

Note: Proportions of sugar, tapioca and cornstarch are based on 5 parts cherries frozen with 1 part sugar.

DOUBLE CHERRY PIE

Doubly good—two kinds of cherries

Pastry for 2-crust pie
- 2 c. pitted tart frozen cherries
- 1 c. pitted dark sweet frozen cherries

- ⅔ c. tart cherry juice
- ⅓ c. sweet cherry juice
- ¼ c. sugar
- 2 ⅓ tblsp. quick-cooking tapioca
- 1 ½ tsp. cornstarch
- 1 tsp. lemon juice

• Thaw cherries until most of the free ice has disappeared. Drain off juices, measure and stir into mixture of sugar, tapioca and cornstarch in saucepan. Heat rapidly until thickening is complete. Boiling is not necessary. Set aside to cool.
• Add cherries and lemon juice to cooled, thickened juice. Pour filling into pastry-lined 9″ pie pan. Cut vents and adjust top crust; flute edges.
• Bake in hot oven (425°F.) 30 to 35 minutes, or until nicely browned. For a brown undercrust, bake on lowest oven shelf.

Note: Proportions of sugar, tapioca and cornstarch are based on 5 parts cherries frozen with 1 part sugar.

GOLDEN PEACH PIE

Sweet perfection in peach pie

Pastry for 2-crust pie
- 3 c. frozen sliced peaches
- 1 c. peach juice
- 1 ½ tblsp. brown sugar
- 1 ½ tblsp. granulated sugar
- 2 ⅓ tblsp. quick-cooking tapioca
- 1 ½ tblsp. cornstarch
- ⅛ tsp. cinnamon
- 1 tsp. lemon juice

• Thaw peaches until most of free ice has disappeared. Drain off the juice, measure and stir it into mixture of sugars, tapioca, cornstarch and cinnamon in saucepan. Heat rapidly until thickening is complete. Boiling is not necessary. Set aside to cool.

· Add peaches and lemon juice to cooled, thickened juice. Pour filling into pastry-lined 9″ pie pan. Cut vents and adjust top crust; flute edges.

· Bake in hot oven (425°F.) 30 minutes, or until nicely browned. For a brown undercrust, bake on lowest oven shelf.

Note: Proportions of sugar, tapioca and cornstarch are based on 5 parts peaches frozen with 1 part sugar.

PEACH-STRAWBERRY PIE

A jewel of a pie in color and taste

Pastry for 2-crust pie
1 ½ c. frozen sliced peaches
1 ½ c. frozen strawberries
 ½ c. peach juice
 ½ c. strawberry juice
3 tblsp. sugar
2 ½ tblsp. quick-cooking tapioca
1 ½ tblsp. cornstarch
1 tsp. lemon juice

· Thaw fruit until most of free ice has disappeared. Drain off the juices and measure, then stir into mixture of sugar, tapioca and cornstarch in saucepan. Heat rapidly until thickening is complete. Boiling is not necessary. Set aside to cool.

· Add fruit and lemon juice to cooled, thickened juice. Pour filling into pastry-lined 9″ pie pan. Cut vents and adjust top crust; flute edges.

· Bake in hot oven (425°F.) 30 to 35 minutes, or until nicely browned. For a brown undercrust, bake on lowest oven shelf.

Note: Proportions of sugar, tapioca

and cornstarch are based on 5 parts peaches frozen with 1 part sugar; 4 parts strawberries frozen with 1 part sugar.

VARIATION

PEACH-BLUEBERRY PIE: Substitute blueberries for strawberries. If blueberries were frozen unsweetened, use ⅓ c. sugar; add water to the combined fruit juices to make 1 c. liquid.

WONDERFUL STRAWBERRY PIE

Top with ice cream for extra festivity

Pastry for 2-crust pie
2 ⅔ c. frozen strawberries
1 ⅓ c. strawberry juice
3 tblsp. sugar
2 ½ tblsp. quick-cooking tapioca
1 ½ tblsp. cornstarch
1 tsp. lemon juice

· Thaw berries until most of free ice has disappeared. Drain off the juice; measure and stir it into mixture of sugar, tapioca and cornstarch in saucepan. Heat rapidly until thickening is complete. Boiling is not necessary. Set aside to cool.

· Add berries and lemon juice to cooled, thickened juice. Pour filling into pastry-lined 9″ pie pan. Cut vents and adjust top crust; flute edges.

· Bake in hot oven (425°F.) 30 minutes, or until nicely browned. For a brown undercrust, bake on lowest oven shelf.

Note: Proportions of sugar, tapioca and cornstarch are based on 4 parts strawberries frozen with 1 part sugar.

CHAPTER 4

CUSTARD AND CREAM PIES

Forks never will cut into creamier and more velvety pies than those made by recipes in this chapter. Here are the really great country pies, royally rich with fresh farm produce—eggs, milk and cream. They are 1-crust versions (with an occasional surprise 2-crust), often graced with tall meringues and other decorative toppings.

True custard pies are made with eggs, milk and sugar, baked with the crust. Cream pies have a custard-type cooked filling, thickened with flour or cornstarch, turned into a baked pie shell. Both kinds are delicious and have their fans.

Pumpkin pies head this family of pies. They're as important as turkey and cranberry sauce for family reunions at Thanksgiving time. You'll want to bake our Pumpkin Pecan Pie with its smooth, spicy filling and crunchy Caramelized Pecan Topping.

Next in popularity, and always the beauty queens, are lemon meringue pies. We have, besides the favorite old versions, some exciting new ones. Black Bottom Lemon Pie, with chocolate painted on its golden pastry shell, is unforgettable in good looks and in its delightful blending of flavors, for instance.

Honorable mention must go to the basic Vanilla Cream Pie recipe, perfected in our Test Kitchens, and to the array of glamorous pies made with it. All are superior.

You'll find hostess-special chocolate pies in this and in Chapter 5.

Do try the coconut pies, made with recipes from country kitchens where they, like holly and mistletoe, are a part of Christmas holiday festivities. Southern chess pie and its cousins, the pecan and other nut pies, make their bow in this chapter. Just turn the pages and you'll find more than a year's supply of marvelous country pies for church suppers and company feasts.

P Stands for Pumpkin . . . and Pie

When ripe pumpkins lie like harvest moons in fields, glow in orange heaps at roadside stands and in winking jack-o'-lanterns, it's time to get out the rolling pin and bake a pie. Pumpkin pie is one of the great autumn dessert glories in country places—and a must for Thanksgiving dinner.

FARM JOURNAL readers say that the pie no longer is a seasonal treat. By using commercially canned pumpkin, a staple in kitchen cupboards, you can have pumpkin pie the calendar around. Some women make their own pumpkin purée and freeze it. Here are the directions they pass along:

Don't let pumpkins freeze before cooking them. The belief that this improves the flavor is a myth. Instead, freezing injures the keeping qualities of raw pumpkins.

So, to freeze pumpkin, prepare it as you would for immediate use. Select sound pumpkins of bright color, heavy for their size. Cut them in halves, remove seeds and strings and arrange cut side up on baking sheets or in shallow pans. Bake in a hot oven (400°F.) until tender, about 1 hour.

Scoop out the pulp and put through a strainer or food mill. Or use your blender if you have one. Pour ⅓ c. water into blender bowl and add 2 c. cut-up, cooked pumpkin. Blend until smooth. Repeat until all pumpkin is blended. Then cook the purée in a shallow pan, stirring constantly, until it is very thick. The boiling evaporates the water added in blending. Use the purée as you do canned pumpkin.

To freeze it, pack in airtight containers, allowing 1″ head space. A pound of pumpkin makes about ¾ c. purée.

The USDA (U. S. Department of Agriculture) has successfully turned pure pumpkin purée into powder, which can be used in pie fillings.

Popular Pumpkin Pies

Pumpkin pie is so popular that every neighborhood has several prize recipes. But all good pumpkin pies have mellow fillings, smooth to the tongue and enriched with eggs and cream or evaporated milk. A blend of spices points up the flavor. (Spice mixes for pumpkin pies are also available.) A shell of tender, flaky pie crust that melts in the mouth is essential to set off the filling.

An Indiana farm cook, who is a pie baker of recognized ability, says there is greater variety in the color and taste of pumpkin pies at bake sales and club and church suppers than other kinds of pies. No two are exactly alike. This indicates the remarkable talent country women have in adding their own touches of genius—aside from the choice of spices, the addition of brown or maple sugar, honey, nuts, grated orange peel, peanut butter, etc.

Taste testers gave our Pecan-Pumpkin Pie excellent ratings, including the comment: "The best pumpkin pie I've ever eaten." You can bypass the caramelized topping if you prefer a whipped-cream trim.

TAWNY PUMPKIN PIE

A FARM JOURNAL *5-star special from our* COUNTRY COOKBOOK

Unbaked 9" pie shell
1 ¼ c. cooked or canned pumpkin
¾ c. sugar
½ tsp. salt
¼ tsp. ginger
1 tsp. cinnamon
1 tsp. flour
2 eggs, slightly beaten
1 c. evaporated milk
2 tblsp. water
½ tsp. vanilla

· Combine pumpkin, sugar, salt, spices and flour in mixing bowl.
· Add eggs; mix well. Add evaporated milk, water and vanilla; mix. Pour into pie shell.
· Bake in hot oven (400°F.) 45 to 50 minutes, or until knife inserted near center comes out clean.

PUMPKIN PECAN PIE

Filling is a mellow golden brown, rich like an old gold coin

Unbaked 9" pie shell
2 eggs, slightly beaten
1 (1 lb.) can pumpkin (2 c.)
¾ c. sugar
½ tsp. salt

1 tsp. cinnamon
½ tsp. ginger
¼ tsp. cloves
1 ⅔ c. light cream or evaporated milk
Caramelized Pecan Topping

· Blend together eggs and pumpkin. Stir in sugar, salt, cinnamon, ginger and cloves. Blend in cream.
· Turn into pie shell. Bake in hot oven (400°F.) 45 to 55 minutes or until knife inserted halfway between center and edge of pie comes out clean. Cool completely on rack.

CARAMELIZED PECAN TOPPING: Combine 3 tblsp. soft butter or margarine, ⅔ c. brown sugar and ⅔ c. coarsely chopped pecans. Gently drop by spoonfuls over cooled pie to cover top. Broil 5" below heat until mixture begins to bubble, about 3 minutes. Watch carefully. (If cooked too long, top will turn syrupy.) Cool on rack.

HONEYED PUMPKIN PIE

Be sure to flute pie-shell edges high to hold the generous filling

Unbaked 9" pie shell, edges fluted high
1 (1 lb.) can pumpkin (2 c.)
½ tsp. ginger
½ tsp. cinnamon
1 tsp. salt
4 eggs, slightly beaten
1 c. honey
½ c. milk
½ c. heavy cream

· In large bowl blend together pumpkin, ginger, cinnamon and salt. Beat in eggs, honey, milk and cream. Pour into pie shell.

· Bake in hot oven (400°F.) until knife inserted 1″ from edge of pie comes out clean, about 50 to 55 minutes. (The filling will set as pie cools.)

GOOD IDEA: Make your pumpkin pie the usual way but use 1 tsp. vanilla and a few drops of lemon extract instead of spices. The pie is a pretty color and the flavor pleases people who do not care for spicy foods.

APPLE BUTTER-PUMPKIN PIE

Mighty good, mighty filling. Serve faintly warm (doesn't weep when cut)

Unbaked 9″ pie shell
1   c. apple butter
1   c. cooked or canned pumpkin
½   c. brown sugar, firmly packed
½   tsp. salt
¾   tsp. cinnamon
¾   tsp. nutmeg
⅛   tsp. ginger
3   eggs, slightly beaten
¾   c. evaporated milk

· Combine apple butter, pumpkin, sugar, salt and spices. Add eggs; mix well. Add milk gradually; mix.
· Pour into pie shell. Bake in hot oven (425°F.) about 40 minutes.

FROSTED PUMPKIN PIE

Decorate spicy, snowy-topped pie with walnuts or bright corn candy

Unbaked 9″ pie shell

Filling:
1 ¾   c. pumpkin
1 ¾   c. milk
3   eggs
⅔   c. brown sugar, firmly packed
2   tblsp. granulated sugar
1 ¼   tsp. cinnamon
½   tsp. ginger
½   tsp. nutmeg
½   tsp. salt
¼   tsp. cloves

Frosting:
½   c. shortening or butter
2 ½   tblsp. flour
¼   tsp. salt
½   c. milk
3   c. sifted confectioners sugar
½   tsp. vanilla

Filling: Measure ingredients in large bowl. Beat until smooth with rotary beater. Pour into pie shell. (Have pastry a little thicker than ⅛″ so it will be crisper.)
· Bake in hot oven (425°F.) 45 to 55 minutes, until a silver knife inserted 1″ from edge of pie comes out clean. The filling may look soft, but it will set later. Let pie cool. Spread with frosting.

Frosting: Melt shortening in saucepan; remove from heat; blend in flour and salt. Slowly stir in milk. Return to heat; cook and stir until mixture has boiled 1 minute. (The frosting may look curdled at this stage.)
· Add confectioners sugar and vanilla. Stir until creamy. (Set pan in ice water to hasten setting of frosting.)
· Spread frosting on cooled pie. Decorate top with walnuts or raisins.

PUMPKIN-MINCEMEAT PIE

Two holiday favorites baked together

Unbaked 9″ pie shell
1   egg, slightly beaten
1   c. canned or cooked pumpkin
⅓   c. sugar
¼   tsp. salt
½   tsp. cinnamon
¼   tsp. nutmeg
¼   tsp. ginger
⅛   tsp. cloves
¾   c. undiluted evaporated milk
2   c. prepared mincemeat

• Combine and blend together egg, pumpkin, sugar, salt, spices and evaporated (not condensed) milk.
• Pour mincemeat into bottom of pie shell, spreading evenly. Spoon pumpkin mixture over mincemeat layer.
• Bake in hot oven (400°F.) 45 to 50 minutes or until knife inserted halfway between edge and center of pie comes out clean.

Squash Pie—Delicate and Delicious

When the yard and fields are white and more snow is falling, most farm women depend on their imagination and cooking skills to fix meals that bring cheer to everyone at the dinner table. "At our house," says a New Hampshire homemaker, "we often celebrate by having our favorite squash pie for dessert. And while our forks are busy, someone, thinking of more pies next year, almost always suggests that we plant more squash in our garden."

New England country kitchens were the birthplace of these smooth, satiny custard pies. Now cooks in all areas, especially if they grow squash, make pies with it. The Butternut, with its yellow-orange flesh, is the top-ranking autumn variety. Buttercups and Blue Hubbards assume a pie role, come December. When there's freezer space, pie bakers like to cook, mash, package and freeze each variety at its flavor peak—and certainly no later than early January, when squash in home storage often need to be sal-

vaged. Then they can make the pies throughout winter and spring.

Squash pies resemble their cousins, pumpkin pies, in appearance and taste. But some New England cooks insist that you use only white sugar in squash and always some brown sugar in pumpkin pies. And they say cloves are taboo in squash-pie fillings. Thus, the custard is milder in taste than the pumpkin and you get more of the vegetable's flavor. Here's the recipe named by a country cook in honor of a snowstorm, but you'll like it equally well when autumn leaves are brilliant or jonquils are blooming by the front porch. It's a winner.

SNOWSTORM SQUASH PIE

Delicate custard in crisp pastry is the vegetable gardener's tasty reward

Unbaked 9″ pie shell
1¾   c. strained, mashed, cooked squash
1   c. sugar
1   tsp. salt   *more*

1   tsp. cinnamon
½   tsp. nutmeg
½   tsp. ginger
3   eggs
1½   c. milk
1   tblsp. butter or margarine,
     melted

· Combine squash, sugar, salt and spices.

· Blend in eggs, milk and butter. Pour into pie shell.
· Bake in hot oven (400°F.) 50 minutes, or until silver knife inserted in filling 1" from pie's edge comes out clean. Cool. Serve slightly warm or cold.

Potato Pies Made with Sweets

When we asked our readers for their treasured pie recipes, the mail brought us directions for several intriguing sweet potato pies from southern kitchens. Every pie baker labeled her contribution just plain Potato Pie. That's because people, south of the Mason and Dixon line, refer to the sweets as potatoes, the whites as Irish potatoes.

The sweet potatoes used in southern recipes were the varieties with a light reddish or coppery skin and a rather moist, bright, orange-yellow interior. You'll notice that in one of the recipes sliced potatoes bake in a pastry envelope. Quite a welcome discovery for northern women who commonly use only the puréed or mashed potatoes in pie. Requests come to FARM JOURNAL kitchens every year from northern readers wanting the recipe for a wonderful sliced sweet potato pie they enjoyed on a trip in the South—usually in Virginia or Kentucky.

Farm women have been making pies with this vegetable (it's a rich source of vitamins A and C) for many years. Sweet potatoes were grown commercially in Virginia as long ago as the mid-1600s. Our collection of sweet potato pie recipes that follows includes the great favorites of the countryside, updated.

During the harvest season this vegetable has a truly fresh taste. To prolong this superior fall flavor, some homemakers cook and freeze sweet potatoes then, for winter and spring pies. You can either bake or cook the unpeeled vegetable in salted water just until tender, then cool, peel, purée it and package and freeze. Dried sweet potato flakes also have been developed by research and are available for convenient use the year around.

SWEET POTATO CUSTARD PIE

Velvety custard with a fascinating, subtle flavor all its own

Unbaked 9" pie shell
2   eggs, slightly beaten
¼   c. sugar
½   tsp. salt
¼   tsp. nutmeg
¼   tsp. cinnamon

1 tsp. grated orange peel
1 ¾ c. milk
2 ½ c. peeled and grated raw sweet potato, lightly packed
1 tblsp. melted butter or margarine

· Combine eggs, sugar, salt, nutmeg, cinnamon, orange peel and milk. Add sweet potatoes, grated just before adding to egg-milk mixture. Stir in butter.
· Pour into pie shell; bake in hot oven (400°F.) until a silver knife inserted in filling 1″ from edge of pie comes out clean, about 45 to 50 minutes. Serve slightly warm or cold.

SLICED SWEET POTATO PIE

Flaky pastry envelops rich, spicy, orange-colored filling--it's luscious!

Pastry for 2-crust pie
1 ½ lbs. sweet potatoes (4 medium)
1 c. light brown sugar
½ tsp. cinnamon
⅛ tsp. nutmeg
½ tsp. ginger
¼ tsp. salt
6 tblsp. butter or margarine
½ c. heavy cream

· Boil sweet potatoes until half-cooked, 15 to 20 minutes. Peel and slice thinly.
· Mix sugar, spices and salt.
· Place a layer of sweet potatoes in pastry-lined 9″ pie pan, sprinkle with some of the sugar-spice mixture and dot with a little butter. Continue until all ingredients are used, dotting top with butter. Add cream. Adjust top crust; flute edges and cut vents.
· Bake in hot oven (425°F.) 30 to

40 minutes. If potatoes are still not tender, reduce temperature to 350°F. and continue baking until they are done.

PURÉED SWEET POTATO PIE

For a special occasion, top pie with whipped cream, sprinkle with walnuts

Unbaked 9″ pie shell
2 c. sweet potato purée
2 eggs, slightly beaten
¾ c. sugar
½ tsp. salt
½ tsp. ginger
½ tsp. nutmeg
1 tsp. vanilla
1 ⅔ c. light cream or evaporated milk
½ c. butter or margarine, melted

· Bake sweet potatoes until tender, peel and mash. Make sure all lumps are removed, straining if necessary.
· Mix all ingredients together and pour into pie shell. Bake in hot oven (400°F.) 50 minutes or until a silver knife inserted in filling 1″ from edge of pie comes out clean.

GRATED SWEET POTATO PIE

Blindfold them and most people think they're eating extra-good pumpkin pie

Unbaked 8″ pie shell
½ c. brown sugar
¼ tsp. salt
¼ tsp. cinnamon
¼ tsp. nutmeg
⅛ tsp. cloves (optional)
1 c. milk
2 eggs, slightly beaten   *more*

1 ½ c. finely grated, raw sweet po-
        tatoes, lightly packed
1   tsp. lemon juice
1   tblsp. butter or margarine,
        melted

· Combine brown sugar, salt, cinnamon, nutmeg and cloves. Stir in milk
and eggs. Add sweet potatoes, grated

just before using, lemon juice and
butter.
· Pour into pie shell and bake in hot
oven (425°F.) until a silver knife inserted in filling 1″ from edge of pie
comes out clean, about 45 to 50 minutes. (Filling in center may still look
soft but it will set later.) Serve slightly
warm or cold.

Custard Pies at Their Country Best

If you live south of the Mason and
Dixon line, you probably call them
Egg Custard Pies; north of it, just
plain Custard Pie. By either name
they're famous, country-kitchen desserts. A sprinkling of nutmeg traditionally tops the pie. Some cooks grate
whole nutmegs to give their pies a
gourmet touch.

Women know that the perfect custard pie is an achievement. This is because the filling requires a low baking
temperature; the crust, if it's to be
flaky, a high temperature. One way to
surmount the difficulty is to bake the
custard and the crust separately at the
ideal temperatures for each and then
combine them (see our Best-Ever
Custard Pie).

The cardinal rule to heed is to avoid
overcooking, which produces a watery
or "weeping" custard. Test the filling
for doneness with a silver knife, when
specified in the recipes.

When you are in a hurry, try our
quick pies, Speedy Custard and Easy
Lemon Custard. One stays in the oven
about 15 minutes and the other, half
an hour. Both are surprisingly good,
considering the baking time required.

Cool all custard pies 30 minutes on
wire racks and then refrigerate until
mealtime. But you'll find the crust will
taste better if pie is taken from refrigerator and left at room temperature
while the main dinner course is eaten.
This is true of all refrigerator pies.

BEST-EVER CUSTARD PIE

Guarantee: a crisp undercrust

Baked 9″ pie shell
½   c. sugar
½   tsp. salt
2 ½ c. milk, scalded
1   tsp. vanilla
4   eggs, slightly beaten
½   tsp. nutmeg

· Add sugar, salt, warm milk and
vanilla to eggs. Pour into buttered 9″
pie pan. Sprinkle with nutmeg. Set in
shallow pan containing water (water
should reach halfway up sides of pie
pan). Bake in moderate oven
(350°F.) until silver knife inserted
halfway between edge and center of
custard comes out clean, 30 to 35 min-

utes. The center of custard may look a little soft, but it will set later. (Overbaking will make the custard pie watery.) Remove from oven and cool on rack at room temperature until lukewarm.

· Carefully loosen custard around edge of pan with small spatula and gently shake pan to loosen custard completely. Tilt the custard over the cooled pie shell, holding the edge of custard directly above far edge of shell. Slip the custard into the pie shell, pulling the pan back to you until all the custard is in the shell. Let custard settle in place.

CHOCOLATE-FROSTED CUSTARD PIE: When Best-Ever Custard Pie is cold, spread on your favorite chocolate frosting made with confectioners sugar. Or mix ½ c. sifted confectioners sugar with ⅛ tsp. salt and 2 tblsp. cream until smooth. Blend in 1 square unsweetened chocolate, melted, and 2 tblsp. melted butter.

VARIATIONS

COCONUT CUSTARD PIE: Omit nutmeg and add 1 c. flaked coconut to the custard. Sprinkle a little coconut on top and bake. Or sprinkle 1 c. flaked or shredded coconut over bottom of pie shell just before adding custard.

RICH CUSTARD PIE: Use 1½ c. milk and 1 c. heavy cream instead of 2½ c. milk. For a sweeter pie, use ⅔ c. sugar instead of ½ c. in custard filling.

MAPLE NUT CUSTARD PIE: Drizzle a little maple-blended syrup over top of cold custard pie and sprinkle with chopped walnuts or almonds.

COUNTRY-KITCHEN CUSTARD PIE

This filling, smooth as velvet, is rich in eggs, milk and cream

Unbaked 9″ pie shell
 4   eggs
 ⅔   c. sugar
 ¼   tsp. salt
 1½ c. milk, scalded
 1   c. light cream, scalded
 1   tsp. vanilla
 ½   tsp. nutmeg

· Chill pie shell thoroughly.
· Beat eggs slightly; then beat in remaining ingredients, except nutmeg. Pour into well-chilled pie shell with high fluted edge. Sprinkle on nutmeg.
· Bake in hot oven (400°F.) until silver knife inserted 1″ from edge of pie comes out clean, 25 to 35 minutes. (Baking too long makes a watery custard pie.) Cool on rack 30 minutes and refrigerate until ready to serve.

SPEEDY CUSTARD PIE

Bakes quickly, in about 15 minutes

Unbaked 9″ pie shell
 4   eggs, slightly beaten
 ½   c. sugar
 ¼   tsp. salt
 1½ tsp. vanilla
 2½ c. milk, scalded
Nutmeg

· Thoroughly mix eggs, sugar, salt and vanilla; slowly stir in scalded milk. Pour at once into pie shell. Dust lightly with nutmeg.
· Bake in very hot oven (475°F.) 5 minutes, then at 425°F. for 10 minutes, or until knife inserted halfway between center and edge of pie comes out clean. Serve cool or chilled.

EASY LEMON CUSTARD PIE

Busy country pie baker's delight

Unbaked 8" pie shell
¾ c. sugar
¾ c. water
⅓ c. lemon juice
1 tsp. grated lemon peel
¼ tsp. salt
3 eggs
Nutmeg

· Chill pie shell.
· Combine sugar, water, lemon juice and peel, salt and eggs in mixing bowl. Beat at medium speed 7 to 8 minutes.
· Place pie shell on oven rack. Pour egg mixture into it. Bake in hot oven (425°F.) 20 minutes. Reduce temperature to 250°F. (very slow) and continue baking 10 minutes. Remove from oven and sprinkle with nutmeg. Cool before serving.

BUTTERMILK PIE IN CORNMEAL PASTRY

One of our best Southern pies

Unbaked Cornmeal Pie Shell
3 eggs, separated
1 c. sugar
1 tblsp. butter
¼ c. flour
2 c. buttermilk
¼ tsp. grated lemon peel
2 tblsp. lemon juice
Meringue (3 egg whites)

· Beat yolks, adding sugar gradually.
· Cut butter into flour; add buttermilk, lemon peel and juice. Fold in yolks.
· Pour into 9" Cornmeal Pie Shell.
· Bake in hot oven (425°F.) 10 minutes; reduce temperature to 350°F. and bake 20 to 25 minutes. Cool.
· Pile meringue lightly over cooled filling (see Perfect Meringue for Topping Pies, Chapter 9). Bake in moderate oven (350°F.) 12 to 15 minutes.

CORNMEAL PIE SHELL: Sift together 1 c. sifted flour and ½ tsp. salt; stir in ½ c. cornmeal. Cut in ½ c. shortening until mixture resembles fine crumbs. Stir in ⅓ c. grated Cheddar cheese; sprinkle ¼ c. water over mixture gradually, mixing lightly with fork. Shape into ball; flatten on lightly floured surface. Roll to about ⅛" thickness. Line 9" pie pan; trim and flute edge. Fill and bake as directed.

Creamiest Cream Pies in the Country

Farm women make the world's best cream pies. For two reasons: they almost always have the necessary ingredients in their kitchens, and they have lots of practice—the pies taste so wonderful that they're favorites.

A Colorado ranchwoman says she bakes cream pies for church sales because they are spoken for by the time she delivers them. Her husband sums

Fix and freeze Cherry Mix *at cherry-picking time to make Cherry-Coconut Ice Cream Pie (recipes, pages 164, 165) and other desserts. Pineapple, tart cherry and coconut flavors blend delightfully in this pie. Keep one in the freezer.*

New variations of Vanilla Cream Pie, *long a country favorite. Here our basic recipe is piled with Strawberry Sponge, and Chocolate Cream Pie with Coconut Macaroon Topping—extra tasty. You will find the recipes on pages 119, 120.*

up his regard for the dessert by saying: "My definition for good is different from Webster's. To me, good is the kind of cream pie my wife bakes."

If your cream pies must wait a few hours before serving, cool them on wire racks for 30 minutes and then refrigerate. It is important to keep them refrigerated until serving time. Return leftovers promptly to refrigerator. These precautions guard against danger of food poisoning, which exists to a larger extent in milk-egg mixtures than in other foods, especially in hot and humid weather.

Cream Filling Pointers

Use a heavy saucepan and stir the filling constantly while it cooks, to prevent scorching.

Do not undercook the filling or it will have a raw, starchy taste.

If you have trouble with lumping, try the paste method of adding cornstarch (see basic recipe for Vanilla Cream Pie).

BROWN-BUTTER BUTTERSCOTCH PIE

For a real treat, sprinkle chopped toasted nuts on whipped cream top

Baked 9" pie shell
6 tblsp. butter
1 c. dark brown sugar
1 c. boiling water
3 tblsp. cornstarch
2 tblsp. flour
½ tsp. salt
1⅔ c. milk

3 egg yolks, slightly beaten
1 tsp. vanilla
Whipped cream

• Melt butter in heavy skillet over low heat. Watch carefully. When golden brown, add brown sugar; cook, stirring constantly, until mixture comes to a boil. Stir in water and remove from heat.
• In saucepan mix cornstarch, flour and salt. Blend in milk, stirring until smooth. Stir in brown-sugar mixture. Cook over medium heat, stirring constantly, until mixture comes to a boil. Boil 1 minute longer. Remove from heat.
• Stir a little of hot mixture into egg yolks; then blend into hot mixture. Boil 1 minute. Remove from heat. Add vanilla. Cool, stirring occasionally.
• Pour into cool pie shell and chill.
• To serve, spread top with whipped cream.

Note: If you prefer to top pie with meringue made with 3 egg whites (see Perfect Meringue for Topping Pies, Chapter 9), you need not cool filling before pouring it into pie shell.

VANILLA CREAM PIE

A FARM JOURNAL *5-star basic recipe*

Baked 8" pie shell
½ c. sugar
3 tblsp. flour
1 tblsp. cornstarch
¼ tsp. salt
1½ c. milk
3 egg yolks, slightly beaten
1 tblsp. butter or margarine
1 tsp. vanilla   *more*

• Combine sugar, flour, cornstarch and salt in top of double boiler. Mix with wooden spoon. Blend in milk gradually, then add egg yolks. Add butter.

• Place over rapidly boiling water so pan is touching water. Cook until thick and smooth, about 7 minutes, stirring constantly. Scrape down sides of pan frequently.

• Remove from heat. Add vanilla. Stir until smooth and blended, scraping sides of pan well. Pour hot filling into pie shell.

Note: Quantities may be doubled and filling cooked for 2 (8") pies at the same time.

VARIATIONS

CHOCOLATE CREAM PIE: Melt 1½ squares unsweetened chocolate in milk in top of double boiler. Set aside to cool. Then proceed as directed for Vanilla Cream Pie filling, using the chocolate-milk mixture and increasing sugar from ½ to ¾ c. Especially good topped with Coconut Macaroon Topping (Chapter 9).

BUTTERSCOTCH CREAM PIE: Substitute ¾ c. brown sugar for granulated sugar and increase butter to 2 tblsp. Proceed as directed for Vanilla Cream Pie.

BLACK BOTTOM PIE: Add 2 tsp. unflavored gelatin to dry ingredients. Cook filling as directed in recipe for Vanilla Cream Pie. Add ½ c. hot filling to ½ c. semisweet chocolate pieces; stir until they melt and mixture is smooth. Spread chocolate mixture in bottom of baked 9" pie shell. Cover and set remaining filling aside. Add ¼

tsp. salt to 3 egg whites; beat until frothy. Gradually add 3 tblsp. sugar, beating until stiff peaks form. With beater, beat half of this meringue into cream filling until mixture is smooth. Fold remaining half of meringue into mixture. Spread on chocolate layer in pie shell. Chill pie several hours before serving.

CHERRY CREAM PIE: Add 2 tsp. unflavored gelatin to dry ingredients and cook filling as directed for Vanilla Cream Pie. Remove from heat; cover and set aside. Add ¼ tsp. salt to 3 egg whites; beat until frothy. Gradually add 3 tblsp. sugar, beating until stiff peaks form. Beat half of meringue into cream filling until mixture is smooth. Fold remaining half of meringue into mixture. Spread 1 c. commercially canned or homemade cherry pie filling on bottom of baked 9" pie shell. Cover with cream filling. Chill several hours before serving.

STRAWBERRY SPONGE CREAM PIE: Drain 1 (10 oz.) pkg. partially thawed frozen strawberries. If necessary, add water to make ½ c. juice. Combine 2 tblsp. cornstarch and 1 tblsp. sugar in small saucepan; slowly add juice, stirring to make smooth paste. Cook over low heat, stirring constantly until mixture is thick and clear. Remove from heat and stir in strawberries. Set aside. Prepare filling for Vanilla Cream Pie, reducing flour to 2 tblsp. and egg yolks to 2. Pour into baked 9" pie shell. Beat egg whites at high speed until frothy. Gradually add 3 tblsp. sugar, beating at high speed until very stiff peaks form. Fold thickened fruit into egg whites. Spread evenly on hot cream filling, sealing to crust all around. Bake in moderate oven (350°F.) about 30 minutes. Cool before serving.

RASPBERRY CREAM PIE: Follow directions for Strawberry Sponge Cream Pie, substituting raspberries for strawberries.

BLUEBERRY CREAM PIE: Follow directions for Strawberry Sponge Cream Pie, substituting blueberries for strawberries. Add 1 tsp. lemon juice to berries.

VINEGAR PIE

Ranch-kitchen pie—truly delicious

Baked 9″ pie shell
3   egg yolks, beaten
1   c. sugar
¼   tsp. salt
1 ¾ c. boiling water

¼   c. cider vinegar
¼   c. cornstarch
¼   c. cold water
1   tsp. lemon extract
Meringue (3 egg whites)

• Place egg yolks in top of double boiler; add sugar and salt. Gradually add boiling water, stirring constantly. Add vinegar and cornstarch dissolved in cold water. Cook over boiling water until thick and smooth, about 12 minutes.

• Remove from heat. Add lemon extract. Stir until filling is smooth and blended, scraping sides of pan.

• Pour hot filling into pie shell. Top lukewarm filling with meringue (see Perfect Meringue for Topping Pies, Chapter 9), spreading to edges and sealing to crust. Bake in moderate oven (350°F.) 12 to 15 minutes, or until meringue is lightly browned.

Elegant Pie for Special Occasions

The good Utah cook, who shares her recipe for this superb, company dessert, says: "When you cut the pie, little, tempting dribbles of caramel sauce follow the knife. Tiny rivulets of the caramel run down the sides of the wedges on the tall and handsome filling. Guests are impatient to taste."

CELESTIAL VANILLA PIE

This high pie has unusual, delicate fluffy filling with caramel on top

Baked 9″ pie shell
4 ½ tblsp. cornstarch
1   c. sugar
1 ½ c. boiling water

½   tsp. salt
3   egg whites
1 ½ tsp. vanilla
Caramel Sauce
½   c. heavy cream, whipped
½   square unsweetened chocolate, coarsely grated

• Combine cornstarch and ¾ c. sugar in saucepan. Add boiling water, stirring constantly; continue to cook and stir until thick and clear, 10 to 12 minutes.

• Add salt to egg whites and beat until stiff. Add 3 tblsp. of remaining sugar and vanilla, beating until egg whites are creamy.   *more*

• Pour hot cornstarch mixture over egg whites, beating constantly. Cool slightly and pour into pie shell, heaping filling high. Chill at least 2 hours.
• Just before serving, spoon thin Caramel Sauce over filling in pie to cover; then top with whipped cream sweetened with remaining 1 tblsp. sugar. Sprinkle with grated chocolate.

CARAMEL SAUCE: Melt 2 tblsp. butter in small saucepan. Add 1¼ c. firmly packed brown sugar and 2 tblsp. dark corn syrup. Stir and cook over medium heat 1 minute. Remove from heat and add ½ c. light cream or top milk. Cook and stir until sugar is dissolved, then simmer 1 minute longer. Remove from heat and add ½ tsp. vanilla. Cool. Dilute with cream if necessary; the caramel sauce should be fairly thin. Makes 1 cup.

Heirloom American Pie

Most people today prefer updated cream pies, in which cooked filling is put in already baked pie shells—pies certain to have crisp, flaky crusts. Here's a pioneer pie, however, created in farm kitchens along the Wabash River during covered-wagon days. This baked cream pie enjoyed great prestige in the prairie states.

It's an heirloom recipe used today almost entirely by homemakers who learned to like it at their grandmothers' tables. We include the recipe primarily for its historic interest, a reminder of what pies were like a century ago. . . . Also for women who've searched for the recipe for a rich, cream pie their grandmothers used to make by mixing the filling in an unbaked pastry shell. (Their way of cutting down on dishwashing!)

HOOSIER CREAM PIE

Shallow, rich pie from frontier days

Unbaked 8″ pie shell
½ c. brown sugar
½ c. granulated sugar
2 tblsp. flour
2 c. light cream
½ tsp. vanilla

• Combine sugars and flour, mixing well. Stir in cream and vanilla. Pour into thoroughly chilled pie shell.
• Bake in hot oven (400°F.) until silver knife inserted halfway between center and edge of pie comes out clean, about 25 to 30 minutes. Cool on rack and refrigerate until serving time.

Cream Pie Filling that Freezes

If you've tried freezing cream pies you may have been disappointed. The fillings often separate, or become grainy or spongy.

Home economists at Texas Technological College worked on this problem, trying different thickeners. They found that fillings thickened with cornstarch, plus a small amount of gelatin, freeze and store successfully for 1 month with no changes in texture.

They had best results when they froze the filling and the baked pastry shells separately. To serve, they recommend putting the frozen filling in the baked shell, spreading it with meringue, then browning. (Egg whites left over from filling may also be frozen and used for meringue.) By changing the layer that goes over the frozen filling, you can serve delicious pies of different flavors. Here's the recipe the Texas home economists developed to freeze successfully:

CREAM PIE FOR FREEZING

Makes 3 pie fillings—saves time

2 tsp. unflavored gelatin
6 c. milk
2 c. sugar
9 tblsp. cornstarch
½ tsp. salt
6 egg yolks, beaten
6 tblsp. butter or margarine
3 tsp. vanilla

· Soften gelatin in ¼ c. milk.
· Scald remaining milk. Add the combined sugar, cornstarch and salt; continue heating rapidly until boiling, stirring constantly.
· Stir about ½ c. of the hot mixture into egg yolks; pour back into saucepan; simmer 5 minutes more.
· Stir in gelatin mixture; add butter and vanilla. Pour into three 8″ pie pans; freeze. (Frozen filling will be right diameter to fit 9″ shell.)
· Remove from pan, wrap in moistureproof freezer material; return to freezer.

To Bake: Place unthawed filling in baked 9″ pastry shell. You may cover it with a fruit or coconut layer (see variations), then top with meringue, making sure it touches crust all around. Bake in moderate oven (375°F.) about 10 to 12 minutes. (For best results, avoid heating the filling completely through.) Cool.

MERINGUE: Beat 3 egg whites (fresh or thawed frozen) with ¼ tsp. cream of tartar until frothy; beat in 6 tblsp. sugar, a little at a time. Beat until meringue stands in firm peaks. Spread on frozen filling at once.

PASTRY FOR FREEZING: Recipes using ⅓ c. shortening to each cup of flour are recommended by the Texas home economists at Texas Technological College. Pastry made with less fat did not freeze as well; neither was oil pastry at its best when frozen.

VARIATIONS

BANANA CREAM PIE: Slice 2 ripe bananas over frozen filling; sprinkle with 1 tblsp. confectioners sugar. Cover with meringue and bake.

STRAWBERRY OR PEACH CREAM PIE: Arrange 1½ c. sliced strawberries or peaches over frozen filling; sprinkle with 3 tblsp. confectioners sugar; cover with meringue and bake.

COCONUT CREAM PIE: Sprinkle 1½ c. flaked coconut over frozen filling; cover with meringue and bake.

FRENCH STRAWBERRY PIE

Glossy glazed berries on top hide the surprise, a rich custard layer

Baked 9″ pie shell
⅓ c. sugar
3½ tblsp. cornstarch
6 egg yolks, slightly beaten
2 c. milk, scalded
1 tsp. vanilla
1 (12 oz.) jar currant jelly
1 pt. fresh strawberries

· Combine sugar, cornstarch and egg yolks in saucepan. Gradually stir in the milk, while bringing to a boil. Cook, stirring constantly, 1 minute.

· Remove from heat and add vanilla. Cool and chill.

· Melt the currant jelly over heat. Cool until it is about ready to set. Brush the inside of pie shell with part of the jelly. Spoon in custard filling.

· Arrange stemmed, washed and drained strawberries, pointed ends up, on top of pie. Spoon remaining currant jelly over berries to glaze them. Chill a few hours before serving.

Beautiful Lemon Pies

Lemon pies of many kinds come to country tables. With their buttercup-yellow, tart-sweet filling and white, gold-tipped meringue, they're tempting at meal's end. Many farmers consider such a pie the perfect finish for a fish dinner, but the tart flavor also pleasantly rounds out a dinner with poultry or meat on the platter.

Notice our method of thickening Best-Ever Lemon Meringue and Vanilla Cream Pies with cornstarch blended with water to make a smooth paste, added to the boiling mixture. Give it a trial—you'll have gratifying results.

BEST-EVER LEMON MERINGUE PIE

A FARM JOURNAL *5-star special*

Baked 9″ pie shell
1½ c. sugar
1½ c. water
½ tsp. salt
½ c. cornstarch
⅓ c. water
4 egg yolks, slightly beaten
½ c. lemon juice
3 tblsp. butter
1 tsp. grated lemon peel
4 egg whites
¼ tsp. salt
½ c. sugar

· Combine sugar, 1½ c. water and salt in saucepan; heat to boiling.

· Mix cornstarch and ⅓ c. water to make smooth paste; add to boiling mixture gradually, stirring constantly; cook until thick and clear. Remove from heat.

· Combine egg yolks and lemon juice; stir into thickened mixture. Return to heat and cook, stirring constantly, until mixture bubbles again. Remove from heat. Stir in butter and lemon peel. Cover and cool until lukewarm.

· For meringue, add salt to egg

whites; beat until frothy. Gradually add ½ c. sugar, beating until glossy peaks are formed. Stir 2 rounded tblsp. of meringue into lukewarm filling.

• Pour filling into cool pie shell. Pile remaining meringue on top and spread lightly over filling, spreading evenly to edge of crust.

• Bake in slow oven (325°F.) about 15 minutes, or until lightly browned. Cool on rack at least 1 hour before cutting.

GOOD IDEA: Store extra grated lemon and orange peel in a tightly covered small jar, placed in refrigerator. It stays fresh a long time and saves getting out the grater when you need a small amount of peel.

BLACK BOTTOM LEMON PIE

Brand-new taste thrill—chocolate and lemon—you've no idea how good it is

Baked 9" pie shell
2 oz. semisweet chocolate
4 eggs, separated
¼ c. lemon juice
3 tblsp. water
1 tsp. lemon peel
1 c. sugar

• Melt chocolate over hot water. Spread evenly over bottom of cool pie shell.

• In top of double boiler, beat egg yolks until thick and lemon-colored. Add lemon juice and water, mixing well. Then stir in lemon peel and ½ c. sugar. Cook over hot (not boiling) water, stirring constantly, until thick,

about 12 minutes. Remove from hot water.

• Beat egg whites until frothy. Add remaining ½ c. sugar gradually, beating constantly until stiff, glossy peaks form. Fold half of this mixture into egg-yolk mixture. Pour over chocolate in pie shell.

• Spoon remaining egg-white mixture into pastry tube and make a lattice design on top of filling.

• Bake in slow oven (325°F.) 10 to 15 minutes, or until lightly browned. Cool on wire rack.

LEMON MERINGUE PIE SUPREME

Our best lemon pie for freezing from our FREEZING & CANNING COOKBOOK

Baked 9" pie shell
7 tblsp. cornstarch
1 ½ c. sugar
¼ tsp. salt
1 ½ c. hot water
3 egg yolks, beaten
2 tblsp. butter or margarine
1 tsp. grated lemon peel
½ c. fresh lemon juice
Meringue (3 egg whites)

• Mix cornstarch, sugar and salt in saucepan; gradually stir in hot water. Cook over direct heat, stirring constantly, until thick and clear, about 10 minutes.

• Remove from heat. Stir ½ c. hot mixture into yolks; stir this back into hot mixture. Cook over low heat; stirring constantly, 2 to 3 minutes. Remove from heat; stir in butter. Add lemon peel and juice, stirring until smooth. Cool. Pour into pie shell.

more

· Spread meringue on filling, making sure it touches inner edge of crust all around pie (see Perfect Meringue for Topping Pies, Chapter 9).

· Bake in moderate oven (350°F.) 15 minutes, or until delicately browned. Cool on wire racks.

· Place in freezer. When frozen, slip into plastic bag or wrap in moisture-vaporproof freezer material. Seal, label, date and return to freezer. Recommended storage time: up to 1 month.

· To serve, remove from freezer 2 to 3 hours before serving.

A Pie to Remember

If you had the pleasure of visiting a grandmother who baked pies almost every day of the week, you'll need no introduction to Lemon Whey Pie. Old-time country cooks had the remarkable knack of using the foods in their kitchens—of avoiding waste. They salvaged the whey, left when making cottage cheese, in several dishes to extend the then scarce and more expensive lemon juice. And of all their whey concoctions, the meringue pie made with the clear, tart, yellow whey was the best.

The pie our recipe produces is a first cousin of lemon meringue pie. They look alike and have somewhat the same delicate taste, although whey imparts an indescribable fullness of flavor that appeals especially to some country people.

If you ever make fresh cottage cheese in your kitchen and have the whey, you may want to bake the pie the way old-fashioned cooks did with a pastry pie shell. Or you may prefer to pour the filling into a baked and cooled graham cracker crust. Broil the meringue-topped pie about 10″ below the heat until the snowy peaks are tinged with gold. Be sure to cool Lemon Whey Pie away from drafts and then chill it before serving. At mealtime, grandmothers hurried to their beds of mint to get a few sprigs to garnish the tops of these pies—a trick you may want to follow if mint grows in your garden.

LEMON WHEY PIE

An old-fashioned FARM JOURNAL *favorite from* COUNTRY COOKBOOK

Baked 8″ pie shell
1½ c. whey
1   c. sugar
3⅓ tblsp. cornstarch
2   eggs, separated
1½ tblsp. butter
½ tsp. salt
¼ c. lemon juice
1   tsp. grated lemon peel
Meringue (2 egg whites)

· Bring 1 c. whey to a boil. Mix sugar and cornstarch and add to remaining cold whey to make a smooth paste. Combine mixture with hot whey and cook until thick, stirring constantly.

· Combine thickened mixture with slightly beaten egg yolks, butter, salt, lemon juice and peel.

· Cook 2 minutes. Pour into pie shell.

· Top with meringue (see Perfect Meringue for Topping Pies, Chapter 9) and bake in moderate oven (350°F.) 12 to 15 minutes. Cool away from drafts.

LEMON CHEESE PIE

Cheerful-looking, like sunshine in winter—lemon tang is refreshing

Crust:

1	c. sifted flour
½	tsp. salt
⅓	c. shortening
1	egg, slightly beaten
1	tblsp. lemon juice
1	tsp. grated lemon peel

Filling:

1 ¼	c. sugar
¼	c. cornstarch
1	c. water
1	tsp. grated lemon peel
⅓	c. lemon juice
2	eggs, separated
½	c. softened cream cheese (4 oz.)

Crust: Sift flour with salt; cut in shortening until mixture resembles coarse cornmeal. Combine egg with lemon juice and peel; sprinkle over flour mixture and mix lightly with fork until dough holds together. Roll out and fit into a 9″ pie pan; flute edge and prick over entire surface with a 4-tined fork. Bake in hot oven (400°F.) until pie shell is golden brown, about 12 minutes. Cool.

Filling: Combine 1 c. sugar with cornstarch; add water, lemon peel and juice, and egg yolks, slightly beaten. Stir until smooth. Cook, stirring constantly, until mixture thickens. Remove from heat and blend in cream cheese. Cool thoroughly.

· Beat egg whites until soft peaks form. Gradually add remaining ¼ c. sugar, beating until stiff peaks form. Slowly fold into lemon mixture. Turn into pie shell and chill thoroughly. Makes 6 or 8 servings.

Cut This Pie at the Table

Some pies are so pretty it's a shame to cut them in the kitchen. Lemon Fluff Pie is a wonderful example. Fluffy, gold-tipped meringue forms a collar around edge of pie, framing the pale-yellow filling in the center. Carry the dessert to the table and let everyone feast on its beauty while you cut the wedges. You'll enjoy watching the expressions of anticipation everyone has when your knife gets busy—the eager waiting to get into the act.

LEMON FLUFF PIE

Filling is light as a sunny cloud and it's just tart enough to please

Baked 9″ pie shell	
4	eggs
Grated peel of 1 lemon	
¼	c. fresh lemon juice
3	tblsp. water
1	c. sugar

· Separate eggs, putting whites in mixing bowl and yolks in top of double boiler.

· Beat yolks until thick, gradually stir in lemon peel and juice, water and ½ c. sugar. Cook over hot water until thickened, stirring constantly. Remove from hot water.

· Beat egg whites until stiff; beat in remaining ½ c. sugar (1 tblsp. at a time). Continue beating until whites are glossy and pile well.

· Fold half the whites into warm yolk mixture; when evenly blended, empty into pie shell, smoothing surface.

· Spoon remaining meringue to make a crown around edge of pie (make sure it touches crust).

· Bake in slow oven (325°F.) long enough to brown meringue lightly, about 15 minutes.

Mother-Daughter Lime Pies

A Midwestern farm woman, who went to Florida on vacation, returned home with a treasured recipe for Key West Lime Pie. She bakes the pie several times a year and says: "It tastes as good in our farm home as it did in its native, tropical setting. I think mine is even more attractive because I add a few drops of food color to tint the filling a pretty lime green."

She shared the prized recipe with her daughter, the mother of several young children, who bakes the pie for "occasions." But, ordinarily, she fixes a Short-Cut Lime Pie, with a no-cook filling. She says: "It's so much quicker and easier to make than Mother's kind."

Both recipes follow—they're typical of other recipes for traditional and short-cut versions that you'll find for other pies in this Cookbook. Around our Test Kitchens we often refer to them as Mother-Daughter recipes.

KEY WEST LIME PIE

Tropical pie has refreshing, tangy taste; a cool, lime-green filling

Baked 9" pie shell
⅓   c. cornstarch
1 ½ c. sugar
¼   tsp. salt
1 ½ c. water
3   egg yolks, beaten
¼   c. fresh lime juice
1   tblsp. grated lime peel
Few drops green food color
Meringue (3 egg whites)

· Combine cornstarch, sugar and salt in saucepan; gradually add water, stirring until smooth. Bring to a boil over medium heat, stirring constantly, and boil 1 minute.

· Remove from heat and quickly add one half the hot mixture to the egg yolks, mixing well. Return to the hot mixture, blending thoroughly.

• Bring the mixture to a boil, stirring, over medium heat. Boil 1 minute longer.

• Remove from heat; stir in lime juice and peel and food color to make filling a delicate green. Pour into cool pie shell at once. Completely cover with meringue (see Perfect Meringue for Topping Pies, Chapter 9).

• Bake in moderate oven (350°F.) 12 to 15 minutes, or until meringue is golden. Cool on wire rack away from drafts, at least 1 hour before cutting.

SHORT-CUT LIME PIE

You can fix it in the morning and chill it to serve in the evening

Baked 8" pie shell
1 (15 oz.) can sweetened con-
        densed milk
1 tsp. grated lime peel
⅓ c. lime juice
1 drop green food color
2 egg yolks
Meringue (2 egg whites)

• Combine sweetened condensed milk (not evaporated milk), lime peel and juice and food color; blend until smooth and thick. Stir in egg yolks and blend well.

• Pour into pastry shell and top with meringue (see Perfect Meringue for Topping Pies, Chapter 9).

• Bake in moderate oven (350°F.) 12 to 15 minutes, or until lightly browned. Cool away from drafts 2 to 3 hours before cutting.

SATINY FRESH COCONUT PIE

This special-occasion pie is worth the time and effort required to make

Baked 9" pie shell
1 c. sugar
½ c. cornstarch
¼ tsp. salt
3 c. milk, scalded
3 egg yolks, beaten
1½ tsp. vanilla
2 c. grated fresh coconut
1 c. heavy cream, whipped

• Combine sugar, cornstarch and salt in saucepan. Gradually add milk, stirring until mixture is smooth. Bring to a boil over medium heat, stirring constantly. Boil, stirring, 2 minutes. Remove from heat.

• Stir half of hot mixture into egg yolks; combine with rest of hot milk mixture in saucepan. Cook, stirring, over low heat until mixture boils and is thick enough to mound from spoon, about 5 minutes.

• Turn into bowl. Add vanilla and 1 c. coconut. Place waxed paper directly on filling and refrigerate at least 1 hour. Spread in pie shell and refrigerate at least 3 hours.

• To serve, spread with whipped cream and sprinkle with remaining coconut.

Note: Grate coconut by hand or cut coconut meat in small cubes and add, ¼ to ½ c. at a time, in blender bowl. Blend until fine.

FLAKED COCONUT PIE: Follow directions for Fresh Coconut Pie, substituting 2 (3½ oz.) cans flaked coconut for fresh coconut.

FRESH GRATED COCONUT PIE

Never-fail recipe for your party—custard is made with packaged mix

Partially baked 10″ pie shell
2   (3 ¼ oz.) pkgs. vanilla pudding
      mix
⅔   c. sugar
⅛   tsp. salt
2   eggs, well beaten
2 ½ c. milk
1   c. coconut milk
2   tblsp. butter
4   c. finely grated fresh coconut
1   tsp. almond extract
2   tblsp. sugar

• Combine pudding mix, ⅔ c. sugar and salt in top of double boiler. Stir in eggs, milk and coconut milk. Cook over boiling water until very thick. Add butter and 3 c. coconut; cook about 5 minutes longer. Remove from heat; add almond extract.
• Pour into warm pie shell, baked 4 to 5 minutes in very hot oven (450°F.). Reduce oven temperature to 425°.
• Sprinkle top of pie with remaining coconut mixed with 2 tblsp. sugar.
• Bake 20 minutes.

COCONUT PIE

Nutmeg makes the difference in this unusual, marvelous, all-coconut pie

Unbaked 9″ pie shell
4   egg whites
1   tsp. nutmeg
⅛   tsp. salt
2   tsp. vanilla extract
2   c. sifted confectioners sugar

1 ½ c. flaked coconut
2   c. milk, scalded
2   tblsp. butter or margarine

• In top of double boiler, combine 2 egg whites, nutmeg, salt, vanilla, sugar, coconut, milk and butter. Stir over hot (not boiling) water 5 minutes, or until mixture has slightly thickened (do not overcook). Remove from heat; cool to room temperature.
• Beat remaining 2 egg whites *only* until they stand in soft, stiff peaks (do not beat too stiff). Fold into cooled coconut mixture. Empty into pie shell.
• Bake in very hot oven (450°F.) 10 minutes; reduce heat to moderate (350°F.) and bake 30 to 40 minutes longer, or until filling is firm in center. Serve cold.

COCONUT MACAROON PIE

Country cupboards always have makings for this favorite, all-season pie

Unbaked 9″ pie shell
¼   c. chopped pecans (optional)
2   eggs, slightly beaten
½   c. water
1 ½ c. sugar
¼   c. flour
¼   tsp. salt
1   (3 ½ oz.) can flaked coconut
      (1 ⅓ c.)
½   c. butter or margarine, melted
      (1 stick)

• Sprinkle pecans over bottom of pie shell. Combine remaining ingredients; pour into pie shell.
• Bake in slow oven (325°F.) until golden brown, and almost set, about 45 minutes. Cool.

Fluffy Pineapple Pie

You may wander any place in this world in search of a beautiful, extra-delicious dessert to spring on guests, but you'll have a hard time surpassing this meringue pie. The secret is folding part of the meringue into the sunny-yellow, pineapple-scented and -flavored custard filling. It's a gorgeous tall pie, guaranteed to bring compliments to the cook.

FLUFFY PINEAPPLE PIE

Enchanting in appearance and taste

Baked 9" pie shell
1 ⅓ c. sugar
⅓ c. cornstarch
1 ⅔ c. canned pineapple juice
5 eggs, separated
2 tblsp. butter or margarine
½ tsp. salt
½ tsp. cream of tartar

· Blend ¾ c. sugar, cornstarch and pineapple juice together. Cook, stirring, until mixture begins to thicken. Continue cooking over low heat, stirring often, until mixture is clear and very thick, about 10 minutes. Blend a little of the hot mixture into egg yolks, well beaten. Return to hot pineapple mixture and cook 2 to 3 minutes longer. Remove from heat. Beat in butter. Cool.

· Beat egg whites, salt and cream of tartar until soft peaks form when beater is lifted. Gradually beat in remaining sugar until stiff peaks form.

· Gently fold about half the meringue mixture into cooled pineapple custard. Turn into pie shell.

· Swirl remaining meringue over top of pie, completely covering filling.

· Bake in moderate oven (350°F.) until lightly browned, about 15 minutes. Cool completely before cutting.

BANANA MERINGUE PIE

Pie cuts best if cooled 4 hours

Baked 9" pie shell
⅓ c. sifted flour
⅔ c. sugar
¼ tsp. salt
2 c. milk, scalded
3 eggs, separated
¼ c. butter or margarine
1 tsp. vanilla
3 medium bananas
Meringue (3 egg whites)

· Combine flour, sugar and salt in saucepan. Blend scalded milk in slowly. Cook, stirring constantly, over medium heat until mixture thickens and boils. Continue cooking and stirring 1 minute.

· Remove from heat and add a little hot mixture to beaten egg yolks. Quickly stir into mixture in saucepan. Return to medium heat and cook, stirring constantly, 3 minutes or until it thickens again and mounds slightly.

· Remove from heat and add butter and vanilla, stirring until butter is melted. Cool while you make meringue (see Perfect Meringues for Topping Pies, Chapter 9).   *more*

• Slice peeled firm bananas into pie shell, making an even layer. Pour luke-warm filling over bananas. Spoon meringue over filling and spread over top, making sure it touches inner edges of crust all around.

• Bake in moderate oven (350°F.) until peaks of meringue are golden brown, about 12 minutes.

GRAPEFRUIT CUSTARD PIE

Top of pie bakes to rich red-orange— filling is tasty and sweet-tart

Unbaked 9" pie shell
1   c. sugar
2 ½ tblsp. flour
1 ½ tblsp. soft butter or margarine
⅛   tsp. salt
3   eggs, separated
1   medium grapefruit
1   tsp. grated orange peel
1   c. light cream

• Combine sugar, flour, butter and salt in bowl; add egg yolks and mix thoroughly.

• Ream grapefruit; do not strain juice. You should have about 1 c. juice and pulp.

• Stir grapefruit juice into sugar mixture; add orange peel and light cream, mixing well.

• Beat egg whites until they form soft peaks when beater is lifted; fold into grapefruit mixture. Pour into pie shell.

• Bake in moderate oven (350°F.) until filling is set and browned on top, about 45 to 50 minutes. Cool on rack.

RHUBARB CUSTARD PIE

Tangy rhubarb in rich creamy custard is an early spring farm-style treat

Unbaked 9" pie shell
Filling:
1 ½ lbs. rhubarb (about 4 c.)
¾   c. sugar
2   tblsp. flour
1   tblsp. lemon juice
⅛   tsp. salt

Topping:
3   eggs
1   c. heavy cream
2   tblsp. butter or margarine, melted
¼   tsp. nutmeg
2   tblsp. sugar

Filling: In bowl, combine rhubarb, cut in ¼" slices, sugar, flour, lemon juice and salt. Toss to mix and turn into pie shell. Bake in hot oven (400°F.) 20 minutes.

Topping: Beat eggs slightly in bowl; stir in cream, butter and nutmeg to blend. Pour over hot rhubarb in pie shell.

• Bake 10 minutes; sprinkle with sugar. Bake 10 minutes more, or until pie's top is browned. Cool on rack before cutting.

RHUBARB-ORANGE CUSTARD PIE

One of FARM JOURNAL'S best recipes

Pastry for 1-crust pie
3   eggs, separated
1 ¼ c. sugar
¼   c. soft butter or margarine
3   tblsp. frozen orange juice concentrate

¼ c. flour
¼ tsp. salt
2½ c. rhubarb, cut in ½" pieces
⅓ c. chopped pecans

· Beat egg whites until stiff; add ¼ c. sugar gradually, beating well after each addition.
· Add butter and juice concentrate to egg yolks; beat thoroughly. Add remaining 1 c. sugar, flour and salt; beat well.
· Add rhubarb to yolk mixture; stir well. Gently fold in meringue. Pour into pastry-lined 9" pie pan (make high-fluted rim); sprinkle with nuts.
· Bake in hot oven (400°F.) 40 to 50 minutes. Cool.

CUSTARD CRUNCH MINCE PIE

Excellent variation for mincemeat

Unbaked 9" pie shell
1 c. sugar
2 tblsp. flour
⅛ tsp. salt
3 eggs, slightly beaten
¼ c. butter or margarine, melted
½ c. chopped walnuts
1 c. prepared mincemeat

· Blend dry ingredients and slowly add to eggs. Add remaining ingredients; mix well.

· Pour into pastry and bake in hot oven (400°F.) 15 minutes. Reduce heat to 325°F. and bake 30 minutes.

QUINCE CUSTARD PIE

An old-time FARM JOURNAL *favorite from our* COUNTRY COOKBOOK

Unbaked 9" pie shell
2 large ripe quinces
½ c. sugar
1 tsp. lemon juice
¼ tsp. nutmeg
¼ tsp. cinnamon
2 tblsp. melted butter or margarine
3 eggs, separated
1 c. milk, scalded
Meringue (3 egg whites)

· Peel and quarter quinces. Cook, covered, in small amount of water, until tender; drain. Put through food mill (should yield 1 c.). Add sugar, lemon juice, nutmeg, cinnamon and butter.
· Beat egg yolks until thick; add milk. Add to quince mixture. Pour into pie shell.
· Bake in hot oven (400°F.) until custard sets, about 50 minutes.
· Top with meringue (see Perfect Meringue for Topping Pies, Chapter 9) and bake in moderate oven (350°F.) 12 to 15 minutes. Cool away from drafts.

Out-of-the-Cupboard Pie

If you have canned apricots and pears on your cupboard shelves, here's a fascinating pie you can bake for a refreshing surprise some frosty day.

The farm woman who shares the recipe calls it a Winter Pie. The sour cream custard is creamy and the fruit juicy and tasty.

APRICOT-PEAR PIE

Apricot halves in the lemon-yellow custard look like small harvest moons

Unbaked 9″ pie shell
1 ½ c. drained apricot halves (1 lb. can)
1 ½ c. drained pear halves (1 lb. can)
¾ c. sugar
1 tblsp. flour
2 tblsp. butter or margarine
3 eggs
1 c. dairy sour cream
3 tblsp. lemon juice
2 tsp. grated lemon peel
Mace

• Arrange fruits (thoroughly drained) in bottom of pie shell, saving out 6 apricot halves.
• Combine sugar, flour and butter in bowl; blend in unbeaten eggs, beating well. Add sour cream, lemon juice and peel. Blend well.
• Pour over fruit in pie shell. Arrange apricot halves, cut side down and evenly spaced, on filling. Sprinkle lightly with mace.
• Bake in hot oven (400°F.) 30 minutes.

Chess and Nut Pies

Chess pies, of English descent, came first to plantation kitchens. Later, clever cooks came up with pecan pies. The appeal of the rich nut desserts is so great that women all over the country learned to make them, using the nuts that were most available in their neighborhoods—Missouri's Black-Walnut Pie, for instance. Usually, the pies are puffed up when taken from the oven, but the filling falls as it cools and has a jellylike consistency.

Peanuts are not nuts, but their name and the marvelous, inexpensive pies you can make with them (Farmer's Peanut Pie, to name one) entitles them to space in this Cookbook. The same goes for Oatmeal Pie, which some cooks call mock-nut pie. The oatmeal, when baked, has a texture and flavor that suggests nuts.

A farm-kitchen rule is never to package or store peanuts with other nuts. If you do, all the nuts will take on the peanut flavor.

Tree nuts are especially easy to freeze. Just see that they are clean. Wash them quickly and drain. Then crack the shells and remove the nuts. Pack them tightly in frozen-food containers or polyethylene bags of fairly heavy strength. They will keep up to a year stored at 0°F.

HEIRLOOM CHESS PIE

Southern-origin pie rich with farm foods—now it's enjoyed everywhere

Unbaked 9″ pie shell
¼ c. butter
½ c. granulated sugar
1 c. brown sugar, firmly packed
⅛ tsp. salt
3 eggs
1 tsp. vanilla

2   tblsp. flour
½   c. cream
1   c. chopped pecans

• Cream butter. Add sugars and salt; cream thoroughly. Add eggs, one at a time, beating well after each addition. Stir in remaining ingredients.
• Pour mixture into pie shell.
• Bake in moderate oven (375°F.) until a silver knife inserted halfway between edge and center of filling comes out clean, about 40 to 50 minutes. Do not overbake. Serve slightly warm or cold.

PINEAPPLE CHESS PIE

Luxurious pie—butter, eggs and sour cream blend with pineapple in filling

Pastry for 1-crust pie
1   (13½ oz.) can pineapple chunks
1   tblsp. flour
½   c. butter
½   c. granulated sugar
½   c. brown sugar, firmly packed
2   tsp. vanilla
¼   tsp. salt
3   eggs
½   c. dairy sour cream
Whipped cream (optional)

• Line 9" pie pan with pastry, fluting edge. Prebake in hot oven (425°F.) 5 minutes. Remove from oven.
• Drain pineapple well; sprinkle with flour.
• Cream butter with sugars, vanilla and salt until fluffy. Beat in eggs, one at a time, until mixture is smooth. Stir in sour cream and pineapple. Filling may separate slightly, but it becomes smooth during baking.
• Turn into pie shell, mounding in center. Brown in slow oven (325°F.) 50 to 60 minutes. Remove from oven and cool thoroughly.
• When ready to serve, garnish pie with rim of whipped cream.

LEMON CHESS PIE

Shimmery and golden inside, nut brown on top—a state fair prizewinner

Unbaked 9" pie shell
2   c. sugar
1   tblsp. flour
1   tblsp. cornmeal
4   eggs
¼   c. butter, melted
¼   c. milk
4   tblsp. grated lemon peel
¼   c. lemon juice

• Combine sugar, flour and cornmeal in large bowl. Toss lightly with fork to mix. Add eggs, butter, milk, lemon peel and lemon juice. Beat with rotary or electric beater until smooth and thoroughly blended. Pour into pie shell.
• Bake in moderate oven (375°F.) 35 to 45 minutes, or until top is golden brown. Cut pie while warm.

Note: A thin layer of the filling originally was baked in tart shells. It's a strong-flavored sweet filling, and should be shallow. A topping of unsweetened whipped cream takes away some of the potency of the filling.

RAISIN CHESS PIE

California ranch cook adds raisins to chess pie with tasty results—try it

Unbaked 9″ pie shell
½ c. butter or margarine
1   c. sugar
¼ tsp. salt
3   eggs
1   c. chopped walnuts
1   c. chopped raisins
1   tsp. vanilla

· Cream butter, sugar and salt thoroughly. Add eggs, one at a time, beating well after each addition.
· Blend in walnuts, raisins and vanilla. Turn into pastry-lined pie pan.
· Bake in moderate oven (375°F.) 10 minutes. Reduce heat to 325°F. and bake 30 to 35 minutes longer.

Walnut Pie—Missouri Style

Missouri, especially in Ozark country, has more than its share of fabulous pie bakers. Anyone who lives or visits the beautiful hill section, knows how extra-good the nut pies are when made with native black walnuts. A farm homemaker in the "show me" state sent this recipe which produces a pie you'll be proud to serve and everyone will be delighted to eat.

BLACK-WALNUT PIE

So rich you can cut pie in 8 servings; so delicious no one will want you to

Unbaked 9″ pie shell
½ c. granulated sugar
½ c. brown sugar

1   c. light corn syrup
3   tblsp. butter or margarine
3   eggs, slightly beaten
1   c. chopped black walnuts
1   tblsp. granulated sugar
1   tblsp. flour

· Combine ½ c. granulated sugar, brown sugar and corn syrup in saucepan. Heat just to boiling. Remove from heat and add butter. Stir until butter melts.
· Gradually stir hot mixture into eggs. Stir in black walnuts.
· Combine 1 tblsp. sugar and flour. Sprinkle evenly over bottom of pastry-lined pie pan. Turn walnut mixture into pastry.
· Bake in moderate oven (350°F.) until top is browned, 45 to 50 minutes.

RAISIN BLACK-WALNUT PIE

Best seller in a Home Demonstration Club's booth at a Virginia county fair

Unbaked 9″ pie shell
3   eggs, beaten
¾ c. light brown sugar
¼ c. soft butter or margarine
1   c. dark corn syrup
½ c. crushed black walnuts
1   tsp. vanilla
1   c. seedless raisins

· Combine eggs, sugar and butter, beating until thick and fluffy. Add corn syrup; beat until fluffy. Add walnuts and vanilla; add raisins, beating gently.

• Turn into pie shell. Bake in moderate oven (375°F.) until firm in the center, 30 to 40 minutes.

BLENDER PECAN PIE

The easiest pecan pie to make and one of the best—a good freezer

Unbaked 8″ pie shell
2   eggs
⅔   c. sugar
½   tsp. salt
½   c. light corn syrup
2   tblsp. butter or margarine, melted

1   tsp. vanilla
1   c. pecans
12   pecan halves

• Put eggs, sugar, salt, corn syrup, butter and vanilla in blender bowl and blend well.
• Add 1 c. pecans and blend just enough to chop nuts coarsely.
• Pour into pie shell. Place pecan halves on top.
• Bake in hot oven (425°F.) 15 minutes; reduce heat to 350°F. and continue baking until top is lightly browned, about 30 minutes.

Holiday Pie Has Sales Appeal

Here's a pie with a good sales record. For 25 years, it's been much in demand at the USDA cafeteria bake shop, especially during winter's holly season. Workers in the government offices like to buy these pies every year to tote home for holiday entertaining. The bakers have to hustle to fill all the orders.

One characteristic of the USDA Pecan Pie is that the luscious filling makes a fairly shallow layer. Washingtonians prefer it this way. They say it's too rich for a deep filling.

We begged the recipe for you. If you carry this pie to a church or other community supper or serve it to the family and friends, you'll get compliments on it. You can bake it in a 9″ pie pan, if you wish, and use the surplus filling in two small tarts.

USDA PECAN PIE

You can make this your bake-sale special. It has sales appeal

Unbaked 10″ pie shell
4   eggs
1   c. sugar
⅛   tsp. salt
1½   c. dark corn syrup
2   tblsp. plus 1 tsp. melted butter
1   tsp. vanilla
1   c. pecan halves

• Preheat oven to 350°F.
• Beat eggs just until blended, but not frothy. Add sugar, salt and corn syrup. Add cooled melted butter and vanilla, mixing just enough to blend.
• Spread nuts in bottom of pie shell. Pour in filling.   *more*

• Place pie in oven. Reduce heat to 325°F., at once. Bake 50 to 60 minutes. Makes 8 to 10 servings.

PECAN PUFF PIE

This puffy-topped, chocolate-nut pie deserves a place of honor in meals

Baked 9″ pie shell

Chocolate Filling:

1	(6 oz.) pkg. semisweet chocolate pieces
½	c. evaporated milk or light cream
½	tsp. vanilla

Pecan Meringue:

½	c. sifted flour
½	tsp. salt
4	egg whites
1	c. light brown sugar, firmly packed
1	c. chopped pecans
3	tblsp. melted butter or margarine
1	tsp. vanilla
½	c. pecan halves

Chocolate Filling: Place chocolate pieces in top of double boiler. Melt over hot water.

• Add evaporated milk and vanilla. Blend thoroughly.

• Spread in a layer over bottom of pie shell and fill with Pecan Meringue.

Pecan Meringue: Sift flour; measure; sift again with salt.

• Beat egg whites until they form soft peaks.

• Gradually add brown sugar, beating until it holds firm peaks.

• Fold in flour, chopped pecans, butter and vanilla.

• Spread over chocolate layer. Arrange pecan halves around edge of pie to make a wreath.

• Bake in slow oven (325°F.) 50 to 60 minutes. Cool. Serve with whipped cream or ice cream.

OATMEAL PIE

Many who eat this think it's pecan pie, it's so rich and luscious

Unbaked 9″ pie shell

¼	c. butter or margarine
½	c. sugar
½	tsp. cinnamon
½	tsp. cloves
¼	tsp. salt
1	c. dark corn syrup
3	eggs
1	c. quick-cooking rolled oats

• Cream together butter and sugar. Add cinnamon, cloves and salt. Stir in syrup.

• Add eggs, one at a time, stirring after each addition until blended. Stir in rolled oats.

• Pour into pie shell and bake in moderate oven (350°F.) about 1 hour, or until knife inserted in center of pie comes out clean.

Note: During baking, the oatmeal forms a chewy, "nutty" crust on top —pie is rich, delicately spiced.

ORANGE PECAN PIE

Orange flavor doesn't shout—just sings —in this rich plantation pie

Unbaked 9″ pie shell

1	c. sugar
1	tsp. salt

1   tblsp. flour
1   c. dark corn syrup
3   eggs, beaten until foamy
½   c. orange juice
1   tblsp. grated orange peel
1 ½ c. broken pecans

• Combine sugar, salt and flour. Add syrup, eggs, orange juice and peel.
• Stir in pecans and pour into pie shell. Bake in moderate oven (375°F.) 40 to 50 minutes, or until filling is set and pastry is browned.

DATE PECAN PIE

A FARM JOURNAL *5-star recipe*

Unbaked 9" pie shell
1   c. dairy sour cream
3   eggs, beaten
1   c. sugar
1   tsp. cinnamon
¼   tsp. salt
¾   c. dates, cut in pieces
½   c. chopped pecans
Whipped cream or ice cream

• Combine sour cream, eggs, sugar and seasonings in a bowl; mix well. Add dates and pecans. (Put dates and nuts through food chopper to save time.) Blend well. Pour into pie shell.
• Bake in moderate oven (375°F.) 30 minutes, or until filling is set and browned. Serve spread with whipped cream or small scoops of vanilla ice cream. Makes 8 servings.

FARMER'S PEANUT PIE

Good-tasting, easy to make, inexpensive dessert men especially enjoy

Unbaked 10" pie shell
4   eggs

¼   tsp. salt
1   c. dark corn syrup
1   c. light corn syrup
2   tblsp. melted butter or margarine
1   c. salted peanuts

• With rotary or electric beater, medium speed, beat together eggs, salt and corn syrups. Add melted butter.
• Sprinkle peanuts over bottom of pie shell. Pour in egg mixture.
• Bake in moderate oven (350°F.) until lightly browned, 45 to 50 minutes. Cool thoroughly before serving. Makes 8 servings.

CHOCOLATE BITTERSWEET PIE

Chocolate favorite—satiny, smooth filling, extra-rich, extra-tasty

Baked 9" pie shell
1   (12 oz.) pkg. semisweet chocolate pieces
¼   c. milk
¼   c. sugar
⅛   tsp. salt
4   eggs, separated
1   tsp. vanilla
Whipped cream

• Combine chocolate, milk, sugar and salt in top of double boiler. Cook over hot water until mixture is blended and smooth. Cool slightly.
• Add egg yolks, one at a time, beating after each addition. Stir in vanilla. Beat egg whites until stiff peaks form. Fold into chocolate mixture, blending well.   *more*

· Pour into cool pie shell. Let set at least 2 or 3 hours. To serve, spread with thin layer of whipped cream. Makes 8 to 10 servings.

SANTIAGO CHOCOLATE PIE

Cook's trick—fold nuts and raisins or dates into the whipped-cream topping

Baked 9″ pie shell

Filling:

3	squares unsweetened chocolate
3½	c. milk
⅔	c. sifted cake flour
¾	c. sugar
¾	tsp. salt
1	egg or 2 egg yolks
2	tblsp. butter or margarine
1½	tsp. vanilla

Topping:

½	c. heavy cream
2	tblsp. sugar
¼	c. chopped raisins or dates
¼	c. broken nuts

Filling: Combine chocolate and milk in top of double boiler. Cook over hot water until chocolate melts. Beat with a rotary beater until smoothly blended.
· Sift flour; measure; sift again with sugar and salt.
· Add a small amount of chocolate mixture, stirring until smooth. Return to double boiler and cook until thickened, stirring constantly. Then cook 10 minutes longer, stirring occasionally.
· Beat the whole egg or egg yolks. Add a little of hot mixture, stirring vigorously. Return to double boiler; cook 2 minutes, stirring constantly.
· Remove from boiling water. Add butter and vanilla. Cool slightly.
· Pour into pie shell. Chill.
Topping: Whip cream until slightly thick. Add sugar and whip until just stiff. Fold in raisins or dates and nuts. Spread over top of filling.

Note: Instead of whipped cream, the pie may be topped with meringue.

Postscript Pies

Here are four 2-crust cream pies signing off a chapter otherwise filled almost entirely with 1-crust specials. They're unusual and taste-rewarding— too good to miss.

DOUBLE CRUST LEMON PIE

Here's an updated version of the sunny lemon pie Mother used to make

Pastry for 2-crust pie

¼	c. cornstarch
¼	c. water
1½	c. boiling water
1½	c. sugar
2	tblsp. grated lemon peel
1	tblsp. butter or margarine
2	eggs, slightly beaten
¼	c. lemon juice

· Blend cornstarch with ¼ c. water. Add boiling water. Cook and stir over medium heat until mixture comes to a boil and is very thick and clear. Add sugar, lemon peel and butter. Cool.

• Stir in eggs and lemon juice. Turn into pastry-lined 9″ pie pan. Adjust top crust, flute edges and cut vents.
• Bake in moderate oven (375°F.) for 30 minutes, then in hot oven (425°F.) until top of pie is golden, 5 to 10 minutes. Cool on rack before serving.

DOUBLE SURPRISE LEMON PIE

Unusual—fresh-tasting lemon slices in filling and sugared top crust

Pastry for 2-crust pie
1 ¼ c. sugar
2 tblsp. flour
⅛ tsp. salt
¼ c. butter or margarine
3 eggs
1 tsp. grated lemon peel
1 medium lemon
½ c. water
2 tsp. sugar
½ tsp. cinnamon

• Combine 1¼ c. sugar, flour and salt. Cream butter until soft and blend with sugar mixture.
• Add 3 well-beaten eggs, reserving 1 tsp. egg white for topping.
• Grate lemon peel; then peel lemon, discarding white membrane. Cut lemon in paper-thin slices (should be ⅓ c.). Add lemon peel and slices and water to sugar mixture. Pour into pastry-lined 8″ pie pan.
• Adjust top crust, flute edges and cut vents. Brush with reserved egg white and sprinkle with mixture of sugar and cinnamon.
• Bake in hot oven (400°F.) 30 to 35 minutes, or until pie is golden.

SQUARE LEMON PIE

Choice combination—coconut pastry and tangy, tart-sweet lemon filling

Coconut Pastry:
1 c. sifted flour
1 tsp. baking powder
1 c. sugar
⅛ tsp. salt
1 c. flaked coconut
½ c. butter or margarine

Filling:
½ tsp. unflavored gelatin
2 tblsp. water
1 lemon, juice and grated peel
⅔ c. sugar
2 eggs, slightly beaten
1 tblsp. butter or margarine

Pastry: Sift together flour, baking powder, sugar and salt. Mix in coconut. Cut in butter until mixture resembles coarse crumbs.
Filling: Add gelatin to water. Combine lemon juice (there should be ¼ c.), lemon peel (1 tsp.), sugar and eggs in saucepan. Cook over low heat, stirring constantly, until mixture is thick. Remove from heat. Add butter and softened gelatin; stir until gelatin is dissolved. Chill.
• Press half of pastry mixture into a well-greased 9″ square pan. Spread cold lemon filling on top. Then sprinkle reserved half of pastry mixture on top, distributing it evenly.
• Bake in moderate oven (375°F.) until lightly browned, about 25 minutes. Makes 9 servings.

2-Crust Nut Pie Marvel

Call this dessert a pie or tart, whichever you prefer. It's a joy both to the hostess and to her guests, especially if they're fond of almonds. Different and distinctive. Better have pencils and paper ready for your guests—they'll want to copy the recipe for Sugar Custard Pie to make for parties.

SUGAR CUSTARD PIE

Almond fans rave about this unusual pie with its shallow, rich filling

Crust:

 1 c. sifted flour
 ¼ tsp. salt
 ½ c. butter
 1 egg

Filling:

 2 eggs
 1 c. sugar
 1 tsp. vanilla
 ¼ tsp. almond extract
 1 c. sliced blanched almonds, lightly toasted

Crust: Sift flour and salt into mixing bowl. Cut in butter until particles are fine. Beat egg slightly and add to flour-butter mixture. Toss with fork to blend. Gather into ball and knead lightly. Divide into 2 balls, one slightly larger than the other. Chill 15 minutes.

Filling: Beat eggs for filling until light; gradually add sugar, beating until mixture is light and thick. Beat in vanilla and almond extract. Fold in almonds.
· Line 9″ pie pan with larger ball of dough rolled 1½″ larger than pie pan. Turn custard filling into it. Adjust top crust (remaining ball of dough, rolled), flute edges and prick entire surface with 4-tined fork to prevent dough from bulging during baking. (Sprinkle top with a little sugar, about 1 tsp., if desired.)
· Bake in moderate oven (350°F.) until golden brown, about 30 minutes. Serve cool or warm. Makes 8 servings.

CHAPTER 5

REFRIGERATOR AND ICE CREAM PIES

Here's a whole chapter of dessert beauties—pie recipes to delight the hostess. You will find great variety when you leaf through the pages—both in the fillings and the crusts. And you will notice that they have one thing in common: They are pies you make ahead and chill before serving.

The refrigerator pie family is large. Chiffon pies with their billows of fluffy filling in crisp crumb, pastry, coconut and other kinds of crusts, are universal favorites. With a can of mandarin oranges in your cupboard, for instance, you can make a gorgeous chiffon pie on short notice—our Golden Nugget Orange Pie. Bavarian pies, with whipped cream folded into their fruity fillings, are among the many refrigerator specials that contain gelatin.

Ice cream pies—so popular on the farm now that home freezers make ice cream available all the time—get special attention in this book. They can be as simple as Strawberry Social Ice Cream Pie or as elaborate as the Alaska pies with ice cream in a crust topped with a tall meringue and frozen for quick browning at mealtime. Do try our Lemon-Layered Alaska Pie and enjoy its enthusiastic reception. Feast your family and friends on the other glamorous lemon pies, including the one made with pink lemonade, which we've nicknamed Fourth of July Pie.

You'll marvel at our fabulous collection of chocolate pies—Chocolate Pie Spectacular, to name one, with flecks of shaved chocolate in the filling and chocolate sauce drizzled on top. And look at the angel pies with their crunchy meringue crusts and fillings out-of-this-world, as angel pies should be. Notice the cheese pies to make in home kitchens—worthy rivals of those made by professional hotel chefs.

Many of these picture pies create a sensation and will make you famous for your desserts. Some of the fanciest take time to make, but can be made at your convenience—hours, and in some instances, days before dinner.

Chiffon Pies—Light as Sea Foam

Chiffon pies need no introduction to farm cooks—they know how beautiful and refreshing the dessert can be. And they have worked out rules for making these pretty pies.

The first step is to dissolve gelatin and sugar in fruit juice or other liquid over heat. The next is to chill the mixture until it mounds slightly when dropped from a spoon. Test frequently. Then it's time to beat egg whites until they form glistening, stiff peaks and fold them into the gelatinized filling. If this mixture mounds, spoon it into the crust; if it doesn't, chill it briefly to the mounding stage. The secret of fluffy chiffon pies is not to let the gelatin mixture get too firm before folding in egg whites (and whipped cream, if it is used). Chill pie until firm before cutting.

Many chiffon pies go to the country table crowned with whipped cream. If you want to freeze a chiffon pie, do not add whipped cream until serving time. Freeze the unwrapped pie until firm and then place it in a freezer bag or enclose it in freezer wrap; label, date and return to freezer. To serve, unwrap pie and let it stand in food compartment of refrigerator from 1 to 1½ hours.

Note: Use egg whites from washed, uncracked eggs for making chiffon pies (and other dishes in which the egg whites are not cooked). Refrigerate the pies immediately after they're made. Heed these precautions to avoid the possibility of salmonellosis, food poisoning caused by food-borne bacteria, sometimes via raw whites from cracked or unclean eggs.

LEMON CHIFFON PIE

Refreshing dessert after a heavy meal

9″ Graham Cracker Crumb Crust (Chapter 2)
1   envelope unflavored gelatin
1   c. sugar
⅛   tsp. salt
4   eggs, separated
⅓   c. lemon juice
⅔   c. water
1   tsp. grated lemon peel
½   c. heavy cream, whipped

• Combine gelatin, ½ c. sugar and salt; mix well. Beat egg yolks, lemon juice and water together. Stir into gelatin mixture and cook, stirring constantly, over medium heat about 5 minutes, or until mixture just comes to a boil.

• Remove from heat, stir in lemon peel and chill until mixture is partially set. Stir occasionally while chilling.

• Beat egg whites until soft peaks form; then beat in the remaining ½ c. sugar gradually. Continue beating until stiff peaks form. Fold into lemon mixture.

• Spoon into pie shell. Chill several hours, or until set. At serving time, spread with whipped cream (sweeten lightly with confectioners sugar, if desired) and garnish with shaved chocolate or chocolate candy shot (jimmies).

FRESH RASPBERRY CHIFFON PIE

A pie with cool, billowy filling that refreshes on sultry summer days

Baked 9" pie shell
1½ envelopes unflavored gelatin
¼ c. water
4 eggs, separated
1 tblsp. lemon juice
¾ c. sugar
2 pts. fresh raspberries
⅛ tsp. salt
¾ c. heavy cream, whipped

· Soften gelatin in cold water.
· Combine egg yolks, lemon juice and ½ c. sugar in small saucepan. Heat slowly, stirring constantly, until mixture is thickened slightly, and coats the back of a metal spoon. Remove from heat and add softened gelatin to the hot mixture; stir to dissolve.
· Put 1½ pts. raspberries through a sieve to make a purée (you should have 1 c. purée). Stir into gelatin mixture and cool until it mounds slightly when dropped from a spoon. (Do not let it get too firm.)
· Beat egg whites with salt until frothy. Gradually beat in remaining ¼ c. sugar and continue beating until meringue is stiff and shiny, but not dry.
· Fold into raspberry mixture along with whipped cream, reserving about one third of the whipped cream. Pour into pie shell and chill a few hours.
· To serve, decorate with remaining whipped cream and berries.

VARIATION

FROZEN RASPBERRY CHIFFON PIE: Substitute 1 (10 oz.) pkg. frozen raspberries for fresh raspberries.

APPLESAUCE CHIFFON PIE

Something new made with applesauce —pie with light, richly spiced filling

9" Graham Cracker Crumb Crust (Chapter 2)
1 envelope unflavored gelatin
¼ c. water
2 eggs, separated
½ c. sugar
¼ tsp. salt
¼ tsp. nutmeg
⅛ tsp. cinnamon
⅛ tsp. ginger
1¼ c. thick applesauce
1¼ c. milk
1 tblsp. lemon juice
Whipped cream (optional)

· Soften gelatin in water.
· Beat egg yolks; add 2 tblsp. sugar, salt, nutmeg, cinnamon, ginger, applesauce and milk. Cook over hot water until mixture thickens, about 15 minutes.
· Remove from heat, add gelatin and stir until it dissolves. Cool. Add lemon juice.
· Beat egg whites until frothy; gradually add remaining 6 tblsp. sugar, beating until glistening, stiff peaks form.
· Fold into applesauce mixture and chill until it mounds a little when dropped from a spoon.
· Spoon into pie shell and chill until firm. Serve garnished with whipped cream or, if you prefer, save out some of the crumb mixture when making Graham Cracker Crumb Crust and sprinkle over top of pie.

FARMSTEAD EGGNOG PIE

Festive pie on light side to serve at end of a hearty holiday dinner

Baked 9" Graham Cracker Crumb
    Crust (Chapter 2)
1   envelope unflavored gelatin
½   c. sugar
⅛   tsp. salt
3   eggs, separated
1 ¼ c. light cream
1   tsp. vanilla
½   tsp. nutmeg
Whipped cream (optional)

• Combine gelatin, ¼ c. sugar and salt.
• Beat egg yolks, stir in cream and gelatin mixture. Cook in double boiler over hot, not boiling, water, stirring constantly, until mixture coats metal spoon (about 12 minutes). Remove from heat, stir in vanilla and cool until mixture mounds when dropped from a spoon. Beat just enough to make smooth.
• Beat egg whites until frothy; gradually add remaining ¼ c. sugar, beating until glossy, stiff peaks form. Fold into gelatin mixture. Pour into crust and sprinkle with nutmeg. Chill until set. Serve topped with whipped cream.

VARIATIONS

STRAWBERRY FLUFF PIE: Fold 1 c. ripe strawberries, sliced, into filling. Garnish pie with whipped cream and berries.

BANANA FLUFF PIE: Line crust with sliced bananas before pouring in the filling.

COCONUT FLUFF PIE: Fold ½ c. flaked coconut and ½ c. heavy cream, whipped, into filling. Omit nutmeg.

EGGNOG PIE GLACÉ: Just before serving, spread top of pie with whipped cream and drizzle on melted currant or other tart, colorful jelly.

ORANGE DREAM PIE

Tawny toasted coconut rings the top of billowy yellow-gold filling

Baked 9" pie shell
1   envelope unflavored gelatin
¾   c. sugar
⅛   tsp. salt
1   c. hot water
3   eggs, separated
1   (6 oz.) can frozen orange juice
    concentrate
2   tblsp. lemon juice
3   tblsp. toasted coconut

• Combine gelatin and ½ c. sugar and salt in top of double boiler. Add hot water and stir over boiling water until gelatin is dissolved. Stir gradually into beaten egg yolks. Return to double boiler and cook, stirring constantly, until mixture thickens and coats metal spoon.
• Remove from heat and add orange juice concentrate and lemon juice. Chill until mixture starts to set.
• Beat egg whites until frothy. Add remaining ¼ c. sugar gradually and continue beating until stiff peaks form. Beat orange mixture until stiff peaks form. Fold egg whites into orange mixture. Turn into pie shell; sprinkle coconut around edge of pie for decorative touch. Chill several hours.

Note: Substitute a coconut pie shell (see Chapter 2) for baked pie shell.

¾ c. sugar

⅛ tsp. salt

½ c. heavy cream, whipped

¼ c. flaked coconut

Gorgeous Mandarin-Orange Pie

This golden pie is a real beauty. The bright pieces of fruit in a sunny yellow custard make it a picture pie. And while this one needs no fancy trim, it's surprising how pompons of whipped cream, sprinkled with shreds or flakes of coconut and garnished with a few orange segments transform the pie into a special-occasion treat.

The small oranges, of Chinese origin, are deep orange in color. Most of the supply in our supermarkets is canned in Japan. Their miniature segments add both flavor and brightness to salads and desserts. They're a beautiful garnish.

Toasted coconut makes an unusual, appealing trim, but the fluffy, white coconut also is attractive. Now that you can buy toasted coconut in packages, it's easy to use. Just keep it in the cupboard near a can of mandarin oranges and you'll have the makings for this marvelous tasting pie at your finger tips.

· To syrup from drained mandarins add enough water to make 1 c.

· Soften gelatin in ¼ c. cold water.

· Beat egg yolks until light and fluffy; stir in sugar, salt and orange syrup mixture. Cook until thickened, stirring constantly. Add softened gelatin and stir until it is dissolved. Cool.

· Reserve several mandarin segments (at least 6) for garnishing. Cut remaining segments in small pieces and fold gently into custard mixture.

· Beat egg whites until they form soft peaks; fold into fruit-custard mixture. Pour into cool pie shell. Chill until set.

· To serve, top each wedge of pie with a spoonful of whipped cream and at least one reserved mandarin segment. Sprinkle with coconut. You can sweeten whipped cream with 1 tblsp. sugar, if you like.

GOLD NUGGET ORANGE PIE

A light, tall, fluffy and handsome chiffon pie that tastes wonderful

Baked 9″ pie shell

1 (11 oz.) can mandarin oranges, drained

1 tblsp. lemon juice

1 envelope unflavored gelatin

¼ c. cold water

4 eggs, separated

MANDARIN-APRICOT PIE

Guaranteed to brighten any meal with festive color and tasty flavor blend

2 tblsp. butter or margarine

2 c. flaked coconut

1 (11 oz.) can mandarin oranges, drained

2 c. apricot nectar

1 (6 oz.) pkg. lemon flavor gelatin, or 2 (3 oz.) pkgs.

½ c. heavy cream, whipped

· Spread butter evenly on bottom and sides of 9″ pie pan. Pat coconut evenly in pan to make a pie shell. Bake in slow oven (300°F.) 15 to 20 minutes, or until coconut is delicately toasted. Cool.

• Meanwhile, measure syrup drained from mandarins. Add it to apricot nectar. Add enough water to make 3 c. Bring juices to a boil and dissolve gelatin in hot mixture. Cool; then chill until mixture starts to thicken. Fold in mandarin segments, reserving a few for garnishing. Pour mixture into cool pie shell and refrigerate until firm.

• To serve, garnish with reserved mandarin segments and dollops of whipped cream.

CHERRY CHIFFON PIE

Pink and pretty—uses canned cherries

Baked 9″ pie shell
2 tsp. unflavored gelatin
2 tblsp. cold water
1 (1 lb. 4 oz.) can tart cherries
4 eggs, separated
¼ tsp. salt
¾ c. sugar
1½ tsp. grated lemon peel
Whipped cream (optional)

• Soften gelatin in water. Drain cherries, reserving juice. Beat egg yolks and add juice from cherries (¾ c.), salt and ½ c. sugar. Cook over low heat until thickened, stirring constantly. Stir in softened gelatin and stir until it is dissolved. Cool slightly and add lemon peel and drained cherries (1½ c.).

• Beat egg whites until soft peaks form when beater is lifted. Gradually add remaining ¼ c. sugar, 2 tblsp. at a time, beating thoroughly after each

addition. Beat until stiff peaks form. Fold into gelatin mixture. Pile lightly in pie shell and chill until firm.

• When ready to use, garnish each serving with whipped cream.

SOUR CREAM PUMPKIN PIE

Add excitement to party refreshments with this tasty layered pumpkin pie

Baked 9″ pie shell
1 envelope unflavored gelatin
¼ c. cold water
3 eggs, separated
⅓ c. granulated sugar
1¼ c. pumpkin purée, canned or homemade
½ c. dairy sour cream
½ tsp. salt
1 tsp. cinnamon
¼ tsp. cloves
¼ tsp. nutmeg
¼ tsp. ginger
¼ c. granulated sugar
1 c. heavy cream, whipped
1 c. sifted confectioners sugar
1 tsp. vanilla, or ½ tsp. vanilla and ½ tsp. rum extract
½ c. chopped pecans

• Soften gelatin in water.
• Beat egg yolks with ⅓ c. sugar until thick and lemon-colored. Add pumpkin, sour cream, salt and spices. Cook over medium heat, stirring constantly, until mixture comes to a boil. Reduce heat and cook 2 minutes, stirring constantly. Remove from heat and stir in softened gelatin. Stir until gelatin is dissolved. Cool.
• Beat egg whites until frothy; add ¼ c. sugar gradually, beating until

stiff peaks form and sugar is dissolved. Fold into pumpkin mixture.

• To whipped cream, add confectioners sugar and vanilla, mixing well.

• Spoon half of pumpkin mixture into cool pie shell; then spread half of whipped cream mixture on top. Repeat. Sprinkle with pecans. Chill at least 2 hours before serving. Makes 8 servings.

Short-Cut and Traditional Chiffon Pies

In any beauty contest for chiffon pies, color-gay apricot, orange and lime entries would have a good chance of winning prizes. They're lovely to look at when made either by the short-cut or traditional method. And they're refreshing.

Today's clever cooks often have two sets of recipes, one to use when they're busy and minutes are short, the other for traditional "from scratch" when there's less rush. Here are three pies with two recipes for each. The quick versions are from our TIMESAVING COOKBOOK. We reprint them in this chapter along with the traditional recipes so you can make the pie that fits best into the time you have to fix the dessert.

Try each of the six pies and compare them! See whether your family can tell the difference.

TRADITIONAL APRICOT CHIFFON PIE

Filling the color of sunset clouds—reprinted from TIMESAVING COOKBOOK

Baked 9" pie shell
½ lb. dried apricots (1 ½ c.)
1 ½ c. water
1 c. sugar
1 envelope unflavored gelatin
4 egg yolks, slightly beaten
2 tblsp. lemon juice
4 egg whites
½ tsp. cream of tartar
⅛ tsp. salt
¼ tsp. almond extract
Toasted coconut

• Soak apricots in water 1 hour; cook, covered, until tender; drain. Put through food mill or sieve to make 1 c. purée.

• Blend together ½ c. sugar, gelatin, egg yolks, lemon juice and apricot purée; cook until mixture comes to boil. Cool by setting pan in cold water until mixture mounds slightly when dropped from spoon.

• Beat egg whites, cream of tartar and salt until frothy. Gradually add remaining ½ c. sugar and extract; beat until stiff and glossy. Fold into cool apricot mixture. Pile into pie shell, swirling top. Chill several hours. Garnish with drifts of toasted coconut.

VARIATIONS

Make the following as you would Apricot Chiffon Pie, omitting apricots, water and lemon juice: *more*

LIME PIE: Blend ½ c. sugar, gelatin, ⅔ c. water and ⅓ c. lime juice with yolks. Add 1 tblsp. grated lime peel and 3 or 4 drops green food color before cooling. Fold into egg white mixture.

ORANGE PIE: Blend ½ c. sugar, gelatin and 1 c. orange juice with yolks as directed in Lime Pie. Add 1 tblsp. grated orange peel and, if desired, red and yellow food color before cooling, to step up orange color. Fold into egg white mixture. Garnish with shredded orange peel.

SHORT-CUT APRICOT CHIFFON PIE

Double-quick to make and tasty, too

Baked 9″ pie shell
1   (3 oz.) pkg. lemon chiffon pie filling
½   c. boiling water
1   c. apricot nectar
⅛   tsp. almond extract
Red and yellow food color
⅓   c. sugar
Toasted coconut

• Thoroughly dissolve pie filling in water. Beat in nectar, almond extract and 3 drops each of the two food colors (makes orange hue). Add sugar and beat until mixture stands in peaks.
• Pile filling into pie shell; swirl top. Chill until set. Garnish with coconut. (You can buy packaged toasted coconut.)

VARIATIONS

Thoroughly dissolve lemon chiffon pie filling in ½ c. boiling water, and proceed as follows:

SHORT-CUT LIME PIE: Beat in ¼ c. each frozen limeade concentrate and cold water; add 4 drops green food color. Add ⅓ c. sugar; beat until mixture stands in peaks. Spoon filling into pie shell; swirl top. Chill until set.

SHORT-CUT ORANGE PIE: Beat in juice of 1 orange plus cold water to make ½ c.; add 1 tsp. grated orange peel and 3 or 4 drops red food color. Add ⅓ c. sugar; beat until peaks form. Spoon filling into pie shell; swirl top. Chill until set. Garnish with shredded peel from ½ orange.

Lemon Accents Superior Flavors

Country pie bakers have the lemon habit—it's a touch of genius they rely on to produce extra-good eating. They add lemon juice or grated peel—sometimes both—to many pie fillings to enhance flavors. When you are looking at recipes in this book, notice the frequency with which lemon appears in the list of ingredients. Lemons have the remarkable ability of bringing out the best taste in many foods, including other fruits.

It's the reason many farm women keep cans of frozen lemonade concentrate in their freezers. The custard in the two recipes, Lemon Coconut and Fruit Cocktail Pies, owes its marvelous taste to the frozen concentrate. Both pies are handsome. And in both of them the tangy lemon taste glorifies the coconut and canned fruit cocktail.

LEMON COCONUT PIE

Lemon-flavored custard is creamy—smooth, fluffy, delicate and tasty

Baked 9" pie shell
1   envelope unflavored gelatin
½   c. cold water
3   eggs, separated
⅛   tsp. salt
1   (6 oz.) can frozen lemonade concentrate (⅔ c.)
½   c. sugar
1   c. flaked or shredded coconut

· In top of double boiler, soften gelatin in water. Add egg yolks, slightly beaten, and salt. Place over boiling water and cook, stirring constantly, until mixture thickens, about 7 minutes. Remove from heat and stir in unthawed frozen lemonade. Stir until mixture thickens. (The custard usually sets fast and needs no chilling.)
· Beat egg whites to soft peaks; stir in sugar, 2 tblsp. at a time, beating well after each addition. Beat until stiff peaks form. Fold into gelatin mixture; then fold in coconut, reserving a little to sprinkle on top of pie. Drop a spoonful of mixture into pie shell. It should mound. If it doesn't, chill, stirring a few times, until it will mound. Turn into pie shell and chill pie until firm before cutting.

FRUIT COCKTAIL PIE: Omit coconut in Lemon Coconut Pie and add canned fruit cocktail instead. Drain 1 (1 lb.) can fruit cocktail. You will have about 1½ c. fruit. Save out a little of it to make a wreath on top of pie at serving time; fold remainder of fruit cocktail into pie filling.

SILVER CREAM PIE

A different lemon pie—a dessert that makes friends and wins compliments

Baked 9" pie shell
4   eggs, separated
1   c. sugar
1   lemon, juice and grated peel
½   envelope unflavored gelatin (1 ½ tsp.)
¼   c. cold water
Whipped cream

· Beat egg yolks with ½ c. sugar and lemon juice and peel. Cook in double boiler until thick and creamy, stirring constantly.
· Soften gelatin in water; then stir into hot lemon mixture until it is dissolved. Cool.
· Beat egg whites until frothy, then gradually add remaining ½ c. sugar, beating until stiff; fold in gelatin mixture. Pour into pie shell and chill 2 hours or longer.
· To serve, garnish, if desired, with whipped cream and sprinkle with silver dragées or grated unsweetened chocolate.

DOUBLE-LEMON AMBROSIA PIE

Layer of fluffy white is topped with deeper lemon yellow—a glamorous pie

Coconut Butter Crust:
⅓   c. soft butter
1   egg yolk
1   c. sifted flour
1   (3 ½ oz.) can flaked coconut (1 ¼ c.)   *more*

Filling:

1 ⅓ c. sugar
1 ¼ c. water
½ tsp. salt
⅓ c. cornstarch
¼ c. water
2 eggs, separated
⅓ c. lemon juice
2 tblsp. butter
1 tsp. grated lemon peel
1 envelope unflavored gelatin
¼ c. cold water
1 c. light cream

Crust: Cream butter and egg yolk together. Add flour, mixing thoroughly. Work coconut into dough.
• Pat mixture into 9″ pie pan, bringing up on sides and fluting edge. Chill 30 minutes.
• Bake in moderate oven (350°F.) 25 to 30 minutes, or until light brown.

Filling: Combine sugar, 1¼ c. water and salt in saucepan; heat to boiling. Combine cornstarch and ¼ c. water to make smooth paste; add to boiling mixture gradually, stirring constantly and cooking until thick and clear. Remove from heat.
• Combine slightly beaten egg yolks and lemon juice; add to thickened mixture and stir well. Return to heat and cook, stirring constantly, until mixture bubbles again. Remove from heat. Stir in butter and lemon peel. Take out 1 c. filling and set aside.
• Soften gelatin in ¼ c. water; add to remaining filling, stirring until dissolved. Stir in light cream. Refrigerate until mixture begins to set. Beat until mixture is smooth.

• Beat egg whites to form stiff peaks. Fold into refrigerator-cooled and thickened lemon mixture. Pour into cooled pie shell. Refrigerate until set. Then spread reserved cup of filling over top. Refrigerate until serving time.

LEMON-PLUS PIE

Orange and lemon flavors share honors in this make-ahead treat

Baked 9″ pie shell
1 envelope unflavored gelatin
¼ c. cold water
4 eggs, separated
½ c. lemon juice
3 tblsp. orange juice
¾ c. sugar
¼ tsp. salt
1 tsp. grated lemon peel
⅔ c. sugar
⅔ c. heavy cream

• Soften gelatin in water.
• In top of double boiler, beat egg yolks until thick and lemon-colored. Add juices and mix well. Stir in sugar and salt. Cook over hot (not boiling) water until slightly thickened (about 10 minutes). Remove from heat; stir in lemon peel and gelatin. Chill until mixture begins to set (about 1 hour). Beat until smooth.
• Beat egg whites until frothy. Gradually add ⅔ c. sugar, beating until glossy peaks are formed.
• Whip cream and fold into egg whites. Then fold into thickened lemon mixture. Spoon into cool pie shell. Refrigerate several hours before serving.

PINK LEMONADE PIE

Pink of perfection—this delicious, unusual refrigerator cream pie

8" Vanilla Wafer Crumb Crust (Chapter 2)
1 (6 oz.) can frozen pink lemonade concentrate
¾ c. water
1 envelope unflavored gelatin
¼ c. sugar
1 c. heavy cream
Few drops of red food color
¼ c. vanilla wafer crumbs

· Chill crumb crust.
· Thaw lemonade and combine with ½ c. water.
· Soften gelatin in remaining ¼ c. water; dissolve over hot water.
· Add dissolved gelatin and sugar to lemonade; stir until sugar dissolves. Chill until mixture is thick but not set (about 1 hour).
· Whip thickened gelatin mixture until light and fluffy. Then whip cream and fold into lemon mixture. Add food color to make mixture a delicate pink. Pour into chilled crust. Sprinkle with ¼ c. wafer crumbs. Chill.

PINEAPPLE POSY PIE

Yellow flowers with cherry centers trim this pie that's gay as a festival

9" Graham Cracker Crumb Crust (Chapter 2)
1 (6 oz.) can frozen pineapple juice concentrate
1 envelope unflavored gelatin
¼ c. cold water
4 egg yolks, beaten until thick and creamy
½ c. sugar
¼ tsp. salt
2 tblsp. finely grated orange peel
4 egg whites
¼ c. sugar
⅔ c. heavy cream, whipped

· Thaw pineapple juice and simmer until it is reduced to ½ c. (or until the total is ⅓ less). Cool.
· Soften gelatin in water at least 5 minutes.
· Add egg yolks to pineapple juice; add gelatin and ½ c. sugar. Place in double boiler. Cook 10 minutes, stirring often. Remove from heat. Add salt and orange peel. Mix well and chill until mixture thickens, but do not let it set. It usually takes about 45 minutes.
· Beat egg whites until frothy, then gradually add ¼ c. sugar while continuing to beat. Beat until stiff peaks form. Fold in whipped cream. Fold egg white mixture into pineapple filling and spoon into cool pie shell.
· At serving time, garnish, if desired, with 6 pineapple flowers. To make flower, arrange 5 drained pineapple tidbits around a maraschino cherry.

Note: A coconut pie shell may be used instead of the crumb crust. See recipe for Coconut Pie Shell (Chapter 2).

PINK RHUBARB PIE

For dieting pie eaters—nonfat dry milk substitutes for whipped cream

Baked 9" low-calorie pie shell (Chapter 2)   *more*

Filling:

3 c. (½" cubes) fresh rhubarb (about 1 lb.)
¼ c. water
¼ c. sugar
1 (3 oz.) pkg. strawberry flavor gelatin
¼ c. ice water
¼ c. nonfat dry milk

Topping:

¼ c. ice water
1 tblsp. lemon juice
½ tsp. vanilla
¼ c. nonfat dry milk
Banana

Filling: Combine rhubarb, water and sugar in saucepan; cover and cook about 5 minutes, or until rhubarb is just tender, but a little firm. There should be 2 c. cooked rhubarb.

· Add gelatin to hot rhubarb and stir until it is dissolved. Reserve ¾ c. of this mixture for glaze. Cool at room temperature.

· Chill remaining rhubarb mixture (for filling) until slightly thickened.

· Measure into bowl ¼ c. ice water and sprinkle on ¼ c. nonfat dry milk. Beat with rotary or electric beater until stiff enough to hold peaks. Fold in chilled rhubarb filling. Pour into pie shell.

· Spoon over the pie the ¾ c. gelatin mixture reserved for glaze. It should be cool, but not cold enough to start congealing. Chill pie again until filling is set.

Topping (prepare at serving time): To the ice water, add lemon juice and vanilla. Sprinkle nonfat milk over water mixture. Beat with rotary or electric beater until mixture holds peaks. Spoon over pie and garnish with banana slices.

PEANUT BUTTER PIE

A FARM JOURNAL *5-star recipe favorite from our* COUNTRY COOKBOOK

Baked 9" pie shell
1 envelope unflavored gelatin
1 c. cold water
3 egg yolks, well beaten
½ c. sugar or light corn syrup
½ tsp. salt
½ c. smooth peanut butter
½ tsp. vanilla
3 egg whites, unbeaten
½ c. heavy cream, whipped (optional)
Peanut halves
Chocolate pieces

· Soften gelatin in ¼ c. water.

· Combine egg yolks, ¼ c. sugar, ¼ c. water and salt in top of double boiler; blend. Add gelatin.

· Place over boiling water; beat constantly with rotary beater until thick and fluffy (about 5 minutes). Cool.

· Place peanut butter in bowl; add remaining ½ c. water gradually; beat until smooth. Add vanilla to egg yolk mixture; blend into peanut butter. Chill until slightly thickened, but still syrupy (10 to 15 minutes).

· Beat egg whites until foamy; add remaining sugar gradually, beating until stiff. Fold into peanut butter mixture. Turn into pie shell. Chill until firm.

· To serve, cover top with thin layer of whipped cream, if desired. (Cream is pretty but does detract a bit from the peanut flavor.) Decorate with "daisies" of peanut halves with chocolate pieces for centers.

Note: Crumb crust may be substituted for baked pastry pie shell.

ORANGE-MINCEMEAT PIE

Keep a baked pie shell in the freezer to make this mincemeat Bavarian pie

Baked 9" pie shell
  1   (9 oz.) pkg. mincemeat
  ½   c. water
  1   (3 oz.) pkg. orange flavor gelatin
  1   c. hot water
  ¼   c. chopped walnuts
  1   c. heavy cream, whipped

· Crumble mincemeat into a saucepan. Add ½ c. water and cook, stirring, until lumps are broken and mixture comes to a boil. Boil vigorously 1 minute. Cool.

· Dissolve gelatin in hot water. Chill until spoonful of mixture mounds slightly. Fold in mincemeat and walnuts, then whipped cream.

· Pour into pie shell. Chill until firm. (Garnish with additional whipped cream if you wish.)

ORANGE-LIME PIE

An orange and green hostess dessert

  2   (9") baked pie shells
  1   (3 oz.) pkg. orange flavor gelatin
  1   (3 oz.) pkg. lime flavor gelatin
  3   c. boiling water
  2   envelopes unflavored gelatin
  1   c. orange juice
  4   (11 oz.) cans mandarin oranges, drained
  2   c. heavy cream
  4   tblsp. sugar

· Prepare orange and lime gelatins as directed on package, but use only 1½ c. water each. Pour each into an 8" layer cake pan. Chill until firm.

· Sprinkle unflavored gelatin over orange juice to soften. Stir over hot water until dissolved. Chill until partially thickened. Stir cut-up orange segments into gelatin.

· Beat cream until stiff. Fold sugar into whipped cream, and fold into orange juice-gelatin mixture.

· Cut firm orange and lime gelatin into ½" cubes. Fold into whipped cream mixture; then spoon lightly into pie shells. Chill at least 3 hours before cutting, but use within 8 hours. Serve garnished with additional whipped cream, if desired, or with a few orange and green gelatin cubes (reserved). Makes 2 pies.

COFFEE-AND-CREAM PIE

You can garnish this rich pie with toasted almonds instead of coconut

Baked 9" pie shell
  2   c. heavy cream
  ½   c. sugar
  3   tblsp. instant coffee powder
  ⅛   tsp. salt
  ½   tsp. vanilla
  1   envelope unflavored gelatin
  ¼   c. cold water
  ½   c. toasted coconut

· Combine heavy cream, sugar, coffee, salt and vanilla in large mixer bowl. Beat until thick.

· Soften gelatin in water; heat over hot water until thoroughly dissolved.

· Gradually add the dissolved gelatin to the cream mixture and continue beating until well blended. Pour into pie shell. Sprinkle coconut over top. Chill at least 1 hour before serving. Makes 8 servings.

APRICOT COCONUT PIE

No fuss to make, mighty good to eat

9" Toasted Coconut Pie Shell
   (Chapter 2)
1   envelope unflavored gelatin
⅓   c. sugar
⅛   tsp. salt
1   (12 oz.) can apricot nectar
    (1½ c.)
1   tsp. lemon juice
4   drops almond extract
2   egg whites

• Combine gelatin, sugar and salt. Heat apricot nectar to boiling point. Add to gelatin mixture and stir until gelatin is dissolved. Add lemon juice and almond extract.

• Chill until mixture starts to thicken (consistency of unbeaten egg white). Beat egg whites until soft peaks form, fold into gelatin mixture and beat with rotary beater until mixture mounds when dropped from spoon. Turn into chilled pie shell. Garnish with a little coconut and chill.

RED AND GREEN CHRISTMAS PIE

This showy dessert will say Merry Christmas to all who sit at your table

2   (8") Graham Cracker Crumb
    Crusts (Chapter 2)
1   (3 oz.) pkg. lime flavor gelatin
2   c. hot water
1   c. sweetened canned grapefruit
    juice
1   (3 oz.) pkg. cherry flavor
    gelatin
1   c. orange juice

1   envelope unflavored gelatin
¼   c. cold water
1   c. pineapple juice
½   c. sugar
1   tsp. vanilla
½   c. heavy cream, whipped

• Dissolve lime gelatin in 1 c. hot water; add grapefruit juice. Pour into a shallow pan; chill. Dissolve cherry gelatin in remaining 1 c. hot water; add orange juice. Pour into a shallow pan; chill.

• Soften unflavored gelatin in ¼ c. cold water. Heat pineapple juice to boiling; add softened gelatin and stir until it is dissolved. Chill until mixture thickens (a little thicker than unbeaten egg white). Add sugar and vanilla to whipped cream and fold into pineapple-gelatin mixture.

• Cut lime and cherry gelatins in small cubes with a knife. Fold into pineapple and whipped-cream mixture, saving out a few cubes of both colors.

• Spoon into pie shells. Chill. To serve, garnish with reserved gelatin cubes and, if desired, with whipped cream. Makes 2 pies, 12 to 16 servings.

Note: You can substitute water for the grapefruit and orange juices; the pie will be less fruity in flavor, however.

MERRY CHRISTMAS PIE

A favorite holiday pie of many women who like to bring it to the table, uncut

Baked 9" pie shell
1   envelope unflavored gelatin
1   c. sugar

¼ c. flour
¼ tsp. salt
1 ¾ c. milk
½ c. heavy cream
¾ tsp. vanilla
¼ tsp. almond extract
3 egg whites
1 (3 ½ oz.) can flaked coconut
Maraschino cherries

· Combine gelatin, ½ c. sugar, flour and salt in medium-size saucepan. Gradually stir in milk. Cook over low heat, stirring constantly, until mixture comes to boil. Remove from heat, cool. If mixture becomes too stiff, beat with mixer or rotary beater until smooth.

· Whip cream; fold it, the vanilla and almond extract into cooked mixture.

· Beat egg whites until frothy. Gradually add remaining ½ c. sugar, beating until egg whites are stiff but not dry. Fold egg whites and coconut into gelatin mixture. Turn into pie shell. Chill 3 to 4 hours, or until firm. To serve, decorate with pieces of maraschino cherries.

GRAPE BAVARIAN PIE

A royal Western-ranch version of year-round Concord grape pie

Walnut Crumb Crust
1 envelope unflavored gelatin
¾ c. cold water

1 (6 oz.) can frozen grape juice
   concentrate
1 c. heavy cream, whipped

· Sprinkle gelatin over water in saucepan. Stir over low heat until gelatin dissolves. Remove from heat.

· Add grape juice concentrate. Stir until it is melted.

· Chill just until gelatin mixture is syrupy, about 5 minutes. Fold gelatin mixture into whipped cream. Pour mixture into crust. Chill until firm.

WALNUT CRUMB CRUST: Mix 1⅓ c. fine graham cracker crumbs, ¼ c. finely chopped walnuts, ½ tsp. each cinnamon, allspice and nutmeg and ¼ c. sugar. Blend in 6 tblsp. soft butter or margarine until mixture is crumbly. Press evenly onto bottom and sides of well-greased 9″ pie pan.

VARIATIONS

· For grape juice, substitute 1 (6 oz.) can frozen fruit juice concentrate—orange, tangerine, lemonade, limeade or cherry-lemon punch.

· For heavy cream, substitute 1 (6 oz.) can evaporated milk, whipped (freeze milk until ice crystals form around edge of bowl before whipping); or 1 (2 oz.) pkg. dessert topping mix, whipped; or ⅓ c. nonfat dry milk whipped with ⅓ c. ice water and 1 tblsp. lemon juice.

Company Pie to Make Ahead

Apple Cider Pie, regardless of where you bake it, will live up to the reputation it enjoys in a Michigan fruit-growing neighborhood where it originated. Orchard people and their friends give the pie a top rating. You can fix it in the morning, put it in the refrigerator and forget it until dinner- or suppertime.

APPLE CIDER PIE

At mealtime decorate with scoops of whipped cream and a few red candies

Baked 9" pie shell
1 ½ c. apple cider
2   tblsp. red cinnamon candies (red hots)
1   (3 oz.) pkg. lemon flavor gelatin
2   large apples
1   c. heavy cream, whipped

• Heat ¾ c. apple cider (apple juice if cider is not available) with red candies to boiling, stirring until candies are melted. Remove from heat, add gelatin, stirring until it dissolves. Add remaining ¾ c. cider. Chill until mixture thickens slightly.
• Quarter apples; peel, core and grate directly into gelatin. Stir after each apple quarter is grated to coat the apple with gelatin immediately.
• Fold in whipped cream.
• Pour into cooled pie shell. Chill until firm, at least 2 hours.

Exciting Chocolate Pies

You'll find wide variety in our chocolate refrigerator pies. Some of them are fancy enough to show off when you entertain and want to impress your guests. Others are simpler and ideal for family and less pretentious company meals. All are rich, but they're the kind chocolate lovers will rave about.

Do try all of the recipes to find out which ones please you most. In all the pie fillings in this Cookbook that call for unsweetened chocolate, packets of unsweetened liquid chocolate product for baking may be substituted. Just press the creamy mixture into the filling and skip the measuring and melting. The contents of each 1 oz. packet equal 1 square of unsweetened chocolate.

It's a good idea to remove chilled pies from the refrigerator about 20 minutes before serving. Just set them on the counter in the kitchen when you sit down to enjoy the main course.

These chocolate pies are excellent in plain pastry shells or Graham Cracker Crumb Crusts if you can't take time to make some of the more elaborate crusts.

CHOCOLATE PIE SPECTACULAR

A hostess' dream come true

Pecan Crumb Crust:
1   c. fine graham cracker crumbs
½   c. finely chopped pecans
⅓   c. brown sugar, firmly packed
⅓   c. melted shortening

Filling:
1   envelope unflavored gelatin
¼   c. cold milk
⅔   c. sugar
2   eggs, separated
¼   tsp. salt
1 ¼ c. scalded milk
1   tsp. vanilla
1   c. heavy cream, whipped
1   square semisweet chocolate, shaved
Chocolate Topping

Crust: Combine ingredients and press firmly into 9″ pie pan. Make even layer on bottom and sides of pan. Bake in slow oven (300°F.) 10 minutes. Cool.

Filling: Soften gelatin in cold milk.

• Combine ⅓ c. sugar, slightly beaten egg yolks, salt and scalded milk. Cook, stirring, over very low heat until mixture coats a metal spoon. Remove from heat, blend in softened gelatin and vanilla.

• Chill until mixture begins to thicken. Beat until light. Beat egg whites until frothy; gradually add remaining ⅓ c. sugar, beating until glossy, firm peaks form. Fold into gelatin mixture. Fold in whipped cream and shaved chocolate. Heap filling into cool Pecan Crumb Crust. Chill until firm. Drizzle on Chocolate Topping. Refrigerate or freeze until serving time. Cut in wedges with sharp knife. Makes 6 to 8 servings.

CHOCOLATE TOPPING: Heat ½ (6 oz.) pkg. semisweet chocolate pieces (½ c.) and 2 tsp. butter or margarine over hot, not boiling, water, until chocolate is just melted. Remove from heat; add 1 tblsp. hot water and stir until smooth. Immediately drizzle over top of pie.

CHOCOLATE MALT PIE

Crunchy nuts on smooth chocolate-malt filling make a distinctive pie

Baked 9″ pie shell
½ lb. large marshmallows (32)
½ c. milk
⅛ tsp. salt
½ c. semisweet chocolate pieces, ½ (6 oz.) pkg.

1 c. heavy cream
¼ c. chocolate malted milk powder
1 tsp. vanilla
⅓ c. chopped walnuts

• Combine marshmallows, milk and salt in top of double boiler. Cook over water, stirring constantly, until marshmallows are melted. Remove from heat.

• Add chocolate pieces, stirring until they are melted. Cool.

• Whip cream until stiff. Fold malted milk powder and vanilla into cream. Then fold into marshmallow mixture and pour into pie shell. Sprinkle walnuts over top. Chill several hours before serving.

CHOCOLATE TOFFEE PIE

This elegant, luscious pie topped with fruited Apple Snow—unusual

Toffee Crust

Filling:
1 (6 oz.) pkg. semisweet chocolate pieces
¼ c. water
2 tsp. instant coffee powder
3 egg yolks
⅛ tsp. salt
6 tblsp. sugar
3 egg whites
2 tsp. vanilla

Apple Snow:
1 egg white
⅓ c. sugar
1 tsp. finely grated lemon peel
⅛ tsp. salt
1 large unpeeled apple, freshly grated (1 c.)   *more*

Filling: Combine chocolate and water; melt chocolate over hot, not boiling, water. Add coffee powder and set aside to partially cool.

· Combine egg yolks, salt and 2 tblsp. sugar; beat until thick and lemon-colored. Combine slightly cooled chocolate and egg yolk mixtures, beating constantly. Cook in double boiler, stirring, 3 minutes. Remove from heat and cool 30 minutes.

· Beat egg whites until frothy; gradually add remaining 4 tblsp. sugar and vanilla, beating until glossy, firm peaks form. Fold egg whites into chocolate mixture; spoon into cool Toffee Crust. Chill until set.

Apple Snow: Beat egg white until foamy. Gradually add sugar, beating constantly. Blend in lemon peel and salt. Add apple; beat at least 10 minutes with electric mixer.

· Spread on filling in pie shell; sprinkle on reserved baked crumbs (from crust recipe). Refrigerate until serving time. Serve the same day. Makes 6 to 8 servings. Tint Apple Snow with a few drops of red food color for a most attractive pie.

TOFFEE CRUST

1   c. sifted flour
½   tsp. salt
1   tsp. granulated sugar
⅓   c. shortening
¼   c. brown sugar, firmly packed
¾   c. chopped pecans
1   square unsweetened chocolate, grated
1   tblsp. water
1   tsp. vanilla

· Sift together flour, salt and granulated sugar. Cut in shortening until mixture resembles small peas. Blend in brown sugar, pecans and chocolate. Mix well, reserving 1 tblsp. mixture. Add water and vanilla to remainder of mixture and press into well-greased 8″ pie pan, moistening fingers if necessary, to make pie shell.

· Bake in moderate oven (375°F.) 15 minutes. During last 5 minutes, bake the 1 tblsp. reserved crumb mixture, spread in a pan. Cool crust.

MOCHA PECAN PIE

Light and airy pecan treat for guests

Coffee Nut Crust
1   envelope unflavored gelatin
1   c. cold water
3   tblsp. cocoa
1   c. sugar
2   tsp. instant coffee powder
3   eggs, separated
1   tsp. vanilla
½   tsp. rum extract (optional)
¼   tsp. salt
¾   c. finely chopped pecans
½   c. heavy cream, whipped
Pecan halves for garnish

· Soften gelatin in ¼ c. water.
· Combine in saucepan cocoa, ¾ c. sugar, ¾ c. water and coffee powder, stirring to dissolve sugar. Bring to a boil and cook gently 4 to 5 minutes, stirring constantly. Remove from heat.
· Pour a little of hot mixture over slightly beaten egg yolks, mix and stir into remaining hot mixture. Cook until mixture thickens, about 5 minutes, stirring constantly. Remove from heat. Add vanilla, rum extract and softened gelatin. Stir until gelatin is dissolved. Chill until mixture mounds slightly when dropped from a spoon.
· Combine egg whites and salt and

beat until frothy; add remaining ¼ c. sugar gradually, beating until glossy, stiff peaks form.

• Fold pecans into gelatin mixture; then fold in egg whites. Spoon into cool Coffee Nut Crust. Chill until firm.

• To serve, garnish with spoonfuls of whipped cream arranged around edge of pie, placing a pecan half on each spoonful of whipped cream. Serves 8.

COFFEE NUT CRUST

7 tblsp. shortening
1 tsp. instant coffee powder
3 tblsp. hot water
1 tsp. milk
1 ¼ c. sifted flour
½ tsp. salt
¼ c. finely chopped pecans

• Combine softened shortening, coffee powder dissolved in hot water and milk. Whip with fork until thick and smooth. Combine flour and salt with shortening mixture. Roll between 2 (12″) squares waxed paper; peel off top paper and sprinkle with 2 tblsp. finely chopped pecans, leaving 1″ border plain. Replace paper and gently roll pecans into dough. Turn pastry over and repeat, using remaining 2 tblsp. pecans. Remove top paper.

• Fit into 9″ pie pan, remove paper; flute and prick pastry with fork.

• Bake in very hot oven (450°F.) 12 to 14 minutes. Cool in pan on rack.

MINTED CHOCOLATE PIE

Two-tone party pie you fix ahead— blend of flavors makes it outstanding

Baked 9″ pie shell
1 envelope unflavored gelatin
¾ c. sugar
2 c. milk
3 eggs, separated
1 tblsp. cornstarch
½ c. heavy cream, whipped
2 squares unsweetened chocolate, melted
¼ tsp. peppermint extract
Chocolate candy shot (jimmies)

• Combine gelatin and ½ c. sugar in top of double boiler. Gradually stir in milk and cook over boiling water until milk is scalded.

• Beat egg yolks with cornstarch to blend well. Gradually stir half of milk mixture into egg yolks. Return to double boiler and cook over boiling water, stirring constantly, until mixture is thickened. Cool, then chill until mixture starts to set.

• Beat egg whites until frothy. Beat in remaining ¼ c. sugar gradually, beating until stiff peaks form. Beat chilled custard mixture until fluffy. Fold in egg whites, then whipped cream.

• Divide mixture in half. Fold chocolate into one half and mint extract into other half. Spread chocolate filling into pie shell; chill 5 minutes. Top with mint filling. Chill several hours before serving. Garnish top with chocolate shot or shaved chocolate.

CHOCOLATE CHERRY PIE

This pie captures that marvelous taste of chocolate-coated cherries

9″ Vanilla Wafer Pie Shell (Chapter 2)
½ c. butter

more

¾ c. sugar
1 square unsweetened chocolate, melted and cooled
1 tsp. vanilla
2 eggs
2 tblsp. chopped maraschino cherries
Whipped cream
Maraschino cherries (whole)

· Cream butter and sugar together until smooth. Blend in chocolate and vanilla.
· Add eggs, one at a time, beating 5 minutes after each addition. Stir in chopped cherries.
· Spread into pie shell and chill 3 to 4 hours. Serve topped with whipped cream, garnished with maraschino cherry flowers. Makes 8 servings.

Note: To make cherry flowers, slit cherries from stem end almost to opposite end 8 times, spacing slits evenly.

CHOCOLATE PEPPERMINT-CANDY PIE

A beauty in looks and taste—pretty pink filling frosted with chocolate

Baked 9″ pie shell
1 envelope unflavored gelatin
¼ c. cold water
2 eggs, separated
1 ¼ c. milk
½ c. crushed peppermint-stick candy
½ c. heavy cream, whipped
Few drops red food color
⅛ tsp. salt
¼ c. sugar
Chocolate Topping

· Soften gelatin in water.
· Combine egg yolks with milk. Cook in top of double boiler or over low heat until mixture coats a metal spoon.
· Add gelatin and candy. Stir until both are dissolved. Chill until slightly thickened.
· Fold in cream and food color.
· Add salt to egg whites. Beat until they hold soft peaks. Add sugar gradually, beating until stiff.
· Fold in pink mixture.
· Pour into baked pie shell; chill until firm.
· Spread with Chocolate Topping.

CHOCOLATE TOPPING

1 ½ squares unsweetened chocolate
6 tblsp. butter or margarine
6 tblsp. confectioners sugar
1 egg yolk
1 tsp. water
¼ c. pecan halves

· Melt chocolate.
· Cream together butter and sugar. Add chocolate and egg yolk. Add water and mix thoroughly.
· Spread over top of pie. Garnish rim with pecan halves.

Note: Chocolate Topping won't crack if knife is dipped in hot water. Or leave pie at room temperature for 20 minutes before cutting.

TWO-TONE PIE

Black-and-white spectacular pie

Baked 9″ pie shell
1 envelope unflavored gelatin
¼ c. cold water

2   c. milk, scalded
4   eggs, separated
1   c. sugar
2   tblsp. cornstarch
2   squares unsweetened chocolate
2   tsp. vanilla
¼   tsp. cream of tartar

• Soften gelatin in water.
• Add milk to egg yolks and beat with rotary beater.
• Mix ½ c. sugar and cornstarch; add to milk and eggs. Cook in top of double boiler or over low heat until thickened, stirring constantly. Remove from heat. Reserve 1 c. of mixture.

• Add gelatin to remaining mixture and stir until gelatin is dissolved.
• Melt 1½ squares chocolate and add to reserved cup of cream filling. Add 1 tsp. vanilla and beat with rotary beater. Cool. Pour chocolate filling into pie shell and chill.
• Beat egg whites until frothy; add cream of tartar and beat until stiff; add remaining sugar gradually, beating until stiff. When gelatin mixture is slightly thickened, fold in egg whites and remaining vanilla.
• Pour into pie shell, covering the chocolate layer. Chill thoroughly. Grate remaining ½ square chocolate. Sprinkle over top.

Praiseworthy Ice Cream Pies

When man first topped his wedge of pie with ice cream, he discovered one of this country's best dessert combinations. And the cook who first put ice cream into a pie shell and topped it with crushed, red-ripe strawberries or glossy chocolate sauce created a fabulous dessert.

Take your pick of our ice cream pies, fancy or plain, and then, using them as guides, try other combinations. It's difficult to go wrong when you put pastry and ice cream together, but you do need a freezer or a freezing compartment in the refrigerator to insure success.

Precaution: When topping ice cream pies with meringue that's browned quickly in a very hot oven, use especial care to select unbroken eggs, washed clean. (The meringue is not baked long enough to destroy the bacteria that cause salmonellosis, a form of food poisoning.)

LEMON-LAYERED ALASKA PIE

Spectacular dessert for a party—ready to brown quickly at serving time

Baked 9″ pie shell
6   tblsp. butter
1   tsp. grated lemon peel
⅓   c. lemon juice
⅛   tsp. salt
1   c. sugar
2   eggs
2   egg yolks
1   qt. vanilla ice cream
Meringue (3 egg whites)

• Melt butter in top of double boiler. Add lemon peel and juice, salt and sugar. Combine eggs and egg yolks and beat slightly. Stir into butter mixture and cook over boiling water, beating constantly with a wire whisk until thick and smooth. Cool.

· Spread half of ice cream over bottom of cooled pie shell. Freeze firm. Spread half of cooled lemon mixture over ice cream. Freeze firm. Cover with remaining ice cream; freeze firm. Cover with remaining lemon mixture; freeze firm.

· Spread fluffy meringue on pie, completely covering filling (see Perfect Meringue for Topping Pies, Chapter 9). Make certain meringue extends to edges. Pie may be frozen and baked later or baked at once.

· To bake, place pie on board. Put into extremely hot oven (500°F.) 3 to 5 minutes, or until meringue is lightly browned. Serve immediately. Makes 6 servings.

PUMPKIN PIE ALASKA

A showy dessert to serve on special occasions. It's as good as it looks

Unbaked 10″ pie shell
1   egg
3   egg yolks
1½ c. dark brown sugar
1   tsp. cinnamon
1   tsp. pumpkin pie spice
½   tsp. salt
¼   tsp. nutmeg
¼   c. maple syrup
1   (1 lb.) can pumpkin (2 c.)
1½ c. evaporated milk
1   pt. butter brickle ice cream
Brown Sugar Meringue

· Beat egg and egg yolks slightly. Blend in sugar, spices, maple syrup,

pumpkin and milk. Pour into pie shell. Bake in hot oven (425°F.) 45 minutes. Cool and then chill thoroughly.

· Line 9″ pie pan with waxed paper. Press ice cream evenly into pie pan; return to freezer and freeze until solid.

· At serving time, turn ice cream out on top of pie. Spread Brown Sugar Meringue over top, sealing well at edges. Bake in extremely hot oven (500°F.) until lightly browned, 2 to 3 minutes. Serve at once. Makes 8 servings.

BROWN SUGAR MERINGUE

3   egg whites
¼   tsp. cream of tartar
2   tsp. vanilla
⅓   c. brown sugar

· Combine egg whites and cream of tartar. Beat until soft peaks form. Add vanilla. Gradually add sugar, beating until stiff peaks form.

FROZEN CHERRY MIX

Extends cherries if crop is short— freeze it for use in pies all winter

5   qts. stemmed tart red cherries
2   (1 lb. 4 oz.) cans crushed pineapple, drained
8   c. sugar
8   tsp. ascorbic acid powder
2   tsp. cinnamon
⅛   tsp. cloves
2   (1¾ oz.) pkgs. powdered fruit pectin

· Pit cherries, chop coarsely. (Fruit and juice should measure about 12 cups.)

· Drain juice from cherries and reserve.

· Add pineapple to cherries.

· Combine sugar, ascorbic acid powder and spices. Add to cherries and pineapple; mix well. Let stand to dissolve sugar.

· Combine pectin and cherry juice in large saucepan. Heat to a full rolling boil; boil 1 minute, stirring constantly. Add to cherry mixture; stir for 2 minutes. Ladle into containers. Seal. Allow to stand at room temperature until set (about 8 to 10 hours). Freeze. Makes 10 pints.

CHERRY-COCONUT ICE CREAM PIE

A new cherry pie from our Test Kitchens—perfect blend of flavors

1 ⅓ c. flaked coconut
2 tblsp. butter or margarine, melted
¼ c. graham cracker crumbs
2 tblsp. sugar
1 qt. vanilla ice cream
1 c. Frozen Cherry Mix

· Combine coconut and butter; mix well. Add crumbs and sugar, mixing thoroughly. Press firmly on bottom and sides of 8″ pie pan. Bake in moderate oven (375°F.) 10 to 12 minutes, or until lightly browned. Cool.

· Soften ice cream and spread in coconut shell. Spread Frozen Cherry Mix over top and freeze.

· Thaw just enough to soften so that pie may be cut in wedges.

PINK PARTY PIE

A FARM JOURNAL *5-star recipe—a favorite in our* TIMESAVING COOKBOOK

Baked 9″ Pink Pie Shell
1 qt. strawberry ice cream
1 (10 oz.) pkg. frozen strawberries
Meringue (2 egg whites)
Few drops red food color

· Pile softened ice cream into cool pie shell and spread evenly. Freeze overnight.

· To serve, heat oven to extremely hot (500°F.). Meanwhile, make meringue (see Perfect Meringue for Topping Pies, Chapter 9), tinting it a pretty pink.

· Arrange berries over ice cream and top with meringue, covering filling completely so heat will not melt ice cream.

· Set pie on wooden breadboard in extremely hot oven (500°F.) and bake about 5 minutes, or until lightly browned. Serve immediately.

PINK PIE SHELL: Make pastry (or use pie-crust mix), adding enough red food color (about 4 drops) to the water to make pink crust.

VARIATION

FRESH STRAWBERRY PINK PIE: Substitute fresh for frozen berries. Place 2 c. ripe berries in baked pie shell, cover with 1 pt. vanilla ice cream and then with pink meringue. Brown meringue as directed for Pink Party Pie. Or use 1 c. each frozen strawberries and sliced peaches for an exotic pie.

STRAWBERRY MARSHMALLOW PIE

Pretty pie with strawberry-pink top-knot—a hostess special

Baked 9" pie shell
16   marshmallows
2   tblsp. strawberry juice
Few drops red food color
2   egg whites
¼   tsp. salt
¼   c. sugar
¾   qt. vanilla ice cream
1   c. fresh strawberries, sliced

· Melt marshmallows in strawberry juice over low heat, folding with spoon until mixture is smooth. Add food color and cool.

· Combine egg whites and salt; beat until frothy. Add sugar gradually and beat until they hold glossy, stiff peaks. Then gently whip in cooled marshmallow mixture.

· Fill pastry pie shell with ice cream, spreading evenly. Cover with strawberries. Top with marshmallow mixture swirled attractively. Hurry to broiler and broil to brown lightly.

· Tuck a few choice unstemmed berries in marshmallow swirls and serve at once.

Note: The country cook who cherishes this recipe and shares it finds it is convenient to spread the slightly softened ice cream in the pie shell, then freeze it until firm.

STRAWBERRY ICE CREAM PIE

One of the best strawberry pies. It's often called Strawberry Parfait Pie

Baked 9" pie shell
1   (3 oz.) pkg. strawberry flavor gelatin
1¼   c. boiling water
1   pt. vanilla ice cream
1½   c. sliced fresh strawberries, sweetened to taste (about ¼ c. sugar)
Whipped cream

· Dissolve gelatin in boiling water in 2 qt. saucepan. Add spoonfuls of ice cream gradually, stirring until it is melted. Chill until mixture is thickened, but do not let it set. Fold in strawberries.

· Pour into pie shell and chill until firm, 25 to 35 minutes. Serve garnished with whipped cream and, if desired, a few whole or sliced berries.

VARIATIONS

DOUBLE STRAWBERRY: Use strawberry instead of vanilla ice cream.

FROZEN STRAWBERRY: Use 1 (10 oz.) pkg. frozen strawberry halves, drained, instead of fresh berries and use strawberry juice for part of water. Use vanilla ice cream.

RASPBERRY: Use raspberry flavor gelatin and fresh raspberries, sweetened to taste (about ¼ c. sugar) and vanilla ice cream.

PEACH: Use lemon flavor gelatin, sliced fresh peaches, sweetened to taste (about ¼ c. sugar) and vanilla ice cream. Add ¼ tsp. almond extract.

ORANGE-BANANA: Use orange flavor gelatin, ½ c. sliced bananas, ½ c. drained fresh orange sections, 2 tsp. grated orange peel and vanilla ice cream. Garnish pie with puffs of whipped cream, banana slices and a little diced orange.

MERINGUE: At serving time, omit whipped cream. Top pie with a meringue made with 2 egg whites (Chapter 9). Seal well around pastry edges. Place in preheated broiler for 3 minutes, just long enough to lightly brown meringue. Serve at once.

LEMON: Use lemon flavor gelatin, 1 tsp. grated lemon peel, 3 tblsp. lemon juice and vanilla ice cream. Garnish pie with whipped cream, strips of lemon peel and, if you have them, a few fresh mint leaves.

POPCORN ICE CREAM PIE

Novel party dessert teen-agers like

2   qts. unsalted popped corn
1   c. toasted coconut
1   c. sugar
1   c. light corn syrup
½   c. butter or margarine
¼   c. water
2   tsp. salt
1   tsp. vanilla
1   qt. vanilla ice cream
Chocolate sauce (optional)

· Put popped corn and coconut in large buttered bowl.
· Combine sugar, syrup, butter, water and salt in heavy saucepan. Bring to a boil over medium heat, stirring until sugar melts. Continue cooking until mixture reaches hard crack stage (290° to 295°F.). Remove from heat and stir in vanilla.
· Pour syrup in fine stream over popped corn, stirring until all kernels are evenly coated.
· Divide in half and pat mixture on 2 greased baking sheets or pizza pans to make 2 (10") rounds. Cool. Mark both circles with knife in wedge-shaped servings.
· Spread one layer with ice cream and top with second layer. Store in freezer. Cut in wedges to serve. Pass chocolate sauce to pour over. Makes 8 servings.

FROSTED ICE CREAM PIE

People of all ages are enchanted with this gala 3-layer frozen pie

9" Chocolate Wafer Crumb Crust
   (Chapter 2)
1½ pts. vanilla or peppermint-stick
   ice cream
Chocolate Frosting

· Fill chilled crust with ice cream, softened at room temperature just enough to spread. Freeze.
· When pie is frozen, quickly spread Chocolate Frosting on top of ice cream and return to freezer for several hours or overnight. Makes 6 servings.

CHOCOLATE FROSTING: In double boiler, over hot, not boiling, water, melt 2 squares unsweetened chocolate. Remove from heat. Gradually beat in ½ c. confectioners sugar and 1 tblsp. hot water. Add 1 egg, beating thoroughly, and 3 tblsp. soft butter or margarine, 1 tblsp. at a time. Beat until smooth.

VARIATIONS

· Use graham cracker or other crumb crusts instead of Chocolate Wafer Crumb Crust.
· Substitute different flavors of ice cream for the vanilla or peppermint stick.

STRAWBERRY SOCIAL PIE

Simple, but oh so good

Baked 9" Graham Cracker Crumb
  Crust (Chapter 2)
1   qt. strawberry ice cream
1   pt. fresh strawberries
Heavy cream, whipped

· Let ice cream soften slightly at
room temperature. Spread into cool
crumb crust. Place in freezer.
· To serve, cut in wedges and garnish
with ripe strawberries, sweetened, and
whipped cream.

VARIATIONS

PEACH ICE CREAM PIE: Substitute vanilla or peach ice cream for strawberry ice cream. Serve with sliced,
sweetened peaches and whipped
cream. If peaches must stand in refrigerator before serving, add a commercial color protector to them as directed
on label. Or sprinkle with lemon
juice.

PEACH-BLUEBERRY ICE CREAM PIE:
Top crumb crust, filled with peach
ice cream, with blueberries, crushed
lightly and sweetened. Whipped cream
garnish is optional.

BLUEBERRY ICE CREAM PIE: Fill Gingersnap Crumb Crust (Chapter 2)
with vanilla ice cream. Serve topped
with crushed and sweetened blueberries.

GINGER PEACH ICE CREAM PIE: Serve
vanilla ice cream or lemon sherbet in
Gingersnap Crumb Crust (Chapter 2)
and top with sweetened sliced peaches.

Note: Choose your favorite ice cream
and crumb crust for these homey ice
cream pies. Instead of topping with
sweetened fruit or berries, top with a
meringue (3 egg whites and 6 tblsp.
sugar), spreading to edges. Place on
board and brown in extremely hot
oven (500°F.). Serve with chocolate
or other sweet sauce, or freeze for use
later.

Pies with Ice Cream Crusts

Among the recipes that our readers
rate high are the double ice cream
treats—ice cream for the crust and in
the filling. Women tell us they use
these recipes year after year, especially to serve guests.

These desserts originated in the
kitchen of a Kansas farm homemaker
and made their debut in our COUNTRY
COOKBOOK. Their long record of success prompted us to bestow our high-

est honor—they rank among FARM
JOURNAL's 5-star specials. The pies not
only taste remarkably good, but they
also are quite easy to fix. And they're
handy to keep in the freezer to bring
out when you need a wonderful dessert.

Some women tell us they pass a
sweet sauce to pour over the wedges
of pie. And one hostess offers her party
guests a choice of sauces and a variety

of chopped nuts so they can have the fun of dressing up their pie servings. Almost all the farm women who wrote us about these frozen pies said they vary the pie shells by using different kinds of ice cream. So let imagination be your guide!

ICE CREAM PIE SHELL

· Line 8″ pie pan with 1 pt. vanilla or favorite ice cream flavor. For a more generous "crust," use 1½ pts. Cut ice cream in ½″ slices; lay on bottom of pan to cover. Cut remaining slices in half; arrange around pan to make rim. Fill spots with ice cream where needed. With tip of spoon, smooth "crust." Freeze until firm before adding the filling.

CRANBERRY NUT PIE

The gala, all-around favorite is one of FARM JOURNAL'S *5-star specials*

Ice Cream Pie Shell
2 c. fresh or frozen raw cranberries
1 c. sugar
1 c. heavy cream
½ c. chopped nuts

· Put cranberries through food chopper, using fine blade. (Grind your cranberries frozen—less juicy.) Add sugar; let stand overnight.
· Whip cream. Mix cranberries and nuts. Fold in whipped cream. Pour into Ice Cream Pie Shell. Freeze. To serve, cut in wedges.

CHOCOLATE PEPPERMINT PIE

Use pink-and-white peppermint ice cream shells to hold chocolate filling

2 Pink Peppermint Ice Cream Pie Shells
1 tblsp. cocoa
½ c. sugar
1 (4 oz.) pkg. chocolate pudding mix
1 tsp. vanilla
2 c. heavy cream

· Combine cocoa and sugar. Add to pudding mix and prepare as directed on package. Cool; add vanilla.
· Whip cream and fold into chocolate mixture. Pour into Peppermint Ice Cream Pie Shells. Freeze. To serve, cut in wedges.

BUTTERSCOTCH PECAN PIE

Flavor blend makes this pie memorable

2 Ice Cream Pie Shells
¼ c. brown sugar
1 (4 oz.) pkg. butterscotch pudding or pie filling mix
1 tsp. vanilla
2 c. heavy cream
½ c. chopped pecans

· Add sugar to pudding mix. Prepare as directed on package. Cool; then add vanilla.
· Whip cream. Add nuts to butterscotch mixture. Fold in whipped cream. Pour into Ice Cream Pie Shells. Freeze. To serve, cut in wedges.

VARIATION

· Omit nuts and use butter-pecan ice cream shell.

SPICY PUMPKIN PIE

A frozen pie that's spiced just right

Ice Cream Pie Shell
1   c. cooked or canned pumpkin
1   c. sugar
¼   tsp. salt
¼   tsp. ginger
1   tsp. cinnamon
¼   tsp. nutmeg
1   c. heavy cream

• Mix together pumpkin, sugar, salt and spices. Cook over low heat 3 minutes. Cool.
• Whip cream; fold into pumpkin mixture. Pour into Ice Cream Pie Shell. Freeze. To serve, cut in wedges.

FROZEN STRAWBERRY VANILLA PIE

Good as strawberries and ice cream

2   Ice Cream Pie Shells
1   (10 oz.) pkg. frozen strawberries, sliced (use fresh ones in season)
2   c. heavy cream
¼   c. confectioners sugar
½   tsp. vanilla
Red food color

• Partially thaw berries.
• Whip cream; add sugar, vanilla and food color. Fold in strawberries. Pour into Ice Cream Pie Shells. Freeze. To serve, cut in wedges.

SWEET 'N' TART LEMON PIE

Marvelous team: lemon and ice cream

Ice Cream Pie Shell
3   eggs
½   c. sugar
¼   tsp. salt
¼   c. lemon juice
1   c. heavy cream

• Beat together 1 whole egg and 2 yolks. Add sugar, salt and lemon juice. Cook over low heat, stirring constantly until thick. Cool.
• Beat egg whites until stiff; then whip cream (no need to wash beaters). Fold cream into lemon mixture. Next, fold in whites. Pour into Ice Cream Pie Shell. Freeze. To serve, cut in wedges.

NO-COOK PIE

When the weather is warm and appetites need tempting, make an All Ice Cream Pie for a supper treat. Here are directions:
• Chill a 9″ pie pan in freezer about 10 minutes. Set a pint carton of chocolate ice cream on the kitchen counter to soften during this 10 minutes. Spoon the slightly softened ice cream smoothly on bottom and sides of chilled pie pan to make pie shell. Return to freezer to freeze firm. Then spread slightly softened strawberry ice cream in chocolate ice cream pie shell. Return to freezer to freeze firm.
• Top the pie with slightly softened vanilla ice cream to make a snowy coverlet. Sprinkle with chopped nuts, if desired. Freeze at least 1 hour before serving. Cut in wedges. If you have chocolate or other sweet dessert sauce in the refrigerator, pass it for pouring over dessert.

Angel Pies Deserve Their Name

Angel pies have crisp, golden meringue crusts and cream or ice cream fillings. They are a glamorous way to use egg whites. Whipped cream and fruits are among the favorite other ingredients. These are elegant desserts not difficult to perfect if recipe directions are followed.

You can freeze the meringue crusts successfully (see Chapter 2).

CHOCOLATE ANGEL PIE

A FARM JOURNAL *5-star special and a favorite from* COUNTRY COOKBOOK

Walnut Meringue Pie Shell
- ¾ c. semisweet chocolate pieces
- ¼ c. hot water
- 1 tsp. vanilla
- ⅛ tsp. salt
- 1 c. heavy cream, whipped

· Melt chocolate pieces in double boiler over not, not boiling, water. Add hot water, vanilla and salt. Cook and stir until smooth. Cool.

· Fold in whipped cream and pour into Walnut Meringue Pie Shell. Chill 4 hours or overnight. Spread thin layer of whipped cream over top when serving, if desired.

WALNUT MERINGUE PIE SHELL: Combine 3 egg whites, ⅛ tsp. salt, ¼ tsp. cream of tartar and ½ tsp. vanilla. Beat until soft peaks form. Add ¾ c. sugar gradually, beating until very stiff and sugar is dissolved. Spread over bottom and sides of greased 9″ pie pan. Build up sides. (Use cake decorator for fancy edge.) Sprinkle ⅓ c. chopped pecans or walnuts on bottom of pie shell. Bake in very slow oven (275°F.) 1 hour. Cool.

CHOCOLATE-BAR ANGEL PIE

A most delicious chocolate-almond pie to make a day before your party

- 9″ Meringue Pie Shell (Chapter 2)
- 3 (1 ½ oz.) milk-chocolate almond candy bars
- 3 tblsp. water
- 1 tsp. vanilla
- 1 c. heavy cream, whipped

· Melt candy bars with water; add vanilla and cool. Fold into whipped cream (sweeten whipped cream with sifted confectioners sugar, if desired). Pour into Meringue Pie Shell. Chill 24 hours. Makes 6 to 8 servings.

CHERRY ANGEL PIE

Elegant and fancy-looking dessert for special occasions—tastes scrumptious

- 10″ Meringue Pie Shell (Chapter 2)
- 1 (1 lb. 4 oz.) can sweetened frozen cherries, thawed
- 1 envelope unflavored gelatin
- ¼ c. cold water
- ¼ c. confectioners sugar   *more*

½   tsp. vanilla
1   c. heavy cream, whipped
½   c. shredded coconut
¼   c. chopped pecans

• Simmer cherries 5 minutes. Drain and cool. Soften gelatin in cold water. Heat 1 c. cherry juice to boiling. Add softened gelatin and stir until it is dissolved. Remove from heat, cool and chill until mixture thickens to the consistency of syrup. Beat until fluffy.

• Beat confectioners sugar and vanilla into whipped cream. Fold into gelatin mixture. Fold in cherries, coconut and nuts. Spread into cooled Meringue Pie Shell. Chill several hours. Makes 8 servings.

ORANGE ANGEL PIE

Showy dessert to fix ahead for guests

9"   Meringue Pie Shell (Chapter 2)
4   egg yolks
1   whole egg
⅔   c. sugar
¼   c. frozen orange juice concentrate
1   tblsp. lemon juice
1   c. heavy cream, whipped

• Beat egg yolks and whole egg until thick and lemon-colored. Beat in sugar, concentrated orange juice and lemon juice. Cook over simmering

water, stirring constantly, until thick. It should be thick enough to mound slightly when dropped from spoon. Chill, stirring several times.

• Fold whipped cream into cold orange mixture. Pile into Meringue Pie Shell. Chill at least 12 hours or overnight. Garnish at serving time, if desired, with spoonfuls of extra cream (½ c.), whipped. Makes 6 to 8 servings.

LEMON ANGEL PIE

Gay as a daisy—meringue holds white-capped billows of lemon filling

9"   Meringue Pie Shell (Chapter 2)
4   egg yolks
½   c. sugar
¼   c. lemon juice
1   tblsp. grated lemon peel
1   c. heavy cream, whipped

• Beat egg yolks until thick and lemon-colored. Gradually beat in sugar. Stir in lemon juice and peel. Cook over simmering water, stirring constantly, until mixture is thick, about 5 to 8 minutes. Mixture should be thick enough to mound slightly when dropped from spoon. Cool.

• Spread cool lemon mixture into Meringue Pie Shell. Top with whipped cream. Chill 12 hours or overnight. Makes 6 to 8 servings.

Soda Cracker Pie Shells

Good country cooks make many pie crusts with graham cracker crumbs. Some of them also use soda and round buttery crackers in egg whites

to produce crisp, meringue-type pie crusts. Here are three recipes typical of many cracker desserts made in farm kitchens.

RANCH-STYLE PEACH PIE

Peaches and cream in crisp pie shell

3   egg whites
1   c. sugar
12 soda crackers, crushed (⅓ c.)
½   c. finely chopped pecans
¼   tsp. baking powder
1   tsp. vanilla
2   c. heavy cream
1   (1 lb.) can peach halves

· Beat egg whites until soft peaks form when beater is lifted. Add sugar, 2 tblsp. at a time, beating after each addition. Beat to stiff peaks.
· Fold in crackers, pecans, baking powder and vanilla. Spread on bottom and sides of a greased 9″ pie pan.
· Bake in slow oven (325°F.) 30 minutes. Cool.
· An hour or two before serving, whip cream. Drain peaches and slice very thin. Save out a few peach slices for garnishing. Alternate layers of cream and peaches in pie shell, having top layer of the cream. Place in refrigerator. Just before serving, garnish top of pie with reserved peach slices. Makes 6 to 8 servings.

VARIATION

· Substitute fresh peaches, sliced and lightly sweetened, for the canned fruit.

Note: The Montana ranchwoman who shares this recipe often puts the canned peaches and whipped cream in the crust and refrigerates overnight.

EASY PECAN PIE

Party pie with crisp cracker-nut crust from our TIMESAVING COOKBOOK

20 round buttery crackers, crushed
1   c. chopped pecans
1   c. sugar
3   egg whites
1   tsp. vanilla
½   c. heavy cream, whipped
½   c. flaked or shredded coconut

· Combine crackers, pecans and ½ c. sugar.
· Beat egg whites until stiff; gradually beat in remaining sugar and vanilla. Fold into cracker mixture.
· Spread on bottom and sides of greased 9″ pie pan to make pie shell. Bake in slow oven (325°F.) 30 minutes. Cool.
· Fill with whipped cream and sprinkle with coconut just before serving.

VARIATION

EASY WALNUT PIE: Substitute walnuts for pecans.

DATE-NUT PIE

Tasty with dates, ice cream and nuts from our TIMESAVING COOKBOOK

12 soda crackers, crushed
½   c. chopped walnuts
12 dates, chopped
3   egg whites
½   tsp. baking powder
¾   c. sugar
½   tsp. vanilla
1   pt. vanilla ice cream   *more*

• Combine crackers, nuts and dates. Beat egg whites until frothy; add baking powder. Continue beating, adding sugar gradually, until mixture forms stiff peaks. Beat in vanilla.
• Fold cracker mixture into egg whites. Spread on bottom and sides of greased 9″ pie pan to make pie shell.
• Bake in slow oven (325°F.) 25 to 30 minutes. Fill with spoonfuls of vanilla ice cream just before serving.

Country Cheese Pies

Serving slices of cheese with pie is a farm custom of long standing. Now pie fillings containing cheese, usually cream and cottage types, are becoming favorites. Here are recipes for some of them—pies that inspire bouquets to the cook.

OHIO CHEESE PIE

Prediction: This is the best cheese pie you've ever made or tasted

Crust:
2 ½ c. graham cracker crumbs
½ c. melted butter or margarine
1 tsp. cinnamon
⅓ c. sugar

Filling:
1 (12 oz.) carton cottage cheese
2 (8 oz.) pkgs. cream cheese
1 ½ c. sugar
4 eggs, beaten
1 tsp. vanilla
1 tblsp. lemon peel
⅓ c. lemon juice

Topping:
½ pt. heavy cream
1 pt. dairy sour cream
3 tblsp. sugar

Crust: Combine ingredients, mixing well. Pat into 2 (9″) cake pans. Bake

5 minutes in hot oven (400°F.). Cool. *Filling:* Sieve cottage cheese. Combine with other ingredients and whip until stiff. Pour into crust-lined pans; bake in moderate oven (350°F.) 30 minutes. Cool.
Topping: Whip heavy cream until very stiff. Combine with sour cream and sugar; spread over top. Chill. Makes 12 servings.

HAWAIIAN CHEESE PIE

Cooling and nourishing summer pie— flute shell high to hold filling

Baked 9″ pie shell
1 (1 lb. 4 oz.) can crushed pineapple
½ c. sugar
⅛ tsp. salt
1 envelope unflavored gelatin
2 eggs, separated
1 c. cottage cheese
1 tsp. grated lemon peel
2 tblsp. lemon juice
½ c. heavy cream, whipped
⅓ c. flaked coconut

• Drain pineapple, reserving syrup. Combine ¼ c. sugar, salt, gelatin, ¾ c. pineapple syrup and slightly beaten egg yolks. Cook over low heat, stirring constantly, until mixture thickens slightly and coats metal spoon. Remove from heat.

• Press cottage cheese through sieve. Stir cheese, pineapple, lemon peel and juice into gelatin mixture.

• Beat egg whites until frothy. Gradually beat in remaining ¼ c. sugar, beating until stiff peaks form. Fold egg whites and whipped cream into pineapple mixture. Pour into pie shell and garnish with coconut. Chill until firm before serving.

CHOCOLATE CHEESE PIE

Heavenly, but serve small portions to the dieters at your table

9" Chocolate Graham Crust
1 (6 oz.) pkg. semisweet chocolate pieces
1 (8 oz.) pkg. cream cheese, softened
¾ c. light brown sugar
⅛ tsp. salt
1 tsp. vanilla
2 eggs, separated
1 c. heavy cream, whipped

• Melt chocolate over hot (not boiling) water; cool about 10 minutes.

• Blend cream cheese, ½ c. sugar, salt and vanilla. Beat in egg yolks, one at a time. Beat in cooled chocolate. Blend well.

• Beat egg whites until stiff but not dry. Gradually beat in ¼ c. sugar; beat until stiff and glossy.

• Fold chocolate mixture into beaten whites. Fold in whipped cream.

• Pour into chilled crust, reserving ¼ of mixture for decorating. Chill until filling sets slightly. With tapered spoon, drop reserved mixture in mounds over top of pie. Chill overnight. Makes 8 servings.

CHOCOLATE GRAHAM CRUST: Mix thoroughly 1½ c. graham cracker crumbs, ¼ c. brown sugar, ⅛ tsp. nutmeg, ⅓ c. melted butter or margarine and 1 square unsweetened chocolate, melted. Press into 9" pie pan. Chill until firm.

SHORT-CUT CHOCOLATE CHEESE PIE

This dieters' version of the preceding recipe has less filling, fewer calories

9" Chocolate Graham Crust (see preceding recipe)
1 (6 oz.) pkg. semisweet chocolate pieces
1 (3 oz.) pkg. cream cheese, softened
¼ c. light brown sugar
1 (2 oz.) pkg. dessert topping mix

• Melt chocolate over hot (not boiling) water. Remove from heat. Stir in the cheese until it is blended. Stir in sugar.

• Prepare topping mix as directed on package; blend ½ c. into chocolate mixture. Fold in remaining topping.

• Spread filling in crust. Chill overnight. Makes 8 servings.

RASPBERRY-CHEESE PIE

A show-off pie for little effort—fix it several hours ahead

Baked 9" pie shell
1 (3 oz.) pkg. raspberry flavor gelatin
2 tblsp. sugar
1¼ c. hot water   *more*

1 (16 oz.) pkg. frozen raspberries
1 (3 oz.) pkg. cream cheese
2 tblsp. milk
Sweetened whipped cream

· Dissolve gelatin and sugar in hot water. Add unthawed berries and stir to break them up. Gelatin thickens as berries thaw.
· Blend cream cheese with milk. Spread over bottom of cool pie shell.
· Pour partially set gelatin mixture over cheese in pie shell. Refrigerate until set.
· Serve garnished with spoonfuls of whipped cream.

FROZEN ORANGE PIE

Country cook's dream come true: this exciting pie ready in freezer

Baked 10" Graham Cracker Crumb
   Crust (Chapter 2)

4 eggs, separated
¾ c. sugar
1 tblsp. grated orange peel
¼ c. orange juice
1 c. heavy cream, whipped

· Beat egg yolks slightly; combine with sugar, orange peel and juice. Cook over boiling water, stirring constantly, until thickened. Cool.
· Fold stiffly beaten egg whites and whipped cream into the cooled orange mixture. Pour into crust. Chill.
· Freeze pie. Remove from freezer, package in moisture-vaporproof wrapping and return to freezer.
· Let stand at room temperature 10 minutes before serving. Do not thaw completely. Makes 8 servings.

Pie Inspired by Hawaiian Cooks

We've discovered a make-ahead pie that tastes like Grandmother's gingerbread, layered with banana slices and crowned with whipped cream. That means it's really good. You can get the pie ready in the morning and refrigerate it for noontime or evening guests.

The banana and ginger combination is a favorite in Hawaiian homes, where big-leafed banana trees with their bunches of pale-yellow fruit often grow near kitchen doors.

BANANA GINGER PIE

Serve frosty cold with hot coffee

9" Gingersnap Crumb Crust (Chapter 2)
1   envelope unflavored gelatin
⅔   c. sugar
¾   c. water
1   tsp. grated lemon peel
3   tblsp. lemon juice
3   medium bananas
2   egg whites, unbeaten
Whipped cream

· Mix gelatin and sugar in top of double boiler; add water. Place over boiling water and cook, stirring constantly, until gelatin is dissolved. Remove from heat.

· Add lemon peel and juice and 1 c. mashed bananas (2 bananas) to gelatin mixture and chill until mixture mounds when dropped from a spoon. Add egg whites and beat with rotary beater until mixture begins to hold its shape. (If necessary, chill briefly until mixture mounds when dropped from spoon.) Spoon into crust and chill. At serving time, peel and slice remaining banana; dip slices in lemon juice. Spread top of pie with whipped cream and garnish with banana slices.

STRAWBERRY TORTE PIE

Low-calorie meringue takes whipped cream role in this luscious berry pie

Baked 9″ pie shell
2 (10 oz.) pkgs. frozen strawberries

⅓ c. sugar
1 tblsp. lemon juice
2 tblsp. cornstarch
Few drops red food color
2 egg whites
¼ c. sugar
⅛ tsp. salt

· Thaw berries and drain, reserving juice. To the juice (about 1 c.) add ⅓ c. sugar, lemon juice and cornstarch. Cook over low heat until thickened; add food color to intensify berry color. Cool glaze.

· Beat egg whites until frothy; gradually add ¼ c. sugar, beating until glistening, stiff peaks form. Spoon into cool pie shell, spreading high on sides to make hollow in center.

· Arrange berries spoke fashion in center of lined pie shell. Pour glaze over berries. Chill in refrigerator 1 hour or longer. Makes 8 servings.

Apricot Refrigerator Pie

One forkful of this pie and you'll want to praise the country cook in California's apricot-growing Santa Clara Valley who invented the recipe. If you like dried apricots, here's a dessert that does the golden fruit justice. Be sure to cook the apricots until very tender, evaporating most of the liquid around them. This really great pie deserves care in making. It's easy to fix, but do heed the little details that make for perfection.

APRICOT LAYER PIE

Tart-sweet, extra-delicious pie you can make the day before serving

Crumb Walnut Pie Shell
1½ c. dried-apricot purée (1½ c. dried apricots)
½ c. granulated sugar
¼ c. soft butter or margarine
1 egg
2 c. sifted confectioners sugar

more

1 c. heavy cream, whipped
2 tblsp. fine graham cracker
   crumbs

· Cook apricots in water to barely cover until very tender, about 1 hour, and drain thoroughly; stir to make a smooth purée. Then stir in granulated sugar. Cool.
· Beat butter until creamy; beat in egg. Gradually add confectioners sugar and beat until smooth. Spoon into Crumb Walnut Pie Shell and spread to make a smooth layer.

· Spoon apricot purée evenly over layer of confectioners sugar mixture.
· Spoon fluffy whipped cream over apricots, completely covering them. Sprinkle on graham cracker crumbs. Refrigerate overnight or at least 4 hours. Makes 8 servings.

CRUMB WALNUT PIE SHELL: Toss 1¼ c. fine graham cracker crumbs, ⅓ c. melted butter and ⅓ c. chopped walnuts together. Press over bottom and sides of 9″ pie pan.

CHAPTER 6

DEEP-DISH AND CAKE PIES, COBBLERS AND DUMPLINGS

You'll feel right at home when you read the recipes in this chapter—they're heirloom desserts, adapted by each generation of new country cooks, and almost every family has inherited a few. We give you a roundup of our readers' and our own favorites.

Deep-dish pies are just right for people who like double the amount of fruit filling and half as much pastry as in the regular 2-crust pie. Try the richly colored Deep Peach-Plum Pie for a summer treat. It's a classic example of wonderful, two-fruit flavor and color blends.

When the purple lilac plumes brush against the garden fence, make our Rhubarb Cobbler. And when leaves of all colors are feathering down and the cranberry harvest is on, make Apple-Cranberry Cobbler—a treat. Wintry weather has its cobblers, too. What dessert could be more heartening on a cold day than our sunny Peach-Apricot Cobbler? Remember that all cobblers are quick desserts. They have biscuit, batter or pastry toppings, and sometimes allow you your choice.

Whole peeled and pitted peaches or cored and peeled apples, baked in pastry, are famous old-time meal endings. Like deep-dish pies and cobblers, dumplings are bowl desserts, often served with cream.

If you've never made or eaten cake baked in a pie shell, you've an exciting experience coming up. Try our delicate, sweet-tart Lemon Cake-Pie. Or serve Blueberry Funny Cake-Pie when you entertain. It's bound to create conversation.

Boston Cream Pie is pie in name only. The 1-layer cake, split and filled with soft custard or whipped cream, is served in wedges like pie. Today's homemakers bake two layers at a time, serving one and freezing the other. If the superlatives of our taste testers mean anything, Superb Boston Cream Pie deserves your attention.

Deep-Dish Pies—Luscious

Among the pleasantries of country kitchens is the serving of freshly baked deep-dish pies—apricot, cherry, peach, boysenberry or whatever fruit is at its seasonal height. Cut through the flaky, crisp crust with your serving spoon and dip into the bubbling, jewel-toned fruit juices and fruit. Ladle the fragrant dessert into individual bowls and take them to the table along with a pitcher of light cream. The family's welcome for your offering will be ample reward for the effort spent.

Even the inexperienced cook excels with these pies. She need not blush over a soggy undercrust. The pastry bakes on top of the filling and gives the juices no opportunity to destroy its golden crispness.

Basic Directions for Deep-Dish Fresh Fruit Pies

· Roll pastry for 1-crust pie into 10" square. Cut several vents or prick with 4-tined fork for the escape of steam during baking.

· Double the filling for a 9" fruit or berry pie. Place filling in 9" square pan. Adjust top crust, fold a little of the edge under and flute just inside edge of pan.

· Bake in a hot oven (425°F.) 40 to 50 minutes, or until lightly browned and the filling starts to bubble through the vents. Serve warm with cream, whipped cream, ice cream or a sauce.

Note: If you use a deep 10" pie pan instead of a square pan, cut rolled pastry in 11" circle. Cut vents and place on top of filling; trim and flute edge, pulling points of fluting over outer rim of pie pan to fasten crust.

Fillings for Deep-Dish Pies

BERRY: Look in Chapter 3 for 2-Crust Fresh Berry Pies. Double the ingredients for filling to make a deep-dish berry pie baked in 9" square pan.

CHERRY: Use 8 c. pitted tart fresh cherries, 2⅔ c. sugar, ⅛ tsp. salt, ⅔ c. flour and 3 tblsp. butter or margarine.

PEACH: Use 8 c. sliced and peeled fresh firm peaches, 2 c. sugar, ⅛ tsp. salt, 2 tblsp. less flour than for Cherry Filling, ½ tsp. cinnamon and 3 tblsp. butter or margarine.

APRICOT: Substitute sliced unpeeled apricots for peaches and follow directions for Peach Filling.

Note: Very tart berries or fruit may require more sugar.

DEEP-DISH APPLE PIE

Country pie to eat with a spoon—it's juicy, mellow and spiced just right

Pastry for 1-crust pie
1   c. sugar
¼   c. flour
½   tsp. cinnamon
⅛   tsp. nutmeg
⅛   tsp. salt
8   c. sliced peeled apples
1   tblsp. lemon juice
2   tblsp. butter or margarine

• Combine sugar (amount of sugar depends on tartness of apples, but you may need 1½ c.), flour, cinnamon, nutmeg and salt in 9″ × 9″ × 2″ pan. Add apples and lemon juice. Stir to combine. Dot with butter and top with pastry, rolled 1″ larger than top of pan. Cut steam vents; trim and flute edge just inside edge of pan. Or pull points of fluting over outer rim of pan to fasten crust.

• Bake in hot oven (425°F.) until apples are tender and crust is browned, about 50 minutes. Serve warm or cool in bowls with light cream or topped with scoops of vanilla ice cream. Or top pie with whipped cream and drizzle with Cinnamon Syrup (recipe follows). Makes 8 servings.

Note: You can bake pie in a 9″ × 12″ × 2″ baking pan. Use 12 c. sliced apples and 2 c. sugar. Fold a little of top pastry edge under and flute just inside edge of pan.

CINNAMON SYRUP: In a small saucepan over heat stir constantly ¼ c. each cinnamon candies (red hots) and water until candies dissolve. Partially cool at room temperature to drizzle over pie at serving time.

APPLE-PORK PIE

This old-fashioned succulent apple pie often is called Sunday Supper Pie

Pastry for 1-crust pie
8   c. sliced peeled apples
20   pieces salt pork (1″ × 1″ × 1″ cube)
1   c. sugar
½   tsp. cinnamon
¼   tsp. nutmeg
¼   tsp. salt

• Place apples in 8″ × 8″ × 2″ pan.
• Cut a 1″ cube of salt pork in 5 slices and then cut each slice in 4 pieces.
• Combine pork with sugar, cinnamon, nutmeg and salt. Sprinkle over apples.
• Roll pastry into square ½″ larger than top of pan. Place over apples. Fold pastry under and flute against inside edge of pan. Cut steam vents in top.
• Bake in hot oven (425°F.) 50 minutes, or until apples are tender. (Cover top crust with foil if it starts to brown too much.) Serve warm or cold with cheese. Makes 6 servings.

DEEP-DISH PEACH PIE

Summer's golden special—make it of ripe fruit; serve fresh from oven

Pastry for 1-crust pie
2   c. sugar
½   c. flour   *more*

½ tsp. cinnamon
½ tsp. mace
8 c. sliced peeled fresh peaches
3 tblsp. butter

• Roll pastry into a 10″ square. (Invert pan, before adding filling, over pastry and cut crust in a straight line 1″ beyond edge of pan.)
• Combine sugar, flour, cinnamon and mace. Stir gently into ripe peaches. Pour into a 9″ × 9″ × 2″ pan. Dot with butter.
• Place pastry over peaches. Fold edge of crust under and flute against inside edge of pan. Cut steam vents.
• Bake in hot oven (425°F.) until lightly browned, about 40 to 50 minutes. Serve warm with cream, whipped cream or vanilla ice cream. Serves 9.

PEACH-PLUM PIE

Juicy, deep-dish summer pie; a beauty in color and in taste

Pastry for 1-crust pie
2 c. sliced peeled peaches
2 c. quartered red plums
1 c. sugar
¼ c. flour
½ tsp. cinnamon
2 tblsp. butter or margarine
Cream or ice cream

• Place fruits in an 8″ × 8″ × 2″ pan.
• Combine sugar, flour and cinna-

mon; sprinkle over fruits. Dot with butter.
• Roll pastry into a 9″ square; place over filling. Trim off excess pastry to make even around the edge. Fold edge of crust under and press against inside of pan. Cut steam vents.
• Bake in hot oven (425°F.) 35 to 40 minutes. Serve warm with cream or ice cream. Makes 6 servings.

DEEP-DISH PEAR-MINCEMEAT PIE

Bake this juicy pie with cheese crust on a frosty day—enjoy compliments

Cheese Pastry for 1-crust pie (Chapter 2)
4 large pears (3 c. sliced)
¼ c. sugar
1 tblsp. flour
¼ tsp. salt
1 ½ c. prepared mincemeat
1 tblsp. lemon juice
2 tblsp. butter

• Arrange pear slices in bottom of 8″ × 8″ × 2″ baking dish. Combine sugar, flour and salt; sprinkle over pears. Cover with mincemeat, sprinkle with lemon juice and dot with butter.
• Roll pastry about 1″ larger than top of baking dish. Place pastry on fruit. Fold a little of the pastry under; crimp edges and cut slits.
• Bake in hot oven (425°F.) 35 to 40 minutes. Serve warm. Serves 6.

Tangy Lemon-Plus Pie (*at right, above*) *is garnished with marshmallows snipped and dipped in yellow sugar. Black Bottom Lemon Pie combines unusual flavors —exotic. Notice its lattice meringue.* (*The two pie recipes, pages 152, 125.*)

"My wife bakes the best pies," *says the Indiana farmer who requests this Frosted Big Apple Pie above all others for his birthday—good for a crowd, it serves 24, and Strawberry Glacé Pie whenever he can get it (pages 54, 68).*

Cobblers You'll Want to Make

Cobblers are a busy woman's quick and hearty dessert standby. Take any fruit filling and top with soft biscuit dough, pour-on batter or pricked pastry cutouts. Bake the dessert while you get the remainder of the meal.

There's one important rule—have the fruit filling hot when you add topping. Bake at once. Availability of fruits need be the only limit to the kinds of cobblers you make. Use ripe fruit in season, canned and frozen the rest of the time.

Fresh Fruit Cobblers (Basic Directions)

• Mix together in saucepan ⅔ to 1 c. sugar, depending on natural sweetness of fruit or berries, and 1 tblsp. cornstarch. Stir in 1 c. boiling water gradually. Bring to a boil and boil 1 minute.

• Add prepared fresh fruit (include juice) and pour into a 10″ × 6″ × 2″ baking dish or a 1½ qt. casserole. Dot with 1 tblsp. butter or margarine and sprinkle with ½ tsp. cinnamon or ¼ tsp. nutmeg.

• Make soft dough this way: Sift together 1 c. sifted flour, 1 tblsp. sugar, 1½ tsp. baking powder and ½ tsp. salt. Blend in ¼ c. shortening until mixture resembles cornmeal. Stir in ½ c. milk to make a soft dough.

• Drop spoonfuls of dough over hot fruit filling. Bake in hot oven (400°F.) about 30 minutes. Serve in bowls with cobbler juices and cream. Makes 6 servings.

VARIATIONS

BLACKBERRY COBBLER: Use ¾ c. sugar.

BOYSENBERRY COBBLER: Use ¾ c. sugar.

CANNED FRUITS IN COBBLERS: Use 1 (1 lb. 13 oz.) can fruit (2½ c.) instead of fresh fruit. Omit water and use only ½ c. sugar.

SWEET CHERRY COBBLER: Add 2 or 3 drops of almond extract to filling made with pitted sweet cherries.

Note: Slice peeled fresh peaches; pit and cut fresh apricots in halves.

CHERRY COBBLER

Homespun dessert that's a snap to fix

1   (1 lb. 4 oz.) can pitted tart
      cherries, undrained (2 c.)
½   c. sugar
1   tblsp. quick-cooking tapioca
2   tblsp. butter
⅛   tsp. salt
4   drops almond extract
Cobbler Topping

• Combine cherries, sugar and tapioca. Cook, stirring constantly, until mixture is thick and clear, about 15 minutes. Stir in butter, salt and almond extract.

· Pour hot mixture into 10″ × 6″ × 1½″ baking dish. Add Cobbler Topping at once.

· Bake in hot oven (400°F.) about 20 minutes, or until crust is browned. Serve warm with cream or vanilla ice cream. Makes 6 servings.

Note: If you like more cherry filling, double the recipe, but use the same quantity of Cobbler Topping.

COBBLER TOPPING: Sift together 1 c. flour, 1 tblsp. sugar, 1½ tsp. baking powder and ¼ tsp. salt. Cut in ¼ c. butter or margarine until mixture resembles coarse crumbs. Mix ¼ c. milk and 1 slightly beaten egg. Add all at once to dry ingredients. Stir just to moisten. Drop by spoonfuls on hot cherry mixture. Bake as directed in Cherry Cobbler recipe.

VARIATION

RHUBARB COBBLER: To 4 c. rhubarb, cut in 1″ pieces, add 1 c. sugar and 2 tblsp. cornstarch, mixed together. Add 1 tblsp. water and bring to a boil. Cook and stir about a minute. Add 2 tblsp. water. Pour into 8″ round baking dish. Dot with 1½ tblsp. butter. Add Cobbler Topping to hot rhubarb filling as directed for Cherry Cobbler, only add 2 tsp. grated orange peel to flour in making topping. Bake in hot oven (400°F.) 20 minutes, or until crust is browned. Serve with cream or vanilla ice cream. Makes 6 servings.

APPLE COBBLER

This juicy cobbler calls for hearty appetites—also cups of hot coffee

1	c. sugar
2	tblsp. cornstarch
⅛	tsp. salt
½	tsp. cinnamon
1	c. water
2	tblsp. butter or margarine
5	c. thinly sliced peeled apples

Orange Biscuit Topping

· Blend sugar, cornstarch, salt and cinnamon in large saucepan. Add water, bring to a boil, stirring constantly. Add butter and apples. Pour into 8″ × 12″ × 2″ baking dish.

· Meanwhile, prepare Orange Biscuit Topping. Arrange biscuits on top of hot apple mixture. Bake in hot oven (400°F.) 20 to 25 minutes, or until apples are tender and biscuits are golden. Serve hot in bowls with whipped cream, vanilla ice cream or Fluffy Orange Sauce (Chapter 9). Makes 6 to 7 servings. (It's a good idea to cover cobbler with foil during first 15 minutes of baking.)

ORANGE BISCUIT TOPPING: Combine 1½ c. prepared biscuit mix and 3 tblsp. sugar. Add ½ c. milk to make soft dough. Roll ½″ thick and cut with 3″ biscuit cutter. Cut each round in half and arrange on top of cobbler, around edge and in center. Sprinkle tops of biscuits with 2 tblsp. sugar and 1½ tsp. grated orange peel.

APRICOT DUMPLINGS

For a change, combine canned apricots and peaches in these dumplings

Crust:
     2 c. biscuit mix
     2 tblsp. sugar
    ⅔ c. milk

Filling:
     1 (1 lb. 14 oz.) can apricot halves
     2 tblsp. sugar
     2 tsp. grated orange peel
     2 tblsp. butter
Apricot Syrup

Crust: Combine biscuit mix and sugar. Add milk all at once and stir to a soft dough. Beat vigorously 20 strokes. Place on a floured board and knead 8 to 10 times. Roll in a 15″ × 10″ rectangle and cut in 6 (5″) squares. (Dough will be soft.)

Filling: Place 3 drained apricot halves in center of each square. Sprinkle 1 tsp. sugar and a little grated orange peel over apricots on each square; dot with butter. Pull corners of squares over apricots and press seams to seal. Carefully place dumplings, seams up, in baking pan; bake in moderate oven (375°F.) about 25 minutes, or until lightly browned.

• Serve in bowls, spooning Apricot Syrup over each serving. Garnish with any remaining apricots. Pass a pitcher of cream or top with vanilla ice cream. Makes 6 dumplings.

APRICOT SYRUP: Combine syrup drained from apricots with 1 tblsp. honey and ½ tsp. cinnamon. Bring to a boil. Makes about 1 cup.

LEMON-APPLE COBBLER

Early spring dessert—lemon and nutmeg complement apple flavors

Pastry for 1-crust pie
    ½ lemon, grated peel and juice
    ½ c. water
    ¾ c. sugar
     2 tblsp. flour
    ⅛ tsp. salt
    ¼ tsp. nutmeg
     4 c. peeled apple slices
     2 tblsp. butter or margarine

• Simmer lemon juice and peel with water about 5 minutes.
• Combine sugar, flour, salt and nutmeg. Blend into lemon mixture.
• Cook, stirring constantly, until mixture is thickened. Add apples and butter. Pour into a 6″ × 10″ × 2″ pan or 9″ pie pan. Cover top with rolled pastry and flute against pan. Cut steam vents.
• Bake in hot oven (400°F.) until apples are tender and crust is golden, about 35 minutes. Serve in bowls with cream or ice cream. Makes 5 servings.

Note: You may want to bake two of these cobblers if you're feeding hungry people.

APPLE-CRANBERRY COBBLER

Autumn's apples and cranberries are flavor mates in biscuit-topped dish

Filling:
     6 c. sliced peeled apples
    1½ c. cranberries
    1¼ c. sugar
     3 tblsp. quick-cooking tapioca
     2 tblsp. orange juice   *more*

1   tsp. grated orange peel
¼   tsp. salt
¼   tsp. cinnamon
2   tblsp. butter or margarine, melted

Topping:

1   c. biscuit mix
⅓   c. milk
2   tblsp. butter or margarine, melted
2   tblsp. sugar

Filling: Combine apples, cranberries, sugar, tapioca, orange juice and peel, salt and cinnamon. Turn into a 2 qt. casserole. Dot with butter.

• Cover and bake in hot oven (425°F.) 30 minutes.

Topping: Combine biscuit mix, milk, butter and sugar. Stir with fork until just moistened. Drop by tablespoonfuls on hot fruit mixture. Bake uncovered until topping is browned the way you like it, 15 to 18 minutes.

• Serve warm in dessert bowls with half-and-half or light cream. Makes 6 servings.

RED PLUM COBBLER

Tart-sweet, color-bright fruit makes an especially delicious cobbler

2   c. sliced pitted red plums
1   c. sugar
2   tblsp. cornstarch
1   c. water
1   tblsp. butter
½   tsp. cinnamon
2   c. prepared biscuit mix
2   tblsp. sugar
⅔   c. milk

• Preheat oven to hot (400°F.).

• Combine plums, sugar and cornstarch in saucepan. Add water and cook, stirring constantly, until mixture comes to a boil. Remove from heat and stir in butter and cinnamon.

• Pour into greased 1½ qt. casserole. Place in hot oven while you prepare biscuit topping.

• Combine biscuit mix and sugar. Add milk and stir to make a soft dough with fork; beat 20 strokes. Drop by spoonfuls on top of hot plum mixture. Place in hot oven (400°F.) and bake 25 minutes or until biscuit topping is brown and juice is bubbly. Serve warm in bowls, topped with juices from cobbler and ice cream, or pass a bowl of whipped cream. Makes 6 servings.

Note: This recipe was tested with Santa Rosa plums. You can peel this fruit if you wish—dip it in boiling water, when skin cracks remove and peel with knife like a tomato.

Springtime Pie in Winter

You don't have to wait to see the first robin of the season to have this refreshing dessert—not if you have frozen rhubarb in your freezer, or can find it in your supermarket. Pink cubes, teamed with juicy, sweet winter pears and rich biscuit topping, make a festive cobbler. Serve it warm in bowls with light cream. This is a dessert your family will ask you to repeat again and again.

PEAR-RHUBARB COBBLER

Red hots nip fruits with cinnamon and make them blush attractively

Filling:
- 1 (10 oz.) pkg. frozen rhubarb
- 3 ripe pears, any variety
- 2 tblsp. water
- ¼ c. sugar
- 2 tblsp. cornstarch
- ¼ tsp. cinnamon
- 1 tblsp. red cinnamon candies (red hots)
- ⅛ tsp. salt
- 1 ½ tblsp. butter or margarine

Crust:
- 1 ¼ c. biscuit mix
- 1 tblsp. sugar
- 2 tblsp. melted butter or margarine
- ½ c. milk

Filling: Thaw package of rhubarb.
• Wash, core and peel pears; cut into ½″ cubes. Add to rhubarb along with water.
• Combine sugar, cornstarch, cinnamon, cinnamon candies (red hots) and salt. Add to fruit.
• Pour into greased 8″ square baking dish. Dot with butter. Cover and bake in hot oven (400°F.) 10 minutes, or until bubbling.
Crust: Combine biscuit mix and sugar; add butter and milk. Mix with a fork.
• Drop by spoonfuls on hot fruit mixture. Sprinkle additional sugar on top.
• Continue baking until biscuit is done, 15 to 20 minutes. Makes 6 servings.

Note: If frozen rhubarb is unsweetened, increase sugar to ⅔ c.

FRESH PEACH COBBLER

A summer version of peaches and cream with Honeyed Cream on top

- 1 ½ tblsp. cornstarch
- ¼ to ⅓ c. brown sugar
- ½ c. water
- 4 c. sweetened sliced peeled peaches
- 1 tblsp. butter
- 1 tblsp. lemon juice
- Batter Topping
- 1 tblsp. granulated sugar
- Spiced Honeyed Cream

• Mix cornstarch, sugar and water. Add peaches and cook until mixture is thickened, about 15 minutes. Add butter and lemon juice. Pour into an 8″ round baking dish.
• Drop spoonfuls of Batter Topping on top hot peach mixture. Sprinkle with sugar. Bake in hot oven (400°F.) 40 to 50 minutes. Serve warm, in bowls, with Spiced Honeyed Cream (recipe follows). Makes 6 servings.

BATTER TOPPING

- ½ c. sifted flour
- ½ c. sugar
- ½ tsp. baking powder
- ¼ tsp. salt
- 2 tblsp. soft butter
- 1 egg, slightly beaten

• Combine all ingredients and beat with spoon until batter is smooth.
• Drop by spoonfuls on hot peach mixture, spreading evenly. It spreads over peaches during baking.
• Bake as directed in Fresh Peach Cobbler.

SPICED HONEYED CREAM: Beat 1 c. heavy cream until thick. Add 2 tblsp. honey and ½ tsp. cinnamon. Beat to mix. Makes 1⅔ cups.

PEACH-APRICOT COBBLER

Two fruits produce wonderful flavor

Filling:

    1   (1 lb. 13 oz.) can sliced peaches
    1   (8 ¾ oz.) can apricot halves
    ½   c. sugar
    1   tblsp. cornstarch
    1   tblsp. butter or margarine
    ¼   tsp. cinnamon

Topping:

    1   c. sifted flour
    1   tblsp. sugar
    1 ½ tsp. baking powder
    ½   tsp. salt
    3   tblsp. shortening
    ½   c. milk

Filling: Drain peaches and apricots, reserving juices. Add enough peach juice to apricot juice to make 1 c.

· Combine sugar and cornstarch in saucepan. Blend in juice and cook over medium heat, stirring constantly, until mixture comes to a boil. Cook 1 minute longer.

· Remove from heat and stir in butter and cinnamon. Add fruits to thickened juice and pour into 1 ½ qt. casserole. Place in hot oven (400°F.) while you prepare topping.

Topping: Sift together flour, sugar, baking powder and salt. Cut in shortening until mixture resembles coarse crumbs. Stir in milk to make a soft dough.

· Drop by spoonfuls over hot fruit. Bake in hot oven (400°F.) until top is lightly browned, about 30 minutes. Serve warm with cream. Makes 6 servings.

CONCORD GRAPE COBBLER

From our FREEZING & CANNING COOKBOOK—*filling freezes successfully*

Biscuit Lattice

    10 c. stemmed and washed grapes
    2   c. sugar
    2 ½ tblsp. quick-cooking tapioca
    ¼   tsp. salt
    ⅛   tsp. cinnamon
    2   tblsp. lemon juice
    1   tblsp. butter

· Slip skins from grapes; set aside. Heat pulp to boiling; rub through coarse sieve or food mill to remove seeds. Discard seeds.

· Combine sugar, tapioca, salt and cinnamon. Add lemon juice and grape pulp. Cook until thickened, stirring.

· Remove from heat; add skins; mix.

· Pour into 8″ square baking pan. Dot with butter. Add Biscuit Lattice.

· Bake in hot oven (400°F.) about 20 minutes, or until lattice crust is golden. Makes 9 servings. This filling will make 2 (8″ or 9″) pies.

BISCUIT LATTICE

    1 ½ c. sifted flour
    2 ¼ tsp. baking powder
    1   tblsp. sugar
    ¼   tsp. salt
    ¼   c. butter or margarine

¼ c. milk
1 egg, slightly beaten

• Sift together dry ingredients.
• Cut in butter. Make well in center; add milk and egg all at once; stir with fork into soft dough. Turn out on lightly floured pastry cloth and knead dough 10 times. Roll dough into 7″ × 9″ rectangle; cut in seven (9″) strips. Place 4 strips on hot filling one way, lattice other 3 strips opposite way. Start with center strip. Bake as directed in recipe for Concord Grape Cobbler.

To Freeze Cobbler Filling: Pour hot filling into 8″ square foil-lined baking pan; cool and freeze.
• Remove block of filling from pan; overwrap and return to freezer. Recommended storage time: 3 to 4 months.
To Serve: Return unthawed filling to pan. Dot with butter. Bake in hot oven (400°F.) about 35 to 40 minutes until bubbling hot, stirring occasionally.
• Remove from oven, cover with Biscuit Lattice; return to oven and bake about 20 minutes. Serve warm.

Dumplings Made with Pie Crust

Pastry and fruit bake together in many forms of fruit desserts. Among the all-time greats are dumplings— tender, juicy fruit in flaky, golden pastry jackets. With farm families, apple dumplings outrank all the rest. We give you two recipes for this treat. In one, you wrap the pastry around the apples, making an especially attractive dessert. You'll find a picture of this kind of dumpling in this book. In the other, you simply lay the pastry over the apples after they're in the baking pan, shaping it around the fruit. Both crusts are exceptionally crisp.

Vanilla ice cream, whipped cream and cream-to-pour are the traditional fruit-dumpling accompaniments. Some farmers say slices of cheese belong with dumplings. And there are country cooks who spice and slightly sweeten the pour cream.

APPLE DUMPLINGS

It's the method of adding pastry jackets that's different—try it

2 c. sifted flour
1 tsp. salt
⅔ c. shortening
⅓ c. cold water
6 medium apples
1 tsp. cinnamon
¼ tsp. nutmeg
1 c. sugar
4 tblsp. butter or margarine
2 tblsp. lemon juice
1 c. hot water

• Combine flour and salt. Cut in shortening until about the size of small peas. Add cold water, a little at a time, mixing with fork until particles form a ball when pressed together. Roll out on lightly floured board ⅛" thick. Cut in 6" circles.

· Peel and core apples; place 2" apart in greased casserole or 13" × 9" × 2" pan. Combine cinnamon, nutmeg and ½ c. sugar. Divide mixture and put in centers of apples. Dot with 2 tblsp. butter.

· Fit pastry circle over each apple, barely tucking it under. Prick pastry in several places. Bake in very hot oven (450°F.) about 25 minutes. Reduce heat to 350°. Remove from oven.

· Meanwhile, combine remaining ½ c. sugar, lemon juice and remaining 2 tblsp. butter; add hot water. Simmer 5 minutes. Pour over dumplings; return to oven at once and continue baking 15 minutes, or until apples are tender. Serve warm or cold with cream or vanilla ice cream. Makes 6 servings.

Note: No chance of dumplings having a soggy undercrust. There's no pastry under the apples.

APPLE DUMPLINGS DE LUXE

One of FARM JOURNAL'S *best recipes reprinted from* COUNTRY COOKBOOK

Pastry for 2-crust pie
3   tblsp. butter or margarine
¾   tsp. cinnamon
¾   tsp. allspice
¾   tsp. nutmeg
⅓   c. sifted brown sugar
8   medium apples, peeled and cored
3   tblsp. orange marmalade
1 ½ c. boiling water
1 ½ c. granulated sugar
3   tblsp. fruit juice (orange, lemon, pineapple, apricot, etc.)

Red food color (optional)
Cream or Strawberry Hard Sauce

· Make paste of butter, spices and brown sugar.

· Roll out pastry ⅛" thick; cut into eight (6") squares. Place apple in center of each; put marmalade (or jelly) in cavity, and spread spicy paste over each apple.

· Moisten edges of pastry; bring points together over apple; seal sides firmly. Roll leftover pastry; cut into "streamers" to lay across tops of dumplings.

· Place in large greased baking dish, about 11" × 15"; bake in moderate oven (375°F.) 30 minutes.

· While apples are baking, make syrup of water, granulated sugar and fruit juice; simmer to dissolve sugar. Pour over apples; bake 10 to 20 minutes more, basting frequently, to give attractive glaze. A little color may be added to syrup. Serve warm with cream or Strawberry Hard Sauce (Chapter 9). Makes 8 servings.

PEACH DUMPLINGS

Country cook's rule: Chill pastry-wrapped peaches before baking

Pastry for 2-crust pie
6   medium peaches
6   tblsp. granulated sugar
6   tblsp. butter or margarine
Cinnamon or mace
1   c. brown sugar
½   c. water

· Roll pastry in a rectangle about ⅛" thick. Cut in 6 squares.

· Peel and pit firm, ripe peaches, using care to keep peaches whole. Fill cavity in each peach with 1 tblsp. granulated sugar and 1 tblsp. butter.

Place peaches in center of pastry squares and mold pastry around peaches to cover completely. Dust lightly with cinnamon. Place dumplings in a deep pan. Bake 10 minutes in hot oven (425°F.).

· Meanwhile, combine brown sugar and water; cook, stirring, about 5 min-utes. Spoon some of syrup over dumplings. Reduce heat to moderate oven (350°F.) and continue baking, 40 to 50 minutes, basting every 10 minutes with a little of the syrup. Serve cold or warm with pitcher of cream, whipped cream or spoonfuls of vanilla ice cream. Makes 6 servings.

Cakes That Are Called Pies

Baking cake batter in pastry was an Early American custom. And the dividing line between cakes and pies was very thin—Boston Cream Pie, for instance. (Washington Pie is similar but has jelly filling.) Most of these farm desserts originated in New England and Pennsylvania Dutch country kitchens, but the recipes traveled with pioneers seeking their fortunes in the fertile heartlands and on to the Pacific shores.

Many of the old recipes have been abandoned with changes in diet patterns. We are including a few examples of these desserts that still are popular—too delicious to give up. They are adapted to the kinds of meals served in country homes. See if you don't agree that they're worth preserving in our culture.

SUPERB BOSTON CREAM PIE

This French version will make two cakes—freeze one and serve the other

3 eggs
1 ½ c. sugar
1 ¾ c. sifted cake flour
½ c. water
2 tsp. baking powder
¼ tsp. salt
1 c. heavy cream, whipped

· Beat eggs 2 minutes, using electric mixer on medium speed. Add sugar gradually and beat about 3 minutes. Add 1 c. cake flour and beat 1 minute longer. Mix in water with few rotations of beaters.

· Sift remaining ¾ c. cake flour, baking powder and salt together twice. Add to batter; beat 1 minute.

· Grease and flour 2 (9″) round layer-cake pans. Divide batter evenly between them.

· Bake in slow oven (325°F.) 30 minutes. Remove from pans; cool thoroughly.

· Split one cake layer in half crosswise and put together with whipped cream. Wrap and refrigerate overnight. Just before serving, dust top with confectioners sugar. Makes 6 to 8 servings.

· Wrap and freeze remaining cake layer. When ready to use, split and fill like first layer.

Note: You will need to double the amount of heavy cream for filling if you serve both the cake layers instead of freezing one for future use.

BOSTON CREAM PIE

A FARM JOURNAL *5-star special from our* COUNTRY COOKBOOK

2   c. sifted cake flour
1 ¼ c. sugar
2 ½ tsp. baking powder
1   tsp. salt
⅓   c. shortening
1   c. milk
1   tsp. vanilla
¼   tsp. almond extract (optional)
1   egg, unbeaten
Custard Cream Filling
Chocolate Icing (optional)

· Sift dry ingredients into mixing bowl. Add shortening, milk, vanilla and almond extract. Beat 2 minutes (mixer at medium speed) or 300 strokes by hand.
· Add egg; beat 2 minutes as before. Pour into two greased 8″ or 9″ round layer pans.
· Bake in moderate oven (350°F.) 25 to 30 minutes. Makes 2 layers. Use one to make Boston Cream Pie; freeze the other.
· Split cooled cake layer in crosswise halves. Spread Custard Cream Filling over lower half. Cover with top half. Dust with confectioners sugar, or spread with Chocolate Icing.

CUSTARD CREAM FILLING

1   c. milk, scalded
½   c. sugar
3   tblsp. cornstarch
⅛   tsp. salt
2   eggs, slightly beaten
1   tblsp. butter or margarine
1   tsp. vanilla

· Gradually add milk to mixture of sugar, cornstarch and salt. Cook slowly, stirring constantly, until mixture thickens (about 10 to 15 minutes).
· Add about ½ c. hot mixture to eggs and blend; carefully combine both mixtures and cook about 3 minutes, stirring constantly.
· Remove from heat; blend in butter and vanilla. Cool. Makes 1¼ cups.

CHOCOLATE ICING

2   tblsp. butter or shortening
2   squares melted chocolate
¼   tsp. salt
½   tsp. vanilla
2 ¼ c. sifted confectioners sugar
¼   to ⅓ c. milk

· Blend together shortening, chocolate, salt and vanilla. Add sugar alternately with milk. Beat until smooth. If thinner glaze is desired, add a little more liquid.

FILLING VARIATIONS

BANANA: Spread Custard Cream Filling between halves of cooled split cake layer. Cover custard with banana slices (1 medium to large banana, sliced and sprinkled with lemon juice) and top with remaining cake.

PINEAPPLE: Combine 1 c. cooled filling with ½ c. drained crushed pineapple just before spreading between split cake. Pineapple may also be added to Coconut Filling.

ORANGE-PINEAPPLE: Add 1 tsp. grated orange peel to pineapple filling.

COCONUT: Add ⅔ c. flaked or cut shredded coconut to custard filling.

WASHINGTON PIE: Bake cake as for Boston Cream Pie. Put cool, split layers together with jelly; sprinkle top generously with confectioners sugar. Serve cut in wedges like pie.

Lemon Pie That's Different

Cooks in Pennsylvania Dutch communities turn out excellent pies that have a close kinship to cakes. Lemon Cake-Pie is one tasty example. Flaky pastry holds the cheerful yellow filling with a lovely, rich red-orange top, the color that develops in browning. Most acceptable dessert for a rather heavy meal. Truly delicate and delicious.

LEMON CAKE-PIE

Three-layered pie—crisp pastry holds custard layer with cakelike topping

Unbaked 9" pie shell
1   c. sugar
1   tblsp. butter
2   eggs, separated
2   tblsp. flour
1   lemon, grated peel and juice
1   c. milk

· Cream together sugar and butter. Beat egg yolks and add to creamed mixture. Add flour, grated lemon peel (2 tsp.) and lemon juice (3 tblsp.) and milk.
· Beat egg whites until stiff, but not

dry, peaks form. Fold into lemon mixture. Pour into pie shell.
· Bake in very hot oven (450°F.) 10 minutes; reduce heat to 325°F. and bake 20 minutes longer, or until filling sets and top is browned.

BLUEBERRY FUNNY CAKE-PIE

You can keep the makings for this winter dessert treat in your cupboard

Unbaked 10" pie shell
¼   c. butter
¾   c. sugar
1   egg
1 ¼ c. sifted cake flour
1   tsp. baking powder
½   tsp. salt
½   c. milk
1   tsp. vanilla
Blueberry Sauce
Vanilla ice cream

· Cream butter; add sugar and mix thoroughly. Add egg and mix well. Sift flour with baking powder and salt; add alternately with milk to creamed mixture. Add vanilla.
· Pour batter into pie shell. Gently pour lukewarm Blueberry Sauce over top.
· Bake in moderate oven (375°F.) 35 to 40 minutes, or until cake tests done. Serve warm with vanilla ice cream. Makes 8 servings.

BLUEBERRY SAUCE: Thoroughly drain 1 (15 oz.) can blueberries, saving 1 tblsp. juice. Combine the 1 tblsp. juice with 1 tblsp. lemon juice, ½ c. sugar and blueberries. Heat just until sugar is dissolved. Cool to lukewarm.

OLD-FASHIONED DATE PIE

Rich but delicious winter dessert

1   c. sugar
3   tblsp. flour
2   tsp. baking powder
1   c. pitted chopped dates
1   c. chopped walnuts
2   eggs, beaten
Sweetened whipped cream

· Sift together sugar, 3 tblsp. flour and baking powder.
· Dredge dates and walnuts with remaining 1 tblsp. flour. Add to beaten eggs.
· Fold in sugar mixture. Pour into greased 9″ pie pan.
· Bake in moderate oven (350°F.) 40 to 50 minutes. Cut in wedges and serve warm or cold with sweetened whipped cream. Makes 8 servings.

Shoofly Pie for Coffee Parties

This famous Pennsylvania Dutch molasses pie, sometimes called a molasses cake, has many variations, but there are three important versions. One is dry—gingerbread baked in a pastry shell. It's favored for dunking in coffee. Number two is put together in the pastry with alternate layers of crumbs and a molasses mixture. The third, and the charm, at least for most gourmets, is the pie with what Pennsylvania Dutch cooks call "a moist zone." We give you our recipe for the third type.

Important points to heed in baking this historical pie are (1) use level measurement of shortening, not butter, to avoid a soggy crust, and (2) work fast once you combine the baking soda and hot water so you won't lose the leavening properties before the pie reaches the oven.

SHOOFLY PIE

Originally a breakfast pie—favored now for coffee party refreshments

Pastry for 2-crust pie
2   c. sifted flour
½   c. sugar
½   tsp. baking soda
¼   c. shortening
1   c. light molasses or cane syrup
1   tsp. baking soda
1   c. hot water

· Line 2 (8″) pie pans with pastry; flute edges.
· Combine flour, sugar, ½ tsp. baking soda and shortening and mix to make crumbs. Divide crumbs evenly between 2 pastry-lined pie pans and spread in smooth layers.
· Combine molasses, 1 tsp. baking soda and hot water. Pour over crumbs in pie pans.
· Bake in moderate oven (375°F.) 40 minutes. Makes 10 to 12 servings.

CHAPTER 7

TARTS AND TURNOVERS

Tarts and turnovers show up at parties, picnics and on the company dinner table, but they're equally at home in family meals. And no pies come in greater variety of size, shape and fillings than these miniatures.

Turnovers serve a double purpose. Fill them with meat and they're sandwiches (Ranchers' Beef Turnovers, Chapter 10). Bake fruit mixtures in them, they're dessert. Cut the pastry in circles, fold, they're half-moons; in squares, they're pocketbooks. Try serving Mincemeat, Frosted Mincemeat or Date-Walnut Turnovers with coffee when you entertain at Christmastime. Our man-sized, husband-pleasing Raisin or Apple Turnovers are fine for family dinners. They're mighty popular as lunch-box tuck-ins, too.

As party pickups, tiny tarts make wonderful easy-to-serve—and eat-finger food. What would delight guests more at a tea party than our Honeyed Lemon or Pecan Tarts? And what would please the family more on a snowy day than big, juicy Concord Grape Tarts with that fresh-from-the-vine taste? We tell you how to make tart shells of all sizes.

We're including in this chapter directions for making French Puff Pastry, because it has been the base for fancy party food for many years, all over the world. If you're skeptical of your ability to make French pastries, you'll find that our recipes give exact instructions. They take time, of course, but aren't difficult. A tray of homemade Napoleons, Cream Twists and Butterflies will charm and impress guests.

Many tarts are at their best assembled shortly before serving. With baked pastry shells on hand and fillings ready in the refrigerator, putting them together and adding a garnish is quick, easy and rewarding.

One big reason for the popularity of these self-contained servings of pie is that they are all ready to bring out—no last-minute cutting of pies or difficult transfer of cream-filled wedges. Just the thing for crowds, for receptions or company refreshments.

Pastry for Tarts

While most homemakers think of tarts as party food because they look so festive, they're one of the best ways to salvage leftover pastry scraps. Look in Chapter 2 for directions on how to freeze unbaked and baked tart shells. You also will find, in the same chapter, detailed recipes for making the shells. Read them before using the tart recipes that follow. And try some of the interesting kinds of pastry designed especially for these little pies.

You can vary the size and shape of tarts by shaping the pastry on aluminum foil (Chapter 2). This way you can make the 2- or 3-bite size or pastries large enough to take the place of pieces of pie in a meal.

We also baked some of our tart shells over inverted muffin-cup pans.

The number of tart shells a recipe yields depends primarily on how thick you roll the pastry and the size of muffin-cup pans and pastry-lined foil circles.

Glamorous Fruit Tarts

Fruit-filled tarts are the largest family in the world of small pastries. That's why we start this chapter with recipes that feature the gifts of orchards, berry patches and citrus groves.

We're repeating a suggestion to remind you again of the many exciting surprises you can introduce in tarts with different kinds of crusts. Cheese Pastry and fruit fillings are fast friends. And tart shells shortened with butter have many boosters in the hostess crowd (see Chapter 2). Or do as many women do and use your own make of pie crust, or a packaged mix, and depend on the fillings to provide color brightness and piquant flavors.

APRICOT TARTS

Wonderful way to serve the tawny-orange fresh fruit to summer guests

1 ¼ c. fine graham cracker crumbs
½   c. sugar
½   c. butter
½   tsp. cinnamon
1 ½ c. ripe apricot quarters
2   tsp. lemon juice
⅛   tsp. salt
2   drops almond extract
1   c. heavy cream, whipped

· Mix crumbs with ¼ c. sugar, butter and cinnamon in bowl.

· Arrange 12 paper baking cups in muffin-cup pan. Divide crumb mixture evenly in them. Press crumbs against bottom and sides of paper cups to make a firm crust. Place in refrigerator until thoroughly chilled.

· Gently mix ripe apricots with lemon juice, salt, almond extract and remaining ¼ c. sugar. Fold into whipped cream. Spoon lightly into crumb crusts. Chill until serving time, or freeze, wrap and return to freezer for use within a week. Let thaw at room temperature about 30 minutes before serving.

CONCORD GRAPE TARTS

They're made with bottled grape juice but have a vineyard-fresh taste

Tart shells (pastry for 2-crust pie)
 - ¼   c. cornstarch
- ½   c. sugar
- ¼   tsp. salt
- 4   egg yolks, beaten
- 1   (1 pt. 8 oz.) bottle grape juice (3 c.)
- 1½ tblsp. butter
- 1   tblsp. lemon juice
- Meringue (4 egg whites)

· Combine cornstarch, sugar and salt in saucepan.

· To egg yolks gradually add grape juice, mixing well and blend into cornstarch-sugar mixture, stirring until smooth. Cook over medium heat, stirring constantly; boil 5 minutes. Remove from heat.

· Stir in butter and lemon juice. Cover and cool.

· Fill baked tart shells; top with meringue (see Perfect Meringue for Topping Pies, Chapter 9), sealing to edges. Bake in moderate oven (350°F.) 12 to 15 minutes. Makes about 12 (3½") tarts.

GOOD COUNTRY-KITCHEN IDEA: "Line cool tart shells with a thin layer of cream cheese," suggests a Georgia homemaker. "I soften the cheese by beating in a little orange or pineapple juice before spreading it. Next, I cover cheese layer with fresh or frozen fruit or berries. Strawberries and peaches are my family's favorites. Then I melt a little jelly and spoon it over the fruit for an attractive glaze. The brighter the jelly is in color, the prettier the tarts are. Sometimes I use apple jelly which I've tinted with a few drops of food color."

Cherry Tarts for Tea Party

When you want a tray of color-bright tarts to serve along with cookies and tea, try these attractive and easy-to-make miniature tart shells filled with red cherries. The Ohio farm woman who sent us the recipe says her young granddaughter is proud of the tarts she makes. They're glamorous enough to give junior cooks the feeling of real accomplishment. You'll find plenty of uses for any leftover cherry pie filling—as topping for ice cream, vanilla and tapioca puddings and slices of unfrosted cake, for instance.

CHERRY TARTS

Pick-up tarts to eat like cookies—they're colorful, delicious, inviting

1   c. flour
½   c. butter or margarine
1   (3 oz.) pkg. cream cheese
Canned cherry pie filling

· Mix flour, butter and cream cheese to make dough. Wrap in waxed paper and refrigerate at least 2 hours, or overnight. (If overnight, let stand at room temperature ½ hour before rolling.)
· Roll to ¼″ thickness and cut in 12 circles (about 2½″) and 24 rings the same size, using doughnut cutter. Moisten edge of a circle with water and lay one ring on it. Moisten edge of ring and place second ring on top of it. Press edge of tart with a sharp fork. Repeat until all pastry is used.
· Place on baking sheet and bake in very hot oven (450°F.) 7 minutes. Cool.
· Fill tarts with prepared cherry pie filling. Makes 12 tarts.
· For added appeal, top each tart, just before serving, with 1 tsp. sweetened whipped cream.

VARIATION

MINCEMEAT TARTS: Fill cooled tart shells with mincemeat pie filling instead of cherry. Garnish with a little whipped cream.

CHEESE PARTY TARTS

Make them one day and chill; garnish prettily and serve the next day

Crust:
2   c. sifted flour
½   c. sugar
¼   tsp. salt
2   tsp. grated lemon peel
½   tsp. vanilla
1   c. soft butter or margarine
2   egg yolks

Filling:
2   (8 oz.) pkgs. cream cheese
1   (3 oz.) pkg. cream cheese
¾   c. sugar
1 ½ tblsp. flour
⅛   tsp. salt
½   tsp. grated lemon peel
⅓   tsp. vanilla
2   eggs
1   egg yolk
2   tblsp. light cream

Crust: Combine flour, sugar, salt, lemon peel and vanilla. Cut in butter and egg yolks with pastry blender until well blended.
· Put about ¼ c. mixture in each of 10 well-greased 5 oz. custard cups. Pat mixture evenly into bottom and sides to line cups. (Dip fingers in water to keep them from sticking.)
· Chill at least 1 hour.
Filling: Beat softened cream cheese until light and fluffy. Gradually add mixture of sugar, flour and salt, beating smooth after each addition. Beat in lemon peel and vanilla. Add eggs, one at a time, and egg yolk, beating well after each addition. Beat in cream.
· Spoon into lined custard cups.

• Bake in extremely hot oven (500°F.) 10 minutes. Reduce heat to 350°F. and continue baking until golden brown, 20 to 25 minutes. (There will be cracks in cheese filling.)

• Cool at room temperature. Carefully remove from custard cups and chill thoroughly.

• To serve, top with a little dairy sour cream and a spoonful of colorful jam, jelly or fruit preserves. Or top with fresh or frozen fruit. Makes 10 tarts.

Note: These tarts are suggestive of cheesecake baked in individual pastry shells.

SPEEDY FRUIT TARTS

Warm-from-the-oven family dessert

½ c. soft butter or margarine
2   c. biscuit mix
6   tblsp. boiling water
1   (1 lb. 5 oz.) can raspberry pie
    filling

• Cut butter into biscuit mix. Add boiling water and stir to make a ball.

• Press about 2 tblsp. dough on bottom and sides of 12 muffin-cup pans, forming a shell about ⅛″ to ³⁄₁₆″ thick. Bake in hot oven (425°F.) 6 minutes.

• Remove from oven and fill each biscuit cup with 2 tblsp. raspberry pie filling. Return to oven and bake 8 minutes longer. Serve warm. Makes 12 tarts.

Note: Substitute cherry, apricot-pineapple and other kinds of canned pie fillings for raspberry.

PRUNE-APRICOT TARTS

Recipe from our COUNTRY COOKBOOK —*too good to leave out of this book*

Pastry for 2-crust pie
1 ½ c. dried prunes
1   c. dried apricots
½   c. sugar
½   tsp. salt
1   tsp. cinnamon
½   tsp. nutmeg
¾   c. prune liquid
Orange Cream Dress-Up

• Rinse and drain prunes. Cook in boiling water to cover, about 15 minutes; drain, reserving ¾ c. liquid. Remove pits.

• Rinse and drain apricots; do not cook.

• Chop and combine fruits; add sugar, salt, spices and prune liquid; bring to boil. Simmer until thickened, about 5 minutes.

• Roll out pastry and cut in 5″ circles. Place on foil rounds the same size as pastry. Put about 3 tblsp. filling in center of each circle. Moisten edges and pinch together in about 6 or 7 pleats.

• Bake in hot oven (425°F.) 15 to 18 minutes. Top tarts with Orange Cream Dress-Up. Makes about 9 tarts.

ORANGE CREAM DRESS-UP: Whip ½ c. heavy cream; fold in ¼ c. sieved cottage cheese. Add ¼ tsp. grated orange peel. Chill. Spoon on tarts just before serving.

VARIATIONS

PRUNE-APRICOT TURNOVERS: Place the filling on half of each pastry circle, fold over and seal edges by pressing with tines of fork or with handle of teaspoon. Make a few slits in top of turnovers. Follow baking directions for Prune-Apricot Tarts.

These turnovers freeze well. Cool thoroughly, wrap and freeze. To serve, heat in a moderate oven (350°F.). Top with Orange Cream Dress-Up. Makes about 9 turnovers.

PRUNE-APRICOT PIE: Bake filling for Prune-Apricot Tarts in a 2-crust (9″) pie.

MINCE TARTLETS

You'll be ready for holiday guests with these tartlets in the freezer

Pastry for 2 (2-crust) pies
1   (1 lb. 6 oz.) can mince pie filling
Sugar

· Divide pastry in fourths. Roll out, one at a time, on lightly floured surface. Cut in circles with 3″ cookie cutter.
· Place half the circles on baking sheet. Top each with 1 tblsp. mincemeat. Place other half pastry circles on tops. Seal edges together by pressing with tines of fork. Prick top of each tartlet for steam vent. Sprinkle with sugar.
· Bake in moderate oven (375°F.) until lightly browned, about 30 minutes. Makes 20 to 22 tartlets.

FRUIT-OF-THE-MONTH TARTS

One of our FARM JOURNAL'S California readers is praised in her neighborhood for her glamorous way of serving seasonal and drained canned fruits in tart shells. She dips the prepared fruits in melted currant jelly to glaze them. Then she places them in tart shells, spoons whipped cream on top and serves the dessert at once. If the fruit needs to be extended, she first lines the tart shells with vanilla pudding and pie filling, prepared by package directions, or with softened and whipped cream cheese.

Among the favorite fresh fruits for these exotic tarts are: strawberries, blueberries, pitted sweet cherries, grapes, peach halves, chunks of fresh pineapple, thick banana slices, nectarine halves and pears, cut in lengthwise halves and then in two crosswise. Canned apricots and peach halves also are good.

The tarts must be assembled at mealtime. They are not a make-ahead dessert.

SPECIAL SUNDAE TARTS

Like to use your imagination in cooking? If you do, here's your chance to try out some of your ideas. You don't need recipes to make fascinating sundae tarts. All you must have is fruit or berries, ice cream and the spirit of adventure.

Just before mealtime, fill tart shells about three fourths full of prepared fruit. Experiment with sliced strawberries or peaches; lightly sweetened raspberries or blueberries; frozen or drained, canned pineapple chunks; diced bananas dipped in lemon juice or mixed with diced oranges; thick applesauce; rhubarb sauce; cooked and cut-up prunes or dried apricots, or a combination of the two; or frozen strawberries and peaches.

Top the fruit with scoops of ice cream or fluffs of whipped cream and garnish attractively until the tarts look like ice cream sundaes. You can spoon on the ice cream, sweetened, crushed berries, diced peaches or other fruit in the tart shells; or top with chopped maraschino cherries, flaked coconut, chopped nuts or chocolate shavings, for instance.

Try different kinds of ice cream, too. Try peach ice cream on raspberry tarts, peppermint stick on applesauce, strawberry on pineapple, prune and apricot tarts. Pour chocolate sauce on banana tarts. You'll get some wonderfully good flavor and color combinations—and plenty of good eating.

STRAWBERRY CREAM TARTS

French Pastry Cream plus fresh berries make glamorous pastries

Tart shells (pastry for 2-crust pie)
1   recipe Pastry Cream
½   c. currant jelly
1   pt. strawberries

· Spoon Pastry Cream (in this chapter) into baked tart shells, dividing it equally.
· Melt currant jelly over low heat.
· Place four ripe berries, pointed ends up, in each tart shell. Spoon currant jelly over berries. Refrigerate until time to serve. Makes about 12 (3″) tarts.

Note: Assemble the tarts the day you serve them.

STRAWBERRY TARTS

Set out a tray of these delicious beauties at your next buffet supper

Tart shells (pastry for 1-crust pie)
1 ½ pts. fresh strawberries
¼   c. sugar
½   c. currant or red apple jelly
Few drops red food color
½   c. heavy cream, whipped

· Slice half of strawberries (1½ c.). Place in bowl and add sugar. Cut remaining berries in lengthwise halves.
· Stir jelly in small pan over medium heat until it melts. Add food color to deepen color.
· Assemble tarts shortly before serving. Spoon about 3 tblsp. sliced berries into each baked tart shell. Top with berry halves. Spoon on melted jelly and garnish with whipped cream. Makes about 6 (3½″) tarts.

CHOCOLATE CRINKLE CUPS

Party dessert for Junior High set

· Melt 2 tblsp. semisweet chocolate pieces at a time over hot (not boiling) water. As soon as melted, spread chocolate over inside of fluted cupcake papers. Set in muffin pans; freeze at once until firm, about 15 minutes; peel off the paper and return cups to freezer until ready to serve.
· At serving time, fill them with ice cream or sherbet and garnish with fruit. One (6 oz.) pkg. semisweet chocolate pieces makes about 8 crinkle cups.

Note: Junior High cooks will like to make these. Their mothers will enjoy serving them to guests, too.

HONEYED LEMON TARTS

Garnish at serving time with coconut—finger food for your next tea party

Tart shells (pastry for 2-crust pie)
 1 c. sugar
 ¼ c. butter
 ½ c. lemon juice
 1 tblsp. grated lemon peel
 2 eggs, beaten

· Combine sugar, butter, lemon juice and peel and eggs. Cook in double boiler over hot water until mixture thickens.
· Pour into baked tart shells. Makes about 20 (2″) tarts.

Note: Filling for Best-Ever Lemon Meringue Pie (Chapter 4) may be served in tart shells. Garnish with whipped cream puffs.

ORANGE SURPRISE TARTS

The surprise is the chocolate liner under the fluffy filling—different

Tart shells (pastry for 2-crust pie)
 1 (4 or 5 oz.) milk-chocolate bar
 2 tblsp. light cream
 3 egg yolks, slightly beaten
 ¼ c. orange juice
 1 tsp. lemon juice
 ½ c. sugar
 ⅛ tsp. salt
 1 c. heavy cream, whipped
 1 tblsp. grated orange peel
Orange segments

· Melt chocolate bar with cream over hot water. Stir until smooth. Cool slightly and spread in tart shells.
· Place egg yolks in double boiler.

Gradually add orange and lemon juices, stirring constantly. Stir in sugar and salt. Cook over hot water, stirring constantly, until mixture thickens. Remove from heat and cool.
· Carefully fold cream, whipped very stiff, and orange peel into orange mixture. Chill. Just before serving, spoon into baked tart shells. Garnish tops with orange segments. Makes about 10 (4″) tarts.

CURRANT COCONUT TARTLETS

Party guests will like these dainty old-fashioned-tasting teatime treats

Pastry (Pecan Tartlets)
 ⅔ c. currants (dried)
 4 tsp. butter
 ⅔ c. brown sugar, firmly packed
 1 small egg, beaten
 ⅓ tsp. vanilla
 ⅓ tsp. nutmeg
 ⅓ c. flaked coconut

· Wash currants and cover with boiling water. Let stand a few minutes. Drain and while still hot, add butter, brown sugar and egg. Stir in remaining ingredients and drop mixture into pastry for Pecan Tartlets in this chapter. (It's a good idea to cover tartlets the first 10 minutes of baking with sheet of aluminum foil.)
· Bake in moderate oven (350°F.) 15 minutes; reduce oven temperature to 250° and continue baking 10 minutes longer. Makes about 3 dozen.

Note: To garnish tartlets, add polka dots of Orange Cheese Topping (Chapter 9) shortly before serving.

Light-as-Chiffon Tarts

You can heap the cloudlike fillings of chiffon pies in tender, flaky tart shells with confidence the dessert will make a glorious meal ending. Many of the fillings are colorful and all of them are attractive garnished at serving time with whipped cream. They contain fewer calories than most tarts, which adds to their high favor with weight-conscious people.

We give you recipes for Strawberry and Pumpkin Chiffon Tarts, but don't stop with them. Turn to Chapter 5 and select other fillings from the recipes for chiffon pies. The filling for a 9″ pie is the right amount for 12 (3″) tart shells.

STRAWBERRY CHIFFON TARTS

Fresh as spring—and luscious

Tart shells (pastry for 2-crust pie)
- 1 pt. fresh strawberries
- ¾ c. sugar
- 1 envelope unflavored gelatin
- ¼ c. cold water
- ½ c. hot water
- 1 tblsp. lemon juice
- ⅛ tsp. salt
- 1 c. heavy cream
- 2 egg whites
- 12 strawberries

• Crush 1 pt. berries (you will have 1¼ c.); cover with ½ c. sugar and let stand 30 minutes.

• Soften gelatin in cold water; dissolve in hot water. Cool. Add crushed berries, lemon juice and salt. Chill until mixture mounds when dropped from spoon. Test frequently while chilling.

• Fold in ½ c. cream, whipped. Beat egg whites until frothy; gradually add remaining ¼ c. sugar, beating until glossy, firm peaks form. Fold into strawberry mixture. Spoon into tart shells and chill until firm.

• To serve, garnish with remaining ½ c. cream, whipped, and whole berries. Makes about 12 (3″) tarts.

VARIATION

STRAWBERRY CHIFFON PIE: Spoon filling into 9″ Graham Cracker Crumb Crust.

PUMPKIN CHIFFON TARTS

Sweet and spicy holiday dessert

Tart shells (pastry for 2-crust pie)
- 1 envelope unflavored gelatin
- ¾ c. light brown sugar, firmly packed
- ½ tsp. salt
- 1 tsp. pumpkin pie spice
- 3 eggs, separated
- ¾ c. milk
- 1¼ c. canned pumpkin
- ⅓ c. granulated sugar
Whipped cream
Amber Caramel Sauce (Chapter 9)

• Combine gelatin, brown sugar, salt and spice in saucepan. Combine egg yolks and milk; stir into gelatin mixture. Cook, stirring constantly, until mixture comes to a boil. Remove from heat; add pumpkin. Chill mixture until it mounds slightly when dropped from spoon. Test frequently for mounding stage.

• Beat egg whites until frothy; add sugar and beat until glossy, stiff peaks form.

• Fold pumpkin mixture into egg whites. Spoon into tart shells. Chill until firm. Serve topped with whipped cream; pass Amber Caramel Sauce to pour over. Makes about 12 (3″) tarts.

VARIATION

PUMPKIN CHIFFON PIE: Spoon filling into a 9″ Graham Cracker Crumb Crust.

RAINBOW TARTS: One farm hostess delighted her guests at a springtime tea party by serving a tray of tarts, colorful as the season's blossoms. For filling tart shells she used Lime, Orange (Chapter 5), Lemon and Strawberry (Chapter 7) Chiffon Pie fillings. The garnishes were tiny fresh mint leaves on the lime, small canned mandarin orange sections, drained, on the orange, coconut on the lemon and ripe strawberries on the strawberry tarts.

Nuts Provide Flavor and Texture

Come with us to another sweet world of party-spirit tarts—a quartet of little pies in which nuts are important. Notice that Individual Chess Pies are rich and luscious with farm foods, eggs and cream, with raisins and lemon juice adding to their tastiness. Some people call them Chess Tarts. By any name, they're indisputably delicious.

Make Pecan Tartlets at your leisure and freeze until needed. Then you'll have refreshments for your party or drop-in guests as quickly as you can make coffee. Heavenly Tarts are miniature Lemon Angel Pies, with no cutting required at serving time.

The filling for Mocha Tarts carries that wonderful blend of chocolate and coffee flavors, with nuts as garnish. Your guests will be talking about how good they are, long after your party.

INDIVIDUAL CHESS PIES

Buttery-rich, nut-raisin filling—delightful contrast to flaky pastry

Tart shells (pastry for 2-crust pie)
½   c. butter or margarine
1   c. sugar
4   eggs, separated
½   c. chopped walnuts or pecans
1   c. chopped raisins
1   tblsp. lemon juice
Meringue (2 egg whites)

• Cream butter; add sugar and mix until light and fluffy. Beat yolks of 2 eggs and 2 whole eggs together and add to sugar-butter mixture. Add nuts and raisins. Stir in lemon juice and cook in double boiler over hot water until thick and dark brown in color, about 15 minutes. Cool.

· Pour into baked tart shells; top with meringue (see Perfect Meringue for Topping Pies, Chapter 9). Brown in moderate oven (350°F.) 12 to 15 minutes. Makes about 8 (4″) tarts.

Note: Serve these rich pies cold, never warm.

PECAN TARTLETS

Delicious—serve them like cookies

1   c. butter or margarine
2   (3 oz.) pkgs. cream cheese
2½ c. unsifted flour
¾   tsp. salt
1½ c. chopped pecans
1   c. brown sugar, firmly packed
2   eggs, slightly beaten
2   tblsp. melted butter or margarine
½   tsp. vanilla
½   c. light corn syrup

· Soften 1 c. butter and cheese. Blend in half the flour at a time and ½ tsp. salt; shape pastry into two 2″ diameter rolls; wrap and chill overnight.
· Slice pastry into 36 portions; press into 2″ muffin-cup pans. Line cups; do not make rims.
· Place half the nuts in lined cups.
· Using a rotary beater, gradually add sugar to eggs. Add melted butter, remaining ¼ tsp. salt and vanilla. Stir in syrup. Pour into tart shells.
· Sprinkle with remaining nuts. Bake in moderate oven (350°F.) about 20 minutes. Makes 3 dozen.

Note: For tiny bite-size tarts, bake in paper bonbon cups. Have pastry at room temperature when you line cups.

HEAVENLY TARTS

You can make these a day ahead

1½ c. sugar
¼   tsp. cream of tartar
4   eggs, separated
3   tblsp. lemon juice
1   tblsp. grated lemon peel
1   pt. heavy cream

· Sift together 1 c. sugar and cream of tartar. Beat egg whites until soft peaks form; add sugar mixture gradually and continue beating until very stiff. Spoon in mounds on baking sheet covered with heavy ungreased paper; shape cups (6 to 8) with spoon.
· Bake in very slow oven (275°F.) 1 hour. Remove from paper and cool.
· Beat egg yolks slightly, stir in remaining ½ c. sugar, lemon juice and peel. Cook in top of double boiler until very thick, 8 to 10 minutes. Cool.
· Whip cream, combine half of it with lemon-egg mixture and use to fill meringue shells. Cover with remaining whipped cream. Place in refrigerator for 24 hours. Makes 6 to 8 servings.

MOCHA TARTS

For a special party, omit walnuts and top with chopped pistachio nuts

Tart shells (pastry for 1-crust pie)
½   c. chopped walnuts
1   (4 oz.) pkg. instant chocolate pudding and pie mix
1   tsp. instant coffee powder
¾   c. milk
1   c. dairy sour cream

· Sprinkle ¼ c. walnuts in baked tart shells.   *more*

· Beat together pudding mix, coffee powder and milk until smooth. Fold in sour cream. Spoon into tart shells.

Sprinkle remaining ¼ c. nuts on top. Chill. Makes about 6 (3½″) tarts.

Good Ideas from Our Test Kitchens

TART FILLINGS: Line tart shells with packaged pudding and pie filling mix, softened cream cheese, whipped cream or packaged whip mix. Fill with perfect pieces of fresh, frozen or canned fruits.

BANANA TARTS: Fill tart shells with sieved apricot preserves and top with banana slices. Glaze bananas with some of the preserves, melted over heat.

SHERBET TARTS: Scoop balls of lime sherbet or sherbets of other flavors with melon scoop; place on tray and freeze. Put the firm, colorful sherbet balls in tiny tart shells just before serving.

FRUIT TURNOVERS: Use 3″ squares or circles of pastry and ½ tsp. berry or fruit preserves to make tiny turnovers.

Turnovers Tote Successfully

Turnovers travel well—in lunch boxes, picnic hampers and packages for potluck meals—or wherever you go, taking along food to share with friends. You can bake these individual pies several days or weeks ahead and freeze them. They'll thaw on the way.

You may prefer to freeze turnovers before baking, especially if you're going to serve them at home. To bake frozen turnovers, unwrap, place on a baking sheet and bake on the lower shelf in a hot oven (425°F.) until golden, about 20 to 25 minutes. Serve them as the occasion dictates—sprinkled with sifted confectioners sugar; frosted; faintly warm, with ice cream; with a dessert sauce poured over.

Picnic Cherry Turnovers, for in-stance, may be sugar-glazed when served out in the yard or in a park, but when you're having them for at-home company, hot Cherry Sauce spooned over them adds color and double-cherry taste. We give you recipes for both Sugar Glaze and Cherry Sauce.

Turnovers are extremely adaptable pies. Farmers almost always will settle for them as a dessert or snack any day and any place if there's plenty of coffee to sip with them.

Notice to cooks: Remember that the critical point in making turnovers is to be certain you have a tight seal around the edges. This will prevent juices from escaping during baking.

DATE AND WALNUT TURNOVERS

Add these dainties to tray of Christmas cookies for a new taste treat

Pastry for 2-crust pie
24 whole fresh dates, pitted
½ c. walnut pieces
2 tblsp. sugar
1 tsp. cinnamon

• Divide pastry in half. Roll each half into a 10″ × 9″ rectangle. Cut into 2½″ × 3″ rectangles.
• Stuff dates with walnuts and wrap each date in pastry rectangle; press edges to seal and tuck the ends under.
• Combine sugar and cinnamon. Dip tops of turnovers in sugar-cinnamon mixture. Bake on baking sheet in hot oven (425°F.) until golden brown, about 12 minutes. Makes 24 turnovers.

PICNIC CHERRY TURNOVERS

Just right for toting to picnics and in lunch boxes—a finger-food pie

Pastry for 2-crust pie
1 (1 lb.) can drained pitted tart cherries (about 1 ¾ c.)
½ c. sugar
1 tblsp. quick-cooking tapioca
⅛ tsp. salt
4 drops almond extract
Few drops red food color
1 tblsp. butter or margarine
Sugar Glaze

• Combine cherries, sugar, tapioca and salt in medium saucepan; cook and stir over medium heat until mixture comes to a boil; let simmer about 5 minutes. Remove from heat; add almond extract, food color and butter. Cool.
• Divide pastry dough in half and roll each in a large square. Cut each in 4 (6″) squares. Put about ¼ c. cherry mixture in center of each square of pastry. Moisten edges and fold over each square to make a triangle. Seal edges by pressing with a floured fork. Cut slits in turnovers over filling to permit steam to escape. Place on an ungreased baking sheet.
• Bake in hot oven (425°F.) 12 to 15 minutes, or until light golden brown. Remove from oven and brush, while warm, with Sugar Glaze. Makes 8 (6″) turnovers.

SUGAR GLAZE: Combine ½ c. sifted confectioners sugar, 1 tblsp. water and 1 drop vanilla. Brush on hot turnovers.

VARIATION

• Omit Sugar Glaze and serve warm with Cherry Sauce—makes turnovers rival cherry pie.

CHERRY SAUCE

1 (1 lb.) can pitted tart cherries
⅔ c. sugar
3 tblsp. cornstarch
⅛ tsp. salt
2 tblsp. butter or margarine
Few drops red food color

• Drain cherries, reserving juice. Add water, if needed, to make 1 ⅓ c. juice.
• Combine sugar, cornstarch and salt in saucepan; gradually stir in cherry

juice. Cook mixture, stirring constantly, over medium heat until it boils and is thickened and clear, about 6 minutes.

• Add butter, stirring until it melts, and a few drops of red food color. Stir ½ c. drained cherries into the sauce. Serve warm over Picnic Cherry Turnovers. Makes about 2 cups.

RAISIN-ORANGE TURNOVERS

Keep a supply in freezer to serve with hot coffee—extra-good flavor team

Pastry for 2-crust pie
1 ¾ c. seedless raisins
1 ¾ c. water
¼ c. orange juice
⅓ c. brown sugar, firmly packed
1 tblsp. quick-cooking tapioca
½ tsp. cinnamon
¼ tsp. salt
1 tblsp. vinegar
1 tblsp. butter
2 tsp. grated orange peel

• Combine raisins, water and orange juice in saucepan. Bring to a boil; boil 5 minutes. Add sugar, tapioca, cinnamon and salt. Cook, stirring, until mixture again comes to a boil. It should be thick. Remove from heat, add vinegar, butter and orange peel. Cool.

• Roll out pastry very thin (less than ⅛" if possible). Cut in 6" circles or 5" squares. Moisten edges with cold water. Place 2 to 3 tblsp. filling on one side of each square or circle of pastry; fold over and seal edges with fork. Make slits with sharp knife in tops of turnovers for escape of steam. Bake in hot oven (425°F.) about 20 minutes. Makes 8 to 10 turnovers.

Note: You can give the turnovers a glistening top with the following Apricot Glaze or plain Sugar Glaze (see Picnic Cherry Turnovers).

Apricot Glaze: Combine ¾ c. apricot preserves and ¼ c. water. Stir over medium heat until preserves melt. Put through sieve and spoon over slightly warm Raisin-Orange Turnovers.

Old-Fashioned Half-Moons

Maybe you've never fried pies, but your grandmother, especially if she lived south of the Mason and Dixon line, rated these turnovers from the kettle a great winter dessert. Today's cooks often fry them in the electric skillet. A rather tart fruit filling contrasts delightfully with the sugar-sprinkled, flaky pastry. Serve the turnovers, often called Half-Moons, either hot or cold. And tuck them in a packed lunch for a much appreciated treat.

FRIED PIES

Southern country-kitchen specials

Pastry for 2-crust pie
1 ½ c. cooked dried apricots or prunes, mashed and sweetened to taste

• Roll pastry ⅛" thick. Cut in 5" circles. On each pastry round place about 1 ½ tblsp. fruit mixture. Fold pastry

to make half-moons; press edges together with fork tines to seal. Prick
tops in several places.
• Fry turnovers in deep hot fat
(375°F.) until light brown, about 3
minutes. Drain on paper towels and
sprinkle with sifted confectioners
sugar. Makes about 12.

FROSTED MINCEMEAT TURNOVERS

Tasty change from mincemeat pies

Pastry for 2-crust pie
  1 c. prepared or homemade
      mincemeat
  ¼ c. diced peeled apples
Confectioners Sugar Frosting

• Roll pastry about ⅛" thick and cut
in 4½" circles.
• Combine mincemeat and apples.
Place about a tablespoon of mixture
on each pastry circle. Fold over to
make half-moons and seal edges with
4-tined fork. Prick tops.
• Bake in a very hot oven (450°F.)
about 15 minutes, or until browned.
• Spread tops while slightly warm
with Confectioners Sugar Frosting.
Makes 15.

CONFECTIONERS SUGAR FROSTING:
Combine ¼ c. soft butter or margarine, ½ tsp. vanilla and 1 c. sifted confectioners sugar. Blend in water, a
little at a time, to make frosting of
spreading consistency.

APPLE TURNOVERS

Spicy apples in pastry pocketbooks

Pastry for 2-crust 10" pie
  4 c. diced peeled apples
  ⅛ tsp. salt
  ⅔ c. sugar
  ½ tsp. cinnamon
  ¼ tsp. nutmeg
  1 tblsp. lemon juice
  6 tblsp. soft butter
Milk

• Combine apples, salt, sugar, cinnamon, nutmeg and lemon juice.
• Divide pastry in half and roll one
half to make 11" square. Dot with 3
tblsp. butter, fold over and roll out
again to make an 18" × 12" rectangle. Cut in 6" squares. Repeat with
second half of dough.
• Place about ⅓ c. apple mixture on
each square of pastry; fold over and
seal edges by pressing with 4-tined
fork. Prick tops of turnovers. Brush
with milk.
• Bake in hot oven (400°F.) until
golden, about 25 to 30 minutes. Serve
warm or cold. Top with vanilla ice
cream or whipped cream, if desired.
Makes 1 dozen.

Note: You can bake half the turnovers and freeze the other half to bake
later.

DATE-WALNUT TURNOVERS

*Make these dainties to serve with an
assortment of holiday cookies*

Pastry for 2-crust pie
  1 c. finely cut dates
  ¼ c. chopped walnuts   *more*

⅛ tsp. salt
½ tsp. grated orange peel
¼ c. orange juice
Orange Glaze

• Roll pastry ⅛″ thick and cut in 4½″ circles.
• Combine dates, walnuts, salt, orange peel and juice; stir to blend. Place about a tablespoon of date mixture on each pastry circle. Fold over, seal edges by pressing with 4-tined fork. Prick tops.

• Bake in very hot oven (450°F.) until browned, about 12 minutes. Cover tops while slightly warm with Orange Glaze. Makes 15.

ORANGE GLAZE: Combine 1 c. sifted confectioners sugar, ⅛ tsp. salt and 1 tsp. grated orange peel in bowl. Blend in 1½ to 2 tblsp. orange juice until mixture has the consistency of a glaze. Spread on turnovers.

Special Tarts from Overseas

Banbury Tarts are raisin turnovers, as English as the hot tea that usually accompanies them. Named for the town northwest of London, where they originated, they're as famous as the town's Banbury Cross of the nursery rhyme. Keep some of these turnovers in your freezer to serve on afternoons when a neighbor stops by for a visit. They are satisfying and encourage good talk.

BANBURY TARTS

You can make the filling ahead and store in refrigerator if convenient

Pastry for 2-crust pie
1½ c. raisins
1 tsp. grated lemon peel
⅛ tsp. salt
¾ c. sugar

1 c. water
4 soda crackers, finely crushed
1 tblsp. butter or margarine
2 tblsp. lemon juice

• Combine raisins, lemon peel, salt, sugar, water and cracker crumbs. Cook slowly, stirring occasionally, until about the consistency of jam (about 30 minutes). Stir in butter and lemon juice. Cool.
• Roll pastry ⅛″ thick. Cut in 4″ circles, using a bowl, jar lid or cardboard circle for pattern. Place 1 tblsp. raisin mixture in center of each pastry circle. Fold over, moisten edges with cold water, seal edges with 4-tined fork. Prick tops.
• Bake in very hot oven (450°F.) until pastry is lightly browned, about 12 minutes. Serve warm or cold with cheese. Makes 15 to 16.

Elegant French Pastries

Imagine what excitement a woman making French pastries in her kitchen would have created a generation ago! Now you can bake them whenever you please. Just use our recipe for Basic Puff Pastry (Chapter 2). It's a simplified version that gives professional results. You need to have patience, willingness to follow techniques and will power to resist changing the specified ingredients. It's really not difficult, just time consuming.

Busy women don't do the work these special pastries take all at one time. You can freeze the pastry, pre-shaped if you like, and use it any time within a month. Or you can refrigerate pastry, wrapped in aluminum foil, for two or three days before shaping. When you are about ready to entertain, you can bake the pastries, garnish and freeze them for a few days.

We give you recipes for five of the most famous French pastries. And we include a filling recipe, Pastry Cream, also borrowed from the French. It's one of the most delicious tart fillings ever invented. You can make it a day ahead, too; cover and refrigerate, folding in whipped cream when you fill the tarts.

Notice our recipe for Strawberry Cream Tarts, also in this chapter. In this delicacy, an exquisite color picture, we combine Pastry Cream and ripe strawberries in tart shells made with plain pastry, so you can use the filling—even if you don't want to tackle the ethereal Basic Puff Pastry.

Set a large tray of assorted French pastries on the table when you have a coffee, tea or dessert party. It will add plenty of talk, sprinkled with pretty adjectives, to the occasion. Your guests will be flattered to have a chance to help themselves to the flaky, fragile and crisp pastries that once were enjoyed almost exclusively by European royalty.

NAPOLEONS

Elegant—the pride of French menus

½ recipe Basic Puff Pastry (Chapter 2)
Glaze
Nuts
1 recipe Pastry Cream

· Roll chilled pastry on lightly floured surface in 6″ × 15″ rectangle ¼″ thick.

· With sharp knife cut in half, lengthwise. Slant knife slightly as you cut so that one surface of each strip will be broader than the other. (This is important because if they are straight, the tops will be smaller when they puff up.)

· Rinse chilled baking sheet with cold water. Place pastry strips on it with broader surface up. Prick with fork. Chill 30 minutes.

· Bake in hot oven (425°F.) 15 minutes. Turn strips with spatula. Reduce heat to 350° and bake 15 minutes, or until puffed and a rich golden color. Cool.

· Split cool strips to make 3 layers each. Choose the two most attractive for tops. Place them on a rack over tray. Spoon glaze over; let dry at room temperature. Repeat with second coat of glaze. Top with slivered or chopped nuts. Or, if you prefer, decorate with pastry tube, allowing glaze to dry at least 1 hour before decorating. (See Chocolate Stripes.)

· Spread Pastry Cream on two un-glazed pastry layers and stack them. Top with a glazed and decorated strip. Repeat this procedure with remaining two strips and top with other decorated strip. Chill at least 30 minutes. Cut each stacked pastry strip in 6 slices. Makes 12.

GLAZE: Combine 1 c. sifted confectioners sugar, ¼ tsp. vanilla, ⅛ tsp. salt and 1½ to 2 tblsp. water.

Note: Bake pastry ahead and freeze, if you wish. Combine with Pastry Cream the day you serve Napoleons. Refrigerate until serving time.

VARIATION

JOSEPHINES: When the two baked strips are split to make 3 layers each, spread top one with thin confectioners sugar frosting and sprinkle with chopped nuts. Stack remaining two layers together with Pastry Cream and add tops. Frosting substitutes for glaze.

CHOCOLATE STRIPES: French chefs omit nuts and pipe 5 lengthwise chocolate stripes on glazed tops of Napoleons for a finishing touch. If you want

to try this decorative trim, melt 1 square unsweetened chocolate and mix with 2 tsp. butter. Use the small, straight pastry tube (for writing) to make stripes. Pull a wood toothpick crosswise through Chocolate Stripes at ½" intervals, alternating the direction each time. This gives the classic "wavy" effect on Napoleons.

PASTRY CREAM

Rich, delicious filling for many tarts

3   egg yolks, beaten
½   c. sugar
⅛   tsp. salt
2   tblsp. flour
2   tsp. cornstarch
1   c. light cream
1   tsp. vanilla
¼   c. heavy cream

· Combine egg yolks, sugar, salt, flour and cornstarch in top of double boiler. Gradually stir in light cream.

· Cook over boiling water, stirring constantly, until mixture thickens so it will pile slightly when dropped from spoon. Remove from heat and stir in vanilla. Place waxed paper or saran or other plastic wrap directly on top of mixture. Cool.

· When cold, beat heavy cream until stiff. Fold into custard. Makes 1¾ cups.

BUTTERFLIES

Pastry has many buttery, delicate, crisp layers—immeasurably thin

½   recipe Basic Puff Pastry
      (Chapter 2)
Sugar

• Roll chilled pastry on board lightly sprinkled with sugar (granulated), to make rectangle ¼" thick. Fold in half. Sprinkle with more sugar and roll again into rectangle ⅛" thick.

• Trim pastry edges straight with sharp knife. Do not use a sawing motion; make a straight, clean, swift cut. Cut pastry into quarters.

• Sprinkle the quarters lightly with cold water, then with sugar. Stack; then cut into 3" × ½" strips. Pick up each strip and give it one twist. Place on chilled baking sheet and press lightly. Chill 30 minutes.

• Bake in hot oven (425°F.) 12 minutes. Reduce heat to 275°F. and bake 10 to 15 minutes, or until golden. Remove immediately from baking sheet. Makes 18 to 20.

PALM LEAVES

A famous French pastry farm cooks can make—guaranteed to impress

½ recipe Basic Puff Pastry
    (Chapter 2)
Sugar

• Roll pastry on surface, sprinkled lightly with sugar, to a rectangle ½" thick. Sprinkle with sugar. Turn over and roll into a rectangle three times as long as it is wide and ⅜" thick. Sprinkle ¼ c. sugar over pastry.

• Fold ends of dough so that they meet in the middle; flatten slightly. Fold folded edges again to meet in the middle and flatten slightly.

• Now fold together lengthwise as you would in closing a book. Press together slightly and refrigerate at least

30 minutes. Then cut in 3 equal portions.

• Chill 2 baking sheets. Remove one from refrigerator and rinse with cold water. Place each pastry roll on its side and slice crosswise in ⅜" slices. Arrange 12 slices on baking sheet. Chill 30 minutes. Repeat process using other baking sheet and remainder of pastry.

• Bake one sheet at a time. Place in a very hot oven (450°F.) 5 minutes. Reduce temperature to 350°. Quickly turn pastry over, spreading leaf ends apart slightly with spatula. Continue baking until golden and crisp, 15 to 20 minutes. Cool on wire rack. Makes about 24.

CREAM TWISTS

These pastries are the famed French cornets—elegant cream-filled "horns"

½ recipe Basic Puff Pastry
    (Chapter 2)
1 egg white, slightly beaten
Granulated sugar
Whipped cream, sweetened
Walnuts
Shaved chocolate

• Make twist molds by wrapping strips of aluminum foil around 12 round wood clothespins to cover each completely.

• Roll pastry to 18" × 12" rectangle, ¼" thick. Cut lengthwise into 12 (1") strips.

• Wrap each strip, overlapping slightly, around a foil-covered clothespin. Do not stretch pastry. Place on baking sheet lined with brown paper.

• Brush with beaten egg white and

sprinkle lightly with sugar. Chill 30 minutes.

· Bake in hot oven (425°F.) 10 minutes. Reduce temperature to 350° and continue baking 20 minutes, or until pastry puffs and is golden. While hot, carefully push foil-covered clothespins out with handle of wooden spoon. Return "horns" to oven to dry out inside, 3 to 5 minutes. Cool completely before filling.

· Fill with whipped cream, using pastry bag and a Number 5 tip, ending with a swirl. Or fill with spoon, gently shaking the cream into the pastry "horn." Sprinkle with chopped walnuts and chocolate shavings.

Note: To freeze Cream Twists, refrigerate unbaked pastry-covered clothespins 30 minutes; wrap individually in foil, leaving clothespins in, and freeze. On the day you serve Cream Twists, unwrap and arrange on baking sheet lined with brown paper. Press gently against paper. Brush pastry with beaten egg white and sprinkle lightly with sugar. Bake in very hot oven (450°F.) 5 to 6 minutes; reduce temperature to 350° and bake until pastry puffs and is golden, 5 to 8 minutes. Carefully push out clothespins. Return "horns" to oven to dry out inside, 3 to 5 minutes. Cool on rack before filling.

Sandwich or Shortcake Tarts

Thrifty women often make these little pastries from scraps of leftover pie crust, but many a hostess bakes a supply of the pastry circles especially for shortcakes or pastry sandwiches. That's because they are so easy to fix —there's no shaping other than cutting with a cookie cutter.

A supply of baked pie crust rounds in the freezer is insurance you'll never want for refreshments when you have company. You can combine them with fruit or filling in the twinkling of an eye. You will be limited only by what you have in your freezer, refrigerator and cupboard—and your imagination.

STRAWBERRY ICE CREAM SANDWICHES

Hostess tip: Just right for the party that's coming up—make them ahead

Pastry for 2-crust pie
2   qts. vanilla ice cream
1   qt. strawberries
Sugar

· Divide pastry in halves and roll each half to ⅛" thickness. Cut in circles with 3" cookie cutter, preferably cutter with scalloped edge.

· Place on ungreased baking sheet

It's apple dumpling time! *Pour on the cream and dip your spoon through the flaky pastry into luscious fruit still faintly warm from the oven. Our pie book wouldn't be complete without Apple Dumplings de Luxe (recipe, page 190).*

and prick several times with four-tined fork. Bake in very hot oven (450°F.) until lightly browned, 5 to 7 minutes.

· Remove to rack. Cool. Wrap and freeze, if desired. Makes 22 circles.

· Place pan or tray in freezer to chill. Open carton of ice cream. Cut off ½" lengthwise slice of ice cream. Put remaining ice cream in freezer while you work with slice. Cut ice cream with 3" cookie cutter with scalloped edge.

· Place a circle of ice cream between two pastry rounds. Put immediately in freezer on chilled pan. Put scraps of ice cream left after cutting circles into chilled bowl and set in freezer.

· Continue in this manner until all the sandwiches are made. Keep in freezer until serving time. Serve topped with strawberries sweetened to taste with sugar. Makes 10 to 11 sandwiches. If you wish to make the sandwiches ahead, freeze them, then cover with airtight wrap and return to freezer.

Note: You will have approximately 3 to 4 c. ice cream scraps left over. Press into bowl, cover with foil or plastic wrap and place in freezer. Use in any way desired.

VARIATIONS

· Use sliced fresh peaches or ripe raspberries instead of strawberries for topping. Substitute other flavors of ice cream for vanilla. Try peach ice cream with raspberry topping.

OPEN-FACE PASTRY TARTS: Spread pastry rounds with softened cream cheese, then with sliced fresh peaches or strawberries, whole raspberries or blueberries. Top with whipped cream. Or top with filling for Vanilla Cream or Chocolate Cream Pie (Chapter 4), or with vanilla or chocolate pudding made from packaged mix, garnishing with whipped cream and a little of the fruit.

LEFTOVER PASTRY TREATS

· Sprinkle rolled pastry with mixture of sugar and cinnamon. Cut in fancy shapes and bake in very hot oven (450°F.) a few minutes, or until lightly browned.

JELLY TARTS: Roll out leftover pastry ⅛" thick. Cut in circles with 3" cookie cutter. Remove centers from half of the pastry rounds with small cutter (about size of a thimble). Prick pastry generously and bake on a baking sheet in a very hot oven (450°F.) a few minutes, or until lightly browned. Remove from oven, cool. Top the plain pastry rounds with those with "windows" in the center. Fill with colorful jelly or fruit preserves.

Fix some for the boys with peanut butter spread on the pastry rounds before adding the circles with center cutouts. Garnish them with jelly.

Two-Fruit hostess specials: *Prune-Apricot Tarts, one ungarnished, the other trimmed with scallops of cream cheese (recipe, page 199), and Strawberry-Pineapple Pie decorated with pastry cutouts (see page 70 for recipe).*

CHAPTER 8

FAST-FIX PIES

All of you have busy seasons when time for baking is short. That's when the quick and easy pie recipes in this chapter will come in handy. Maybe you'll need them most when apple blossoms cloud the air and spring work comes on with a bang, upsetting your cooking schedule and making quick meals a necessity. Or it may be during summer's gardening and food-preserving days or autumn's harvest when you scarcely can get enough time for cooking. Regardless of the season, you'll find the pies made from recipes in this chapter easy to fix and even easier to eat.

You'll notice that some of the recipes call for convenient packaged and canned foods. They do not always make as elegant and delectable pies as some of the more time-consuming "from scratch" recipes in this Cookbook. But we're willing to guarantee that these pies are most acceptable in looks and in taste. If you're serving them to company, you'll be proud of them.

Notice our special Soufflé Pie recipes. They are made by the method FARM JOURNAL home economists best like to use with packaged pie fillings. These are extra-pretty and extra-good pies—Butterscotch Pecan Soufflé Pie, for instance. And as we've mentioned elsewhere in this book, packaged and homemade pie crust mixes are a real help when the cook is in a hurry. So is pastry made with instant-type flour in the electric mixer.

While our fast-fix pies are for busy women who are experienced, excellent pie bakers, they also are for brides and young cooks learning their way around the kitchen. Try Bride's Peach Pie and see if the Praline Topping doesn't make it distinctive and luscious. Make Sunday-Best Banana Pie—we bet you'll agree that the homemaker who invented the recipe has been clever in decorating the pie for the holiday seasons. Don't miss the quintet of quick red cherry pies. And if the weather is hot and company is coming, make no-bake Party Chocolate Pie. No one will guess how little work it is. We promise you compliments on all the pies in this chapter.

Something New—Soufflé Pies

If you're looking for something new and tasty in fast-fix desserts, try our Soufflé Pies. Folding part of the pie filling, made from packaged pudding and pie mix, into the beaten egg whites instead of topping the pie with meringue, distributes flavor throughout the filling. And it's almost no extra work.

You get some charming color contrasts in the layered fillings, too. To see for yourself, start with Butterscotch Pecan Soufflé Pie—you'll like the pie you make. We also predict you'll use the recipe for Butterscotch Pie often, because it has a surprise taste (it's the best way we've discovered in our Test Kitchens for salvaging that half cup of canned pumpkin often left over after baking a pumpkin custard pie).

BUTTERSCOTCH PECAN SOUFFLÉ PIE

Your guests will never guess how easy this pie is to fix—it tastes so good

Baked 8″ pie shell
1 (4 oz.) pkg. butterscotch pudding and pie filling mix
2 c. milk
2 eggs, separated
½ c. chopped pecans, toasted
¼ tsp. salt
¼ tsp. cream of tartar
2 tblsp. sugar

• Combine pudding mix, ¼ c. milk and egg yolks in saucepan. Blend thoroughly. Add remaining milk and cook as directed on package. Remove ½ c. hot filling; cool 10 minutes, stirring several times.

• Stir remaining filling until smooth. Add pecans and pour into pie shell.

• Add salt and cream of tartar to egg whites; beat until frothy. Add sugar gradually, beating until stiff peaks form. Stir the ½ c. hot filling until smooth. Fold into egg white meringue in two parts. Pile on hot filling in pie shell; spread evenly out to edges. Bake in slow oven (325°F.) 20 to 22 minutes, until delicately browned. Cool several hours before serving.

BLACK BOTTOM SOUFFLÉ PIE

Not half the work most black bottom pies are—attractive and tasty

Baked 8″ pie shell
1 (3¼ oz.) pkg. vanilla pudding and pie filling mix
2 c. milk
2 eggs, separated
1 (6 oz.) pkg. semisweet chocolate pieces
¼ tsp. salt
¼ tsp. cream of tartar
2 tblsp. sugar

• Combine pie filling, ¼ c. milk and egg yolks in saucepan. Blend thoroughly. Add remaining milk and cook as directed on package. Remove ½ c. hot filling; cool 10 minutes, stirring several times.

• Add chocolate pieces to remaining hot filling; stir until melted and smooth. Pour into pie shell.

• Add salt and cream of tartar to egg whites; beat until frothy. Add sugar gradually, beating until stiff peaks form. Stir the ½ c. hot filling until smooth. Fold into egg white meringue in two parts. Pile on hot filling in pie shell; spread evenly out to edges. Bake in slow oven (325°F.) 20 to 22 minutes, until delicately browned. Cool several hours before serving.

LEMON GINGER SOUFFLÉ PIE

Brand-new taste experience—lemon and ginger flavors blend in filling

Baked 8″ pie shell
1 (3⅝ oz.) pkg. lemon pie filling
¾ c. sugar
2½ c. water
2 eggs, separated
¼ tsp. ginger
¼ tsp. salt

• Prepare pie filling as directed on package, using ½ c. sugar, water and egg yolks. Remove 1 c. of the hot filling, stir ginger into it and allow to cool 10 minutes.

• Cool remaining filling 5 minutes, stirring several times. Pour into pie shell.

• Add salt to egg whites; beat until frothy. Add remaining ¼ c. sugar gradually, beating until stiff peaks form.

• Stir the 1 c. of warm filling until smooth. Fold into egg white meringue

in two parts. Pile on hot filling in pie shell; spread evenly out to edges.

• Bake in hot oven (400°F.) 10 to 12 minutes, until delicately browned. Cool several hours before serving.

BUTTERSCOTCH PIE

Flavor secret is pumpkin—it mellows the butterscotch-coconut filling

Unbaked 8″ pie shell
1 (4 oz.) pkg. butterscotch pudding and pie filling mix
1 tsp. cinnamon
¼ tsp. nutmeg
¼ tsp. salt
½ c. cooked or canned pumpkin
2 c. milk
2 eggs, slightly beaten
1 c. flaked coconut

• Combine pie filling mix, spices and salt. Add pumpkin and stir until dry ingredients are moistened. Blend in milk gradually. Stir in eggs, blending well. Stir in coconut.

• Pour into pie shell. Bake in very hot oven (450°F.) 10 minutes. Reduce heat to 325° and continue baking 35 to 40 minutes, or until mixture doesn't adhere to knife when tested halfway between center and outer edge of pie. Cool to serve.

CHERRY CREAM PIE

Don't hesitate to serve this fast-fix pie to guests—they'll brag about it

Baked 9″ pie shell
1 (1 lb.) can pitted tart red cherries (water pack)   *more*

1   envelope unflavored gelatin
¼   c. cold water
1   (3 ¼ oz.) pkg. vanilla pudding
     and pie filling mix
2 ½ c. milk
¼   c. sugar
Few drops of red food color
1   (2 oz.) pkg. dessert topping mix
½   tsp. vanilla

· Drain cherries, saving juice.
· Soften gelatin in water.
· Prepare pie filling as directed on package, using 2 c. milk and 2 tblsp. sugar. Remove 1 c. of hot filling; add gelatin to it and stir until dissolved. Add remaining 2 tblsp. sugar and stir in cherry juice slowly. Add food color to tint mixture delicate pink. Cover and chill in refrigerator until partially set (about 1½ hours).
· Stir remaining hot filling until smooth. Add cherries and pour into pie shell. Cover and cool.
· Prepare dessert topping as directed on package, using ½ c. milk and vanilla. Beat partially set gelatin mixture until smooth. Fold into whipped topping. Pile lightly on cherry filling, spreading evenly to edges. Chill several hours before serving.

CHOCOLATE MOCHA PIE

Two different chocolate layers, distinctive with rich mocha taste

Baked 8″ pie shell
1   (4 oz.) pkg. chocolate pudding
     and pie filling mix
2 ½ c. milk
2   tsp. instant coffee powder
2   tblsp. sugar

1   (2 oz.) pkg. dessert topping mix
½   tsp. vanilla

· Prepare pie filling as directed on package, using 2 c. milk. Remove 1 c. of hot filling. Add instant coffee and sugar; stir to dissolve and blend. Chill thoroughly.
· Cool remaining filling 5 minutes, stirring several times. Pour into pie shell. Cool.
· Prepare dessert topping as directed on package, using remaining ½ c. milk and vanilla. Beat chilled cup of filling until smooth. Fold into topping. Pile lightly on cooled filling in pie shell, spreading evenly to edges. Chill several hours before serving.

BLUSHING APPLE PIE

Excellent way to use canned apple-sauce—pie filling is blush-red

8″ Graham Cracker Crumb Crust
     (Chapter 2)
2 ½ c. thick applesauce
¼   c. red cinnamon candies (red
     hots)
Whipped cream

· Combine applesauce and red hots in saucepan. Heat just enough to dissolve candy. Cool thoroughly. Pour into cool crumb crust.
· Chill at least 1 hour. Garnish with whipped cream at serving time.

Note: For an attractive pie, save out ⅓ c. crumb mixture when making crust and sprinkle it over top of pie.

BRIDE'S PEACH PIE

Praline Topping adds a gourmet touch

Baked 8″ pie shell
1   (1 lb. 13 oz.) can sliced peaches
1   tblsp. cornstarch
Few drops almond extract
Praline Topping (Chapter 9)

· Drain peaches. Measure ¾ c. syrup. Add gradually to cornstarch in saucepan, stirring to blend.
· Cook, stirring constantly, until thick and clear. Add almond extract and drained peaches. Cool and pour into pie shell. Top with Praline Topping (Chapter 9).

Jiffy Holiday Pie

The Oregon homemaker who originated the recipe for this banana pie, likes to feature the dessert in her Sunday-best meals—often on holidays. For Halloween, she tints the whipped cream yellow and makes a pumpkin face on it with orange segments. For the Christmas season, she tints the topping a pale green and adds a wreath of tiny candies of many colors. She says she makes the pie in a few minutes, but that no one guesses she hasn't labored much longer over it. She chills the pie at least two hours before serving, often several hours.

SUNDAY-BEST BANANA PIE

Tasty example of a pie created in the home kitchen of an artist-cook

8″ Graham Cracker Crumb Crust

1   (3 ¼ oz.) pkg. vanilla pudding
     and pie filling mix
2   c. milk
2   bananas
1   c. heavy cream
½   tsp. vanilla
¼   c. sugar
3   tblsp. finely chopped walnuts

· Put pudding mix and milk in saucepan; cook as directed on package. Cool 5 minutes, stirring once or twice.
· Slice 1 banana and spread over bottom of crust. Pour on pudding mixture. Chill about 3 hours.
· To serve, slice remaining banana over top of pie. Whip cream; add vanilla and sugar. Spread over pie and sprinkle with walnuts.

HURRY-UP MINCEMEAT PIE

Applesauce blends with mincemeat, lemon juice points up fruity flavors

Pastry for 2-crust pie
1   (1 lb. 12 oz.) jar prepared
     mincemeat (3 c.)
1   c. applesauce
¼   c. lemon juice

· Combine mincemeat, applesauce and lemon juice. Spread in pastry-lined 9″ pie pan. Adjust top crust; flute edges and cut vents.
· Bake in hot oven (400°F.) about 40 minutes, or until pie is golden brown.

QUICK CHERRY PIE

You can make this cherry pie "quick as a cat can blink his eye"

Baked 9" pie shell
1 (15 oz.) can sweetened con-
    densed milk (1 ⅓ c.)
¼ c. lemon juice
1 (1 lb. 4 oz.) can tart cherries
    (1 ½ c. drained)
¼ tsp. almond extract
Coconut

· Blend the condensed milk with
lemon juice. The mixture will thicken
slightly.
· Stir in drained cherries and almond
extract; pour mixture into baked pie
shell. Sprinkle coconut over top. Chill
until ready to serve.

CREAM CHERRY PIE

So easy to fix—so color-gay

Baked 9" pie shell
1 (3 oz.) pkg. cream cheese
¼ c. sugar
½ tsp. vanilla
1 c. heavy cream, whipped
1 (1 lb. 5 oz.) can prepared
    cherry pie filling

· Beat together cream cheese, sugar
and vanilla until light and fluffy. Fold
in whipped cream. Spread evenly in
pie shell.
· Spoon pie filling over top. Chill
thoroughly before serving.

Note: Substitute other canned fruit pie
fillings for the cherry.

CHERRY-CHEESE PIE

*No one will guess this beautiful pie is
a fast-fix one you made ahead*

Pastry for 1-crust pie
1 (1 lb. 6 oz.) can cherry pie
    filling
2 (3 oz.) pkgs. cream cheese,
    room temperature
¼ c. sugar
2 eggs
½ tsp. vanilla
1 c. dairy sour cream

· Line 8" pie pan with pastry and
flute edges. Spread half of cherry pie
filling over bottom of pastry. Bake in
hot oven (425°F.) 15 minutes, or until
pastry is browned.
· Meanwhile, soften cream cheese in
electric mixer. Blend in sugar gradually; beat in eggs and vanilla. Pour this
mixture over hot cherry filling in pie
shell. Reduce oven temperature to
350°F. and continue baking 20 minutes.
· Cool pie and place in refrigerator.
Before serving, spoon sour cream
around rim of pie, and spoon remaining half of cherry pie filling in center.

FROZEN STRAWBERRY PIE

*Good insurance that your dessert
ready in freezer will please guests*

2 (9") Graham Cracker Crumb
    Crusts (Chapter 2)
1 (10 oz.) pkg. frozen strawber-
    ries, thawed
1 c. sugar
2 egg whites
1 tblsp. lemon juice
1 c. heavy cream

• Put berries, sugar, egg whites and lemon juice in mixer bowl; beat 15 minutes at high speed.

• Whip cream and fold into strawberry mixture. Pile high in 9" foil pie pans lined with crumb crusts. Freeze; remove from freezer and place in plastic bags and seal. Serve without defrosting. Makes 2 pies or 10 servings.

VARIATION

FROZEN PEACH PIE: Substitute 1 (12 oz.) pkg. frozen peaches, thawed, for strawberries and follow directions for Frozen Strawberry Pie, adding ¼ tsp. almond extract to the whipped cream.

PARTY CHOCOLATE PIE

A no-bake pie, cool to make in summer—filling is rich and velvety

9" Graham Cracker Crumb Crust (Chapter 2)
1   c. butter or margarine
1 ½ c. sugar
3   squares unsweetened chocolate, melted and cooled
¼   tsp. peppermint extract
2   tsp. vanilla
4   eggs

• Cream butter in electric mixer, adding sugar gradually. Add chocolate, peppermint extract and vanilla, mixing well.

• Add eggs, one at a time, beating with electric beater, 5 minutes after adding each egg.

• Pour mixture into crumb pie shell. Chill at least 2 hours. Makes 10 to 12 servings.

CHOCOLATE-PINEAPPLE PIE

Frosty cold—exciting flavor blend

1   pt. chocolate ice cream
1   (8 oz.) can crushed pineapple, drained
1   pt. pineapple sherbet
Shaved semisweet chocolate

• Spread slightly softened chocolate ice cream on sides and bottom of 9" pie pan, hollowing out in center. Freeze.

• Remove from freezer and spread on pineapple. Freeze.

• Top with pineapple sherbet and shaved chocolate. Freeze.

• Cut in wedges to serve. Makes 6 to 8 servings.

FUDGE NUT CREAM PIE

Creamy and rich with double chocolate flavor of homemade fudge

Baked 9" pie shell
2   (4 oz.) pkgs. chocolate pudding and pie filling mix
3   c. milk
1   (6 oz.) pkg. semisweet chocolate pieces
2   tblsp. butter or margarine
1   tsp. vanilla
½   c. chopped walnuts
½   c. heavy cream, whipped

• Combine pudding mix, milk and chocolate pieces in saucepan. Cook, stirring constantly, over medium heat until chocolate melts and pudding comes to a boil. Remove from heat and blend in butter and vanilla.

more

• Cool 5 minutes, stirring occasionally. Pour into cool pie shell. Sprinkle chopped nuts over pie, but not quite to edges. Chill. Serve garnished with whipped cream, spooned in ring around edge of pie. Serves 6 to 8.

CHOCOLATE PEANUT PIE

You can omit peanuts, but they add flavor and texture to this party pie

Baked 8″ pie shell
1 (4 oz.) pkg. chocolate pudding and pie filling mix
2 tblsp. brown sugar, firmly packed
½ square unsweetened chocolate
2 c. milk
2 eggs, separated
2 tblsp. butter or margarine
⅓ c. chopped salted peanuts
Meringue (2 egg whites)

• Combine pudding mix, brown sugar, chocolate and ¼ c. milk in saucepan. Add egg yolks and blend well. Then add remaining 1¾ c. milk. Cook over medium heat, stirring constantly, until mixture comes to a boil.
• Remove from heat and stir in butter. Cool at least 5 minutes, stirring two or three times.
• Scatter peanuts in cool pie shell. Pour on chocolate mixture and spread evenly. Top with meringue (see Perfect Meringue for Topping Pies, Chapter 9) and bake in moderate oven (350°F.) until delicately browned, (12 minutes). Cool away from drafts.

VARIATION

• Omit salted peanuts and use Peanut Pie Shell (see Chapter 2) instead of plain pastry pie shell.

CALIFORNIA BROWNIE PIE

A make-ahead pie you can refrigerate 2 or 3 days—also a good freezer

3 egg whites
⅛ tsp. salt
¾ c. sugar
¾ c. fine chocolate wafer crumbs
½ c. chopped walnuts
½ tsp. vanilla
Sweetened whipped cream
Shaved unsweetened chocolate

• Beat egg whites and salt until soft peaks form. Gradually add sugar; beat until very stiff.
• Fold in cookie crumbs, nuts and vanilla. Spread evenly in lightly buttered 9″ pie pan.
• Bake in slow oven (325°F.) about 35 minutes. Cool thoroughly.
• Spread with 1 c. heavy cream, whipped and sweetened with 2 tblsp. sugar; garnish with shaved chocolate. Chill 3 to 4 hours.

Note: For speed, use a potato peeler to shave chocolate.

MALLOW BANANA PIE: Slice bananas in baked 9″ pie shell, top with prepared packaged vanilla pie filling, cover with miniature marshmallows and brown lightly under broiler.

When Company's Coming

The generous woman, who shares this recipe, says she often bakes the pie after friends telephone they'll be stopping by. She serves it fresh out of the oven with tea or coffee. Her guests almost always compliment her on how attractive the pie is and someone usually asks: "May I have the recipe?"

AFTERNOON PARTY PIE

Cookielike crust holds colorful jam— you can fix this one in a jiffy

½ c. butter or margarine
½ c. sugar
1 egg
1 c. sifted flour
⅛ tsp. salt
¼ c. chopped almonds or pecans
1 c. red raspberry jam or preserves
½ c. flaked coconut

· Combine butter, sugar and egg and thoroughly mix. Add flour, salt and nuts. Press mixture into a 9″ pie pan. Spread with jam.
· Bake in hot oven (400°F.) until lightly browned, about 15 minutes. Cool on cakerack. (Pie is on the thin side.) Serve sprinkled with coconut. Makes 6 servings.

VARIATION

· Substitute apricot jam or preserves for the raspberry.

WINTER STRAWBERRY-CHEESE PIE

Vary this company dessert with different kinds of fruit preserves

Baked 9″ pie shell
1 (8 oz.) pkg. cream cheese
½ c. sugar
3 eggs, beaten
½ c. milk
1 tsp. vanilla
1 (12 oz.) glass strawberry preserves
Whipped cream

· Combine cream cheese, softened at room temperature, and sugar; mix to blend thoroughly.
· Gradually stir in eggs, milk and vanilla. Pour into pie shell.
· Bake in moderate oven (350°F.) 25 minutes. Cool. Top with strawberry preserves and whipped cream or dairy sour cream. Makes 6 to 8 servings.

SUNDAE PIE

Keep one in the freezer for quick use

Baked 9″ pie shell
1 qt. vanilla ice cream
Chocolate sauce
Chopped nuts

· Spread slightly softened ice cream in cool pie shell. Wrap in aluminum foil and freeze.
· To serve, cut in wedges and pass a

pitcher of chocolate sauce and small dish of chopped nuts for serving on pie.

Note: Vary the dessert by using different kinds of ice cream and sauces.

ANGEL COCONUT PIE

Looks like a party! A hostess sweet that's a real treat—so easy to fix

1   c. crushed graham crackers
½   c. grated or flaked coconut
½   c. chopped nuts (optional)
5   egg whites
1   c. sugar
Whipped cream
9   maraschino cherries

· Combine graham crackers, coconut and nuts. Mix thoroughly.
· Beat egg whites until stiff. Fold in sugar. Fold in cracker, coconut and nut mixture.
· Spread in well-greased 9″ pie pan. Bake in moderate oven (350°F.) 30 minutes.
· To serve, cut in wedges. Top each with whipped cream and a maraschino cherry. Makes 9 servings.

Pie for the Busy Hostess

If you ever return home late on the day you're having company for dinner, here's just the pie for you to have ready in the refrigerator. Everyone will think it's a cheese pie rather than the easy, make-ahead with a packaged mix the basis of the filling. This is a regal beauty with colorful fruit preserves or sliced, fresh fruit on top of the snowy white filling. Add the decorative trim at the last minute. The best part of the dessert is its wonderful taste.

SNOW CREAM PIE

Favorite with the cook, because it's easy; with guests, because it's good

Graham Cracker Crumb Crust (Chapter 2)
1   (3¾ oz.) pkg. instant vanilla pudding
1   c. dairy sour cream
1   c. milk
½   c. strawberry preserves

· Combine pudding mix with liquids (sour cream and milk) as directed on package. Mixture will be quite liquid.
· Pour into 8″ crumb crust. Chill until set, at least 1 hour, or longer.
· To serve, spoon strawberry preserves over top. Or use other fruit preserves or sweetened sliced fruit, like strawberries or peaches. Makes 6 servings.

Note: Use a baked crumb crust.

SPUR-OF-THE-MOMENT HOSTESS IDEA: When company comes on short notice, one farm woman makes peach pie in a few minutes like this: Drain canned peaches thoroughly. Put ¾ c. syrup drained from fruit in saucepan with 1 tblsp. cornstarch. Cook over low heat until mixture thickens and is clear. Add a drop or two of almond extract,

3 drops of red food color and ½ tsp. grated lemon peel. You have a pink, peach glaze.
· Take a baked pie shell from the freezer. Arrange drained peach halves in it. Spoon glaze over fruit. Garnish pie with whipped cream and serve it with pride. Softened vanilla ice cream may be used instead of whipped cream, if it's easier.

Timesaving Pies

Recipes for the following eight pies are from our TIMESAVING COOKBOOK. They are so quick and easy and such good pies that we felt we must include them in our Fast-Fix Pies chapter.

HAWAIIAN PINEAPPLE PIE

Combine pineapple and coconut in a pie for exotic, tropical flavors

1   pkg. refrigerator coconut cookie dough
1   (3 oz.) pkg. vanilla pudding and pie filling mix
⅛   tsp. salt
½   c. water
1   (20 oz.) can crushed pineapple, drained
1   tblsp. butter or margarine
½   c. heavy cream, whipped
⅓   c. flaked or shredded coconut

· Slice cookie dough in ¼″ slices. Arrange slices in 9″ pie pan, first lining bottom of pan, then sides. (Let side slices rest on bottom ones to make higher sides.) Bake in moderate oven (375°F.) until lightly browned, 9 to 12 minutes.

· Meanwhile combine pudding mix and salt in saucepan. Blend in water. Add pineapple and cook over medium heat, stirring constantly, until mixture comes to a full boil. Stir in butter.
· Pour hot filling into pie shell. Cool. Spread whipped cream over top. Sprinkle with coconut.

CRANBERRY-MINCEMEAT PIE

Keep the relish on hand for this pie

Unbaked 9″ pie shell
3   c. prepared mincemeat
1   c. Cranberry Relish

· Combine mincemeat and Cranberry Relish; pour into pie shell.
· Bake in hot oven (400°F.) 35 minutes.

CRANBERRY RELISH: Put pulp and peel of 4 seeded oranges (medium), 2 lbs. cranberries and 4 cored unpeeled apples (medium) through food grinder. Add 4 c. sugar and mix well. Cover and refrigerate. Or pour into glass jars, leaving ½″ head space, seal and freeze. Makes 4 pints.

FROZEN PUMPKIN PIE

Freeze this to serve on short notice

Baked 9″ pie shell
1 qt. vanilla ice cream, slightly softened
1 c. canned pumpkin, or cooked, sieved pumpkin
⅓ c. sugar
½ tsp. salt
1 tsp. cinnamon
½ tsp. ginger
½ tsp. ground cloves
¼ c. chopped walnuts

• Beat together ice cream, pumpkin, sugar, salt and spices with electric beater until well blended.
• Pour into pie shell. Sprinkle with nuts. Freeze until firm. If pie is kept longer, store in a plastic bag. Serve frozen. Makes 6 servings.

DANISH RASPBERRY PIE

Filling makes extra-good dessert, too

Baked 8″ pie shell
1 c. cold water
1 pkg. Danish-dessert mix, currant-raspberry flavor
1 (10 oz.) pkg. frozen raspberries
1 c. heavy cream, whipped

• Add water to Danish-dessert mix. Bring to boil and boil 1 minute, stirring constantly. Add raspberries; cool.
• Pour into cooled pie shell; refrigerate several hours. Garnish with whipped cream.

BROWNIE PIE

Chocolate lovers laud this pie

Unbaked 9″ pie shell
1 (1 lb.) pkg. brownie mix
¼ c. chocolate syrup
¼ c. chopped nuts
Whipped cream

• Prepare brownie mix as directed on package for fudgy brownies. Spread mixture evenly in pie shell. Pour chocolate syrup evenly over top. Sprinkle with nuts.
• Bake in moderate oven (350°F.) 40 to 45 minutes. Serve warm, topped with whipped cream. Makes 10 servings.

NORTH POLE CHERRY PIE

It says: Merry Christmas to all!

Baked 9″ pie shell or crumb crust
1 qt. vanilla ice cream
1 (1 lb. 6 oz.) can cherry pie filling

• Spread slightly softened ice cream in pie shell and freeze. (You may tint ice cream delicate green.)
• An hour before serving, spread filling over top. Return to freezer. Serve quickly.

FROZEN MINCEMEAT PIE

Fix it ahead for holiday meals

Baked 9″ pie shell
1 qt. vanilla ice cream, slightly softened
1½ c. prepared mincemeat

¼ c. chopped nuts
Maraschino cherries, well drained

· Beat together ice cream and mincemeat. Spread into pie shell. Sprinkle with nuts and maraschino cherries, cut in halves.
· Freeze until solid, about 4 hours. If kept longer, place in plastic bag. Serve frozen.

APRICOT PIE À LA MODE

Canned apricots go glamorous in pie

Unbaked 9″ pie shell
1   (1 lb. 13 oz.) can apricot halves, drained

1   tblsp. lemon juice
½   c. flour
¾   c. sugar
¼   tsp. cinnamon
¼   tsp. nutmeg
¼   c. butter or margarine
1   pt. vanilla ice cream

· Spread apricots in pie shell; sprinkle with lemon juice.
· Combine flour, sugar and spices. Mix with butter until crumbly. Sprinkle over apricots.
· Bake in hot oven (400°F.) 40 minutes. Serve warm or cold, topped with scoops of ice cream.

CHAPTER 9

PIE TOPPINGS

Toppings are to pie what frostings are to cake—sweet flavor boosters. Spread slightly warm apple pie with Caramel or Molasses Topping, and see what a remarkable difference that homey country-kitchen taste makes. It gives traditional apple pie an exciting new taste.

Try one of the bake-on toppings—there's Spiced Crust Topping, for instance, that turns gold in the oven and leaves the pie crisp on top. Or spoon a glistening glaze over an open-face fruit pie for a finishing touch (see the glacé pies in Chapter 3). Ladle a sweet sauce like Vanilla Cream, reminiscent in flavor of homemade ice cream on apple pie—or Fluffy Orange Sauce. Spoon Amber Caramel Sauce over Pumpkin Pie.

Don't be surprised, when you stop in a neighbor's kitchen for a friendly visit, to find your hostess with one eye on the oven while a topping broils on a pie—Broiled Marshmallow Topping, so delicious on Chocolate Cream Pie. Peanut Butter Cream Topping broiled on banana pie is equally good.

Our grandmothers depended on handsome meringues, swirled whipped cream and scoops of rich, homemade ice cream to top their pies. Grandfathers also had ideas—they frequently poured thick cream over their wedges of fruit pies. It's only recently that the trend to exciting, new pie toppings has picked up momentum.

Besides this chapter of toppings, you'll find recipes for others throughout this Cookbook along with the pies they enhance—Apple-Raisin Pie spread with Orange Frosting, Peach Cream Pie with Lemon Crumb Topping and Concord Grape Pie with a butter-brown sugar streusel containing rolled oats, for examples. We list locations for these toppings at the end of this chapter to help you find them in a hurry.

While some toppings are on the fancy side, most are simple and homespun, like creamy cottage cheese touched with honey and a dash of ginger —delicious on blueberry, peach and our own Peach-Blueberry combination (Chapter 3). We believe you'll not be able to resist the creative toppings for cream pies worked out in our Test Kitchens—they're that unusual.

Gold-Tipped Meringues

Meringues decorate more 1-crust pies than all other toppings put together. And they glorify more lemon pies than any other kind. That's partly because lemon meringue pies long have been farm favorites. But there are other reasons. Meringues are easy to make, too, and they glamorize pies that are lighter endings for hearty meals than 2-crust specials. Then, the practical cook makes meringues with the egg whites left over from fillings that call for yolks.

To be successful with meringue toppings all you need do is *follow the directions* in our recipes. Do pay special attention to dissolving the sugar in the egg whites and to spreading the meringue over the top of the filling so that it touches the edge of the crust around the pie. To keep the topping high and handsome, the way it comes from the oven, protect it from drafts. Home economists sometimes make a screen of stiff paper to stand up around the pie to divert wandering breezes. Let pie cool on rack at least 1 hour.

You can tint meringue before spreading it on pie, if you wish. We like delicate pink meringue on our Pink Party Pie (Chapter 5). And you can put meringue in your pastry tube and press a fluffy collar around the edge of a pie and a design in the center. One farm homemaker says she sometimes makes a meringue lattice on fruit pies with colorful fillings. Here are her directions: Pipe four strips across pie one way (touching ends to crusts), four the other way, slantwise,

so openings will be diamond-shaped. Broil 8" to 10" from heat until delicately browned, 2 to 3 minutes.

PERFECT MERINGUE FOR TOPPING PIES

For 8" Pie

2   egg whites
¼   tsp. cream of tartar
⅛   tsp. salt
¼   tsp. vanilla
¼   c. sugar

For 9" Pie

3   egg whites
¼   tsp. cream of tartar
¼   tsp. salt
½   tsp. vanilla
6   tblsp. sugar

For 10" Pie

4   egg whites
¼   tsp. cream of tartar
¼   tsp. salt
½   tsp. vanilla
½   c. sugar

• Have egg whites at room temperature to obtain greatest volume. Place them in a medium bowl with cream of tartar, salt and vanilla.
• Beat with electric or hand beater, at medium speed, until entire mixture is frothy. Do not beat until eggs stiffen.
• Add sugar, a little at a time, beating well after each addition. Do not under-

beat. Beat until sugar dissolves to help prevent beading (those brown syrup drops on top). To test, rub some of the meringue between your fingers to see if it's still grainy. (The grains are undissolved sugar.) Continue to beat until stiff, pointed peaks form when you lift beater slowly.

• Place spoonfuls of meringue around edge of pie filling, spreading it so it touches inner edge of crust to seal all around. This prevents shrinkage. Pile remainder of meringue in center of pie and spread to meet meringue around edge. If the filling is not covered completely, the oven heat may cause it to weep. (Stirring the cooked filling may cause it to weep; water will collect under the meringue.) Lift up meringue over pie in points with back of teaspoon.

• Bake in moderate oven (350°F.) 12 to 15 minutes, or until meringue peaks are golden brown. Too long baking may cause weeping. Cool gradually away from drafts.

COUNTRY-STYLE MERINGUE: With egg whites plentiful in farm kitchens, many country pie bakers like to use 5 egg whites and 10 tblsp. sugar to make a high cover on their 9" and 10" pies.

Note: You can substitute 1 tsp. lemon juice for cream of tartar when making meringues for lemon, lime and orange pies. The acid in the juice gives the same result—a wonderful meringue!

Pretty Dress-Ups for Cream Pies

The best way to give pale (but delicious!) cream pies color appeal and extra flavor is to add sweet toppings. This chapter contains several suggestions for fascinating toppings for vanilla-flavored and other cream pies. The directions were developed in our Countryside Kitchens, where taste testers gave them enthusiastic approval and praise.

VANILLA CREAM PIE TOPPINGS

MERINGUE: Combine 3 egg whites, ¼ tsp. salt and ¼ tsp. cream of tartar in small mixing bowl. Beat at high speed until frothy. Gradually add 6 tblsp. sugar, beating at high speed until stiff glossy peaks form and sugar is dissolved. Pile on lukewarm filling, covering evenly out to edges and seal to crust. Bake in slow oven (300°F.) about 20 minutes, or until lightly browned. Cool away from drafts.

JAM MERINGUE: Add ¼ tsp. salt to 3 egg whites. Beat at high speed until frothy. Stir ¼ c. fruit jam until smooth; then add gradually, beating at high speed until stiff glossy peaks are formed. Add a few drops of food color for a delicate color. Spread meringue over lukewarm filling. Bake in slow oven (300°F.) 20 minutes, or until lightly browned.

COCONUT MACAROON TOPPING: Combine 2 slightly beaten egg whites and ⅓ c. sugar. Stir in 1 (3½ oz.) can flaked coconut. Spoon in little mounds all over top of cream filling. Then spread gently to cover completely. Broil 8″ to 10″ from heat, 3 to 4 minutes, or until delicately browned. This browns quickly, so watch carefully.

CONFETTI TOPPING: Combine 1 c. miniature marshmallows, 1 (8½ oz.) can crushed pineapple, well drained (½ c.) and ¼ c. chopped maraschino cherries. Cover cream filling evenly with this mixture. Broil 8″ to 10″ from heat until marshmallows are puffed and soft, but not brown (1 to 2 minutes). Remove from broiler, spread out marshmallows with spatula. Return to broiler until delicate brown (1 to 2 minutes).

Note: You may substitute ½ c. well-drained fruit cocktail for pineapple and cherries in Confetti Topping.

Fluffy Whipped Cream Toppings

No farm woman needs to be reminded how attractive puffs of whipped cream are on pies. But you may have forgotten how your grandmother swirled it on pies and garnished it with homemade jellies or strawberry and other fruit preserves. We borrowed a trick from her for our Snow Cream Pie (Chapter 8)—try it, just in case you've forgotten how pretty and tasty berry preserves are on pie. And we've used jellies, melted, for glazing some of our best 1-crust fruit and berry pies and tarts.

Sweeten whipped cream slightly for topping pies. Add 2 to 4 tblsp. sifted confectioners sugar to 1 c. heavy cream in deep bowl. Chill, then whip until stiff. Makes about 2 cups.

Note: Dairy sour cream frequently substitutes for whipped cream in topping pies. It's one of today's success stories in the food world. The light cream, pasteurized, has a tangy taste and a custardlike consistency, due to the starter or culture added to sour it.

Look up Cherry-Cheese Pie (Chapter 8) and you'll see how fancy sour cream makes this quick-fix pie.

MAPLE CREAM: Whip 1 c. heavy cream. Pour ¼ c. maple syrup in a fine stream over it, carefully folding it in. Cover the top of pumpkin or squash pie with the cream, swirling it attractively.

CREAM LATTICE: Put whipped cream in pastry tube. Press it out on top of a 1-crust pie, making a lattice, or three circles. Or make a collar of whipped cream around edge of pie.

ALMOND CREAM: Chill 1 c. heavy cream, 2 to 4 tblsp. sifted confectioners sugar and ¼ tsp. almond extract in deep bowl. Beat until stiff. Makes about 2 cups. A tasty dress-up for cherry and peach pies!

FLUFFY CARAMEL SAUCE: Add 6 tblsp. brown sugar, firmly packed, and ½ tsp. vanilla to 1 c. heavy cream.

Refrigerate 30 minutes. Whip until stiff. Wonderful on peach, apple and pumpkin pies!

COCOA WHIPPED CREAM: Chill 1½ c. heavy cream, ½ c. sugar and ⅓ c. cocoa in deep bowl. Beat until stiff. Excellent on Vanilla and Banana Cream Pies when serving a crowd (makes enough for 4 pies).

GINGER WHIPPED CREAM: Add 1 tblsp. shaved candied ginger or ½ tsp. powdered ginger to 1 c. heavy cream, whipped.

COFFEE CREAM TOPPING: Chill ¾ c. heavy cream, 2 tblsp. sifted confectioners sugar and 2 tsp. instant coffee powder in bowl. Beat until stiff and fluffy. Marvelous on pumpkin pie and good on any fruit pie.

HONEYED CREAM: Whip 1 c. heavy cream until stiff. Gently stir in about 1 tblsp. strained honey. Extra-good on pumpkin pie.

FLUFFY ORANGE SAUCE

Turns homey cobblers into company fare—especially good on apple cobbler

½ c. sugar
⅛ tsp. salt
½ c. thawed frozen orange juice
     concentrate
2 egg yolks, slightly beaten
1 c. heavy cream, whipped

• Combine sugar, salt and orange juice in saucepan. Cook over low heat, stirring until sugar dissolves.
• Gradually beat a little of the orange mixture into egg yolks. Combine with remainder of hot orange mixture. Cook, stirring constantly, until slightly thickened, about 8 to 10 minutes. Cool.
• About an hour before mealtime, fold in whipped cream. Chill. Makes about 2⅔ cups.

Cheese Makes Pie Extra-Good

Our grandmothers frequently topped fruit pies with spoonfuls of creamy cottage cheese, sprinkled lightly with cinnamon. And men have liked so much to eat Cheddar cheese slices with apple and other fruit pies that the dessert team has gained universal popularity. No clever cook wants to abandon these firmly established customs, but many women also like to find new ways of combining cheese with pie. We give you a few good examples. Try them and then invent a few combinations of your own.

CHEESE CRUST TOPPING

New way to add cheese to apple pie

1 egg white
1 tblsp. grated Parmesan cheese

• Beat egg white until stiff peaks are formed. Fold in cheese.
• Spread over unbaked top crust of apple pie. Bake as directed for regular 2-crust apple pie. Serve warm.

HONEYED CHEESE: Mix 1 tblsp. honey into ½ c. cottage cheese. Add a dash of ginger, if desired. Serve on Peach-Blueberry Pie or on peach and blueberry pies.

ORANGE CHEESE: Soften 1 (3 oz.) pkg. cream cheese with 1 tblsp. orange juice. Spoon on peach or apple pie wedges.

DIFFERENT CHEESE TOPPING: Crumble a little Roquefort or blue cheese on top of apple pie. Return to oven just long enough to heat. A nice change from Cheddar cheese!

FRUIT VELVET TOPPING

Glamorizes vanilla cream pies

2   tblsp. water
3   tblsp. fruit flavor gelatin (strawberry, raspberry or cherry)
1   (3 oz.) pkg. cream cheese
2   tblsp. sugar

⅛   tsp. salt
1   (2 or 2¼ oz.) pkg. dessert topping mix

· Add water to gelatin; dissolve over hot water.
· Have cream cheese at room temperature; stir smooth in small bowl. Add sugar and salt. Add dissolved gelatin gradually, stirring to blend evenly with cheese.
· Prepare dessert topping mix according to package directions. Fold cheese mixture into whipped topping.
· Spread on top of cooled vanilla cream filling in 8″ or 9″ pie shell.
· Refrigerate several hours before serving. For smooth cutting, use warm knife.

VARIATION

· Use ½ c. fruit jam instead of gelatin and water.

Broiled Toppings de Luxe

Some of the most fascinating toppings are broiled after they're spread on ready-to-serve pies. You have to mind what you're doing for a few minutes to see that the topping doesn't brown unevenly or too much. But you'll find it's worth the careful watching for 2 or 3 minutes.

BROILED MARSHMALLOW TOPPING

Excellent on Chocolate Cream Pie

16   marshmallows (¼ lb.)
1   tblsp. milk

¼   tsp. salt
2   egg whites
¼   c. sugar

· Melt marshmallows in milk over hot water; stir until smooth. Let stand over hot water until ready to use.
· Add salt to egg whites; beat until frothy. Add sugar gradually, beating until stiff peaks are formed. Fold in marshmallow mixture. Spread gently over hot cream filling.
· Broil 8″ to 10″ from heat until delicately browned, 2 to 3 minutes. Watch closely, turning to brown evenly.
· Chill thoroughly before serving.

PEANUT BUTTER CREAM TOPPING

Use to top banana pie—a tasty team!

8	marshmallows
1	tblsp. milk
2	tblsp. creamy peanut butter
1/8	tsp. salt
1	egg white
2	tblsp. sugar

• Melt marshmallows in milk over hot water. Add peanut butter; stir until smooth. Let stand over hot water until ready to use.

• Add salt to egg white; beat until frothy. Add sugar gradually, beating until stiff peaks are formed. Fold in marshmallow mixture. Spread gently over hot filling.
• Broil 8″ to 10″ from heat until golden brown, 2 to 3 minutes. Watch closely, turning to brown evenly.
• Chill thoroughly before serving.

Note: Substitute for the meringue in recipe for Banana Meringue Pie (Chapter 4).

Baked-On Pie Toppings

Here are tops for pies that are almost no bother; yet they add distinction, both in flavor and texture. You spread them on the top crust just before you put the pie in the oven to bake. Be sure to notice the different suggestions for types of cookies to use on various kinds of pies in the Cookie Crust Topping recipe.

pie. Mark pieces for cutting while pie is still hot from oven.

Note: Use Butterscotch Nut Cookies on mincemeat; Oatmeal Raisin Cookies on apple; and Sugar Cookies, sprinkled with sugar and cinnamon, on cherry filling.

COOKIE CRUST TOPPING

Clever trick for busy pie bakers

Unbaked pie shell filled with canned
    mincemeat, cherry or apple
    pie filling
1/4 roll commercial refrigerator
    cookie dough (14 slices)

• Slice refrigerator cookie dough in 1/8″ slices; cut slices in quarters. Arrange to cover top of filling in pie shell.
• Bake as directed for regular 2-crust

SPICED CRUST TOPPING

It will make your apple pie a favorite at church suppers and bake sales

1	tsp. cinnamon
1/4	tsp. nutmeg
1/8	tsp. cloves
1	egg white

• Add spices to egg white and beat until stiff peaks are formed.
• Spread over unbaked top crust of apple pie. Bake as directed for regular 2-crust apple pie. Serve warm.

Wonderful Nutty Tops

Nuts add crunchy texture and rich flavors—both in and on pies. Almost any chiffon pie is enhanced by a sprinkling of chopped nuts at serving time —black walnuts do wonders for chocolate pies. This section deals with nut toppings; the nut pies are in Chapter 4.

CARAMELIZED ALMONDS: Place ¼ c. blanched almonds and 2 tblsp. sugar in skillet. Cook, stirring constantly, until golden brown. Pour on greased baking sheet at once. Cool and break apart. Sprinkle over chiffon pies at serving time.

PEANUT CRUNCH CREAM: Chill ½ c. heavy cream, 1 tblsp. sugar and ½ tsp. vanilla in deep bowl. Beat until stiff. Fold in ¼ c. finely crushed peanut brittle. Excellent on pumpkin pie.

PRALINE TOPPING

Wonderful on all kinds of peach pies

3 tblsp. butter
¼ c. brown sugar
⅓ c. coarsely broken walnuts
1 c. corn flakes

• Melt butter, add sugar and boil 2 minutes.
• Add walnuts and corn flakes. Toss lightly to coat all evenly.
• Cool; crumble over fruit filling in baked pie shell. Chill before serving. Makes enough for 1 (8″ or 9″) pie.

BLACK WALNUT-BROWN SUGAR TOPPING: Combine 3 tblsp. melted butter, ½ c. brown sugar and ¼ c. chopped black walnuts. Sprinkle over top of warm apple or peach pie.

Last-Minute Toppings

You spread these toppings on slightly warm 2-crust pies when you serve them. They are simple to make, but rewarding in taste. Here are a few we predict you'll adopt.

CARAMEL TOPPING

New, marvelous-tasting apple pie trim

⅓ c. sugar
⅓ c. water
2 tblsp. butter
1 tblsp. hot water

• Combine sugar and ⅓ c. water in small heavy saucepan. Boil, without stirring, until golden color—10 to 12 minutes.

• Remove from heat; stir in butter immediately. Then stir in 1 tblsp. hot water. Stir until smooth. Pour into bowl and cool until of spreading consistency.

• Spread over crust of slightly warm apple pie when ready to serve.

BUTTER BALLS: Combine 1½ c. sifted confectioners sugar with ½ c. butter, ¼ tsp. vanilla and ⅛ tsp. nutmeg. Thoroughly mix and chill. Spoon on warm 2-crust apple or peach pie servings or shape in balls and arrange on pie. Add color and flavor by scattering on drained and finely chopped maraschino cherries. A sprinkling of chopped walnuts adds delightful texture and flavor.

SOUR CREAM TOPPING: Combine 1 c. dairy sour cream, 2 tblsp. confectioners sugar and 1 tsp. grated orange peel. Mix and chill. Serve with warm peach pie.

MOLASSES TOPPING

Have the 2-crust apple pie warm, the topping very cold—and enjoy it!

¼   c. butter or margarine
1   c. confectioners sugar
⅛   tsp. nutmeg
1 ½ tblsp. light molasses

• Cream butter and sugar until blended and fluffy. Add nutmeg and molasses and beat to mix thoroughly. • Chill or freeze. Spoon on individual servings of warm apple pie. Makes ¾ cup.

Pie à la Mode

With ice cream in the freezer, it's no trick to add topknots of it to individual servings. For a special treat, use homemade ice cream.

Here are four much praised recipes from our FREEZING & CANNING COOKBOOK. Use them to dress up your pies. Recommended storage time is up to 1 month.

Don't get in a rut and use only vanilla ice cream. At least dress it up for taste surprises. Swirl a little prepared mincemeat through it and serve on apple pie. Stir crushed fresh or just-thawed frozen strawberries or red raspberries through the softened ice cream and serve on peach pie.

Top apple pie with one of the nut ice creams—coconut, burnt almond, butter pecan or pistachio—or with coffee ice cream. Spoon peach ice cream

on blueberry pie, strawberry ice cream on peach pie. Let your imagination be your guide and your family the judge of which combinations hit the jackpot.

COCONUT HONEY ICE CREAM

Makes warm peach pie irresistible

1 ½ c. honey
4   eggs, slightly beaten
3   c. heavy cream
2   tsp. vanilla
½   tsp. lemon extract
½   tsp. salt
3   c. milk
1   (3 ½ oz.) can flaked coconut
2   (8 ½ oz.) cans crushed pineapple

• Add honey to eggs; mix well. Add cream, flavorings, salt and milk; stir until well blended. Chill.   *more*

• Pour into freezer can; put dasher and cover in place. Pack chopped ice and coarse salt around can, 4 parts ice to 1 part salt. Turn dasher.

• When partly frozen, add coconut and pineapple; continue freezing until crank turns hard. Remove dasher. Pack in same ice mixture until serving time. Or spoon into freezer containers; seal, label, date and store in freezer. Makes 1 gallon.

VARIATION

• To intensify coconut flavor, add 2 tsp. coconut extract with lemon extract and vanilla.

MARIELLA'S ICE CREAM

Perfect garnish for fruit pies

1	qt. milk, scalded
4	eggs, beaten
2½	c. sugar
2⅓ to 3	c. heavy cream
1	qt. cold milk
2	tblsp. vanilla
¼	tsp. salt
3	drops lemon extract

• Stir hot milk slowly into eggs and sugar; cook slowly over direct heat until thickened, stirring constantly; cool.

• Add remaining ingredients to cooled egg mixture; stir until smooth. Pour into freezer can; put dasher and cover in place. Pack chopped ice and coarse salt around can, using 4 parts ice to 1 part coarse salt; turn dasher until crank turns hard (about 30 minutes with electric freezer). To store,

spoon lightly into airtight freezer containers (do not pack). Seal, label and date. Freeze. Makes about 1 gallon.

VARIATIONS

CHOCOLATE: Stir 1 (5½ oz.) can chocolate syrup into vanilla mixture.

STRAWBERRY: Mix 3 (10 oz.) pkgs. frozen strawberries, thawed, and ½ c. sugar; stir into vanilla mixture; add red food color for pink ice cream.

Note: You can make 4 batches consecutively. By time the custard for the fourth one is cooked, the first is cool enough to put in freezer can. When that gallon is frozen, the second batch is ready for freezing. This assembly line method makes economical use of ice. A 50 lb. bag of cracked ice is enough to freeze 4 gallons. You save time by using the same bowls and pans for each batch. A good selection to make is 2 gallons of vanilla, 1 of chocolate and 1 strawberry.

QUICK VANILLA ICE CREAM

Soften slightly before spooning on pie

1	tblsp. unflavored gelatin
½	c. cold water
7	c. light cream
1½	c. sugar
1	c. evaporated milk
1	tblsp. vanilla

• Sprinkle gelatin over water to soften.

• Scald 2 c. cream; add gelatin and stir to dissolve. Add sugar; stir to dissolve. Add remaining cream, evaporated milk and vanilla; add slowly to gelatin mixture, stirring.

• Pour into 1 gallon freezer container. Pack with 4 parts ice to 1 part coarse salt; freeze. Makes about 3 quarts.

• Pack in rigid containers with tight lids. Label and date. Store in bottom or coldest part of freezer.

VANILLA CUSTARD ICE CREAM

Its homemade taste enhances pies

2 c. sugar
⅛ tsp. salt
¼ c. cornstarch
1 qt. milk
4 eggs, separated
2 tsp. vanilla
1 (13 oz.) can evaporated milk
1 pt. light cream
½ c. milk (about)

• Thoroughly mix sugar, salt and cornstarch; stir into 1 qt. milk, heated just to boiling point. Remove from heat.

• Beat yolks; gradually add 1 c. of the hot milk mixture, beating constantly. Stir egg yolk mixture into remaining hot milk and bring to a boil. Remove from heat; add vanilla, evaporated milk and cream to hot custard. Cool.

• Fold in egg whites, beaten to stiff but not dry peaks. Pour into 1 gallon freezer container. Add remaining milk to fill can ¾ full.

• Pack with 4 parts ice to 1 part coarse salt; freeze. Makes 1 gallon.

• Package in rigid containers with tight lids. Label and date. Store in coldest part of freezer.

Note: Substitute 2 (13 oz.) cans evaporated milk for light cream, if you wish.

Ice Cream Topping—Farm-Style

The Iowa farm woman who contributes this king-size recipe for Ice Cream Topping says she makes it because her family and other people, especially the men who help occasionally with the work, like it so much on pies, cakes, frozen and fresh fruits and many other desserts. With a supply in the freezer, she can make her pie doubly delicious on short notice. And she always has the important ingredients on hand to whip up 6 quarts—milk, eggs and cream. The topping will keep satisfactorily in the freezer up to a month—if it gets a chance!

The mixture is not as fluffy and light as ice cream made in a crank-type freezer. If you put the topping in the refrigerator or on the counter to soften slightly before serving, it is easier to spoon out and is creamier. The flavors have a chance to mellow, too. Storing the cartons in the freezer away from the freezing surface will keep their contents nearer serving consistency. This holds for all ice cream.

It is not a good idea to freeze Ice Cream Topping or other foods in refrigerator trays unless reserved especially for this purpose. Washing trays used both for food and ice cubes prevents easy removal of ice cubes.

ICE CREAM TOPPING

Serve on slightly warm fruit and berry pies for superb desserts

2	envelopes unflavored gelatin
7½	c. milk
12	eggs, separated
3	c. sugar
½	tsp. salt
3	tblsp. vanilla
6	c. heavy cream

· Soften gelatin in ½ c. milk.

· Combine remaining 7 c. milk, slightly beaten egg yolks, sugar and salt. Add softened gelatin. Cook in heavy pan over low heat, stirring constantly, until mixture thickens slightly. Cool.

· Add vanilla and fold in stiffly beaten egg whites. Pour into 13″ × 9″ pan. Cover with foil and place in freezer.

· When frozen, remove from freezer and cut mixture in 6 even blocks. Place 1 block in chilled mixer bowl and return remaining blocks to freezer or refrigerator. When the custard mixture in bowl is barely thawed, beat it until smooth and fluffy.

· Meanwhile, whip 1 c. cream until almost stiff. Fold it into custard mixture and spoon into a quart carton. Return to freezer.

· Repeat with remaining 5 blocks of frozen custard mixture, making 1 qt. Ice Cream Topping at a time.

· To serve, spoon on pieces of pie or other desserts. Makes 6 quarts.

CINNAMON ICE CREAM TOPPING: Blend ¼ tsp. cinnamon into 1 c. slightly softened vanilla ice cream. Spoon on warm apple pie wedges.

Saucy Tops for Pies

Sauces you pass in a pitcher or ladle over pie at serving time provide new taste experiences. The simplest one of all is a pitcher of cream. Just set it on the table and notice how many people will pour it over their pie wedges.

· Combine sugar, syrup and water in small saucepan and bring to a boil. Cook, uncovered, 5 minutes.

· Remove from heat; stir in vanilla. Serve warm or cold. Makes about 1⅓ cups.

AMBER CARAMEL SAUCE

Sweetness to drizzle over whipped cream spread on spicy pumpkin pies

1	c. brown sugar, firmly packed
½	c. light corn syrup
½	c. water
1	tsp. vanilla

VANILLA CREAM SAUCE

Tastes like good homemade vanilla ice cream—spoon over 2-crust fruit pies

1	egg
3	tblsp. sugar
⅛	tsp. salt
¼	c. butter or margarine, melted

½ tsp. vanilla
¾ c. heavy cream

• Beat egg with sugar and salt until fluffy and thick. Beat in butter, a small amount at a time, and stir in vanilla.
• Beat cream until stiff; fold into egg-sugar mixture until all streaks disappear. Chill thoroughly. Makes 2¼ cups.

STRAWBERRY HARD SAUCE

A treasure from a plantation kitchen in Mississippi's fertile Delta region

¼ c. butter or margarine
1½ c. confectioners sugar

2 tblsp. crushed fresh strawberries

• Cream butter until fluffy. Beat in sugar, a little at a time, until blended. Then add strawberries and beat until mixture is smooth. Cover and chill. Spoon on individual pie servings. Makes about 1 cup.

VARIATION

VANILLA HARD SAUCE: Omit strawberries in recipe for Strawberry Hard Sauce and add 1 tsp. vanilla. Cover and chill. Sprinkle lightly with mace or nutmeg when serving on apple pie or dumplings. Makes about 1 cup.

More Wonderful Toppings to Try

Here is a list of toppings included with pie recipes elsewhere in this book. You can find them in the chapters indicated, or check the Index.

Chapter 2: Potato Snowcaps
(Frozen)

Chapter 3: Spicy Pecan
Cinnamon Nut
Brown Sugar Streusel
Cinnamon Jelly Glaze
Brown Sugar Syrup
Marshmallow Sauce
Oat Streusel
Lemon Crumb
Spicy
Orange Frosting
Toasted Oat
Crumbly

Chapter 4: Caramelized Pecan
Caramel Sauce
Pecan Meringue

Chapter 5: Chocolate
Chocolate Frosting
Apple Snow

Chapter 6: Blueberry Sauce
Spiced Honey Cream
Orange Biscuit Topping
Cinnamon Syrup

Chapter 7: Sugar Glaze
Cherry Sauce
Orange Cream Dress-Up
Apricot Glaze

Main-Dish Pies

For a hearty supper hot dish *with plenty of man-appeal, bake colorful Chili con Carne Pie (recipe, page 254). Take your pick of corn bread or mush for "crust." You'll find this a good way to use some of the ground beef stored in your freezer.*

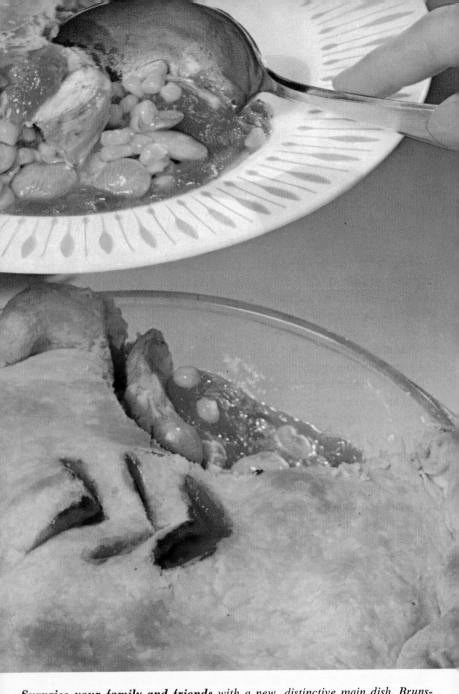

Surprise your family and friends with a new, distinctive main dish, Brunswick Chicken Pie (recipe, page 270)—filling suggests the South's stew of same name. Directions are for two pies: one to freeze, one to serve immediately.

CHAPTER 10

MEAT AND CHICKEN PIES

When fall's first brisk days arrive and harvested vegetables overflow their storage baskets, it's a country custom to get out a rolling pin and fix a meal-in-a-pie. Brimful of fork-tender meat, succulent vegetables and savory gravy, capped with flaky pastry or puffed-up, golden biscuits, meat pies are so satisfying. And they make the cook's work easier, for few accompaniments are needed. Salad or crisp relishes, ice cream or sherbet and a beverage round out the menu.

Notice the variety in our meat pies—especially those made with beef and pork. Our readers, of course, sent us more favorite recipes using ground beef than any other type. They're truly American farm specials. But there are others—Midwestern Casserole Beef Pie with Butter Crumb Biscuits, to name an extra-good one. We believe you'll want to treat your family to it some day soon.

You'll detect intriguing foreign flavors in many pies. That's natural, for Europeans are as fond of these main dishes as we are of steak and potatoes. Exciting recipes for Quebec Pork Pie, Cornish Pasty, English Steak and Kidney Pie and Italian Beef Pie appear in this chapter, among others.

Chicken Pie, Grandmother's wonderful Sunday-dinner standby, has undergone many changes. Crusty, brown Popover Chicken Pie is an example of the new. Double-Crust Chicken Pie represents the traditional—part of its crust bakes in the pie, making dumplings. This old-fashioned Southern chicken dish never will go out of style. And sometime when you're entertaining, or want to surprise the family, try our Individual Chicken-Ham Pies with Rice Crust—delicious!

Be sure to read about the unusual crusts you can make from basic biscuits (Chapter 2). You'll be convinced that while the filling is important, it's often the crust that makes a pie distinctive.

Beef Pies—Hearty and Heartening

Provide a real treat on dark, rainy and cold evenings, when the family seeks the warmth and bright lights of the kitchen at suppertime. Take a brown-topped meat pie from the oven. Let everyone see the rich juices bubbling in the crust's peepholes and savor the aroma. Watch the way everyone hustles around to get ready for supper. No one will forget these home scenes and scents. Psychologists say that pleasing food fragrances are much remembered childhood experiences.

Among the top-ranking meat pies that come to farm tables are the beef and vegetable stews under pastry, biscuits, corn bread or other crusts. You can add your own touches to the fillings or crusts—whatever your family likes. Is it celery, caraway or dill seed, or dill weed? Let the flavors your husband, children and friends appreciate be your guide in converting a homey meat pie into a gourmet dish. Spring a surprise change in flavor occasionally to observe its reception. One country homemaker's stunt is to roll the biscuit dough covering stews in melted butter and fine bread crumbs for golden results. Here is an adapted version of her dish.

1 ½   tsp. salt
⅛   tsp. pepper
¼   c. shortening
2   medium onions, separated in rings
½   c. water
1   can condensed cream of chicken soup
2   c. cubed raw potatoes
Butter Crumb Biscuits
1   can condensed cream of mushroom soup
½   c. dairy sour cream

· Cut steak in 1″ cubes. Dredge with mixture of flour, paprika, ½ tsp. salt and pepper. Place in skillet and brown well in hot shortening. Top with onion rings. Add water and chicken soup. Cover and simmer 45 minutes.

· Add potatoes and remaining 1 tsp. salt. Continue cooking 15 minutes, stirring occasionally.

· Pour hot mixture into 1½ qt. casserole. Top with Butter Crumb Biscuits and bake in hot oven (400°F.) 20 to 25 minutes, or until biscuits are golden.

· Serve with sauce made by heating 1 can mushroom soup and ½ c. dairy sour cream. Makes 6 to 8 servings.

CASSEROLE BEEF PIE

Crumb biscuits atop beef give pie new look and taste—extra-good

2   lbs. round steak
⅓   c. flour
1   tsp. paprika

BUTTER CRUMB BISCUITS

2   c. sifted flour
4   tsp. baking powder
½   tsp. salt
¼   tsp. poultry seasoning
½   tsp. celery seed

½   tsp. onion flakes
¼   c. salad oil
1   c. milk
¼   c. melted butter
1   c. fine bread crumbs

• Sift together into bowl, flour, baking powder, salt and poultry seasoning. Add celery seed and onion flakes; stir in oil and milk. Drop by tablespoonfuls into melted butter, then roll in bread crumbs.

• Place on top hot meat mixture in casserole and bake as directed in Casserole Beef Pie.

STEAK AND ONION PIE

The tantalizing aroma of this pie baking builds eager appetites

Filling:

1   c. sliced onions
½   c. shortening
1   lb. round steak, cut in small
       pieces
¼   c. flour
½   tsp. paprika
⅛   tsp. ginger
⅛   tsp. allspice
2   tsp. salt
⅛   tsp. pepper
2½   c. boiling water
2   c. diced raw potatoes

Egg Crust:

1   c. sifted flour
½   tsp. salt
⅓   c. shortening
1   egg, slightly beaten

Filling: Fry onions slowly in melted shortening, until yellow; remove from fat.

• Roll meat in mixture of flour, spices and seasonings. (Or shake all together in paper bag.) Brown in hot fat.

• Add water; cover and simmer until meat is tender, about 45 minutes.

• Add potatoes and cook 10 minutes longer. Pour into 8″ greased casserole. Place cooked onions on top and cover with Egg Crust.

Egg Crust: Mix flour and salt. Add half of shortening and cut in until as fine as meal. Add remaining shortening and cut in until particles are size of large peas.

• Add egg, mixing thoroughly into a dough. Roll out slightly larger than top of casserole. Make dime-size openings for steam to escape and fit dough over top of casserole; fold under pastry edge and flute.

• Bake in very hot oven (450°F.) 30 minutes. Makes 4 to 6 servings.

STEAK AND KIDNEY PIE

Serve this favorite of English meat-potato-gravy men straight from oven

Pastry for 1-crust pie

1   beef kidney
2   lbs. round steak, cubed
2   tblsp. fat
2   c. chopped onions (2 large on-
       ions)
2   tsp. salt
¼   tsp. pepper
½   tsp. dried thyme
1   bay leaf
2   tsp. Worcestershire sauce
2   c. water
4   c. diced raw potatoes (4 me-
       dium size)
6   tblsp. flour   *more*

· Cover beef kidney with lightly salted water, cover and refrigerate overnight. Drain; cut out tubes and white membrane with scissors. Dice meat.

· Brown kidney and steak in hot fat. Add onions, seasonings and 1½ c. water. Simmer until meat is almost tender, about 1 hour.

· Add potatoes and continue simmering until potatoes are tender, about ½ hour.

· Blend together flour and remaining ½ c. water; stir into meat mixture. Continue cooking and stirring until mixture thickens. Pour into 3 qt. casserole.

· Roll out pastry slightly larger than top of casserole. Place over meat mixture and trim to overhang 1". Fold under and flute against inside edge of casserole. Cut several steam vents in center.

· Bake in hot oven (425°F.) until lightly browned, about 30 minutes. Makes 8 servings.

Note: You can use the milder-flavored veal or lamb kidney instead of beef kidney, if available. You need not soak it overnight in salted water.

DINNER BEEF PIE

Beef and vegetables in tomato gravy make this plump pie wonderful eating

Pastry for 2-crust pie
 2 tblsp. shortening
 1½ c. chopped celery
 1½ c. chopped onions
 1½ c. chopped green pepper
 3 c. beef cubes (1")
 1 can condensed tomato soup
 2 tblsp. prepared mustard
 ¼ c. tomato ketchup
 ¾ tsp. salt

· Heat shortening in skillet, add celery, onions and green pepper; sauté until soft. Stir in beef cubes; cover and simmer 20 minutes. Add soup, mustard, ketchup and salt; heat thoroughly.

· Place meat mixture in pastry-lined 9" pie pan; adjust top crust, flute edges and cut vents.

· Bake in hot oven (425°F.) 40 to 50 minutes. Makes 6 servings.

Note: Green pepper may be omitted; if so, use 2¼ c. each of celery and onion.

Country Pies Filled with Ground Beef

With ground beef almost always on hand in farm home freezers, it's not surprising that much experimentation with it goes on in country kitchens. It is often the main ingredient in savory meat pies. Two country-kitchen tricks that please—fluffs of mashed potatoes topping the pie in lieu of crust; expertly seasoned ground beef pie shells shaped in a pie pan to hold a variety of tempting fillings.

CHEESEBURGER PIE

If your family likes cheeseburgers in buns, watch them go for this pie

Cheese Pastry for 2-crust pie (Chapter 2)
- 1 lb. ground beef chuck
- ½ c. chopped celery
- ¼ c. chopped onion
- 2 tblsp. chopped green pepper
- 1 tsp. salt
- ¼ tsp. pepper
- 1 (8 oz.) can tomato sauce
- 1 tsp. Worcestershire sauce

• Brown beef in skillet, stirring frequently. Add celery, onion, green pepper, salt, pepper, tomato and Worcestershire sauces. Cover and simmer 15 minutes.

• Roll out pastry to 8½″ square by placing 8″ pan on pastry and cutting around it with knife, leaving ½″ margins.

• Place hot meat mixture in 8″ square pan and top with square of pastry, turning under edges.

• Cut remaining pastry into strips and arrange them lattice-style on pastry square, turning under edges.

• Bake in hot oven (400°F.) 30 minutes. Makes 4 servings.

VARIATION

• Use plain pastry for a 1-crust pie instead of Cheese Pastry. Place over top of pie. When baked, sprinkle on ½ c. grated Cheddar cheese and return to oven just long enough to melt cheese.

UPSIDE-DOWN MEAT PIE

Bake this meat loaf under a tent of cheese pastry when you want a change

Pastry for 1-crust pie
- 1 lb. ground beef chuck
- 2 tblsp. instant minced onion
- 1 tsp. salt
- 1 tsp. prepared mustard
- ⅛ tsp. pepper
- ½ c. dry bread crumbs
- 1 egg, beaten
- ⅓ c. milk
- ½ c. ketchup
- Parsley

• Combine beef, onion, salt, mustard, pepper, bread crumbs, egg, milk and ⅓ c. ketchup. Place mixture in greased 8″ round cake pan. Pat meat out to within ½″ of sides of pan.

• Roll pastry out to a scant 10″ circle. Place it over meat, tucking it down around meat and pressing it against bottom of pan. Prick pastry all over with a four-tined fork.

• Bake in hot oven (425°F.) until crust is golden, about 40 minutes. Remove from oven and let stand a few minutes. Run spatula under outer edge of pie. Invert serving plate over top of pie pan. Invert both and lift off pie pan.

• Dot top of meat with remaining ketchup and sprinkle with coarsely snipped (with scissors) parsley. If parsley is not available, add color by scattering shreds of yellow cheese over ketchup-dotted meat pie. Makes 6 servings.

SUCCOTASH-BEEF PIE

Southwesterners will step up flavor by adding a little chili powder to filling

Filling:

1 ½ lbs. ground beef
1 c. chopped onion (1 large)
1 c. chopped celery
3 tblsp. flour
1 (1 lb.) can tomatoes
1 ½ tsp. salt
¼ tsp. pepper
1 tsp. Worcestershire sauce
1 c. grated sharp process cheese
2 (10 oz.) pkgs. frozen succotash

Topping:

1 c. cornmeal, yellow or white
¼ c. flour
1 tblsp. sugar
2 tsp. baking powder
½ tsp. salt
1 egg
½ c. milk
¼ c. butter or margarine, melted

Filling: Cook beef, onion and celery in heavy skillet until beef is browned. Stir in flour. Add tomatoes and cook, stirring, until mixture is thickened and bubbling. Stir in seasonings. Cover and simmer until celery is tender, about 15 minutes; stir frequently. Stir in cheese.

· Combine meat mixture and succotash, cooked by package directions, in 3 qt. casserole. Place in moderate oven (375°F.) while you make topping.

Topping: Combine cornmeal, flour, sugar, baking powder and salt. Blend together egg and milk. Stir into corn-meal mixture. Stir in butter. Spread over meat mixture in casserole.

· Bake until topping is golden, about 30 minutes. Makes 8 servings.

EMPANADAS

Serve with bowls of steaming soup and a fruit or vegetable salad

Pastry for 2 (2-crust) pies
1 tblsp. butter
⅓ c. chopped onion
½ c. peeled chopped tomatoes
¼ c. chopped green pepper
½ lb. lean ground beef chuck
¾ tsp. salt
⅛ tsp. pepper
Few drops Tabasco sauce
1 hard-cooked egg, chopped
1 ½ tblsp. seedless raisins
¼ c. chopped green olives

· Melt butter in skillet; add onion, tomatoes and green pepper and cook over low heat until onion is soft. Stir in beef and cook until no pink remains. Remove from heat and stir in remaining ingredients. Cool.

· Roll out pastry. Cut in 4″ rounds. Place 1 tblsp. filling in center of each round. Brush edges with water and fold over dough, pressing edges together firmly. Cut steam vent in top of each.

· Bake in hot oven (425°F.) until lightly browned, about 15 minutes. Makes about 2½ dozen.

Note: These small meat pies are as popular in South America as hot dogs in the U.S.A. They make different and good snacks.

RANCHERS' BEEF TURNOVERS

You're lucky if you have leftovers, for these make tasty cold sandwiches

1	lb. ground lean beef
½	c. chopped onion
¼	c. chopped green pepper
2¼	c. biscuit mix
1	tsp. salt
¼	tsp. pepper
⅓	c. ketchup
3	tblsp. butter or margarine
⅔	c. milk
1	(10½ oz.) can beef-mushroom gravy (optional)

• Cook beef, onion and green pepper in skillet until beef is browned. Pour off excess fat.

• Add ¼ c. prepared biscuit mix, salt, pepper and ketchup. Cook, stirring frequently, several minutes.

• Cut butter into remaining 2 c. biscuit mix, until mixture is crumbly. Blend in milk. Turn out on board dusted with a little biscuit mix and knead 8 to 10 times.

• Divide dough in half. Roll each half into a 10″ square. Divide each into 4 squares. Top each square with about ⅓ c. beef filling. Fold over corner to corner to make triangles. Seal edges and cut steam vents in top.

• Bake on greased baking sheet in hot oven (400°F.) until browned as desired, about 15 minutes. Serve topped with hot beef-mushroom gravy. Makes 8 turnovers.

Pasty—Family-Size and Individual

Pasty, a meat-and-potato pie adopted from Cornwall, England, is popular in this country, especially in neighborhoods where people of Cornish ancestry live—Mineral Point, Wisconsin, Michigan's Upper Peninsula, Montana's mining areas and other places.

For family use, the pasty usually is large enough to serve everyone at the table. For lunch boxes and picnic hampers, individual turnovers are the rule. They're served cold and are picked up and eaten from the fingers when toted; hot in home meals. It was the custom of miners' wives in Mineral Point to stand in their doorways at mealtime and shake a white cloth to call the men home to eat. This part

of the town, now being restored, is still called Shake-Rag-under-the-Hill. When the men ate at the lead mines, their wives wrapped freshly baked pasties in their shawls and carried them to their husbands.

The most unusual feature of the true pasty is that no steam vents are cut in the pastry that holds the savory meat-and-vegetable filling. For inexperienced cooks this often creates the problem of sealing the pastry so that the steam and juices do not escape. It's an exciting moment when the pasty is cut at the table and a little of the fragrant steam spouts out.

Many American cooks depart from the traditional and cut two slits on top of individual pasties before baking them. A Wisconsin custom with family-size pasties is to cut three-cornered openings about 2″ apart. After the pasty has baked half an hour, and once again during the baking, a little cream is poured into the "windows" to insure a juicy filling.

The "a" in pasty is pronounced as in "dash," although some Americans pronounce it as in "pastry." If they do this in the Cornish neighborhoods of Wisconsin and Michigan, they'll be politely corrected.

We give you two recipes for pasty, the family-size and individual.

AMERICAN PIE-PAN PASTY

The original pasty was a big turnover and wasn't baked in a pie pan

Pastry for 2-crust pie
1   lb. ground lean beef chuck
1 ¾ c. diced raw potatoes
¼   c. finely chopped celery
1   tsp. dried onion flakes
1   tsp. salt
¼   tsp. pepper
½   c. grated Cheddar cheese
Paprika

• Combine meat, potatoes, celery, onion, salt and pepper. Place in pastry-lined 9″ pie pan. Sprinkle with grated cheese.
• Adjust top crust; seal. (Do not cut steam vents in it.) Sprinkle lightly with paprika.
• Bake in moderate oven (375°F.) until top is lightly browned, about 1 hour. Serve hot. Makes 6 servings.

CORNISH PASTIES

The traditional recipe for individual pasties—often packed in lunch boxes

Pastry for 1 (10″) 2-crust pie
2   c. thinly sliced raw potatoes
½   c. thinly sliced onion
½   lb. round steak, thinly sliced and cut in ½″ pieces
1 ½ tsp. salt
⅛   tsp. pepper
2   tblsp. butter or margarine

• Divide pastry in three equal parts. Roll one third to make 8″ × 15″ rectangle. Trim edges and cut to make 2 (7″) squares. Place on baking sheet. Repeat with other two thirds of pastry.
• Arrange layer of potatoes on half of each pastry square, top with layer of onion and then with meat. Sprinkle with salt and pepper and dot with butter.
• Moisten pastry edges with cold water and fold over to make triangles; press edges together to make tight seal. (A tight seal retains steam and makes juicy pasties.)
• Bake in moderate oven (375°F.) 1 hour or until meat is tender. Serve hot with chili sauce, ketchup or pickle relish, or serve cold for sandwiches. Makes 6 pasties.

CHILI CON CARNE PIE

Both corn bread and cornmeal mush make good toppings—take your pick

½   c. chopped onion
1   clove garlic, minced
1 ½ lbs. ground beef
1   (8 oz.) can tomato sauce

1 (1 lb.) can tomatoes (2 c.)
1 (20 oz.) can kidney beans, drained (or Mexican-style chili beans)
1 tblsp. chili powder (or less)
1 tsp. salt
¼ c. grated Parmesan cheese
Corn Bread Topping or Mush Topping

· Sauté onion, garlic and beef. Stir in remaining ingredients, except cheese and Topping; simmer 10 minutes.
· Bake as directed with either Topping. Makes 6 servings.

CORN BREAD TOPPING

¾ c. enriched cornmeal
¼ c. sifted flour
½ tsp. salt
1 ½ tsp. baking powder
1 egg
½ c. milk
¼ c. soft shortening
1 tblsp. chopped parsley

· Sift together dry ingredients. Add egg, milk and shortening. Beat with rotary beater until smooth, about 1 minute. Do not overbeat. Stir in parsley. Place hot filling in shallow 2 qt. baking dish; sprinkle with cheese. Spoon Topping around edge of dish. Bake in hot oven (425°F.) 15 to 18 minutes.

MUSH TOPPING

3 c. water
1 c. enriched cornmeal
1 c. cold water
1 tsp. salt
½ tsp. garlic salt
¼ c. finely chopped onion

· Boil 3 c. water. Mix remaining ingredients; stir into boiling water. Cook until thickened, stirring often. Cover; continue cooking over low heat, 10 minutes for yellow cornmeal, 5 minutes for white cornmeal.
· Line greased 9″ × 9″ × 2″ baking dish with two thirds of mush. Add hot filling; sprinkle with cheese. Top with remaining mush.
· Bake in moderate oven (375°F.), about 30 minutes.

HAMBURGER CORN-PONE PIE

Have for supper with creamed peas, coleslaw and strawberry sundae

1 lb. ground beef
⅓ c. chopped onion
1 tblsp. shortening
¾ tsp. salt
1 to 2 tsp. chili powder
1 tsp. Worcestershire sauce
1 c. canned tomatoes
1 (15 ½ oz.) can kidney beans
Corn-Pone Topping

· Brown beef and onion in shortening, stirring. Drain off excess fat. Add seasonings and tomatoes; cover and simmer over low heat 15 minutes. Add kidney beans and heat to boiling.
· Turn into 10″ pie pan and pour over Corn-Pone Topping to cover meat mixture. Bake in hot oven (425°F.) 15 to 20 minutes. Makes 6 servings.

CORN-PONE TOPPING: Sift together ½ c. flour, ¾ tsp. salt and 2 tsp. baking powder; stir in ½ c. cornmeal. Mix thoroughly. Add 1 egg, ¼ c. salad oil and ½ c. milk or enough milk to make a pour batter.

BEEF-ONION PIE

Biscuits, beef and sour cream make this a fancy main-dish pie for company

Biscuit Pie Shell

2 tblsp. butter or margarine
1 c. sliced onion (1 medium-large)
1 lb. ground beef
1 tsp. salt
⅛ tsp. pepper
1 tblsp. flour
1 c. dairy sour cream
1 egg, slightly beaten
Paprika

• Melt butter, add onion and cook gently 5 minutes. Add beef and stir with fork until meat loses red color. Remove from heat, drain off excess fat and blend in salt, pepper and flour. Cool slightly.

• Spread meat mixture in Biscuit Pie Shell. Bake in hot oven (400°F.) 5 minutes.

• Meanwhile, combine sour cream and egg.

• Remove pie from oven; reduce heat to 350°F. Spread cream-egg mixture over meat filling. Sprinkle with paprika. Return to oven and bake 30 minutes. Makes 5 to 6 servings.

BISCUIT PIE SHELL: Stir ⅓ c. light cream into 1 c. biscuit mix with fork. Roll out soft dough to fit 9″ pie pan.

BLACK-EYE PEAS AND CHILI PIE

Good, easy Texas-style pie with cornbread crust—serve with sliced tomatoes

1 (15 oz.) can black-eye peas (1 ¾ c.)

1 (15 ½ oz.) can chili con carne
½ c. cornmeal
½ c. flour
1 tblsp. sugar
¼ tsp. salt
2 tsp. baking powder
½ c. milk
1 egg
2 tblsp. soft shortening

• Drain peas, reserving liquid. Combine peas with ¼ c. of the reserved liquid and chili con carne in saucepan. Heat.

• Stir together cornmeal, flour, sugar, salt and baking powder. Add milk, egg and shortening. Beat with rotary beater until smooth, about 1 minute. Do not overbeat.

• Place hot chili mixture in a 1½ qt. greased casserole. Spoon cornmeal mixture over top. Bake in hot oven (400°F.) until lightly browned, about 25 minutes. Makes 4 to 6 servings.

Revival of Shepherd's Pie

Many Monday dinners once featured wonderful Shepherd's Pie made with leftover mashed potatoes, roast beef and gravy from Sunday's feast. They first were made with cooked lamb—hence their name. And to this day, many country cooks champion lamb as the perfect ingredient for the classic pie.

"I stopped making Shepherd's Pies several years ago because I never had enough gravy left to fix them," a farm woman said. But she quickly added,

"Imagine how thrilled I was to discover packaged gravy mixes one day while browsing in a supermarket! Since then, the old-fashioned pies have staged a comeback at our house. However I rarely make one the day after we've had roast. Instead, I freeze the leftover meat, potatoes and gravy (each separately) and make the pie several days later. I've found packaged instant potatoes a help in stretching those left over. In fact, I always keep them in the cupboard."

No doubt nostalgia for the excellent Shepherd's Pies our mothers used to make had something to do with it, but the extra-good taste also helps account for today's renewed interest in the meat-and-potato pie. The following recipe will prompt you to revive this dish you may have forgotten.

UPDATED SHEPHERD'S PIE

Leftover beef in this potato topped pie is a hearty dish with husband appeal

1 ½ c. chopped celery
½ c. chopped onion
½ c. water
4 c. cubed cooked beef pot roast
2 c. leftover gravy
½ c. chopped parsley
1 tsp. salt
3 eggs, separated
3 c. seasoned mashed potatoes
¼ tsp. salt
2 tblsp. grated Parmesan cheese
¼ tsp. paprika
1 c. hot gravy

· Put celery, onion and water in covered saucepan; cook until barely

tender. Do not drain. Combine with beef, 2 c. gravy, parsley and 1 tsp. salt in greased 2½ qt. casserole. (If you don't have enough gravy, extend it with gravy mix.)

· Set oven regulator to hot (400°F.). Place casserole in oven to heat while you prepare potatoes.

· Beat egg yolks. Add to mashed potatoes and beat again. (Use instant potatoes, if you wish.)

· Combine egg whites and ¼ tsp. salt. Beat until stiff peaks form. Fold into potatoes and spread over hot meat in casserole. Sprinkle with cheese and paprika.

· Bake until lightly browned, about 25 minutes. Serve with extra gravy. Makes 8 servings.

Note: Follow label directions on 1 (¾ oz.) pkg. gravy mix to make extra gravy.

HAMBURGER-POTATO PIE

Supper's ready! Meat and vegetables topped with potatoes in a hot dish

½ c. chopped onion
1 tblsp. shortening
1 lb. ground beef
½ tsp. salt
⅛ tsp. pepper
1 (1 lb.) can green beans (2 c.)
1 can condensed tomato soup
6 frozen potato Snowcaps (Chapter 2)
Melted butter

· Cook onion in hot shortening until golden; add meat and seasonings;

brown. Add drained beans and soup; heat; pour into 1½ qt. casserole.

• Top with frozen potato Snowcaps; brush with melted butter. Bake in moderate oven (375°F.) 30 minutes, or until Snowcaps are delicately browned. Makes 6 servings.

4-H PIZZABURGERS

Teen-agers like this farm version of pizza that resembles hamburgers

2 lbs. ground beef
1 lb. minced ham luncheon meat, ground
3 (6 oz.) cans tomato paste
1 tblsp. instant onion
1½ tsp. orégano
½ tsp. sage
1½ tsp. salt
¼ tsp. pepper
3 c. grated Mozzarella cheese (12 oz.)
¼ c. dried parsley
14 hamburger buns

• Brown beef in skillet; drain off fat. Add luncheon meat, tomato paste, onion, orégano, sage, salt, pepper and 1 c. grated cheese; mix thoroughly. Cool and refrigerate until needed.

• Split hamburger buns. Place ¼ c. meat mixture on bun half. Spread to cover bun. Sprinkle with 1 tblsp. remaining grated cheese and about ½ tsp. dried parsley. Repeat with remaining bun halves.

• Place on baking sheets and bake in very hot oven (450°F.) about 10 minutes, or until cheese is bubbly. Makes 25 to 28 sandwiches.

VEGETABLE BEEF PIE

Cheese potato puffs brown atop a pie long on flavor, short on fixing time

1 medium onion, chopped
1 lb. ground beef
1 tsp. salt
¼ tsp. pepper
1 tblsp. Worcestershire sauce
¼ tsp. chili powder
1 (1 lb.) can green beans, drained
1 can condensed tomato soup
6 tblsp. warm milk
1 egg, beaten
2 c. mashed potatoes
¼ c. sharp grated cheese

• Brown onion and beef; drain fat. In greased 2 qt. casserole, combine beef mixture with next six ingredients.

• Beat milk and egg into potatoes; spoon in ¼ c. mounds over bean mixture, top with cheese.

• Bake in moderate oven (350°F.) 30 minutes or until heated through. Makes 8 servings.

JIFFY MEAT-POTATO PIE

Welcome variety for meat-and-potato families—easy to fix on busy days

1 lb. ground beef
1 tsp. salt
¼ tsp. pepper
½ c. finely chopped onion
½ c. soft bread crumbs
½ c. milk
1 egg, beaten
1 envelope instant mashed potatoes
¾ c. shredded sharp process cheese

• Combine beef, salt, pepper, onion, bread crumbs, milk and egg. Mix thoroughly and press in bottom and on sides of 9″ pie pan to line. Bake in moderate oven (350°F.) 35 minutes. Drain off excess fat.

• Prepare potatoes as directed on package. (You can cook and mash potatoes if you prefer.) Spread over meat. Sprinkle with cheese. Return to oven and bake until cheese melts, about 10 minutes. Cut in wedges to serve. Makes 4 servings.

BONELESS STEAK PIE

This farm kitchen special makes a meal along with salad and ice cream

2	lbs. round steak, cut in 1″ cubes
2	tblsp. hot fat
1	c. chopped onion
2	tsp. salt
½	tsp. pepper
1	tblsp. Worcestershire sauce
2	tblsp. chopped parsley
1½	c. boiling water
1½	c. sliced carrots
½	c. sliced celery
2	tblsp. flour
¼	c. water
4	c. seasoned mashed potatoes
½	c. process cheese spread

• Brown steak cubes in fat. Add onion and cook until soft. Add salt and pepper, Worcestershire sauce, parsley and boiling water. Cover and simmer slowly 30 minutes.

• Add carrots and celery; continue simmering 45 minutes.

• Blend together flour and ¼ c. cold water. Stir into meat mixture and continue stirring until mixture returns to a boil.

• Pour into greased 2½ qt. casserole. Combine hot, seasoned mashed potatoes (may be made from packaged instant mashed potatoes) and cheese spread, stirring until cheese is blended in. Drop by spoonfuls on hot meat around edge of casserole.

• Bake in moderate oven (350°F.) 30 minutes. Makes 6 servings.

BEEF PIE SUPREME

A favorite of meat-and-potato men— from our COUNTRY COOKBOOK

1½	lbs. beef for stew (boneless shoulder or chuck)
¼	c. flour
1	tsp. salt
⅛	tsp. pepper
3	tblsp. shortening
1	c. water
1	c. canned tomatoes
2	tsp. Worcestershire sauce
6	carrots
12	small onions
3	c. mashed potatoes
⅓	c. process cheese spread
Melted butter or margarine	

• Cut meat into 1½″ cubes.

• Mix flour, salt and pepper; roll meat in mixture to coat all sides.

• Brown meat well in hot shortening; add water, tomatoes and Worcestershire sauce.

• Peel carrots; cut in 1″ crosswise slices. Peel onions; add to meat.

• Cover tightly. Simmer 2 hours. Stir occasionally to avoid sticking.

more

- Pour into greased 2 qt. casserole.
- With mixer, blend together mashed potatoes and cheese spread. Drop by spoonfuls around rim of casserole.

Brush with melted butter. Bake until bubbly hot in moderate oven (375°F.), about 30 minutes. Makes 6 to 8 servings.

Beef Makes the Crust

Pie shells made with ground beef have an enthusiastic following in many farm homes. If you use fairly lean meat, you'll reduce shrinkage during the baking. In Italian Hamburger Pie you have a blend of meat, tomatoes, cheese and seasonings that explains the name and wonderful taste of the pie. Use this main dish when you're in a hurry. Oven time is only half an hour. You will want to double this recipe for some meals. Or use the larger recipe for Italian Beef Pie in this chapter.

bread crumbs, onion, garlic and tomato juice. Press into a 9″ pie pan, lining pan.
- Bake in moderate oven (375°F.) 15 minutes. Drain off fat.
- Cut up tomatoes and place in beef pie crust. Sprinkle with parsley, orégano and cheese. Return to oven and bake 15 minutes. Cut in wedges. Makes 4 servings.

ITALIAN BEEF PIE

Use Italian-style canned tomatoes instead of regular, if available

2   tsp. salt
2   cloves garlic
2   lbs. ground lean beef chuck
⅓   c. fine dry bread crumbs
¼   tsp. pepper
1   medium onion, chopped (about ¾ c.)
2   (1 lb.) cans tomatoes
1   tsp. seasoning salt
¼   tsp. orégano
¼   tsp. basil
½   c. grated Mozzarella or Parmesan cheese

ITALIAN HAMBURGER PIE

Something different, colorful and tasty to do with ever popular ground beef

1   (1 lb.) can tomatoes
1   lb. ground beef chuck
1   tsp. salt
¼   tsp. pepper
½   c. soft bread crumbs
⅓   c. finely chopped onion
1   clove garlic, minced
½   tsp. dried parsley
¼   tsp. orégano
½   c. shredded Mozzarella cheese

- Drain tomatoes, reserving juice. Measure ½ c. juice, adding water if necessary.
- Combine ground beef, salt, pepper,

- Put salt in mixing bowl; add cut cloves garlic and rub to crush. Remove garlic. Add beef, bread crumbs, pepper and onion.
- Drain tomatoes. Measure ¾ c. to-

mato juice, adding water if necessary. Mix into meat mixture. Pat meat mixture into bottom and on sides of a 10″ pie pan.

· Bake in moderate oven (375°F.) 30 minutes, placing a piece of foil slightly larger than pan on oven rack below pan to catch possible drippings.

· Remove from oven; drain off fat. Arrange drained tomatoes in meat pie shell. Top with seasoning salt, orégano, basil and cheese.

· Return to oven and bake 20 minutes longer. Cool a minute or two, drain off drippings and cut in wedges. Makes 8 servings.

MEAT LOAF PIES

Pastry-wrapped bundles of barbecued meat loaves are supper-party specials

Pastry for 10″ 2-crust pie
  1   lb. ground beef chuck
  ½   lb. ground lean pork
  ½   lb. liver sausage
  2   tblsp. finely chopped onion
  2   tblsp. finely chopped green pepper
  1   clove garlic, chopped
1 ½   tsp. salt
  ½   tsp. paprika
  ¼   tsp. pepper
  ⅓   c. bread crumbs
Barbecue Sauce

· Combine beef, pork, liver sausage, onion, green pepper, garlic, salt, paprika, pepper and bread crumbs, mix-

ing thoroughly. Shape mixture into 8 square loaves. Place in greased baking pan. Top each meat loaf with 1 tblsp. Barbecue Sauce.

· Bake in moderate oven (350°F.) 15 minutes. Spoon remaining sauce over loaves and continue baking 20 minutes. Remove from baking pan and cool until lukewarm (or bake in advance, cool and refrigerate).

· Divide pastry in half. Roll each half into 12″ square. Cut in fourths. Place each meat loaf diagonally on a square of pastry so that corners of pastry may be brought up over sides of meat loaves. Seal pastry well. Prick each pastry-wrapped meat loaf two or three times.

· Bake in hot oven (425°F.) 20 minutes. Serve hot or cold. Makes 8 servings.

BARBECUE SAUCE: Combine ½ c. ketchup, ¼ c. vinegar, 2 tsp. Worcestershire sauce, ½ clove garlic, finely chopped, 1 tblsp. grated onion, 1 tsp. prepared mustard and 1 tsp. salt. Stir to mix thoroughly.

GOOD IDEA: If you have leftover beef and vegetable stew, reheat it, turn into casserole and top with biscuits (Chapter 2). Bake in very hot oven (450°F.) 20 to 25 minutes, or until biscuits are done.

· You can add a surprise to this guaranteed-to-please pie by using some of the variations for biscuits listed in Chapter 2.

North-of-the-Border Pork Pie

You don't have to visit Canada or our own adjacent north country to enjoy *tourtière*, the famous holiday pork pie. We have two recipes, both from New England farm kitchens.

The true *tourtière* always contains ground lean pork and mashed potatoes in a delicately spiced filling, but there are many variations. We give you the traditional type, which originated in the Province of Quebec. Usually, the cooks there like to double the amount of spices, using ¼ tsp. cloves and ½ tsp. cinnamon in a 9″ pie. While French-speaking people call it *tourtière*, you'll find it's a real treat in our language as Quebec Pork Pie.

The second version—our Good-Neighbor Pork Pie—is an updated recipe from Vermont, with salt, pepper, garlic and vegetables doing the seasoning. While our Canadian neighbors often serve the pie on New Year's Day and during the winter holiday season, it is hearty and tasty for serving throughout the cold months.

One Vermont homemaker who sent us her best-liked pork pie recipe wrote: "My pie-eating men like *tourtière* because it contains two of their favorite foods, meat and potatoes, baked in an envelope of something they're fond of—flaky pastry."

QUEBEC PORK PIE

You can freeze this pie before baking, or freeze just the filling to use later

Pastry for 2-crust pie
1   lb. ground lean pork
½   lb. ground lean beef
3   tblsp. chopped onion
½   tsp. salt
⅛   tsp. pepper
1   c. water
⅛   tsp. cloves
¼   tsp. cinnamon
1 ½ c. mashed potatoes (2 medium large)

• Combine pork, beef, onion, salt, pepper and water. Cook slowly for 45 minutes. Add cloves and cinnamon; cook 15 minutes longer.

• Add potatoes to meat mixture while hot. Let cool thoroughly, or about 1 hour, so flavors will blend. Turn mixture into pastry-lined 9″ pie pan. Adjust top crust, cut vents and flute edges.

• Bake in hot oven (400°F.) 45 minutes.

GOOD-NEIGHBOR PORK PIE

Brimful of budget meats and savory gravy, capped with golden pastry lid

Pastry for 2-crust pie
6   slices bacon
1   lb. ground lean pork
½   lb. ground veal
1   c. chopped onion
1   clove garlic, minced
¼   c. finely chopped celery
½   tsp. salt
⅛   tsp. pepper
1   beef bouillon cube
¾   c. boiling water
3   tblsp. instant potato flakes

• Chop bacon and cook over medium heat until almost crisp. Add meats, onion, garlic and celery; cook, stirring occasionally, until lightly browned. Drain off excess fat.

• Add seasonings and bouillon cube dissolved in hot water. Cover and simmer 20 minutes.

• Sprinkle 1 tblsp. instant potato flakes over pastry-lined 9″ pie pan. Stir remaining potato flakes into meat mixture. Pour into pie pan, mounding a little in center. Adjust top crust, cut vents and flute edges.

• Bake in hot oven (425°F.) 25 to 30 minutes. Makes 6 servings.

PORK-CRANBERRY PIE

Cranberries give the tender, savory pork a delightfully different taste

2 ¼ lbs. lean pork
¼ c. flour
1 tsp. ground sage
¾ tsp. salt
2 slices bacon, chopped
1 c. ground cranberries
⅓ c. sugar
1 c. hot water
Biscuit Crust

• Cut pork in 2″ cubes. Combine flour, sage and salt and toss pork in flour mixture to coat thoroughly. Pan-fry bacon and pork, browning on all sides. Drain off excess fat. Place hot meats in a 1½ qt. casserole.

• Combine cranberries and sugar. Scatter over meat. Add hot water. Cover and bake in hot oven (400°F.) while making Biscuit Crust. Place bis-

cuit dough on top of meat and continue baking 20 minutes or until crust is as brown as desired. Makes 6 servings.

BISCUIT CRUST: Sift together 1 c. flour, 1½ tsp. baking powder and ½ tsp. salt. Cut in ¼ c. butter or margarine until mixture resembles coarse crumbs. Stir in ⅓ c. milk all at one time. Stir just to moisten. Knead lightly 8 or 10 times. Pat out or roll out the same size as casserole. Cut round of dough in 6 wedges and arrange on top of pork mixture.

SAUSAGE-EGG SUPPER PIE

A good Ohio cook's interpretation of pizza to fix for the family or teens

Unbaked 9″ pie shell
½ lb. bulk pork sausage
¾ c. chopped onion
½ tsp. orégano
¼ tsp. salt
¼ tsp. pepper
4 eggs
½ c. milk
1 c. shredded sharp Cheddar cheese
⅔ c. canned pizza sauce

• Cook sausage and onion together in skillet, breaking up sausage with fork, until sausage is browned and onion is tender. Drain off excess fat. Add orégano, salt and pepper.

• Beat eggs and milk together. Stir in sausage and cheese. Turn into pie shell and bake in very hot oven (450°F.) 15 minutes. Reduce heat to moderate oven (350°F.) and continue baking until filling is set, 10 to 15 minutes.

more

• Remove from oven and spread top of pie with pizza sauce. Return to oven a minute or two to heat sauce. Makes 6 servings.

SAUSAGE-CORN CUPS

Individual tarts with sausage crust baked in and served from a casserole

1 ½ lbs. bulk pork sausage
2   c. prepared stuffing mix
1   (12 oz.) can whole kernel corn, drained
1   can condensed cream of chicken soup
½   c. milk

• Divide sausage into 6 portions; form into cups about 3″ in diameter. Broil about 5 minutes, or until browned. Pierce bottom of sausage cups with fork to let fat drain.
• Combine stuffing mix and corn. (You can make your own bread dressing or stuffing, seasoning it as you like.) Place one third of mixture in shallow baking dish. Top with sausage cups; fill cups with remaining corn mixture. (You can do this ahead, refrigerate and bake later.)
• Combine soup and milk; stir until smooth. Pour over sausage cups. Bake in slow oven (300°F.) for 30 minutes. Makes 6 servings.

BACON-AND-EGG BREAKFAST PIE

Serve with chilled tomato slices and plenty of steaming hot coffee

Pastry for 2-crust pie
12 slices bacon, cooked

6   eggs
¼   tsp. salt
⅛   tsp. pepper
2   tblsp. chopped parsley
1   tblsp. chopped chives or green onion tops
1   can condensed cream of mushroom soup
3   tblsp. milk

• Place half the bacon strips in bottom of pastry-lined 9″ pie pan.
• Carefully break each egg, keeping yolk whole, into cup. Slip, one at a time, on top of bacon. Sprinkle with salt, pepper, parsley and chives or onion tops. Top with remaining bacon slices. Spoon ½ c. mushroom soup, in small dots, over top.
• Cover with top crust, flute edges and cut steam vents.
• Bake in hot oven (425°F.) 30 minutes, or until lightly browned. Cut in wedges and serve hot with mushroom sauce made by heating remaining mushroom soup combined with milk. Makes 6 servings.

Ham-'n'-Eggs Pie

Here's a pie for which you'll have ingredients on hand. You may want to double the recipe if you have more than five people at your dinner table. It's a wonderful pie for a company supper because it's brimful of country-good foods like ham, eggs and milk.

DEEP-DISH HAM PIE

Home-style meat pie—you can dress it up with cheese pastry lattice top

Cheese Pastry for 1-crust pie
(Chapter 2)
¼ c. butter or margarine
¼ c. flour
½ tsp. salt
¼ tsp. dry mustard
⅛ tsp. pepper
1 tsp. instant minced onion
2 c. milk
2 hard-cooked eggs, chopped
2 ½ c. diced cooked ham
1 (8 ½ oz.) can peas, drained

• Melt butter; blend in flour, salt, mustard and pepper. Add onion and milk; cook over medium heat, stirring constantly, until mixture is thick and smooth. Add eggs, ham and peas.
• Pour hot mixture into 2 qt. casserole. Roll pastry dough slightly larger than top of casserole. Place over warm ham mixture and fold edges under. Flute against inside of casserole. Make steam vents.
• Bake in hot oven (425°F.) until top is browned, about 20 minutes. Makes 4 to 5 servings.

CHEESE-HAM PIES

Pies can be readied for baking in a hurry when you return home late

Cheese Pastry for 2-crust pie
(Chapter 2)
2 c. diced carrots
2 c. cubed potatoes
3 c. cubed cooked ham
2 tblsp. ham drippings
1 (4 oz.) can sliced mushrooms, drained
2 tblsp. flour
1 ¼ c. milk
1 tsp. celery seed
¼ tsp. paprika

• Cook carrots and potatoes in salted water until just tender; drain. Arrange in 2 greased 9″ square pans. Divide ham between the 2 pans.
• Heat ham drippings and mushrooms in skillet. Stir in flour until mixture is smooth; add milk and cook until thick and smooth, stirring constantly. Add celery seed and paprika.
• Pour sauce over vegetables and ham in both pans.
• Cover each with pastry, cut vents and flute against pans' edges. Refrigerate until time to bake.
• Bake in hot oven (400°F.) 30 minutes. Makes 12 servings.

CRISSCROSS HAM TAMALE PIE

Widely praised FARM JOURNAL recipe from our COUNTRY COOKBOOK

1 (1 lb.) slice ready-to-eat ham or
2 ½ c. cubed baked ham
3 tblsp. salad oil
¾ c. chopped onion
1 clove garlic, minced
1 ½ tsp. chili powder
2 tblsp. flour
1 green pepper
2 c. tomato juice
1 (4 oz.) can mushroom stems and pieces
2 c. cooked lima beans (fresh, frozen or canned)
1 (14 oz.) pkg. corn muffin mix
½ c. milk
1 egg, beaten   *more*

· Cut ham into 1″ cubes.

· Heat oil in large skillet. Add onion and garlic. Cook 5 minutes. Add the cubed ham. Sprinkle with chili powder and flour. Continue to cook over moderate heat 10 minutes. Stir occasionally.

· Wash pepper. Remove core. Cut into eighths; add to ham along with tomato juice, mushrooms with liquid and lima beans. Bring to boil; reduce heat, cook 2 or 3 minutes, stirring constantly.

· Pour hot mixture into greased 2 qt. casserole. (A shallow one allows more space for topping.) Place in moderate oven (375°F.) while mixing corn muffin topping.

· Blend corn muffin mix with milk and egg. Spoon over hot ham mixture in a wide crisscross pattern.

· Bake 25 minutes, or until topping is golden brown.

· If meat-and-vegetable mixture is made ahead and chilled in refrigerator, heat it in oven until bubbly hot before adding topping. Makes 6 to 8 servings.

TRIPLE MEAT PIE

Company meat pie with 2 crusts—one of ham, the other pastry

Pastry for 2-crust pie
½ lb. ground lean pork
½ lb. ground veal
1   small onion, chopped (½ c.)
¼ c. chopped parsley
¾ tsp. salt
¼ tsp. pepper
2   tsp. Worcestershire sauce
2   egg yolks, beaten
2   egg whites, stiffly beaten
8   slices baked or boiled ham
     (6 oz.)
Cream (optional)

· Combine pork, veal, onion, parsley, salt, pepper, Worcestershire sauce and egg yolks. Fold in egg whites.
· Arrange half slices of ham so they line pastry-lined 9″ pie pan. Spoon pork mixture over them, mounding it slightly.
· Adjust top crust. Brush with cream for shiny top. Cut vents and flute edges.
· Bake in moderate oven (375°F.) 1 hour. Serve either hot or cold. Makes 6 servings.

Country Chicken Pies

Did you ever, as a child, sit wide-eyed and eager while your grandfather dipped a spoon into the superb chicken pie your grandmother brought steaming hot to the table? It's an unforgettable experience—first, the expectancy and then the fulfillment when you tasted. You'll find modernized old-time recipes for exceptional pies in this chapter along with the new.

Some of our chicken pies contain vegetables. While frozen vegetables often are specified because they're usually available in farm homes and are so handy, you can use cooked fresh or canned vegetables if you prefer.

Cooked turkey may be substituted for chicken in any of these pies—and with equally good results. In some farm kitchens there are larger quantities of the ready-to-use turkey than chicken in the freezer. Pies are a good way to use some of the poultry meat.

Try all these chicken pie recipes to determine which one you and your family and friends like most. Don't overlook the miniature chicken liver pies or tarts, a new type of hot sandwich. We predict that you'll never discover a more appetizing use for those chicken livers.

CHICKEN-POTATO PIE

Chicken and pimiento combine tastily in this hearty main dish

1   frozen Pimiento-Potato Pie Shell (Chapter 2)
4   tblsp. melted butter or margarine
2   tblsp. flour
1   c. chicken broth
Salt and pepper
1   (4 oz.) can sliced mushrooms, drained
½   c. diced celery
1   c. diced cooked chicken

· Remove wrap from frozen Pimiento-Potato Pie Shell. Place in casserole in which it was originally shaped. Drizzle with 2 tblsp. of the melted butter. Cover and bake in hot oven (400°F.) 30 minutes. Uncover and bake 30 minutes.
· Meanwhile, combine the remaining 2 tblsp. melted butter and flour in heavy saucepan. Slowly add broth; stir constantly until sauce is smooth and

thick. Season with salt and pepper. Add remaining ingredients; heat. Spoon hot mixture into baked nest for serving. Makes 6 servings.

POPOVER CHICKEN PIE

"Puffed-up" chicken pie is different, new, taste-rewarding and easy to fix

1 ¾   c. flour
2   tsp. salt
¼   tsp. pepper
1   tsp. paprika
8   good-sized pieces fryer chickens (at least 4 lbs.)
⅓   c. vegetable shortening or salad oil
1 ½   tsp. baking powder
4   eggs, slightly beaten
1 ½   c. milk
3   tblsp. melted butter
1   tsp. celery seed

· Combine ¼ c. flour, 1 tsp. salt, pepper and paprika; mix well.
· Use legs and thighs of chicken. Breasts also may be used, but cut them in half. Roll chicken in flour mixture and brown on all sides in shortening. Remove chicken from skillet and drain on paper towels.
· To make batter, sift together remaining 1½ c. flour, baking powder and remaining 1 tsp. salt.
· Blend eggs, milk and butter. Combine flour and egg mixture, beating with rotary beater just enough to make smooth batter. Do not beat more than necessary.
· Pour batter into an 8″ × 12″ × 2″ pan. Arrange browned chicken pieces on top. Sprinkle with celery seed.
· Bake in moderate oven (350°F.) 1

hour, or until puffed and browned. Serve at once. Makes 6 servings.

Note: If you want to serve gravy with the pie, thicken and season chicken broth, if you have it, or heat a can of condensed cream of chicken soup, adding milk for the desired consistency, or use gravy mix. (You can cook the bony chicken pieces in water to make the broth.) If you prefer, bake the chicken pie in a 9" deep pie pan, but you may be able to use only 6 chicken pieces.

CHICKEN AND OYSTER PIE

A Missouri farm woman's delicious way to extend oysters

Pastry for 1-crust pie
3   c. diced cooked chicken
1   c. oysters
6   tblsp. flour
2 ½ c. chicken broth
½   c. finely minced celery

1   tsp. instant onion flakes
1   (10 oz.) pkg. frozen peas and
     carrots
1   tsp. salt
⅛   tsp. pepper
Paprika

• Place alternate layers of chicken and oysters in bottom of greased 2 qt. casserole.
• Blend together flour and ½ c. chicken broth (or cold water). Add to remaining 2 c. chicken broth. Add celery, onion, salt, pepper and peas and carrots. Cook over medium heat, stirring constantly, until mixture comes to a boil. Simmer 5 minutes. Pour over chicken and oysters.
• Roll pastry slightly larger than top of casserole; place over casserole and trim so it overhangs casserole 1". Fold edge of pastry under and flute against inside edge of casserole. Cut steam vents. Sprinkle with paprika.
• Bake in hot oven (425°F.) until pastry is lightly browned, about 30 minutes. Makes 6 servings.

Chicken Pie Southern-Style

You don't have to live in the South to enjoy Double-Crust Chicken Pie, an old plantation masterpiece . . . make it in your own kitchen. A Georgia farm woman won honors with this recipe in a cooking contest. Serve this pie at your next company or community meal—it's easy to tote. Some Southern homemakers like to double the recipe and bake the pie in a dishpan or roaster!

You may want to follow an old Georgia custom and use your favorite buttermilk biscuits instead of the biscuit mix. Molded cranberry salad and butter beans go well with this.

DOUBLE-CRUST CHICKEN PIE

Two crisp, buttery-brown crusts cover tender chickens, dumplings and gravy

2   (2 ½ lb.) broilers
2   tsp. salt
1 ¼ c. butter or margarine

4 c. biscuit mix
1 ⅓ c. milk
½ tsp. pepper
2 c. boiling water

• Cut chicken into serving pieces; sprinkle with salt; set aside 30 minutes.
• Cut ½ c. butter into biscuit mix. Add milk all at once; stir with fork to soften dough. Beat 12 strokes. Divide into four equal parts.
• Roll out one portion of dough to ¼″ thickness (knead each part gently 10 times just before rolling). Cut into 1″ × 2″ strips; lay strips over bottom of buttered 4 qt. baking dish. Top with half the chicken pieces.
• Place ¼ c. butter in lumps between and on pieces of chicken; sprinkle with ¼ tsp. pepper.
• Roll second dough portion and cut as before; lay pastry strips over chicken until covered.
• Place rest of chicken on this pastry, making sure chicken pieces touch edge of baking dish; add ¼ c. butter in lumps and sprinkle with ¼ tsp. pepper.
• Roll third dough portion large enough to cover chicken; seal it to inside of dish. Cut small hole in center of pastry; pour in enough boiling water to barely float the crust (about 2 c.).
• Bake in very hot oven (450°F.) about 15 minutes, or until brown. Remove from oven; spread with 2 tblsp. softened butter.
• Roll remaining dough large enough to cover first crust; place over top, again sealing to side of dish.
• Return to oven 10 minutes, or until second crust is lightly browned. Remove chicken pie from oven; spread with remaining butter.

• Reduce oven to slow (325°F.); bake 45 minutes or until chicken is tender (add more boiling water as before, if needed). Makes 6 to 8 servings.

CHICKEN SPOONBREAD PIE

Pie wears high, puffy, brown topping

Filling:
5 tblsp. chicken fat
¼ c. chopped celery
2 tblsp. chopped onion
5 tblsp. flour
2 ½ c. chicken broth
1 tsp. salt
¼ tsp. monosodium glutamate
⅛ tsp. pepper
1 tsp. dried parsley
2 ½ c. cubed cooked chicken

Spoonbread:
2 c. boiling water
1 c. white cornmeal
2 tblsp. soft butter
1 c. milk
1 tsp. salt
3 tsp. baking powder
4 eggs, well beaten

Filling: Melt chicken fat in bottom of saucepan. (Extend with butter if necessary to make 5 tblsp., or use all butter.) Add celery and onion and cook until soft, but do not brown. Stir in flour. Add chicken broth and cook, stirring constantly, until mixture boils and is thickened. Add salt, monosodium glutamate, pepper and parsley. Stir in chicken and heat.
• Pour into 3 qt. casserole and place in hot oven (400°F.) and let heat while you make Spoonbread.
Spoonbread: Pour boiling water over

cornmeal. Beat in butter, milk, salt, baking powder and eggs. Pour on top of bubbling hot chicken in casserole.
· Bake in hot oven (400°F.) 40 to 45 minutes or until top is browned. Serve at once. Makes 8 servings.

BRUNSWICK CHICKEN PIE

Deep-dish chicken pie inspired by the Deep South's Brunswick Stew

Pastry for 2 (2-crust) pies
1   (4 to 5 lb.) chicken, cut up
2   tsp. salt
2   c. drained whole-kernel corn
2   c. chopped onion
6   c. thick canned tomatoes
4   c. lima beans, fresh or frozen
½   lb. bacon, finely diced
¼   tsp. pepper
¼   tsp. dried thyme
¼   c. soft butter
3   tblsp. flour

· Combine chicken with all ingredients except pastry, butter and flour. Simmer 1 hour. Remove chicken to cool.
· Meanwhile blend butter and flour. Add a little of the stew liquid. Blend; return to stew and cook, stirring constantly, until stew thickens. Cool quickly.
· Remove chicken from bones; cut meat into large pieces and add to cooled stew.
· Line two 2 qt. casseroles with half of pastry. Fill with cooled stew. Top with remaining pastry; seal edges and cut vents in top.
· Cover rim of crust with foil; place in hot oven (425°F.) and bake 15 minutes; reduce heat to 350° and bake

45 minutes. Remove foil and continue baking 15 minutes. Makes 10 to 12 servings.

Note: Unbaked pie freezes well. To bake, place unthawed pie in cold oven. Set oven at hot (425°F.) and bake 30 minutes; reduce heat to 350° and bake about 1½ hours.

LATTICE CHICKEN PIE

Count on this 2-crust pie to make friends and to disappear quickly

1   (3 lb.) broiler-fryer, cut up
3   c. water
3   celery tops
1   tsp. salt
5   peppercorns
Chicken Gravy
1   (10 oz.) pkg. frozen peas, cooked and drained
3   tblsp. chopped pimiento (optional)
2   c. sifted flour
1   tsp. salt
⅓   c. shortening
⅔   c. milk

· Simmer chicken with water, celery tops, 1 tsp. salt and peppercorns until tender, about 1 hour. Remove from broth; cool slightly. Strain broth and make gravy (recipe follows).
· Slip skin from chicken and remove from bones while still warm. Cut into bite-size pieces and combine with peas, pimiento and 2 c. Chicken Gravy.
· Sift flour and 1 tsp. salt in bowl, cut in shortening to make crumbly mixture and stir in milk with fork to make dough that just holds together.

• Turn dough onto lightly floured surface and knead three times; roll two thirds dough in a rectangle about 12" × 16". Fit it into a baking dish 10" × 6" × 2". Spoon chicken mixture into pastry-lined dish.

• Roll remaining third of pastry into a rectangle about 14" × 7" and cut in 9 long strips from ¾" to 1" wide. Lay 5 strips lengthwise over chicken. Cut the remaining 4 strips in half and weave them across long strips to make a lattice. Trim overhang to 1", turn under and flute against edge of baking dish.

• Bake in hot oven (400°F.) 20 minutes; reduce heat to 350° and bake about 30 minutes longer, or until crust is browned. Serve with remaining Chicken Gravy, heated. Makes 5 to 6 servings.

CHICKEN GRAVY: Melt 6 tblsp. butter or margarine over low heat; stir in 6 tblsp. flour, 1 tsp. salt, ⅛ tsp. pepper, 1 tsp. minced onion and ⅛ tsp. dried marjoram leaves. Cook, stirring constantly, until mixture bubbles. Add 3 c. strained chicken broth gradually, stirring constantly, and 1 tsp. lemon juice. Cook until mixture thickens and boils a minute. Stir in 1 c. light cream. Makes about 4½ c.

HIS AND HER CHICKEN PIE

This pie flatters people by giving them their choice of dark or light meat

Filling:

2   (2½ lb.) frying chickens
5   c. water
½   tsp. salt
1   small onion, sliced
1   carrot, sliced
1   celery stalk, diced
½   tsp. monosodium glutamate
1   c. sliced celery
1   (10 oz.) pkg. frozen mixed vegetables
5   tblsp. flour
½   c. light cream
2½ c. chicken broth
1   tsp. salt
⅛   tsp. pepper

Biscuit Crust:

2   c. sifted flour
4   tsp. baking powder
2   tsp. sugar
1   tsp. salt
½   tsp. cream of tartar
½   c. shortening
⅔   c. milk
Olives, pitted ripe and pimiento-stuffed

Filling: Combine chicken pieces, water, ½ tsp. salt, onion, carrot, diced celery and monosodium glutamate in kettle. Cover and simmer until tender (about 1 hour). Drain and reserve broth. Cool chicken in broth; remove meat from bones, separating dark and light meat.

• Cook sliced celery in salted water until just tender. Add mixed vegetables and cook as directed on package. Drain.

• Blend together flour and cream. Combine in saucepan with broth. Add 1 tsp. salt and pepper and cook over medium heat, stirring constantly, until mixture comes to a boil. Stir in celery and mixed vegetables.

• Place ⅓ of broth mixture in bottom of 2 qt. casserole. Fill one side of casserole with dark meat, the other with light meat. Place toothpick in dark meat side to identify. Pour remaining broth over chicken.

• Place in very hot oven (450°F.) until mixture is bubbly hot. Top with biscuits (recipe follows), cut with doughnut cutter and return to oven. Bake until biscuits are golden, 10 to 12 minutes.

• Remove from oven. Place pitted black olives (ripe) in doughnut holes on side of dark meat, removing toothpick. Place stuffed green olives in holes in biscuits on side holding light meat. Serve at once. Makes 6 to 7 servings.

Biscuit Crust: Sift together flour, baking powder, sugar, salt and cream of tartar. Cut in shortening until mixture resembles coarse crumbs. Add milk all at one time and stir until dough follows fork around bowl. Dough should be soft and easy to handle.

• Turn dough onto lightly floured surface and knead by folding over and pressing with palm of hand 8 to 10 times. Pat or roll to about ½″ thickness and cut with doughnut cutter. Arrange on top of chicken pie as directed.

Note: You can use 2 c. cooked light and 2 c. cooked dark meat to make this pie if you have cooked chicken in the freezer. If you do not have chicken broth, commercially canned broth may be used. Frozen peas may be used instead of mixed vegetables.

MAINE CHICKEN PIE

Chicken and gravy under crisp, flaky pastry—a COUNTRY COOKBOOK *favorite*

Pastry for 2-crust pie
1   (5 lb.) whole stewing chicken

1 ½ qts. water
2   tsp. salt
1   small onion
1   carrot
1   stalk celery
¾   tsp. monosodium glutamate
½   c. sifted flour
½   tsp. onion salt
½   tsp. celery salt
Pepper
3 ½ c. chicken broth
2   or 3 drops yellow food color

• Place chicken in large kettle and add next six ingredients, using ½ tsp. monosodium glutamate and 1 tsp. salt. Simmer, covered, until tender, 3 to 3½ hours. Save broth.

• Remove bird to rack. Strip meat from bones, removing in large pieces. Refrigerate when cool.

• Combine flour, onion salt, celery salt, pepper, 1 tsp. salt and ¼ tsp. monosodium glutamate with ½ c. chicken broth. Mix until smooth.

• Heat 3 c. chicken broth to boiling. Add flour mixture, beating with a wire whip to prevent lumping.

• Cook over medium heat, stirring constantly until mixture is smooth and thickened. Add food color.

• Add chicken and blend well.

• Line 9″ deep-dish pie pan with pastry. Fill with chicken mixture. Adjust top crust, cut vents and flute edges.

• Bake in hot oven (400°F.) 45 minutes, or until browned. Makes 6 to 8 servings.

Note: If you want to freeze this pie, cool, wrap, label and place in freezer. Cool filling before pouring in crust to freeze like unbaked pie. Freeze broth for gravy separately.

INDIVIDUAL CHICKEN-HAM PIES

What a marvelous combination! Rice, chicken and ham expertly seasoned

Rice Crust
- 3   tblsp. butter
- ¼   c. flour
- 2   c. chicken broth
- 2   tblsp. chopped parsley
- 2   tsp. salt
- ¼   tsp. pepper
- 3   c. diced cooked chicken
- 1   c. diced cooked ham
- ⅔   c. grated Cheddar cheese

• Melt butter; add flour and blend. Add chicken broth and cook over medium heat, stirring constantly, until mixture comes to a boil and is thickened. Add parsley, salt, pepper, chicken and ham.

• Pour into rice-lined tart pans. Sprinkle the reserved cup of rice mixture over tops of pies. Sprinkle with cheese.

• Bake in moderate oven (350°F.) 20 minutes. Serve in tart pans.

RICE CRUST: Combine 5 c. cooked rice, 2 beaten eggs, ½ c. melted butter, 1 tsp. salt and ⅛ tsp. pepper. Mix thoroughly. Reserve 1 c. mixture. Pat remaining rice mixture over bottom and on sides of 6 greased (6″) tart pans.

VARIATION

ALL-CHICKEN PIES: Omit ham and use 4 c. diced cooked chicken in recipe for Individual Chicken-Ham Pies.

CHICKEN LIVER TARTS

Unusual hot sandwiches to serve with salad or as snack with tomato juice

Pastry for 2 (2-crust) pies
- 1   lb. chicken livers
- 3   tblsp. flour
- ¼   c. chopped onion
- ¼   c. butter or margarine
- 2   tsp. Worcestershire sauce
- ½   tsp. salt
- ⅛   tsp. pepper

Melted butter
- 2   tblsp. Parmesan cheese

Paprika

• Dust chicken livers with flour. Cook with onions in ¼ c. butter. Add Worcestershire sauce, salt and pepper. Remove from heat and chop and mash livers until of spreading consistency.

• Divide pastry in fourths and roll each, one at a time, ⅛″ thick. Cut in 3″ rounds.

• Place half of rounds on baking sheet and top each with 1 tblsp. chicken-liver mixture. Top with other half of pastry rounds and press edges together with tines of fork to seal. Prick tops with fork.

• Brush with melted butter and sprinkle with cheese and paprika. Bake in hot oven (425°F.) 10 to 12 minutes, or until lightly browned. Makes 20 tarts.

Note: Tarts may be made in advance and frozen unbaked. Bake frozen tarts in hot oven (425°F.) 12 to 15 minutes, or until lightly browned. Make smaller tarts to serve as an appetizer.

English Hare Pie

When children have 4-H rabbit projects, their mothers look for recipes to use some of the meat the youngsters produce. Here's a dish adapted by food specialists, U. S. Department of Agriculture. It's an Americanized version with onion and green peppers added—a blend of flavors much enjoyed in many homes.

RABBIT PIE

As English as the Thames—this hare pie has been adapted in this country

Pastry

¼ c. butter or margarine
¼ c. chopped onion
½ c. chopped green pepper
¼ c. sifted flour
4 chicken bouillon cubes
2 c. hot water
Salt
Pepper
3 c. cut-up cooked rabbit meat

• Heat butter in large skillet; add onion and green pepper and cook over low heat about 5 minutes.

• Blend in flour and cook until mixture bubbles. Pour in bouillon, made by dissolving cubes in hot water, stirring constantly. (Use broth in which rabbit was cooked if available, for all or part of bouillon.) Cook until thick and smooth, stirring frequently. Add salt and pepper to taste.

• Add meat to sauce and heat thoroughly. Pour into a 1½ qt. casserole.

PASTRY: Roll out pastry made with 1 c. sifted flour, ½ tsp. salt, ⅓ c. lard and about 2 tblsp. cold water, slightly larger than top of baking dish. Cut slits for steam to escape. Adjust on top of hot rabbit mixture and trim to overhang 1″. Fold under and flute against inside of casserole.

• Bake in hot oven (425°F.) 15 to 20 minutes, or until crust browns and sauce bubbles in vents. Makes 5 to 6 servings.

CHAPTER 11

CHEESE, FISH, SEA FOOD AND VEGETABLE PIES

We're predicting you'll really enjoy drop-in company for lunch when there's a hearty main-course pie practically ready to put in the oven. You can build such appetizing menus around these hot dishes.

Protein foods predominate in these pies—cheese, fish, sea food and eggs. They're good meatless-Friday specials—our Double Corn and Egg Pie, for instance. While the pies are perfect for lunch, they'll serve your whole family well for supper or dinner. Some of them, like Potato and Egg Pie, are hearty breakfast dishes that will start the day right.

If you're having big bowls of steaming beef-vegetable soup, glamorize the meal with our Individual Cheese Tarts or pies. For go-withs, have fruit salad, cookies and a beverage. Take the cookies from the freezer—also the tarts ready for reheating.

Some of the pies in this chapter are ideal for serving when you invite women friends to lunch. Farmhouse Asparagus-Chicken Pie, for instance, is delicious with the green spears arranged in a pastry shell like the spokes of a wheel. And if you're entertaining shrimp fans, do feature this sea food in Shrimp-Cheese Pie or Gulf-Style Shrimp Pie. Don't count the men out —the countryside is filled with farmers who are fond of shrimp. Men also praise our onion pies. One country homemaker says she makes a point of serving piping-hot Herbed Onion and Cheese Pie with sizzling steaks when she's splurging a little for guests. And if your family has little interest in the shiny, purple eggplant from the garden, bake an Eggplant Pie and watch its happy acceptance.

Country cooks show no favoritism in crusts; they use both pastry and biscuit types. Check the ingredients in our recipes—you'll observe most of them are in your cupboard, refrigerator and freezer. So decide on one of the pies in this chapter when you're wondering what to fix for supper.

Win Them to Vegetables with Pies

Farm mothers say that one of the most successful ways of persuading men and children to like vegetables, other than their ever favorite potatoes, is to serve them in pies. Anything held in tender, flaky, golden pastry, or topped by it, has a head start on getting a welcome at farm tables. Once the vegetable is approved in a pie, it also will fare better in other dishes. So pies, country cooks find, are useful in winning friends for garden vegetables.

ONION CHEESE-POTATO PIE

Pretty, tasty economy dish that's especially good with ham or pork

1   frozen Cheese-Potato Pie Shell (Chapter 2)
2   tblsp. melted butter
1   beef bouillon cube
½   c. boiling water
2   c. chopped onions
¼   c. butter or margarine
3   tblsp. flour
1   c. milk
Salt and pepper

• Remove wrap from frozen Cheese-Potato Pie Shell. Place in casserole in which it originally was shaped. Drizzle with melted butter. Cover and bake in hot oven (400°F.) 30 minutes. Uncover and bake 30 minutes.

• Meanwhile, dissolve bouillon cube in boiling water. Add onions; cover and simmer until tender. Drain.

• Melt ¼ c. butter in heavy saucepan. Add flour to make smooth paste. Add milk slowly, stirring constantly until smooth and thickened.

• Season with salt and pepper. Add drained onions. Spoon into baked Cheese-Potato Pie Shell for serving. Makes 6 servings.

CORN-CHEESE PIE

Serve this hearty, hot pie with cold cuts and tomato-lettuce salad

Unbaked 9" pie shell
1   c. light cream
½   tsp. salt
1   egg, beaten
1   green pepper, chopped (¾ c.)
⅓   c. chopped onion
1   (1 lb.) can cream style corn
½   c. fine bread crumbs
2   tblsp. butter or margarine
⅓   c. grated process American cheese

• Blend cream, salt and egg. Stir in green pepper, onion and corn. Turn into pie shell.

• Scatter bread crumbs over top; dot with butter and sprinkle with cheese.

• Bake in moderate oven (375°F.) until filling is set, about 40 to 45 minutes. Let stand 10 minutes before cutting. Makes 6 servings.

DOUBLE CORN AND EGG PIE

A Friday special—serve with a mixed fruit salad and a green vegetable

Pastry for 2-crust pie
1 (1 lb.) can cream style corn
1 (12 oz.) can Mexicorn
2 tblsp. grated onion
½ tsp. salt
⅛ tsp. pepper
4 hard-cooked eggs, sliced
4 oz. process American cheese, thinly sliced

• Combine corns, onion, salt and pepper, mixing well.

• Arrange sliced eggs in pastry-lined 10″ pie pan to make even layer. Top with corn mixture, then with cheese slices.

• Adjust top crust; flute edges and cut steam vents.

• Bake in hot oven (425°F.) 30 minutes. Let stand 5 minutes before cutting. Makes 8 servings.

• Melt 4 tblsp. butter and toss with 1½ c. cracker crumbs. Press into bottom and on sides of 9″ pie pan to make pie shell. Bake in moderate oven (350°F.) 5 minutes. Cool.

• Melt 2 tblsp. butter in skillet. Add onions, separated into rings. Cover and cook over low heat until onions are soft, 10 to 15 minutes. Stir occasionally. Turn into pie shell.

• Beat eggs with milk, salt, pepper, marjoram and thyme. Add cheese. Melt remaining 1 tblsp. butter in skillet in which onions cooked. Add egg mixture and cook over very low heat, stirring constantly, just until cheese melts. Carefully pour sauce over onions. Top with remaining ½ c. cracker crumbs.

• Bake in very hot oven (450°F.) 15 minutes. Reduce heat to 350°F. and continue baking until filling is set, 10 to 15 minutes. Cut in wedges and serve hot. Makes 8 servings.

HERBED ONION AND CHEESE PIE

Superb with grilled steaks and good with barbecued ribs and other meats

7 tblsp. butter or margarine
2 c. cheese-flavored cracker crumbs
3 large onions, thinly sliced (about 3 c.)
2 eggs, slightly beaten
1 c. milk
1 tsp. salt
¼ tsp. black pepper
⅛ tsp. dried marjoram
⅛ tsp. dried thyme
½ c. shredded sharp Cheddar cheese

ONION PIE

A FARM JOURNAL *5-star success—recipe from* COUNTRY COOKBOOK

Caraway Pastry:
1½ c. sifted flour
¾ tsp. salt
1½ tsp. caraway seeds
½ c. shortening
2 to 3 tblsp. water

Filling:
3 c. thinly sliced peeled onions
3 tblsp. melted butter or margarine
½ c. milk
1½ c. dairy sour cream   *more*

1   tsp. salt
2   eggs, well beaten
3   tblsp. flour
Bacon slices

Pastry: Combine flour, salt and caraway seeds. Add shortening; cut into flour until mixture resembles little peas and coarse cornmeal.
• Gradually add water, tossing with fork until mixture forms a ball that follows fork around bowl.
• Turn onto a lightly floured surface; roll to 11½″ circle of ⅛″ thickness. Fit into a 10″ pie pan; flute edge; prick entire surface with 4-tined fork.
• Bake in hot oven (425°F.) 10 minutes, or until lightly browned.
Filling: Sauté onions in butter until lightly browned. Spoon into pie shell.
• Add milk, 1¼ c. sour cream and salt to eggs.
• Blend flour with remaining ¼ c. sour cream. Combine with egg mixture; pour over onions.
• Bake in slow oven (325°F.) 30 minutes, or until firm in center. Garnish with crisp bacon. Serve as a main dish. Makes 8 servings.

SPINACH PIE

See if they won't eat spinach fixed this way—a prizewinning luncheon dish

Unbaked 9″ pie shell
10   bacon slices (about ½ lb.)
¾   c. chopped onion (1 medium)
1   (10 oz.) pkg. frozen chopped
     spinach
4   eggs, slightly beaten
1   c. milk
1   tsp. seasoned salt

• Cut 6 slices bacon in small pieces and pan-fry until crisp. Remove, drain. Cook onion in bacon fat until golden brown. Drain.
• Cook spinach as directed on package. Drain thoroughly.
• Blend eggs, milk and seasoned salt. Add spinach, onion and cooked bacon. Turn into pie shell. Bake in moderate oven (375°F.) until filling is set, 40 to 45 minutes.
• Meanwhile, cut remaining slices of bacon in small pieces and pan-fry until crisp and brown. Drain and sprinkle on top of pie just before serving. Makes 6 servings.

Asparagus and Chicken-Pie Team

Country women long have served asparagus with chicken in special-occasion meals. But we found one farm woman who teams chicken and the green spears in an elegant main-dish pie that her guests praise.

With her Farmhouse Asparagus Pie, she often serves a generous mixed fruit salad in lettuce cups with hot tea or coffee. This 3-piece meal satisfies and it's no trick for the hostess-cook to have everything ready in advance.

By using a 10″ pie pan, you get eight good servings. You can use a 9″ × 9″ × 2″ pan and pastry for a 2-crust pie, but it's more difficult to fit the pastry into the square pan.

These dainty pick-up pies (*see Good Ideas from Our Test Kitchens, page 206*) *are ideal for parties and receptions. Pastry holds fruit and cream fillings, cream cheese glazed with melted jelly, sherbets and ice cream.*

FARMHOUSE ASPARAGUS PIE

Company lunch special—so attractive

Unbaked 10" pie shell
20 fresh asparagus spears or 1
     (10 oz.) pkg. frozen aspara-
     gus spears, cooked
1 ½ c. chopped cooked chicken
 4 slices bacon
 ½ c. shredded natural Swiss cheese
 4 eggs
 1 tblsp. flour
 ½ tsp. salt
 2 c. light cream

 2 tblsp. grated Parmesan cheese
Paprika

• Arrange cooked asparagus in bottom of pie shell, spoke-fashion. Top
with chicken. Cook, drain and crumble
bacon. Scatter it and Swiss cheese over
asparagus and chicken.
• Beat together eggs, flour, salt and
cream; pour over asparagus. Sprinkle
with Parmesan cheese and paprika.
• Bake in moderate oven (375°F.) 45
to 50 minutes or until pie filling is set.
Let stand 10 minutes before cutting.
Makes 8 servings.

Royal Purple Eggplant Pie

Shiny, purple eggplants that you see
in your markets or grow in the garden
make excellent hearty pies. Select a
vegetable that's firm and heavy for its
size. Make sure it's a uniform dark
color, free of blemishes (when eggplant ages, it sometimes shrivels and
develops a bitter taste).

You need not peel the vegetable for
our recipe. Just wash and cut it in
cubes. The seasonings suggest dishes
popular along Mediterranean shores or
in our states bordering the Gulf of
Mexico. It's a pie that cuts nicely and
adds to the prestige of a vegetable
too often neglected in farm kitchens.

EGGPLANT PIE

*People who like Italian pizza espe-
cially enjoy this—teens, for instance!*

Unbaked 9" pie shell
 2 c. cubed unpeeled eggplant

 ¼ c. butter or margarine
 ¾ lb. ground beef chuck
 ½ c. finely chopped onion
 1 clove minced garlic
 1 tblsp. chopped parsley
 ¼ c. chopped celery tops
 1 tsp. salt
 ¼ tsp. orégano
 ⅛ tsp. pepper
 1 (8 oz.) can tomato sauce
 ½ c. shredded Mozzarella cheese

• Place eggplant, washed and cut in
½" cubes, in melted butter in heavy
skillet. Cover and cook over medium
heat 5 minutes. Remove eggplant.
• Place ground beef, onion and garlic
in skillet and cook, stirring, until meat
is browned. Add parsley, celery tops,
seasonings and tomato sauce. Cook
over medium heat 5 minutes, stirring

English Fish Pie, a Friday dish *worthy of company (recipe, page 289). Red-ripe
tomatoes and hard-cooked egg slices are layered with fish and baked under a
crispy top crust of pastry for a deep-dish pie. Wonderfully different fish dish.*

constantly. Stir in eggplant. Partially cool.

• Turn into pie shell. Bake in moderate oven (375°F.) 45 minutes, until pie is golden brown. Sprinkle cheese over top and return to oven a few minutes until cheese melts. Let stand 5 minutes. Makes 6 servings.

liquid into bowl. Stir in clams, milk, eggs, crackers, bacon and seasonings. Turn into pie shell. Dot with butter. Adjust top crust; flute edges and cut vents.

• Bake in very hot oven (450°F.) 15 minutes. Reduce heat to moderate (350°F.) and bake 30 minutes longer or until golden. Makes 6 servings.

A Down-East Pie Special—Try It

You don't have to live near the ocean to enjoy sea food. Here's a Clam Pie you can fix in the heart of the Rocky Mountains or on the Kansas plains. Do try it. While it's a treat at all times, it's especially refreshing on a cool, rainy evening.

CLAM PIE

New England pie special that will make friends in all parts of the country

Pastry for 2-crust pie
2   slices bacon
2   (8 oz.) cans minced clams
¾   c. milk
2   eggs, well beaten
½   c. coarsely broken oyster crackers
1   tsp. onion salt
¼   tsp. pepper
2   tblsp. butter or margarine

• Line 9" pie pan with half of pastry.
• Pan-fry bacon until crisp. Drain and crumble.
• Drain clams. Measure ¾ c. clam

Eggs and Oysters in Pies

Instead of fretting because fresh oysters in landlocked grocery stores frequently are scarce or rather costly, clever cooks contrive to extend the flavor in interesting ways. They often borrow ideas from famous dishes like the Hangtown Fry of California's gold-rush days, in which oysters and eggs share honors.

Hangtown Supper Pies contain the number of eggs required to stretch a pint of fresh oysters to feed six hungry people. The cook, who revived this ranch version, relies on an old country habit of serving the favorite combination of foods in pastry. This time, it's in flaky tart shells so that everyone has his own share. The pastry takes the role of bread in the meal.

These main-dish individual pies are company fare—perfect for the guest who stops in on a snowy winter or rainy spring evening. You can dress up the little pies with garnishes of lemon slices and show off some of your best homemade pickles as accompaniments. Someway the table talk flourishes when these pies are set before family and friends.

HANGTOWN SUPPER PIES

Example of what imaginative country cooks do with a bounty of fresh eggs

6   baked 6" tart shells (pastry for 2-crust pie)
6   slices bacon
1   pt. oysters, drained
½   c. flour
10   eggs
1   tblsp. water
¾   tsp. salt
1 ½ c. fine cracker or bread crumbs
¼   c. milk or cream
⅛   tsp. pepper
¼   c. chopped green pepper
¼   c. chopped chives
2   tblsp. butter

· If tart shells are cold, set them on a baking sheet and warm in moderate oven (350°F.) while preparing other ingredients.
· Fry bacon until almost crisp; roll each slice around a fork to make a curl; drain on paper toweling.
· Roll oysters in flour. Beat 1 egg with water; dip oysters in egg mixture mixed with ½ tsp. salt; roll in crumbs. Pan-fry in bacon fat until golden brown on both sides. Drain and keep warm.
· Beat remaining 9 eggs with milk, add remaining ¼ tsp. salt and pepper. Add green pepper and chives. Melt butter in same skillet used for cooking bacon and oysters. Add egg mixture and scramble just until eggs are set.
· Place eggs in bottom of warmed tart shells; top with warm oysters, then with bacon curls. Garnish with lemon slices and pickles, if desired. Makes 6 servings.

SHRIMP-CHEESE PIE

This is a company lunch tempter but don't bypass the family

Unbaked 9" pie shell
1   (6 oz.) pkg. natural Swiss cheese slices
1   lb. cleaned and cooked shrimp
2   eggs
2   tblsp. flour
1   c. light cream
½   tsp. dried parsley
½   tsp. onion salt
½   tsp. salt
Paprika

· Place half of cheese slices in bottom of pie shell, top with shrimp, then with remaining cheese.
· Blend together eggs, flour, cream, parsley and salts. Pour over cheese. Dust with paprika.
· Bake in hot oven (400°F.) 40 to 45 minutes. Let stand 5 minutes before cutting. Makes 6 servings.

GULF-STYLE SHRIMP PIE

Makes a little shrimp go a long way

½   lb. bacon, diced
⅓   c. milk
1   tblsp. salad oil
1 ½ c. prepared biscuit mix
1   c. cleaned and cooked shrimp
2   tblsp. chopped green onions
1   clove garlic, minced
2   peeled tomatoes, thinly sliced
½   tsp. crumbled dried sweet basil
¼   tsp. salt
⅛   tsp. pepper
1   (6 oz.) pkg. sliced Mozzarella cheese   *more*

• Cook bacon until crisp; drain.

• Stir milk and salad oil into biscuit mix. Mix with a fork. Turn dough on lightly floured surface and roll to fit 9″ pie pan. Crimp edges with fork tines.

• Sprinkle bacon, shrimp, onions and garlic in pie shell. Cover with a single layer of tomatoes. Sprinkle with basil, salt and pepper. Cover with cheese, breaking slices apart to cover tomatoes completely.

• Bake in hot oven (400°F.) 20 to 25 minutes. Serve hot, cut in wedges. Makes 6 servings.

SHRIMP SALAD TARTS

Fruited shrimp salad in pastry shells makes an ideal guest luncheon dish

Cheese Tart Shells:

- 2   c. sifted flour
- 1   tsp. salt
- ½   c. salad oil
- 1   c. grated Cheddar cheese
- 3   tblsp. cold water

Filling:

- ¼   c. mayonnaise
- ¼   c. dairy sour cream
- 4   tsp. lemon juice
- 1   tsp. salt
- ⅛   tsp. dry mustard
- 2   c. chopped cooked shrimp
- 1   c. chopped celery
- ¼   c. finely chopped green onions
- 1   c. seedless green grapes, cut in halves
- 1   medium unpeeled apple, chopped
- ½   c. chopped pecans

Cheese Tart Shells: Combine flour and salt. Cut in salad oil with pastry blender. Stir in cheese. Add water and toss with fork. Form into smooth ball. Divide in half and roll out each half between waxed paper.

• Cut circles to fit over backs of muffin-cup pans. (A 4½″ circle fits over medium muffin-cup pan.)

• Place each circle over back of cup. Pinch several pleats in pastry so it fits against cup. Bake in hot oven (425°F.) until lightly browned, about 12 minutes. Carefully remove from pans and cool. Makes 15 shells.

Filling: Mix together mayonnaise, sour cream, lemon juice, salt and dry mustard. Combine with remaining ingredients. Serve in Cheese Tart Shells. Makes 5 cups.

CONFETTI-CRUSTED CRAB PIE

This luncheon main dish is ever so tasty with crab and corn chips

Corn Chip Crust:

- 2   c. finely crushed corn chips
- 2   tblsp. butter, melted
- 1   tsp. paprika

Filling:

- ½   c. chopped green pepper
- ½   c. finely chopped onion
- ¼   c. butter or margarine, melted
- 3   tblsp. flour
- 1   tsp. salt
- ¼   tsp. pepper
- ½   c. milk
- 1   c. dairy sour cream
- ½   c. sliced pimiento-stuffed olives
- 2   (6 oz.) pkgs. frozen crab meat, thawed and flaked

Crust: Combine corn chips, butter and paprika. Reserve ⅓ c. mixture. Press remainder on bottom and side of 9″ pie pan. Bake in moderate oven (375°F.) 10 minutes. Cool.

Filling: Cook green pepper and onion in butter until soft. Blend in flour, salt and pepper. Add milk and sour cream and cook over very low heat, stirring constantly, until thickened.

· Stir in olives and crab meat. Spoon mixture into cool crust. Sprinkle with reserved crust mixture.

· Bake in moderate oven (350°F.) 15 minutes. Serve hot. Makes 6 servings.

Something Special for Supper

Cheese pie rises to the occasion in grand style when served as the main supper or luncheon dish. In spring, serve with tender, new peas seasoned with light cream. Round out your meal with garden lettuce salad—perhaps the oak-leaf variety—if you don't have the makings for the country special, pale-green and white dandelion leaves! Be sure to cook a little snipped green onion with the peas or dried or fresh chopped parsley for extra seasoning.

Start the meal with glasses of tomato juice; end it with old-fashioned tapioca pudding, vanilla-flavored, made with quick-cooking tapioca or a packaged pudding mix. Spoon pretty, pink rhubarb sauce or sugared strawberries, refrigerated until frosty, over the pudding. And if you have sugar cookies, pass them for a bonus. You'll be as happy over your menu as when you discover the season's first violets!

In autumn or winter, serve this cheese pie with buttered succotash and crisp coleslaw, brightened with cut-up red and green peppers or pimientos. Set off the homespun feast with big raisin-stuffed, baked apples and pass your sugar-sprinkled, dark molasses cookies. Have both coffee and milk to drink.

Cheese pie also makes good summer fare. Serve corn on the cob and sliced ripe tomatoes with it then; for dessert, sugared peaches topped with scoops of vanilla ice cream or red raspberry sherbet.

Such menus are the proper setting for French Cheese Pie, a welcome change from the faithful, but overworked, toasted-cheese sandwiches.

FRENCH CHEESE PIE

The French call it Quiche Lorraine— we call it good by any name

Unbaked 9″ pie shell
 6   slices bacon
 ¾   c. chopped onion (1 medium)
1 ¼ c. grated Swiss cheese
 ¼   c. grated Parmesan cheese
 3   eggs, beaten
1 ½ c. light cream
 ½   tsp. salt
 ¼   tsp. pepper

· Cook bacon until crisp. Remove from skillet and crumble; drain off fat. Return 1 tblsp. fat to skillet; add onion and cook gently until tender, but not browned.   *more*

• Place bacon, onion and cheeses in pie shell. Blend together eggs, cream, salt and pepper. Pour over mixture in pie shell.

• Bake in moderate oven (375°F.) until mixture is firm and lightly browned, about 45 minutes. Makes 6 servings.

Miniature Cheese Pies

Our miniatures of the famous French Quiche Lorraine are tasty and the hostess can make them ahead and refrigerate or freeze for quick reheating. Our recipe has strictly American accents that make this type of hot sandwich most acceptable. If you wish, you can make the pies smaller than specified in the recipe. Then they become appetizers to serve as snacks.

INDIVIDUAL CHEESE PIES

Take the place of hot sandwiches—excellent with salad or for snacks

6   slices bacon
½   c. chopped onion
1 ½ c. grated aged Swiss cheese
       (6 oz.)
2   tsp. flour
1   (4 oz.) can mushroom pieces,
       drained
2   eggs
1   c. light cream or milk
¾   tsp. salt
Pat-in-Pan Tart Shells

• Cook bacon until crisp, remove from skillet, drain and crumble.
• Cook onion in bacon drippings until tender. Remove and drain.
• Combine bacon, cheese, flour and mushrooms. Beat eggs and beat in

light cream and salt; add onion.
• Divide cheese-bacon mixture in 12 Pat-in-Pan Tart Shells. Spoon egg mixture over.
• Bake in hot oven (425°F.) 7 minutes. Reduce heat to 300° and bake until egg mixture is set, 10 to 15 minutes. Cool at least 10 minutes before removing from muffin-pan cups. Serve warm. Or refrigerate if you wish to keep the tarts several hours. Reheat in slow oven (300°F.) until heated through, 10 to 15 minutes. You also can freeze the tarts for reheating when needed.

PAT-IN-PAN TART SHELLS

½   c. soft butter or margarine
1   egg yolk
1 ½ c. sifted flour
½   tsp. salt
2   tblsp. milk

• Cream butter in medium bowl with wooden spoon or electric mixer. Beat in egg yolk. Beat in flour and salt, then milk at low speed.
• Shape dough in ball, wrap in waxed paper. Chill 1 hour in refrigerator or 20 minutes in freezer.
• Divide dough in 12 equal balls. Pat into 2½″ muffin-pan cups to make tart shells. Chill in refrigerator 15 minutes before filling and baking as directed in Individual Cheese Pies.

EVERYDAY CHEESE PIE

Tomato adds color—delicious with scalloped corn and tossed green salad

Unbaked 9″ pie shell
4   oz. Cheddar cheese, grated
6   slices cooked bacon, drained
    and crumbled
1   tblsp. grated onion
1   tomato
3   eggs, beaten
1 ¼   c. milk
½   tsp. salt
¼   tsp. pepper
¼   c. chopped parsley

· Sprinkle cheese over bottom of pie shell. Top with bacon and onion. Cut tomato in 6 wedges and arrange over cheese and bacon, spacing so each serving will have a tomato wedge on top.

· Blend together eggs, milk, salt, pepper and parsley. Pour over cheese.

· Bake in moderate oven (350°F.) until set, 50 to 60 minutes. Let stand 10 minutes before cutting. Makes 6 servings.

Breakfast Pie That Pleases

You may have to stretch your imagination to call this dish a pie. But the country cook who sent us the recipe does. She points out that it's double fast to put together when time is short. The potatoes substitute for regular pie crust so that when the wedges are cut it really looks like pie. Her husband says: "It tastes as good as pie!"

Use either your homemade French fries from the freezer, or those you buy at the supermarket to have handy when you need to get a quick, hearty meal.

POTATO AND EGG PIE

Sleight-of-hand pie—bacon, potatoes and eggs cook quickly in skillet

6   slices bacon, chopped
⅓   c. chopped green onions
1   (1 lb.) pkg. frozen French-fried
    potatoes
2   tsp. salt
8   eggs
⅓   c. light cream or top milk
¼   tsp. pepper

· Cook bacon in 10″ skillet until golden. Add onions and continue cooking until onions are limp and bacon is browned. Remove bacon and onions; drain on paper toweling. Keep warm in low oven.

· Pour bacon drippings from skillet; return 3 tblsp. drippings to skillet. Add frozen French fries, sprinkle with 1 tsp. salt; brown, stirring constantly.

· Beat together eggs, cream, remaining 1 tsp. salt and pepper. Pour over potatoes. Cover pan and cook over low heat about 8 minutes. If top is not set then, lift up edges of mixture and tilt the skillet to let liquid run under. Place under broiler until top is completely set.

· Top with bacon and onions. To serve, cut in wedges. Makes 6 servings.

TUNA SALAD PIE

Excellent selection for women's group luncheon if weather is warm

Baked 9" pie shell
  2   envelopes unflavored gelatin
  1   c. water
  1   can condensed cream of celery
        soup
  ½   tsp. salt
  ½   tsp. dry mustard
  ¼   c. lemon juice
  1   tsp. grated onion
  1   c. salad dressing
  2   (6½ to 7 oz.) cans tuna
  1   c. chopped celery
  1   avocado
  1   tblsp. lemon juice

• Sprinkle gelatin on water in saucepan. Place over medium heat, stirring constantly, until gelatin is dissolved, about 3 minutes. Remove from heat.
• Add soup, salt, mustard, ¼ c. lemon juice, onion and salad dressing. Beat with rotary beater until smooth. Chill, stirring occasionally, until mixture mounds when dropped from spoon. Add tuna and celery.
• Peel avocado and dice half of it. Wrap remaining half well in plastic wrap and refrigerate. Chop first avocado half and stir into salad mixture. Spoon into cool pie shell. Chill until firm.
• To serve, cut remaining avocado half into 8 slices, sprinkle with 1 tblsp. lemon juice and arrange on top of pie. Cut pie in 8 wedges, each trimmed with an avocado slice. Makes 8 servings.

VARIATION

• Add ½ c. chopped cucumber to salad with celery for a cool, refreshing note.

TUNA AU GRATIN PIE

Instead of tuna in the usual casserole, fix a cheese-tuna pie surprise

Unbaked 9" pie shell
  ¼   c. milk
  1   can condensed cream of mushroom soup
  2   tblsp. flour
  ⅓   c. chopped onion
  2   (6½ oz.) cans tuna
  1   (10 oz.) pkg. frozen peas (2 c.)
  4   oz. pimiento cheese, sliced
  1   c. crushed corn chips

• Combine milk, soup, flour and onion in saucepan. Cook, stirring constantly, until mixture comes to a boil.
• Add tuna and peas; cook over low heat, stirring occasionally, until peas can be separated.
• Pour into pie shell. Top with slices of cheese. Sprinkle with corn chips.
• Bake in hot oven (425°F.) 30 minutes. Makes 6 servings.

TUNA PIZZA

Mildly seasoned pizza—a Friday farmhouse special that children ask for

  1   pkg. hot roll mix
  ¼   c. olive or salad oil
  1   clove garlic, crushed
  2   (6½ to 7 oz.) cans tuna
  ½   c. pitted ripe olives, sliced

2 (8 oz.) cans tomato sauce
1 tsp. dried orégano
¼ tsp. dried basil
¼ tsp. salt
⅛ tsp. pepper
1 (6 oz.) pkg. sliced Mozzarella
   cheese

• Prepare roll mix as directed on package. Divide in half. Roll to fit or press into 2 (12″) greased pizza pans or into 2 (12″) rounds on greased baking sheets.

• Combine olive oil and garlic; brush oil over dough. Drain tuna, reserving oil. Arrange tuna chunks evenly over dough circles. Place olive slices in spaces between tuna.

• Combine oil from tuna and any remaining olive oil, tomato sauce and seasonings. Spread over tuna.

• Top with cheese slices, broken into small pieces. Bake in hot oven (425°F.) 20 minutes or until nicely browned around edges. Makes 2 (12″) pizzas.

Friday Pie

Cans of salmon are at home on farm cupboard shelves . . . insurance for many inviting dishes that can be fixed in a hurry. Salmon pie, for instance. The recipe for our pie comes direct from a Wisconsin kitchen. The crust is biscuitlike and flaky; when baked to a golden brown, it complements the red-fleshed fish.

With this main dish serve buttered corn, broccoli, green beans or peas, depending on what you have in the freezer. A plate of relishes and a sunny compote of canned peaches and apricots complete the meal. How about milk or hot cocoa for a refreshing beverage?

SALMON PIE

Run pie in the oven and relax—your quick meal is under control

1 (1 lb.) can salmon
1 tblsp. grated onion

¼ lb. process sharp cheese, thinly
   sliced
1 can condensed cream of celery
   soup
1 c. flour
1½ tsp. baking powder
½ tsp. salt
3 tblsp. shortening
1 egg
½ c. milk

• Drain salmon, reserving liquid. Flake with fork, removing bones and skin. Place in bottom of 9″ pie pan.

• Top with onion, 2 tblsp. salmon liquid and cheese. Spread ⅓ can celery soup over cheese.

• To make crust, sift together flour, baking powder and salt. Cut in shortening until mixture resembles coarse crumbs. Combine egg and ¼ c. milk. Add to dry ingredients and mix only until all the flour is moistened.

• Place on lightly floured board and knead 8 or 10 times. Roll out slightly larger than top of pie pan. Place over salmon mixture and flute edges against edge of pan. Cut a 1″ square out of center of dough for steam vent.

· Bake pie in moderate oven (375°F.) until lightly browned, 25 to 30 minutes. Cut in wedges. Serve topped with sauce made by heating remaining ⅔ can celery soup and ¼ c. milk. Makes 6 servings.

SALMON POTPIE

Suppe⟨r⟩ in a casserole. Extend menu with coleslaw, canned fruit, cookies

3 tblsp. chopped onion
4 tblsp. butter or margarine
¼ c. flour
2 c. milk
½ tsp. salt
⅛ tsp. pepper
1 (1 lb.) can red salmon, broken into chunks
1 c. diced cooked carrots
1 c. frozen peas
½ c. grated cheese
Biscuits for topping (1 c. biscuit mix)

· Sauté onion in melted butter until tender. Add flour and blend. Slowly add milk, stirring constantly. Cook until thickened. Season with salt and pepper. (Or make the sauce of 1 can cream of chicken soup, adding ½ soup can of milk and the sautéed onion.)

· Add salmon chunks, carrots, uncooked peas, and grated cheese. Pour into casserole. Top with rolled biscuit dough, made by package directions, and cut in pielike wedges. (Or use leftover pastry, cut in circles, instead of biscuit dough.)

· Bake in hot oven (425°F.) 20 min-

utes, until biscuits are brown and mixture is bubbly. Makes 4 to 6 servings.

SALMON CUSTARD PIE

Dill adds a tasty flavor note—serve with green or cabbage salad

Unbaked 9″ pie shell
¼ c. chopped green onion
2 tblsp. butter
1 (1 lb.) can salmon
1 tsp. dried dill weed
½ tsp. salt
¼ tsp. pepper
1 c. light cream, scalded
4 eggs, slightly beaten

· Bake pie shell in moderate oven (375°F.) 5 minutes.

· Cook onion in butter until soft. Drain salmon, reserving ¼ c. salmon liquid. Remove bones from salmon.

· Place salmon, dill, salt, pepper and salmon liquid in bowl. Mash with fork until well mixed. Add green onion, cream and eggs. Mix well.

· Pour into pie shell and bake in moderate oven (375°F.) until mixture is set, 35 to 40 minutes. Makes 6 servings.

DEEP-DISH FISH PIE

Delicious example of how country cooks team fish with mashed potatoes

¼ c. chopped onion
¼ c. sliced carrots
½ c. chopped celery
¼ c. chopped parsley
2 tsp. salt
½ tsp. whole peppercorns

2   c. boiling water
1½ lbs. frozen perch fillets, thawed
½   lb. cleaned frozen shrimp
3   tblsp. butter or margarine
3   tblsp. flour
4   c. fluffy seasoned mashed potatoes
1   c. grated Cheddar cheese

• Combine onion, carrots, celery, parsley, salt, peppercorns and boiling water in saucepan. Bring to a boil and boil 5 minutes.
• Add fillets, cover and simmer gently until tender and flaky, 7 to 10 minutes. Remove fish and place in a greased 9″ square pan.
• Add shrimp to fish stock. Cook until water comes to a rolling boil, about 5 minutes. Shrimp will be pink. Remove shrimp and scatter over fish fillets.
• Melt butter in separate saucepan; add flour and blend. Strain fish stock and stir 1½ c. of it into flour mixture. Cook, stirring constantly, until mixture comes to a boil. Pour over fish.
• Combine potatoes with ½ c. cheese. Spread over fish. Bake in moderate oven (350°F.) 30 minutes. Sprinkle remaining cheese over potatoes and return to oven for several minutes until cheese melts. Makes 6 to 8 servings.

ENGLISH FISH PIE

Especially tasty way to serve fish

Pastry for 1-crust pie
2   lbs. fish fillets
3   tblsp. butter
2   tsp. salt
¼   tsp. pepper

2   tblsp. flour
1   c. liquid from cooked fish (add milk to make 1 c.)
3   tblsp. fine cracker crumbs
3   hard-cooked eggs, sliced
2   tomatoes, peeled and sliced
2   tblsp. chopped parsley

• Place fish on rack in shallow pan. Brush with 1 tblsp. melted butter; sprinkle with ½ tsp. salt and pepper. Bake in hot oven (400°F.) 15 minutes, until flaky but firm. Save liquid.
• Melt 2 tblsp. butter in saucepan; add flour and ½ tsp. salt. Stir over low heat. Remove from heat; stir in liquid from fish; cook 5 minutes.
• Sprinkle 9″ buttered pie pan with 1 tblsp. crumbs. Arrange half of fish over crumbs; top with half the egg and tomato slices. Sprinkle with 1 tblsp. parsley, ½ tsp. salt and 1 tblsp. crumbs. Cover with half of sauce.
• Repeat above for second layer.
• Top with pastry; flute edges and cut vents. Bake in hot oven (400°F.) 35 minutes. Makes 6 servings.

PIZZA

A favorite FARM JOURNAL *version taken from* TIMESAVING COOKBOOK

1   pkg. active dry yeast
1   tsp. sugar
1   c. warm water
3   c. flour
½   tsp. salt
2   tblsp. salad oil
1   lb. Mozzarella, Muenster, process Swiss or American cheese

more

Pizza Sauce

1 (3 ¾ oz.) can sardines, drained
½ c. Parmesan cheese (about)
Dried orégano

⅛ tsp. pepper
½ tsp. orégano
1 tblsp. salad oil
Dash red pepper (optional)

• Dissolve yeast and sugar in warm (not hot) water. Beat in half the flour; add salt, oil and remaining flour. Mix well; knead until smooth, adding more flour if needed. Place in lightly oiled bowl; turn dough to oil top. Cover; let rise in warm place (85° to 90°F.) until doubled.

• Divide dough in half; roll each half into circle about 13″ in diameter. Place on oiled pizza pan; fold edge under and build up rim slightly. (Or bake on oiled baking sheet in two 8″ × 12″ rectangles, building up dough edges.) Brush with oil.

• Divide remaining ingredients in half. Shred half the Mozzarella cheese and slice the other half.

• On each circle of dough, sprinkle half the shredded Mozzarella; cover with half the sauce. Top with half the sliced Mozzarella and sardines. Sprinkle with half the Parmesan cheese and orégano. (These ingredients make 3 pizzas instead of 2, if you bake them in an electric skillet—see Quick Pizza for directions for baking in skillet.)

• Bake in very hot oven (450°F.) 20 to 25 minutes (until crusty on bottom). Cut each circle into 6 or 8 wedges. Serve hot.

PIZZA SAUCE

1 clove garlic
1 tsp. salt
1 (6 oz.) can tomato juice
1 (8 oz.) can tomato sauce
½ tsp. sugar

• Put garlic through garlic press or mash to a pulp with salt. Combine with remaining ingredients. Do not cook. Makes 1 cup, enough for 2 (12″) pizzas.

PIZZA TOPPINGS: In place of sardines, use chopped or whole anchovies . . . Italian sausage or salami or cold cuts, cut in strips . . . or ground beef (½ lb. to each pizza), seasoned lightly and sautéed in butter. Circle top of any pizza before baking with slices of fresh or canned mushrooms. . . . Sprinkle with chopped chives or parsley, or garnish with chopped stuffed green olives or strips of ripe ones. . . . Decorate top with pattern of raw onion or green pepper rings dipped in salad oil.

VARIATION

QUICK PIZZA: Prepare 1 (15½ oz.) pkg. assembled ready-to-bake pizza mix (contains yeast, flour mixture, sauce and cheese) as directed on package. (Or use hot-roll mix, following directions for pizza on package.) Roll out dough and fit into an oiled, unheated 11″ or 12″ electric skillet; slightly build up dough edge. Add sauce, cheese and chosen topping. Cover; set dial at 300° to 320°F. (low to medium) and bake with vent closed until dough is set, about 30 minutes. Dough browns on bottom of pizza. Slide out with spatula; cut in squares. Serve hot. Makes 4 to 6 servings.

BISCUIT PIZZA

As easy as 1-2-3 to put together and bake for the teen-age crowd

Crust:

2	c. flour
1	tblsp. baking powder
1	tsp. salt
⅔	c. milk
⅓	c. salad or cooking oil

Filling:

1	(6 oz.) can tomato paste
¼	c. water
1	tsp. dried orégano
½	tsp. salt
⅛	tsp. pepper
1	(8 oz.) pkg. Mozzarella cheese slices, cut in strips

Crust: Sift together flour, baking powder and salt; add milk and oil. Stir with fork until mixture forms a ball. Turn onto lightly floured board and knead 8 to 10 times.

• Roll dough between sheets of waxed paper to fit a 14″ pizza pan or 2 (10″) pie pans.

Filling: Combine tomato paste, water and seasonings. Spread over dough. Place strips of cheese on top.

• Bake in hot oven (425°F.) 15 to 20 minutes. Makes 12 servings.

INDEX